The Rosh Hashanah Anthology

In Memory
of
Joseph H. Lauder

Jo Carole and Ronald S. Lauder
Evelyn and Leonard A. Lauder

PHILIP GOODMAN

The Rosh Hashanah Anthology

The Jewish Publication Society

Philadelphia   Jerusalem
5752/1992

Copyright © 1970 by The Jewish Publication Society of America
First paperback printing, 1992
Introduction © 1992 by The Jewish Publication Society
All rights reserved   Manufactured in the United States of America
Designed by Sidney Feinberg

Library of Congress Catalog Card Information
The Rosh Hashanah Anthology. Philip Goodman, comp.
  1970, 1992.
Cloth, ISBN 0–8276–0023–2   Paper, ISBN 0–8276–0408–4
1. Rosh ha-Shanah.   I. Goodman, Philip, 1911–
BM695.N5G6   394.2'6829'6   74-105069

The editor herewith expresses his sincere appreciation to the following publishers and authors who have kindly granted permission to use the material indicated:

ACUM Ltd., Societe d'Auteurs, Compositeurs et Editeurs de Musique en Israel, Tel Aviv, Israel: "A Sweet New Year," from *My Holidays: Holiday Stories for Children*, by Levin Kipnis, trans. by Israel M. Goodelman, N. Tversky Publishing House, Tel Aviv, 1961; *"Shofarot,"* by Shin Shalom, trans. by Dom Moraes, from *Anthology of Modern Hebrew Poetry*, vol. 2, selected by S. Y. Penueli and A. Ukhmani, Institute for the Translation of Hebrew Literature Ltd., Tel Aviv, 1966.

Ben Aronin, Chicago: "Rosh Hashanah," from *Jolly Jingles for the Jewish Child*, by Ben Aronin, Behrman House, New York, 1947.

A. S. Barnes & Company, Inc., Cranbury, N.J.: "The *Shofar*," from *The Book of Fire: Stories*, by I. L. Peretz, trans. by Joseph Leftwich, 1960; "Kaddish," by Levi Isaac of Berditchev, from *The Golden Peacock: A Worldwide Treasury of Yiddish Poetry*, trans. and ed. by Joseph Leftwich, 1961.

Basic Books, Inc., New York: "The Precentor's Prayer" and commentary, and commentary on "All the World Shall Come to Serve Thee," from PRAYER IN JUDAISM by Bernard Martin, Basic Books, Inc., Publishers, New York, 1968.

Behrman House Inc., New York: "The Ritual Horn of Israel," from *A World Passed By: Scenes and Memories of Jewish Civilization in Europe and North Africa*, by Marvin Lowenthal, 1938; "Rosh Hashanah," from *Jolly Jingles for the Jewish Child*, by Ben Aronin, 1947.

Bloch Publishing Co., New York: "Factors Detrimental to Repentance," from *Duties of the Heart*, by Bachya ben Joseph ibn Pakuda, trans. by Moses Hyamson, 1945; "The Jewish New Year," by Joseph H. Hertz, from *A Book of Jewish Thoughts*, ed. by Joseph H. Hertz, 1926; "The Sacrifice of Isaac," commentary on "Our Father, Our King," and "The Symbolic Ceremony of *Tashlikh*," from *Jewish Feasts and Fasts*, by Julius H. Greenstone, 1945; selections from *Rejoice in Thy Festival: A Treasury of Wisdom, Wit and Humor for the Sabbath and Jewish Holidays*, by Philip Goodman, 1956; "Yow Celebrates Rosh Hashanah in His Own Way," from *Habibi and Yow: A Little Boy and His Dog*, by Althea O. Silverman, 1946; "Simon Observes Rosh Hashanah," from *The Story of Jewish Holidays and Customs for Young People*, by Dorothy F. Zeligs, 1942; "Le-Shanah Tovah," from *Mother Goose Rhymes for Jewish Children*, by Sara G. Levy, 1945; "The Jewish Year," from *Around the Year in Rhymes for the Jewish Child*, by Jessie E. Sampter, 1920; "The New Year," from *A Jewish Child's Garden of Verses*, by Abraham Burstein, 1940.

B'nai B'rith Commission on Adult Jewish Education, Washington, D.C.: "A Uniquely Jewish Concept," by Eliezer Berkovits, from *Great Jewish Ideas*, ed. by Abraham Ezra Millgram, 1964.

The Burning Bush Press, New York: commentary on "He Who Ordains Judgment," from *The High Holy Days: A Commentary on the Prayerbook of Rosh Hashanah and Yom Kippur: Book One*: Rosh Hashanah, by Herman Kieval, 1959. Reprinted by permission of the author and publisher.

Central Conference of American Rabbis, New York: "Prayer for Rosh Hashanah Eve," from *The Union Prayer Book for Jewish Worship: Newly Revised Edition: Part II*, 1962.

Commentary, New York: "The Birthday of the World," by Ernst Simon. Reprinted from *Commentary* by permission of the author and publisher; copyright © 1955 by the American Jewish Committee.

Doubleday & Company, Inc., New York: "The *Shofar* Blower of Lapinishok," by Aaron D. Ogus, from A TREASURY OF JEWISH HUMOR, ed. by Nathan Ausubel. Copyright © 1951, 1967 by Nathan Ausubel. Reprinted by permission of Doubleday & Company, Inc.; "In the Warsaw Ghetto," from NO TRAVELER RETURNS, by Henry Shoskes, ed. with a prologue and an epilogue by Curt Riess. Copyright © 1945 by Henry Shoskes. Reprinted by permission of Doubleday & Company, Inc.

E. P. Dutton & Co., Inc., New York: "New Year in Marseilles," from TRAVELS IN JEWRY, by Israel Cohen. Copyright, 1953, by E. P. Dutton & Co., Inc. Reprinted by permission of the publishers.

Rabbi Ira Eisenstein, New York: "A Search for the Holy Spirit," from *Whither?*, by Mordecai Zeev Feierberg, trans. by Ira Eisenstein, Abelard-Schuman, New York, 1959.

Emmett Publishing Company, Minneapolis: "*Selihot*," "The *Shofar* Calls," and "In the Days of Awe," from *A Rag of Love*, by Ruth F. Brin, 1969.

Feldheim Publishers Ltd., Jerusalem, Israel: "The Principle of Repentance," from *The Gates of Repentance*, by Yonah ben Avraham of Gerona, trans. by Shraga Silverstein, 1967.

Hadassah Magazine, New York: "The *Shofar* Maker," by Paul Rader, and "How Afghan Jews Celebrate Rosh Hashanah," by Reuben Kashani, *Hadassah Magazine*, vol. 50, no. 1 (September, 1968).

Hadassah Zionist Youth Commission, New York: "The *Shofar* Call," by Elma Ehrlich Levinger, from *Poems for Young Judaeans*, 1925.

Harvard University Press, Cambridge: "The Trumpet Feast." Reprinted by permission of the publishers, Harvard University Press, Cambridge, Mass., and THE LOEB CLASSICAL LIBRARY from *Philo*, Volume VII, F. H. Colson, translator.

Hebrew Publishing Company, New York: "Arise from Your Slumber," "Things That Hinder Repentance," and "Ways of Repentance," from *Maimonides' Mishneh Torah*, ed. and trans. by Philip Birnbaum, copyright 1967 by Hebrew Publishing Company; "Put Thy Awe Upon All," "In the Book of Life," and "It Is Our Duty," from *High Holyday Prayer Book*, trans. by Philip Birnbaum, copyright 1951 by Hebrew Publishing Company; "Remember Us Unto Life," "He Who Ordains Judgment," "Our Father, Our King," "The Three *Musaf* Themes," "Supreme King," and "Let Us Declare the Mighty Holiness of This Day," from *The High Holyday Prayer Book*, trans. by Ben Zion Bokser, copyright 1959 by Hebrew Publishing Company.

Herzl Press, New York: "Holy Days in the Holy City," from *Coming Home*, by Rahel Yanait, trans. by David Harris and Julian Meltzer, 1964.

Hill and Wang Inc., New York: "God the Accused," by Elie Wiesel, from NIGHT by Elie Wiesel. English translation © MacGibbon & Kee, 1960. Reprinted by permission of Hill & Wang, Inc.

Holt, Rinehart and Winston, Inc., New York: "A Prayer Without

Words" and commentaries on "Put Thy Awe Upon All," "The Three
Musaf Themes," "Supreme King," and "Let Us Declare the Mighty
Holiness of This Day," from JUSTICE AND MERCY by Max Arzt. Copy-
right © 1963 by Max Arzt. Reprinted by permission of Holt, Rinehart and
Winston, Inc.

Horizon Press, New York: "The Legend of the Jewish Pope," by Micha
bin Gorion, reprinted by permission of the publishers, Horizon Press,
from Popes from the Ghetto: A View of Medieval Christendom, by Joachim
Prinz. Copyright 1966.

Jewish Chronicle, London, England: "Tashlikh," by Isaac Bashevis
Singer, Jewish Chronicle, no. 4,875 (September 28, 1962).

The Jewish Publication Society of America, Philadelphia: selections
from The Torah: The Five Books of Moses: A New Translation . . . According to the Masoretic Text, 1962; selections from The Holy Scriptures
According to the Masoretic Text, 1917; "Three Principles of Divine Law"
and "Elements of Repentance," from Sefer ha-Ikkarim, by Joseph Albo,
trans. and ed. by Isaac Husik, 1929; "The Martyrdom of Rabbi Amnon of
Mayence," from Ma'aseh Book: Book of Jewish Tales and Legends,
trans. by Moses Gaster, 1934; "New Year in Svislovitz," from Forward
from Exile: The Autobiography of Shmarya Levin, trans. and ed. by
Maurice Samuel, 1967; "Happy Birthday, World!,". from What the Moon
Brought, by Sadie Rose Weilerstein, 1942.

Jewish Reconstructionist Foundation, New York: "That We Be Reborn," by Hillel Zeitlin, from Supplementary Prayers and Readings for
The High Holidays: Part I, 1960.

Jewish Social Studies, New York: "The New Year in Cochin," from
"The Jewish Way of Life in Cochin," by David G. Mandelbaum, Jewish
Social Studies, vol. 1, no. 4 (October, 1939).

Jonathan David, New York: "Revival in Sicily," by Samuel Teitelbaum,
from Rabbis in Uniform: The Story of the American Jewish Military
Chaplain, ed. by Louis Barish, 1962.

Rabbi Max D. Klein, Jenkintown, Pa.: "Prayer for Rosh Hashanah
Eve," from Seder Avodah, trans. by Max D. Klein, 1960.

Alfred A. Knopf, Inc., New York: "Ecstasy on the New Year," from
PRINCE OF THE GHETTO, by Maurice Samuel. Copyright 1948 by
Maurice Samuel. Reprinted by permission of Alfred A. Knopf, Inc.;
"Tashlikh in the Warsaw Ghetto," from THE WALL, by John Hersey.
Copyright 1950 by John Hersey. Reprinted by permission of Alfred A.
Knopf, Inc.

Dr. Israel Knox, New York: "An Ethical-Humanist View of Rosh
Hashanah," from "Solemn Days: An Ethical-Humanist View of Rosh
Hashanah and Yom Kippur," by Israel Knox, Point of View, vol. 1, no.
2 (Autumn, 1961); reprinted in The Jewish Spectator, vol. 27. no. 7
(September, 1963).

Fania Kruger, Austin: "Sound of the Trumpet," from The Tenth Jew,
by Fania Kruger, Kaleidograph Press, Dallas, 1949.

Ktav Publishing House, New York: "The Shofar's Message," from
Tell Me about God and Prayer, by Morris Epstein, 1953; "The Boy's
Prayer," from My Holiday Story Book, by Morris Epstein, 1952.

The Macmillan Company, New York: "Secret Services in Warsaw,"
from Scroll of Agony: The Warsaw Diary of Chaim A. Kaplan, ed. and
trans. by Abraham I. Katsh. Copyright © Abraham I. Katsh 1965.

National Women's League of the United Synagogue of America, New
York: "How K'tonton Drove Satan out of the Shofar," from The Adventures
of K'tonton: A Little Jewish Tom Thumb, by Sadie Rose Weilerstein,

1935; "For a Good and a Sweet New Year" and "A Happy New Year," from *The Singing Way: Poems for Jewish Children*, by Sadie Rose Weilerstein, 1946.

The Rabbinical Assembly, New York: "In Praise of Another Year," by Joanne Greenberg, and "Peace and Plenty," by Jules Harlow, from *Yearnings: Prayer and Meditation for the Days of Awe*, ed. by Jules Harlow, copyright 1968 and reprinted by permission of The Rabbinical Assembly.

Rabbi Victor E. Reichert, Cincinnati: "The Month of Tishri," from *The Tahkemoni*, vol. 1, by Judah Al-Harizi, trans. by Victor Emanuel Reichert, Raphael Haim Cohen's Press, Ltd. Publishers, Jerusalem, 1965.

Rev. Abraham Rosenfeld, London, England: "A Propitiatory Prayer," by Solomon ibn Gabirol, from *The Authorised Selichot for the Whole Year*, trans. and annotated by Abraham Rosenfeld, I. Labworth & Co., London, 1957.

Schocken Books Inc., New York: "Kinds of Repentance," reprinted by permission of Schocken Books Inc., from THE MEDITATION OF THE SAD SOUL, by Abraham bar Hayya, trans. by Geoffrey Wigoder. Copyright © 1968 by Geoffrey Wigoder; "The Judgment Day," reprinted by permission of Schocken Books, Inc. from FRANZ ROSENZWEIG: HIS LIFE AND THOUGHT, edited by Nahum N. Glatzer. Copyright © 1953 by Schocken Books Inc.; "The Mouse and the Cock," reprinted by permission of Schocken Books Inc. from THE BRIDAL CANOPY, by S. Y. Agnon. Copyright © 1967 by Schocken Books Inc.; "Rosh Hashanah in Vitebsk, Russia," by Bella Chagall and "*Tashlikh*," by Marc Chagall, reprinted by permission of Schocken Books Inc. from BURNING LIGHTS, by Bella Chagall, with drawings by Marc Chagall. Copyright © 1946 by Schocken Books Inc.

E. S. Schwab, London, England: "In a Rural Community in Germany," from *Jewish Rural Communities in Germany*, by Hermann Schwab, Cooper Book Co., London, 1956.

Simon & Schuster, Inc., New York: "Utilization of Emotion," from *Peace of Mind* copyright © 1946 by Joshua Loth Liebman. Reprinted by permission of Simon & Schuster, Inc.; "Rescue in Denmark on Rosh Hashanah," from *Rescue in Denmark* copyright © 1963, by Harold Flender. Reprinted by permission of Simon & Schuster, Inc.

Isaac Bashevis Singer, New York: "*Tashlikh*," by Isaac Bashevis Singer, London *Jewish Chronicle*, no. 4,875 (September 28, 1962).

The Soncino Press Limited, London, England: "The Day of the Concealed Moon," from *Zohar*, trans. by Harry Sperling and Maurice Simon, 1931–1934; "The Shofar of Rosh Hashanah" and "We All Need *Teshuvah*," from *Horeb: A Philosophy of Jewish Laws and Observances*, by Samson Raphael Hirsch, trans. by I. Grunfeld, 1962; "The Piercing Summons," from *Judaism Eternal: Selected Essays*, by Samson Raphael Hirsch, trans. by I. Grunfeld, 1956; selections from *Midrash Rabbah*, trans. under the editorship of H. Freedman and Maurice Simon, 1939–1951; selections from *The Babylonian Talmud*, trans. under the editorship of Isidore Epstein, 1935–1950. All rights reserved by The Soncino Press Limited.

Union of American Hebrew Congregations, New York: "Days of Awe in an East European Town," from *The Jewish Festivals: From Their Beginnings to Our Own Day*, by Hayyim Schauss, trans. by Samuel Jaffe, 1938.

Union of Orthodox Jewish Congregations of America, New York: commentary by Sidney B. Hoenig on "It Is Our Duty," from *The Orthodox Union*, vol. 8, no. 2 (November–December, 1940).

University of California Press, Berkeley: "*Piyyut* for Rosh Hashanah," by Hayyim Guri, from *Modern Hebrew Poetry: A Bilingual Anthology*, ed.

and trans. by Ruth Finer Mintz. Copyright © 1966. Reprinted by permission of The Regents of the University of California.

The University of Chicago Press, Chicago: "Confession and Penitence" and "Forgive Your Neighbor," from *The Apocrypha*, trans. by Edgar J. Goodspeed, published by The University of Chicago Press. Copyright 1938 by Edgar J. Goodspeed. All rights reserved.

Vallentine, Mitchell & Co. Ltd., London, England: "The Torah and *Haftarah* Portions," from *A Guide to Rosh Hashanah*, by Louis Jacobs, Jewish Chronicle Publications, London. Copyright 1959 by Louis Jacobs.

The Viking Press, Inc., New York: "If Not Higher," by I. L. Peretz, from A TREASURY OF YIDDISH STORIES, edited by Irving Howe and Eliezer Greenberg. Copyright 1954 by The Viking Press, Inc. Reprinted by permission of The Viking Press, Inc.

World Over, New York: "The Miracle of the Shofar," by Alexander Shafran, *World Over*, vol. 8, no. 9 (February 21, 1947).

Yale University Press, New Haven: "A Karaite Interpretation of Repentance," by Aaron ben Elijah, from *Karaite Anthology: Excerpts from the Early Literature*, trans. by Leon Nemoy, 1952; selections from *Pesikta Rabbati: Discourses for Feasts, Fasts and Special Sabbaths*, trans. by William G. Braude, 1968; selections from *The Midrash on Psalms*, trans. by William G. Braude, 1959; "Lapsing Back into Sin" and "Five Degrees of Repentance," from *The Book of Beliefs and Opinions*, by Saadia Gaon, trans. by Samuel Rosenblatt, 1948.

Yeshiva University Press, New York: "Lights of Repentance," from *Rabbi Kook's Philosophy of Repentance*, trans. by Alter B. Z. Metzger, 1968 (*Studies in Torah Judaism*).

Zionist Organisation, Youth and Hechalutz Department, Jerusalem, Israel: "Shofar and Man," by Isaac ben Moses Arama, from *A Handbook for Jewish Youth Leaders: The Month of Elul*, ed. by Shlomo Ketko, 1955.

Zionist Organisation, Youth and Hechalutz Department, Religious Section, Jerusalem, Israel: "Rosh Hashanah in Persia, 1944," by H. Z. Hirschberg, *Igeret Lagolah*, no. 28 (August, 1946).

Zionist Record and S. A. Jewish Chronicle, Johannesburg: "In the Jewish Ghetto of Yemen," by S. Ernst, *South African Jewish Chronicle*, vol. 44 (September, 1946).

מוקדש
לנכדי הצבר
מרדכי
בן אברהם חיים ושרה מינדל

PREFACE

I welcome this opportunity to express my sincere gratitude to all colleagues and friends from whom I obtained assistance in the compilation of this volume. I am particularly indebted to my collaborators who have written original articles at my request: Dr. Joseph Gutmann, professor of art history, Wayne State University, Detroit, who wrote the scholarly article "Rosh Hashanah in Art"; Dr. Alexander Alan Steinbach, editor of *Jewish Book Annual* and *In Jewish Bookland*, who composed the fascinating chapter on "Rosh Hashanah Parables"; and Cantor Max Wohlberg, professor of *Hazzanut*, Cantors Institute of The Jewish Theological Seminary of America, who contributed the erudite essay on "The Music of the Rosh Hashanah Liturgy."

My deep appreciation is extended also to the following persons who have given me helpful suggestions: Aryeh Ben-Gurion, Bet ha-Shitah, Israel; Irene Heskes, staff consultant of the National Jewish Music Council; Dr. I. Edward Kiev, librarian of the Hebrew Union College–Jewish Institute of Religion, New York: Sylvia Landress, director of the Zionist Archives and Library; Rabbi and Mrs. Herbert Parzen, New York; Bernard Postal, director, Public Information, National Jewish Welfare Board; Rabbi Irving Rubin of Congregation Kesher Israel, West Chester, Pennsylvania; Jacob and Ruth Schreiber, Heftzibah, Israel; Dr. Elias Schulman, librarian of the Jewish Education Committee of New York; and Dora Steinglass, chief of the Jewish Division, New York Public Library.

I am most grateful to Dr. Chaim Potok, editor, and Lesser Zuss-
man, executive director, of The Jewish Publication Society of America for encouraging me to undertake the preparation of this volume.
The Society's copy editor, Mrs. Kay Powell, read the manuscript with
painstaking care. Dr. Sidney B. Koenig, professor of Jewish history,
Yeshiva University, kindly consented to examine the manuscript and
offered much helpful criticism and many excellent suggestions. I
benefited greatly from the critical judgment and literary craftsman-
ship that was so graciously given by Dr. Alexander Alan Steinbach.
Words do not suffice to express the appreciation I owe to my wife,
Hanna, a true helpmate in all my literary endeavors.

PHILIP GOODMAN

New York City
Shevat 17, 5730 [1970]

INTRODUCTION

Rosh Hashanah, literally "head of the year," which falls on the first and second days of the autumn month of Tishrei, is now celebrated as the primary Jewish New Year. The Bible originally designated Nisan, the month during which Passover falls, as the "first of the months" (Exod. 12:2) and listed Rosh Hashanah as a festival of the seventh month, "a sacred occasion commemorated with loud blasts" (Lev. 23:24). The Jewish calendar also designates a "New Year of the Trees," the late winter holiday of Tu B'Shevat.

It was common among Semitic peoples to begin the economic year at the fall harvest, when crops were brought to market. Rosh Hashanah probably began as such a harvest festival, marking the beginning of the agricultural cycle. In time, that function became associated primarily with the festival of Sukkot, which falls two weeks after Rosh Hashanah. This season was also the time of the annual coronation of the king. The theme of God's kingship is central to the Rosh Hashanah liturgy.

From late biblical times to our own, Rosh Hashanah has symbolized the season of penitence and renewal, of *teshuvah*—literally, returning to the right path. It marks the beginning of the yearly liturgical cycle. The Jews who returned from Babylonian exile stood listening as Ezra the Scribe read the Torah before them on Rosh Hashanah, reminding them of the ancient traditions, and Nehemiah instructed them to celebrate the holy day with feasting and joy (Neh. 8:1–12).

[xiii

This solemn season begins with a long period of spiritual preparation, which takes place during Elul, the month preceding Tishrei. Special penitential prayers called *selihot* are recited at midnight, the shofar is sounded each morning, and many Jews devote time to studying texts on the theme of repentance and to making atonement for past misdeeds. The ten days that begin with Rosh Hashanah on the first of Tishrei and culminate with Yom Kippur on the tenth are known as *aseret yeme teshuvah*, the Ten Days of Repentance, an especially intensive period focused on making amends for wrongs committed against one's fellow human beings and against God during the previous year.

Rosh Hashanah itself emphasizes several central themes: divine judgment, repentance, and renewal. The Rabbis maintain that the world was created on the first day of Tishrei; Rosh Hashanah is therefore the birthday of the world, *ha-yom ha-rat olam* (Rosh Hashanah 27a). According to the Mishnah, it is also the day that the world is judged and its fate determined for the coming year (Rosh Hashanah 1:2). On this day, God thus reassesses and reaffirms that first act of creation.

Human beings similarly confront judgment and spiritual rebirth during this season. It is a time for heartfelt prayer and intensive soul-searching—called in Hebrew *heshbon ha-nefesh*, literally, taking a moral inventory of the soul. It is a time to restore balance to the human and divine worlds. The metaphor of God weighing our past year's deeds on a scale pervades the Rosh Hashanah liturgy: On this day God judges "who shall live and who shall die . . . who shall be at peace and who shall be tormented." It is probably no coincidence that this season, commemorating as it does the restoration of human and divine equilibrium, occurs during the month of Tishrei, which, from ancient times, has been symbolized by the Zodiac sign of Libra, the Scales, a universal symbol of psychic and cosmic balance.

Another major symbol of this holiday is the Book of Life, in which God is said to inscribe our deeds and to seal our fate for the coming year (Rosh Hashanah 16b). It is customary to greet people and to send them cards during this season, expressing the hope that God will inscribe them for life in the year to come.

The central synagogue ritual of Rosh Hashanah is the sounding of the shofar, the ram's horn, calling the people to repentance and God to merciful forgiveness. The shofar is blown on several occasions during the synagogue service, adding up to a total of one hundred blasts. The *musaf* (additional service) is greatly expanded on this day, focusing on the three themes of *malkhuyot* (kingship), *zikhronot* (remembrance), and *shofarot* (shofar blasts).

Many folk customs have arisen to commemorate this day. It is customary, for example, to eat sweet foods, such as apples dipped in honey, to symbolize hope for a sweet New Year, or round hallahs with raisins, symbolizing our hopes for a sweet, new "round" of the year. It is also traditional to avoid eating certain foods such as nuts (*egoz* in Hebrew), whose numerical equivalence in Hebrew is close to that of the word "sin" *(khet)*. Fish *(dag)* is also avoided because the Hebrew is close to *da'ag*, meaning "worry"; many Sephardic Jews, however, eat fish heads on this holiday to symbolize their wish to head their community in righteousness. A very popular custom is the ceremony of *tashlikh*, casting bread crumbs into a nearby stream or river to symbolize the casting off of our sins, based on the biblical verse: "You will hurl all our sins into the depths of the sea" (Micah 7:19).

The twenty-three sections of *The Rosh Hashanah Anthology* provide valuable resource materials for teachers, rabbis, parents, students, and newcomers to Judaism.

The first five sections—"Rosh Hashanah in the Bible," "Rosh Hashanah in Postbiblical Writings," "Rosh Hashanah in Talmud and Midrash," "Rosh Hashanah in Medieval Jewish Literature," and "Rosh Hashanah in Jewish Law"—present traditional texts for study and historical background. The next four sections—"Selected Prayers," "The Scriptural Readings," "The *Shofar*," and "The Symbolic Ceremony of *Tashlikh*"—focus on ritual and liturgical aspects of the holiday. Other sections—"Rosh Hashanah in Many Lands," "Rosh Hashanah Greeting Cards," "The Culinary Art of Rosh Hashanah," and "Rosh Hashanah Miscellany"—provide fascinating background information highlighting folklore and customs typical of Rosh Hashanah celebrations throughout the world. These selections include many liturgical pieces, songs, recipes, crafts, and customs that will greatly enhance enjoyment and understanding of this festival. Joseph Gutmann's "Rosh Hashanah in Art" and Max Wohl-

berg's "The Music of the Rosh Hashanah Liturgy" demonstrate the
rich aesthetic heritage inspired by this holiday.

The volume also includes numerous illustrations and photographs
that depict scenes and artifacts representative of traditional observances of this holiday.

One of the unique features of this anthology is the abundant selection of both secular and religious literature on the themes of Rosh
Hashanah. These include many Hasidic parables (meshalim), tales,
and teachings, culled from the rich treasury of lore once so popular
in the Eastern European shtetl and today enjoying a remarkable
revival in America, as well as essays by Franz Rosenzweig, Samson
Raphael Hirsch, Rav Kook, and Elie Wiesel. An additional section
presents short stories by modern writers such as I. L. Peretz, Shmuel
Yosef Agnon, and Isaac Bashevis Singer.

Parents and teachers will find in this anthology three sections especially designed for children. There are classic stories such as Sadie
Rose Weilerstein's "How K'tonton Drove Satan out of the Shofar" and
bin Gorion's "The Legend of the Jewish Pope"; a number of poems
suitable for a variety of ages; and a special section of "New Year Programs," including discussion themes, creative dramatics, crafts,
games, and school activities. Many of the recipes from the "The Culinary Art of Rosh Hashanah" can also be adapted for classroom or
home use.

Twenty-five centuries ago, when the Jewish people began to return
from Babylonian exile, they committed themselves wholeheartedly
to rebuilding their community, re-establishing the sacred city of
Jerusalem as their spiritual center. On Rosh Hashanah, Ezra the
Scribe called the people together at the city gate to read the Torah for
the first time since their miraculous return from exile. As the people
listened to Ezra's voice, they burst out weeping, but their leader
Nehemiah restrained them: "Do not be sad, for your rejoicing in the
Lord is the source of your strength" (Neh. 8:10). The passage continues: "The Levites were quieting the people, saying, 'Hush, for the day
is holy; do not be sad.' Then all the people went to eat and drink and
send portions and make great merriment, for they understood the
things they were told" (Neh. 8:11–12).

In recent decades, the High Holy Days—Rosh Hashanah and Yom
Kippur—have assumed an increasingly central place in the religious

life of the American Jewish community, overshadowing the observances of Shabbat and the three pilgrimage festivals of Passover, Shavuot, and Sukkot. This season continues to maintain a strong hold even on those Jews whose observance of traditional Jewish practices has become quite attenuated.

Why?

Perhaps we can find the reason by focusing on the themes so central to this holiday season: human vulnerability, the necessity of taking moral inventory, and the possibility of spiritual rebirth after the repenting of past misdeeds. Yet this very focus on ultimate spiritual questions has somewhat skewed the balance inherent in this season. The High Holy Days are experienced as a time marked by great solemnity, by stern sermons and strict decorum. Like the ancient Israelites returning from foreign exile, we experience primarily sadness as we take stock of our shortcomings over the past year and contemplate our uncertain future.

Yet the liturgy, customs, and teachings of Rosh Hashanah are filled with messages of hope and joy. This day is the Birthday of the World! We hear the shofar blast and awaken from our spiritual stupor. Hearts mended and spirits renewed, we look forward to a bountiful harvest at Sukkot. It is a time to celebrate another year of life.

By studying the treasures in this remarkable anthology, we can prepare ourselves for the New Year, so that we too can be inscribed in God's Book for good and for blessing.

ELLEN FRANKEL

Philadelphia
1992/5752

CONTENTS

ILLUSTRATIONS

The Rosh Hashanah
Anthology

I

ROSH HASHANAH IN THE BIBLE

The Bible alludes to Rosh Hashanah in only a few verses, despite its significant role among the Jewish holy days and festivals. The name appears only once—in Ezekiel 40.1—and in that instance, according to the traditional interpretation, it actually refers to Yom Kippur, which is the beginning of the jubilee year. The Bible stresses that Rosh Hashanah shall be observed on the first day of the seventh month and calls it "a day when the horn is sounded," even though the *shofar* was blown on various other occasions in biblical times.

The themes of Rosh Hashanah—acceptance of God's Kingdom and return to the Torah—are found in the book of Nehemiah. The subject of repentance is treated repeatedly throughout the Bible.[1]

A SACRED OCCASION

The LORD spoke to Moses, saying: Speak to the Israelite people thus: In the seventh month, on the first day of the month, you shall observe complete rest, a sacred occasion commemorated with loud blasts. You shall not work at your occupations; and you shall bring an offering by fire to the LORD.

Leviticus 23.23–25

In the seventh month, on the first day of the month, you shall observe a sacred occasion: you shall not work at your occupations. You shall observe it as a day when the horn is sounded.

You shall present a burnt offering of pleasing odor to the LORD: one bull of the herd, one ram, and seven yearling lambs, without blemish. The meal offering with them—choice flour with oil mixed in—shall be: three-tenths of a measure for a bull, two-tenths for a ram, and one-tenth for each of the seven lambs. And there shall be one goat for a sin offering, to make expiation in your behalf—in addition to the burnt offering of the new moon with its meal offering and the regular burnt offering with its meal offering, each with its libation as prescribed, offerings by fire of pleasing odor to the LORD.

Numbers 29.1–6

BLOW THE HORN AT THE NEW MOON

> Blow the horn at the new moon,
> At the full moon for our feast-day.
> For it is a statute for Israel,
> An ordinance of the God of Jacob.

Psalms 81.4–5

IN THE TIMES OF CYRUS, KING OF PERSIA

And when the seventh month was come, and the children of Israel were in the cities, the people gathered themselves together as one man to Jerusalem. Then stood up Jeshua the son of Jozadak, and his brethren the priests, and Zerubbabel the son of Shealtiel, and his brethren, and builded the altar of the God of Israel, to offer burnt-offerings thereon, as it is written in the Law of Moses the man of God. And they set the altar upon its bases; for fear was upon them because of the people of the countries, and they offered burnt-offerings thereon, unto the LORD, even burnt-offerings morning and evening.

Ezra 3.1–3

IN THE DAYS OF EZRA AND NEHEMIAH

And when the seventh month was come, and the children of Israel were in their cities, all the people gathered themselves together as one man into the broad place that was before the water gate; and they spoke unto Ezra the scribe to bring the book of the Law of Moses, which the LORD had commanded to Israel. And Ezra the priest brought the Law before the congregation, both men and women, and all that could hear with understanding, upon the first day of the seventh month. And he read therein before the broad place that was before the water gate from early morning until midday, in the presence of the men and the women, and of those that could understand; and the ears of all the people were attentive unto the book of the Law. And Ezra the scribe stood upon a pulpit of wood, which they had made for the purpose; and beside him stood Mattithiah, and Shema, and Anaiah, and Uriah, and Hilkiah, and Maaseiah, on his right hand; and on his left hand, Pedaiah, and Mishael, and Malchijah, and Hashum, and Hashbaddanah, Zechariah, and Meshullam. And Ezra opened the book in the sight of all the people—for he was above all the people—and when he opened it, all the people stood up. And Ezra blessed the LORD, the great God. And all the people answered: "Amen, Amen," with the lifting up of their hands; and they bowed their heads, and fell down before the LORD with their faces to the ground. Also Jeshua, and Bani, and Sherebiah, Jamin, Akkub, Shabbethai, Hodiah, Maaseiah,

Kelita, Azariah, Jozabad, Hanan, Pelaiah, even the Levites, caused the people to understand the Law; and the people stood in their place. And they read in the book, in the Law of God, distinctly; and they gave the sense, and caused them to understand the reading.

And Nehemiah, who was the Tirshatha, and Ezra the priest the scribe, and the Levites that taught the people, said unto all the people: "This day is holy unto the LORD your God; mourn not, nor weep." For all the people wept, when they heard the words of the Law. Then he said unto them: "Go your way, eat the fat, and drink the sweet, and send portions unto him for whom nothing is prepared; for this day is holy unto our LORD; neither be ye grieved; for the joy of the LORD is your strength." So the Levites stilled all the people, saying: "Hold your peace, for the day is holy; neither be ye grieved." And all the people went their way to eat, and to drink, and to send portions, and to make great mirth, because they had understood the words that were declared unto them.

And on the second day were gathered together the heads of fathers' houses of all the people, the priests, and the Levites, unto Ezra the scribe, even to give attention to the words of the Law.

Nehemiah 7.73–8.13

ON THE THEME OF REPENTANCE

The LORD spoke to Moses, saying: Speak to the Israelites: When a man or woman commits any wrong toward a fellow man, thus breaking faith with the LORD, and that person realizes his guilt, he shall confess the wrong he has done. He shall make restitution in the principal amount and add one-fifth to it, giving it to him toward whom he is guilty.

Numbers 5.5–7

When all these things befall you—the blessing and the curse that I have set before you—and you take them to heart amidst

the various nations to which the LORD your God has banished
you, and you return to the LORD your God, and you and your
children heed His command with all your heart and soul, just as
I enjoin upon you this day, then the LORD your God, in His
compassion, will restore your fortunes. He will bring you together again from all the peoples where the LORD your God
has scattered you. Even if your outcasts are at the ends of the
world, from there the LORD your God will gather you, from there
He will fetch you. And the LORD your God will bring you to the
land which your fathers occupied, and you shall occupy it;
and He will make you more prosperous and more numerous
than your fathers.

Then the LORD your God will open up your heart and the
hearts of your offspring to love the LORD your God with all your
heart and soul, in order that you may live.

Deuteronomy 30.1–6

When Thy people Israel are smitten down before the enemy,
when they do sin against Thee, if they turn again to Thee,
and confess Thy name, and pray and make supplication unto
Thee in this house; then hear Thou in heaven, and forgive the
sin of Thy people Israel, and bring them back unto the land
which Thou gavest unto their fathers.

I Kings 8.33–34

> Seek ye the LORD while He may be found,
> Call ye upon Him while He is near;
> Let the wicked forsake his way,
> And the man of iniquity his thoughts;
> And let him return unto the LORD, and He will
>   have compassion upon him,
> And to our God, for He will abundantly pardon.

Isaiah 55.6–7

Go, and proclaim these words toward the north, and say:
> Return, thou backsliding Israel,
> Saith the LORD;
> I will not frown upon you;

For I am merciful, saith the LORD,
I will not bear grudge for ever.
Only acknowledge thine iniquity,
That thou hast transgressed against the LORD thy God,
And hast scattered thy ways to the strangers
Under every leafy tree,
And ye have not hearkened to My voice,
Saith the LORD.

Return, O backsliding children, saith the LORD; for I am a
lord unto you, and I will take you one of a city, and two of a
family, and I will bring you to Zion.

Jeremiah 3.12–14

If the wicked turn from all his sins that he hath committed,
and keep all My statutes, and do that which is lawful and right,
he shall surely live, he shall not die. None of his transgressions
that he hath committed shall be remembered against him;
for his righteousness that he hath done he shall live. Have I
any pleasure at all that the wicked should die? saith the LORD
God; and not rather that he should return from his ways, and
live? . . .

Therefore I will judge you, O house of Israel, every one
according to his ways, saith the LORD God. Return ye, and turn
yourselves from all your transgressions; so shall they not be
a stumblingblock of iniquity unto you. Cast away from you all
your transgressions, wherein ye have transgressed; and make
you a new heart and a new spirit; for why will ye die, O house
of Israel? For I have no pleasure in the death of him that dieth,
saith the LORD God; wherefore turn yourselves, and live.

Ezekiel 18.21–23, 30–32

Return, O Israel, unto the LORD thy God;
For thou hast stumbled in thine iniquity.
Take with you words,
And return unto the LORD;
Say unto Him: "Forgive all iniquity,
And accept that which is good; . . .
For in Thee fatherless findeth mercy."

I will heal their backsliding,
I will love them freely;
For Mine anger is turned away from him.

Hosea 14.2–5

Hide Thy face from my sins,
And blot out all mine iniquities.
Create me a clean heart, O God;
And renew a stedfast spirit within me.
Cast me not away from Thy presence;
And take not Thy holy spirit from me.
Restore unto me the joy of Thy salvation;
And let a willing spirit uphold me.
Then will I teach transgressors Thy ways;
And sinners shall return unto Thee. . . .
The sacrifices of God are a broken spirit;
A broken and a contrite heart, O God, Thou wilt
    not despise.

Psalms 51.11–15, 19

Turn Thou us unto Thee, O Lord, and we shall be turned;
Renew our days as of old.

Lamentations 5.21

II

ROSH HASHANAH IN POST-
BIBLICAL WRITINGS

▼▼▼▼▼▼▼▼▼▼▼▼▼▼▼▼▼▼▼▼▼▼▼▼▼▼▼▼▼▼

Among the outstanding postbiblical writings are the
Apocrypha and the works of Philo. For a period of more than
five centuries, from about 330 B.C.E. to about 200 C.E., Jews
in the Diaspora developed significant literary creations in the
Greek language. Foremost among these is the Septuagint, a
Greek translation of the Hebrew Bible by the Jews in Alexandria,
which includes a number of additional or "hidden" books known
as the Apocrypha. Cited below are *The Prayer of Manasseh* and
a selection from *Ben Sira* of the Apocrypha. There is also a
pertinent passage from *The Book of Jubilees*, one of a group
of works of about the same period that are embraced in the
Pseudepigrapha.

Philo of Alexandria (c. 20 B.C.E.–c. 50 C.E.), whose original
thinking has left an indelible impact on the religious philosophy
of Western Europe, did not exert a strong influence on Jewish
life. He is noted for his literal and historical acceptance of
the Bible and for his allegorical interpretations.

▼▼▼▼▼▼▼▼▼▼▼▼▼▼▼▼▼▼▼▼▼▼▼▼▼▼▼▼▼▼

CONFESSION AND PENITENCE

Almighty Lord,
God of our forefathers,
Abraham, Isaac, and Jacob,
And of their upright descendants;
You who have made the heaven and the earth with all their
   system;
Who have fettered the sea with Your word of command;
Who have shut up the great deep, and sealed it with Your
   terrible, glorious name;
Before whom all things shudder, and tremble before Your power,
For the majesty of Your glory is unbearable,
And the anger of Your threatening against sinners is unen-
   durable,
Immeasurable and unsearchable is the mercy You promise,
For You are the Lord Most High,
Tender-hearted, long-suffering, and most merciful,
And regretful of the wickedness of men.
You therefore, Lord of the upright,
Have not ordained repentance for the upright,
For Abraham, Isaac, and Jacob, who did not sin against you;
You have ordained repentance for a sinner like me,
For my sins are more numerous than the sands of the sea,
My transgressions are multiplied, Lord, they are multiplied!
I am unworthy to look up and see the height of the heaven,
For the multitude of my iniquities.
I am weighed down with many an iron fetter,
So that I bend beneath my sins,
And I have no relief,
Because I have provoked Your anger,
And done what is wrong in Your sight,
Setting up abominations and multiplying offenses.
Now therefore I bend the knee of my heart, begging You for
   kindness.
I have sinned, Lord, I have sinned,
And I know my transgressions.

I earnestly beseech You,
Forgive me, Lord, forgive me!
Do not destroy me in the midst of my transgressions!
Do not be angry with me forever and lay up evil for me,
Or condemn me to the lowest parts of the earth.
For You, Lord, are the God of those who repent,
And You will manifest your goodness toward me,
For unworthy as I am, You will save me in the abundance of
  Your mercy,
And I will praise You continually as long as I live,
For all the host of heaven sings Your praise,
And Yours is the glory forever. Amen.

The Prayer of Manasseh[1]

FORGIVE YOUR NEIGHBOR

> Forgive your neighbor his wrongdoing;
> Then your sins will be forgiven when you pray.
> Shall one man cherish anger against another,
> And yet ask healing from the Lord?
> Does he have no mercy on a man like himself,
> And yet pray for his own sins?

Ben Sira 28.2–4[2]

OBSERVING THE STARS

Abram sat up throughout the night on the new moon of the seventh month to observe the stars from the evening to the morning, in order to see what would be the character of the year with regard to the rains, and he was alone as he sat and observed. And a word came into his heart and he said: "All the signs of the stars, and the signs of the moon and of the sun are all in the hand of the Lord. Why do I search them out?"

Book of Jubilees 12.16–17[3]

THE TRUMPET FEAST

PHILO OF ALEXANDRIA

When the opening of the sacred month comes it is customary to sound the trumpet in the temple at the same time that the sacrifices are brought there, and its name of "trumpet feast" is derived from this. It has a twofold significance, partly to the nation in particular, partly to all mankind in general. In the former sense it is a reminder of a mighty and marvellous event which came to pass when the oracles of the law were given from above. For then the sound of the trumpet pealed from heaven and reached, we may suppose, the ends of the universe, so that the event might strike terror even into those who were far from the spot and dwelling well nigh at the extremities of the earth, who would come to the natural conclusion that such mighty signs portended mighty consequences. And indeed what could men receive mightier or more profitable than the general laws which came from the mouth of God, not like the particular laws, through an interpreter? This is a significance peculiar to the nation. What follows is common to all mankind. The trumpet is the instrument used in war, both to sound the advance against the enemy when the moment comes for engaging battle and also for recalling the troops when they have to separate and return to their respective camps. And there is another war not of human agency when nature is at strife in herself, when her parts make onslaught one on another and her law-abiding sense of equality is vanquished by the greed for inequality. Both these wars work destruction on the face of the earth. The enemy cut down the fruit-trees, ravage the country, set fire to the foodstuffs and the ripening ears of corn in the open fields, while the forces of nature use drought, rainstorms, violent moisture-laden winds, scorching sun-rays, intense cold accompanied by snow, with the regular harmonious alternations of the yearly seasons turned into disharmony, a state of things in my opinion due to the impiety which does not gain a gradual hold but comes rushing with the force of a torrent among those whom these things befall. And therefore the law instituted this feast figured by that instrument of war the trumpet, which gives it its name, to be as a thank-offering to God the peace-maker and peace-keeper, Who destroys faction both in cities and in the various parts of the universe and creates plenty and fertility and abundance of other good things and leaves the havoc of fruits without a single spark to be rekindled.

The Special Laws II, 188–192[4]

III

ROSH HASHANAH IN TALMUD
AND MIDRASH

⌄⌄⌄⌄⌄⌄⌄⌄⌄⌄⌄⌄⌄⌄⌄⌄⌄⌄⌄⌄⌄⌄⌄⌄⌄⌄⌄⌄⌄⌄⌄⌄⌄⌄⌄⌄⌄⌄

This chapter includes meaningful selections of ethical messages culled from talmudic and midrashic literature—the vast storehouses of law, commentary, interpretation, legend, and moral imperatives.

References to the New Year are found throughout the Talmud, but *Tractate Rosh Hashanah* is concerned mainly with the rules regarding the calendar year and with the laws relating to the *shofar* and to the New Year service. *Midrash Rabbah*, among other midrashic works, is another major source producing interpretations of the significance of Rosh Hashanah. *Midrash Tehillim* ("Midrash on Psalms"), a compilation developed by accretion from the third to the thirteenth century C.E., presents homilies on verses in the Book of Psalms. *Pesikta Rabbati*, probably redacted during the seventh century, is a collection of discourses for festivals, fast days, and special Sabbaths. *Pirke de-Rabbi Eliezer*, attributed to Rabbi Eliezer, son of Hyrcanus of the first and second centuries C.E., was in all likelihood completed in the ninth century. *Eliyahu Zuta*, an ethical-religious work, was written at the end of the tenth century.

═══════════════════════════════════════

THE FIRST DAY OF THE YEAR AS THE DAY OF JUDGMENT

It was taught in the name of R. Eliezer: "The world was created on the twenty-fifth of Elul." The view of Rav agrees with the teaching of R. Eliezer. For we have learned in the *Shofar* Benediction [the *Zikhronot*, Remembrance passages in the additional service on New Year's Day] composed by Rav: "This day, on which was the beginning of work, is a memorial of the first day, for it is a statute for Israel, a decree of the God of Jacob. Thereon also sentence is pronounced upon countries, which of them is destined to the sword and which to peace, which to famine and which to plenty; and each separate creature is visited thereon, and recorded for life or for death." Thus you are left to conclude that on New Year's Day [the sixth day from the twenty-fifth of Elul], in the first hour the idea of creating man entered His mind, in the second He took counsel with the ministering angels, in the third He assembled Adam's dust, in the fourth He kneaded it, in the fifth He shaped him, in the sixth He made him into a lifeless body, in the seventh He breathed a soul into him, in the eighth He brought him into the Garden of Eden, in the ninth he was commanded [against eating of the fruit of the tree of knowledge], in the tenth he transgressed, in the eleventh he was judged, in the twelfth he was pardoned. "This," said the Holy One, blessed be He, to Adam, "will be a sign to your children. As you stood in judgment before Me this day and came out with a free pardon, so will your children in the future stand in judgment before Me on this day and will come out from My presence with a free pardon." When will that be? *In the seventh month, in the first day of the month* (Leviticus 23.24).

Leviticus Rabbah 29.11

There are four New Years: on the first day of Nisan is the New Year for kings and festivals; on the first of Elul is the New Year for the tithe of cattle (R. Eleazar and R. Simeon say that this is on the first of Tishri); on the first of Tishri is the New Year for reckoning of the years, and for release and jubilee years for planting and [the tithe of] vegetables; on the first of Shevat is the New Year for trees, according to the School of Shammai, but the School of Hillel say it is on the fifteenth of that month.

At four seasons judgment is passed on the world: at Passover in respect of produce; at Pentecost in respect of fruit; at New Year all creatures pass before Him like children at Maron, as it says, *He that fashioneth the heart of them all, that considereth all their doings* (Psalms 33.15); and on Tabernacles judgment is passed in respect of rain.

Rosh Hashanah 1.1–2[2]

On the first of Tishri is New Year for years.

R. Nahman b. Isaac explained the Mishnah to refer to the Divine judgment, as it is written, *From the beginning of the year to the end of the year* (Deuteronomy 11.12), which means, From the beginning of the year sentence is passed as to what shall be up to the end of it. How do we know that this takes place in Tishri? Because it is written, *Blow the horn at the new moon, at the covered time for our feastday* (Psalms 81.4). Which is the feast on which the moon is covered over? You must say that this is New Year; and it is written in this connection, *For it is a statute for Israel, an ordinance for the God of Jacob* (ibid. 5).

Our Rabbis taught: *For it is a statute for Israel, an ordinance for the God of Jacob* teaches that the heavenly court does not assemble for judgment until the court on earth has sanctified the month.

Rosh Hashanah 8a–b

When the ministering angels assemble before God and ask, "When is the New Year and when is the Day of Atonement?"

God says to them: "Why do you ask Me? You and I, let us all go to the court on earth and inquire of them."

Deuteronomy Rabbah 2.14

On what day does the Holy One, blessed be He, judge the [inhabitants of the] world and acquit them? It is on New Year's Day that He judges His creatures and acquits them. For assuredly He desires to acquit His creatures, not to hold them guilty, as is said *As I live, saith the Lord God, I have no pleasure in the death of the wicked* (Ezekiel 33.11), and again *That which the Lord desireth is to make him righteous* (Isaiah 42.21), that is, He desires to declare His creatures righteous. And why does He wish to declare His creatures righteous? Because, according to R. Judah bar Nahman citing Resh Lakish, the Holy One, blessed be He, reasons as follows: When I win I lose, and when I lose I win. I won out over the generation of the flood and I lost, for I had to destroy all the hosts of that generation, as is said *And He blotted out every living substance* (Genesis 7.23). And so it was with the generation of the dispersion of the races of man, and so with the Sodomites. But at the making of the golden calf, Moses won over Me by asking in entreaty, *Lord, why doth Thy wrath wax hot?* (Exodus 32.11), and I then won for Myself all the hosts of the children of Israel. Hence I acquit all My creatures in order not to lose them. It is on New Year's Day that I acquit My creatures. Accordingly, when I judge them, let them be sure to lift up *shofars* and blow them before Me, and I will bring to remembrance in their behalf the binding of Isaac and will acquit them at the judgment. Whence do we know that the blowing of the *shofar* is a reminder to God? From what is read in the lesson for the day, *In the seventh month, in the first day of the month . . . a time of remembrance proclaimed with the blast of horns* (Leviticus 23.24).

Pesikta Rabbati 40.1[3]

R. Judah says: "Man is judged on New Year and his doom is sealed on the Day of Atonement." R. Jose says: "Man is judged every day, as it says, *And thou dost visit him every morning* (Job 7.18).″ R. Nathan says: ″Man is judged every moment, as it says, *Thou dost try him every moment* (ibid.).″

Rosh Hashanah 16a

On New Year Sarah, Rachel and Hannah were remembered on high [and they conceived]; on New Year Joseph went forth from prison; on New Year the bondage of our ancestors in Egypt ceased.

Rosh Hashanah 10b–11a

Shall the *Hallel* [songs of praise] be said on the New Year and on the Day of Atonement? That is not possible because R. Abbahu said: ″The ministering angels said in the presence of the Holy One, blessed be He: 'Why do not the Israelites sing a song before You on the New Year and on the Day of Atonement?' He answered them: 'Is it possible that the King should sit on the throne of judgment, with the books of those destined to live and destined to die before Him, and Israel should sing a song before Me?' ″

Arakhin 10b

How did the Holy One, blessed be He, come to ordain the measure of mercy to go with the measure of justice? R. Hanina said: When the Holy One, blessed be He, wishing to create His world, observed the doings of the wicked—the generation of Enosh, the generation of the flood, the generation of the dispersion of the races of man, the acts of the Sodomites—He no longer wished to create the world. But then the Holy One, blessed be He, returned and observed the doings of the righteous —of Abraham, Isaac, and Jacob, and of all the other righteous. As He returned and observed them, He said: Am I not to create the world because of the wicked? Indeed, I shall create the world—and as for him who sins, it will not be difficult to chastise him. Nevertheless, when He was about to create the world with the measure of justice alone, He could not bring Himself to do so because of the deeds of the righteous, for whom justice alone would be too severe a measure. And when He was about to create it with the measure of mercy alone,

He could not bring Himself to do so because of the deeds of the wicked, for whom mercy alone would be too indulgent a measure. What did He do? He made partners of the two measures, the measure of justice and the measure of mercy, and created the world, as is said *In the day that the Lord [of mercy and the] God [of justice] made heaven and earth* (Genesis 2.4). . . .

Therefore David said: Master of universes, hadst Thou not judged Adam with mercy at the time he ate of the tree, he would not have remained alive for even one hour. And even as Thou didst judge him with mercy, so didst Thou ordain, beginning with him, that this day, New Year's Day, Thou wouldst judge his children with mercy. *For ever, O Lord, Thy word standeth fast* (Psalms 119.89). What is implied by *standeth fast*? Thy word which Thou didst ordain for Adam still stands: even as Thou didst judge him with mercy, so Thou judgest for ever all the generations after him. Hence it is said *For ever, O Lord.*

Pesikta Rabbati 40.2⁴

According to the custom of the world, when two charioteers race in the hippodrome, which of them receives a wreath? The victor. Thus on New Year's Day all the people of the world come forth like contestants on parade and pass before God, and the children of Israel among all the people of the world also pass before Him. Then the guardian angels of the nations of the world declare: "We were victorious, and in the judgment shall be found righteous." But actually no one knows who was victorious, whether the children of Israel or the nations of the world were victorious. After New Year's Day is gone, all the children of Israel come forth on the Day of Atonement and fast thereon, clothed in white and comely garments. But even after the Day of Atonement is gone, still no one knows who was victorious, the children of Israel, or the nations of the world. When the first Day of Tabernacles comes, however, all the children of Israel, they that are grown as well as the little ones, take up their festive wreaths in their right hands and their citrons in their left, and then all people of the world know that in the judgment the children of Israel were proclaimed victorious.

Midrash on Psalms 17.5[5]

THE RIGHTEOUS AND THE WICKED

R. Kruspedai said in the name of R. Johanan: "Three books are opened [in heaven] on New Year, one for the thoroughly wicked, one for the thoroughly righteous, and one for the intermediate. The thoroughly righteous are forthwith inscribed definitively in the book of life; the thoroughly wicked are forthwith inscribed definitively in the book of death; the doom of the intermediate is suspended from New Year till the Day of Atonement; if they deserve well, they are inscribed in the book of life; if they do not deserve well, they are inscribed in the book of death."

Rosh Hashanah 16b

Our Rabbis taught: "A man should always regard himself as though he were half guilty and half meritorious. If he performs one good deed, happy is he for weighting himself down in the scale of merit. If he commits one transgression, woe to him for weighting himself down in the scale of guilt, for it is said, *but one sinner destroyeth much good* (Ecclesiastes 9.18); on account of a single sin which he commits much good is lost to him."

R. Eleazar son of R. Simeon said: "Because the world is judged by its majority, and an individual too is judged by his majority of deeds, good or bad, if he performs one good deed, happy is he for turning the scale both for himself and for the whole world on the side of merit; if he commits one transgression, woe to him for weighting himself and the whole world in the scale of guilt, for it is said, *but one sinner . . .* —on account of the single sin which this man commits he and the whole world lose much good."

R. Simeon b. Yohai said: "Even if he is perfectly righteous

all his life but rebels at the end, he destroys his former good deeds, for it is said, *The righteousness of the righteous shall not deliver him in the day of his transgression* (Ezekiel 33.12). And even if one is completely wicked all his life but repents at the end, he is not reproached with his wickedness, for it is said, *and as for the wickedness of the wicked, he shall not fall thereby in the day that he turneth from his wickedness* (ibid.)."

Kiddushin 40a–b

THE SOUND OF THE *SHOFAR*

R. Abbahu said: "Why do we blow on a ram's horn? The Holy One, blessed be He, said: 'Sound before Me a ram's horn so that I may remember on your behalf the binding of Isaac the son of Abraham, and account it to you as if you had bound yourselves before Me.' "

R. Isaac said: "Why do we sound the horn on New Year? You ask, why do we sound? The All-Merciful has told us to sound!"

Rosh Hashanah 16a

And Abraham lifted up his eyes, and looked, and behold behind him a ram caught in the thicket by its horns (Genesis 22.13). This teaches that the Holy One, blessed be He, showed our father Abraham the ram tearing itself free from one thicket and getting entangled in another. The Holy One, blessed be He, said to Abraham: "In a similar manner are your children destined to be caught by iniquities and entangled in troubles, but they will ultimately be redeemed through the horns of the ram. Hence it is written, *The Lord God will blow the horn* (Zechariah 9.14)." R. Huna son of R. Isaac said: "It teaches that the Holy One, blessed be He, showed Abraham the ram tearing itself free from one thicket and getting entangled in another. The Holy One, blessed be He, said to Abraham: 'In a similar manner are your children destined to be caught by the nations and entangled in troubles, being dragged from empire to empire, from Babylon to Media, from Media to Greece, and from

Greece to Edom [Rome], but they will ultimately be redeemed through the horns of the ram.' Hence it is written, *The Lord shall be seen over them, and His arrow shall go forth as the lightning; and the Lord God will blow the horn* (ibid.)."

Leviticus Rabbah 29.10

Judah son of R. Nahman opened his discourse with the text, *God is gone up amidst shouting, the Lord amidst the sound of the horn* (Psalms 47.6). When the Holy One, blessed be He, ascends and sits upon the Throne of Judgment, He ascends with intent to do [strict] judgment. What is the reason for this statement? *God [of justice] is gone amidst shouting.* But when Israel take their horns and blow them in the presence of the Holy One, blessed be He, He rises from the Throne of Judgment and sits upon the Throne of Mercy—for it is written, *The Lord [of mercy] amidst the sound of the horn*—and He is filled with compassion for them, taking pity upon them and changing for them the attribute of justice to one of mercy.

Leviticus Rabbah 29.3

The *shofar* was created for the welfare of Israel. The Torah was given to Israel with the sound of the *shofar*, as it is said: *When the voice of the* shofar *waxed louder and louder* (Exodus 19.19). Israel conquered in the battle of Jericho with the blast of the *shofar*: *when the people heard the sound of the* shofar *that the people shouted with a great shout, and the wall fell down flat* (Joshua 6.20). Israel will be advised of the advent of the messiah with the sound of the *shofar*: *And the Lord God will blow the* shofar (Zechariah 9.14). And the Holy One, blessed be He, will sound the *shofar* at the time of the ingathering of the exiles of Israel to their place: *And it shall come to pass in that day, that a great* shofar *shall be blown; and they shall come that were lost in the land of Assyria, and they that were dispersed in the land of Egypt; and they shall worship the Lord in the holy mountain at Jerusalem* (Isaiah 27.13).

Eliyahu Zuta 2

ANNULLING THE HARSH DECREE

Three means annul the harsh decree: prayer, charity and repentance.

Jerusalem *Taanit* 65a

R. Yudan in the name of R. Eliezer: Three things—prayer, turning in repentance to God, and charity—avert a harsh decree, as is indicated in a single verse wherein all three are specifically referred to: *If My people, upon whom My name is called, shall humble themselves, and pray* (II Chronicles 7.14). Here the word *pray* refers to prayer; the next words in the verse, *and seek My face* (ibid.), refer to acts of charity, as when Scripture says, *As for me, I shall behold Thy face through charity* (Psalms 17.15); the following words in the verse, *and turn from their evil ways* (II Chronicles 7.14), refer to turning in repentance to God. And with regard to the practice of the three, how does the verse conclude? *Then will I hear from heaven, and will forgive their sin, and will heal their land* (ibid.).

Pesikta Rabbati 52.3[6]

SIGNS AND OMENS

R. Zebid said: "If the first day of the New Year is warm, most of the year will be warm; if cold, most of the year will be cold."

Baba Batra 147a

It has been said that omens are of significance; therefore, a man should make a regular habit of eating, at the beginning of the year, pumpkin, fenugreek, leek, beet, and dates [as these grow in profusion and are symbolic of prosperity].

Horayot 12a

The entire sustenance of man for the year is fixed for him from New Year to the Day of Atonement, except the expenditures for festivals and for the instruction of his children in the Law; if he spent less for any of these he is given less and if he spent more he is given more.

Betzah 16a

It is written, *Seek ye the Lord while he may be found* (Isaiah 55.6). When can an individual find God? Rabbah b. Abbuha said: "These are the ten days between New Year and the Day of Atonement."

Rosh Hashanah 18a

GOD WELCOMES PENITENTS

The Holy One, blessed be He, said: "My hands reach out to the penitent. I turn back no man who gives me his heart in repentance. Hence it is said: *Peace, peace, to him that is far off and to him that is near* (Isaiah 57.19). If any man comes towards Me, I will go towards him, and I will heal him."

Midrash on Psalms 120.7[7]

Penitence is a good characteristic, and the compassion of the Holy One, blessed be He, goes out to mankind when they show penitence.

Numbers Rabbah 2.10

Repentance and meritorious deeds are a protection against punishment. R. Ishmael said: "If repentance had not been created, the world would not exist. However, since repentance has been created, the right hand of the Holy One, blessed be He, is stretched forth to receive the penitent every day, and He says, *Return ye children of men* (Psalms 90.3)."

Pirke de Rabbi Eliezer 43

Israel is sunk in iniquity on account of the evil impulse which is within them, but they do penitence, and God each year pardons their iniquities and renews their heart to fear Him; for it says: *A new heart also will I give you* (Ezekiel 36.26).

Exodus Rabbah 15.6

Just as when a garment becomes soiled, it can be made white again, so can Israel return unto God after they have sinned, by doing penance.

Exodus Rabbah 23.10

If an ordinary person makes use of broken vessels, it is a disgrace for him, but the vessels used by the Holy One, blessed be He, are precisely broken ones, as it is said, *The Lord is nigh unto them that are of a broken heart* (Psalms 34.19).

Leviticus Rabbah 7.2

R. Jassa said: "The Holy One, blessed be He, said to Israel: 'My sons, present to Me an opening of repentance no bigger than the eye of a needle, and I will widen it into openings through which wagons and carriages can pass.' "

Song of Songs Rabbah 5.2

The Holy One, blessed be He, waits for the nations of the world in the hope that they will repent and be brought beneath His wings.

Numbers Rabbah 10.1

Consider the parable of a prince who was far away from his father—a hundred days' journey away. His friends said to him: "Return to your father." He replied: "I cannot: I have not the strength." Thereupon his father sent word, saying to him: "Come back as far as you can according to your strength, and I will go the rest of the way to meet you." So the Holy One, blessed be He, says to Israel: *Return unto Me, and I will return unto you* (Malachi 3.7).

Pesikta Rabbati 44.9[8]

If a man should come and say that God does not receive the penitent, there is Manasseh the son of Hezekiah; let him come and give evidence. For no creature in the world acted so wickedly before Me as he did, yet in the hour of repentance I accepted him; as is borne out by the text, *And he prayed unto Him; and He was entreated of him, and heard his supplication, and brought him back to Jerusalem unto his Kingdom* (II Chronicles 33.13).

Numbers Rabbah 14.1

There were once some highwaymen in the neighborhood of R. Meir who caused him a lot of trouble. R. Meir accordingly prayed that they should die. His wife Beruriah said to him: "How do you conclude that such a prayer should be permitted?" "Because it is written, Let *hattaim* [sins] cease." "Is it written *hotim* [sinners]? It is written *hattaim!* Further, look at the end of the verse: *and let the wicked men be no more* (Psalms 104.35). Since the sins will cease, there will be no more wicked men! Rather pray for them that they should repent, and there will be no more wicked." He did pray for them, and they repented.

Berakhot 10a

THE GREATNESS OF REPENTANCE

R. Hama b. Hanina said: "Great is penitence, for it brings healing to the world, as it is said: *I will heal their backsliding, I will love them freely* (Hosea 14.5)."

R. Levi said: "Great is repentance, for it reaches up to the Throne of Glory, as it is said: *Return, O Israel, unto the Lord thy God* (ibid. 2)."

R. Jonathan said: "Great is repentance, because it brings about redemption, as it is said: *And a redeemer will come to Zion, and unto them that turn from transgression in Jacob* (Isaiah 59.20)."

Resh Lakish said: "Great is repentance, for because of it premeditated sins are accounted as errors, as it is said: *Return O Israel, unto the Lord, thy God; for thou hast stumbled in thine iniquity* (Hosea 14.2)."

R. Samuel b. Nahmani said in the name of R. Jonathan: "Great is repentance, because it prolongs the years of man, as it is said: *And when the wicked turneth from his wickedness . . . he shall live thereby* (Ezekiel 33.19)."

Yoma 86a–b

Great is repentance for it preceded the creation of the world, as it is said, *Before the mountains were brought forth, or ever Thou hadst formed the earth and the world. . . . Thou turnest man to contrition, and sayest, Return, ye children of men*

(Psalms 90.2–3). What was the call to repentance? A voice
from heaven which cried out saying: "Repent, ye children of
men."

Midrash on Psalms 90.12[9]

In the place where penitents stand even the wholly righteous
cannot stand.

Berakhot 34b

These are man's advocates: Repentance and good deeds.

Shabbat 32a

Repentance and good works are as a shield against retribution.

Avot 4.11

Penitence is equal to all the sacrifices of a sinner combined,
for it is written, *The sacrifices of God are a broken spirit*
(Psalms 51.19).

Numbers Rabbah 13.18

If a man repents he converts into pious deeds even the many
sins of which he may be guilty.

Exodus Rabbah 31.1

Were Israel to practice repentance even for one day, forthwith they would be redeemed, and forthwith the scion of David
would come.

Song of Songs Rabbah 5.2

Better is one hour of repentance and good works in this
world than the whole life of the world to come; and better is
one hour of bliss in the world to come than the whole life of
this world.

Avot 4.17

THE TIMING OF REPENTANCE

The gates of prayer are sometimes open and sometimes
locked, but the gates of repentance are always open.

Deuteronomy Rabbah 2.7

R. Eliezer said: "Repent one day before your death." His disciples asked him, "Does then one know on what day he will die?" "Then all the more reason that he repent today," he replied, "lest he die tomorrow, and thus his whole life is spent in repentance. And Solomon too said in his wisdom, *Let thy garments be always white; and let not thy head lack ointment* (Ecclesiastes 9.8)."

Shabbat 153a

Happy is he who repents while he is still [enjoying the full vitality and energy of] a youthful man.

Avodah Zarah 19a

WAYS OF PENITENCE

If one commits a sin and is ashamed of it, all his sins are forgiven him.

Berakhot 12b

At the time when the Temple stood, the altar brought atonement for a person; now a person's table brings atonement for him [through the hospitality shown to poor guests].

Hagigah 27a

IV

ROSH HASHANAH IN MEDIEVAL
JEWISH LITERATURE

Jewish literature of the medieval period is rich in philosophy, poetry, and works of scholarship. It gave birth to
numerous classics that have remained our literary heritage to
this day. The selections in this chapter, arranged in anthological
rather than chronological order, have been taken from the writings of some of the leading medieval Jewish authors.

Saadia Gaon (892–942), who enriched many branches of
Jewish literature and exerted a profound influence on Jewish
thought, outlined ten reasons for blowing the *shofar* on New
Year's Day. These may be found in the *Siddur* (1340) of David
ben Joseph Abudarham and were later included in several
liturgical rituals.

Solomon ibn Gabirol (c. 1021–1058), the illustrious Spanish
moralist, philosopher, and poet, composed a number of prayers
which are included in the *Selihot* (penitential prayers) recited
on the eve of Rosh Hashanah. Rabbi Solomon ben Isaac (1040–
1105)—Rashi—was a prolific commentator on the Bible and
Talmud whose writings are avidly studied to this day.

Bachya ibn Pakuda (c. 1050?–c.1150) wrote *Hovot ha-Levavot* ("Duties of the Heart"), an inspiring treatise on ethical conduct that made a deep impact on Jews which continues even to this day. A twelfth-century Spanish Jewish scholar, Abraham Bar Hiyya, who authored many scientific works in Hebrew, also wrote an ethical treatise, *Hegyon ha-Nefesh* ("Meditation of the Soul"). Moses ben Maimon (1135–1204), popularly called Maimonides and noted as a philosopher, codifier, and physician, wrote *Moreh Nevukhim* ("Guide for the Perplexed"), in which he sought to harmonize philosophy and religion. Judah Al-Harizi (c. 1170–1235), "a celebrated literary genius and intellectual vagabond poet," was the author of *Tahkemoni*, a Hebrew potpourri of prayers, sermons, love ditties, tales of travel, proverbs, and other sundry matters, written in rhymed prose interspersed with poetry.

Jonah ben Abraham Gerondi of Spain (1180–1263) was a noted Talmudist, but he is best known for his ethical writings, particularly *Shaare Teshuvah* ("Gates of Repentance"), a work that strongly influenced later Jewish ethical literature. Moses ben Nahman of Gerona, Spain (1195–c.1270), known as Nahmanides, was a noted Talmudist and commentator. Aaron ben Elijah (died 1369), a Karaite, wrote extensively on the philosophy of religion, law, and biblical exegesis. The excerpt below is from his philosophical work *Etz Hayyim*. Joseph Albo, a fifteenth-century theologian, is noted for his *Sefer ha-Ikkarim* ("Book of Principles"), a medieval philosophical and theological classic which has been exceedingly popular among Jews since its publication. Rabbi Isaac ben Moses Arama (c. 1420–1494), a Spanish Talmudist and philosopher, was the author of *Akedat Yitzhak* ("The Binding of Isaac"), a homiletical classic.

Of a different character is the *Zohar*. Although popularly attributed to Simeon ben Yohai of the second century, it first made its appearance in the thirteenth century through Moses ben Shemtob de Leon. It is the basic work of Cabala, consisting mainly of discursive commentaries on the Bible and teachings on mysticism.

THE MONTH OF TISHRI

JUDAH AL-HARIZI

The first of the months is Tishri, the time when all good things bear fruit, and every heart scales the height of joy. God has created it to interpret the secret of the months. And it became the head over them.

For in it God established the Jewish year and made the moon for seasons. And from it are known the days that are disqualified and proper and how the rest of the fasts and festivals are recorded. And our saintly sages mentioned four New Years, of which Tishri, the splendor of souls, is the first, and from thence it was parted, and becomes four heads. And through it are the reckonings of the feasts and the times and they are for signs, for seasons, and for days and for years. On its first day is a day of mustering and of remembrance—a day of exaltation and pre-eminence, the day when the creatures pass before God as a flock of sheep. This one laments and this one exults. This one finds favor and this one anger. And God warns His prophets in a vision that the Jews should be ready for this day. It is the day on which all who are written for life are counted and numbered for peace. Those who are destined for death are blotted out from the Book of Life.

It is a day that God judges His creatures as wayfarers and wanderers. He says to bring out the Book of Remembrances, the Book of Chronicles, and have them read before the King. It is the day when each man moans with pang and pain and on giving reckoning for his deeds. It is as fire of Tophet for rottenness, for fire comes forth from the "Reckoning."

Happy is the man whose soul will be pure on that day, worthy to behold the countenance of the King. For then he will blossom as a fruitful vine, and his table will be filled with abundance, and his cup running over. Then the drinking will be sweet and good for every moaning soul.

When the days grow short and the hours less and wine calls to creatures—"See how the days grow shorter and the moments

1. *Mahzor.* Germany. First half of 14th century. Bodleian Library, Oxford, Ms. Reggio 1, folio 207v. See Chapter XIII.

2. Miscellany. Northern Italy. Circa 1470. The Israel Museum, Jerusalem. See Chapter XIII.

3. *Mahzor.* Italy. Second half of 15th century. Strasbourg, Collection of Georges Weill. See Chapter XIII.

בְּחַיֵּיכֹן וּבְיוֹמֵיכֹן וּבְחַיֵּי דְכָל בֵּית יִשְׂרָ בְּעַגָלָא וּבִזְמַן קָרִיב וְא

וְאִמְרוּ אָמֵן ׃ יְהֵא שְׁמֵיהּ רַבָּא מְבָרַךְ לְעָלַם וּלְעָלְמֵי עָלְמַיָּא ׃ יִתְבָּרַךְ וְיִשְׁתַּבַּח וְיִתְפָּאַר

וְיִתְרוֹמַם וְיִתְנַשֵּׂא וְיִתְהַדָּר וְיִתְעַלֶּה וְיִתְהַלָּל שְׁמֵיהּ דְּקֻדְשָׁא בְּרִיךְ הוּא לְעֵלָּא

מִכָּל בִּרְכָתָא וְשִׁירָתָא תֻּשְׁבְּחָתָא וְנֶחָמָתָא דַּאֲמִירָן בְּעָלְמָא וְאִמְרוּ אָמֵן ׃

תִּתְקַבַּל צְלוֹתְהוֹן וּבָעוּתְהוֹן דְּכָל יִשְׂרָ קֳדָם אֲבוּהוֹן וּבִשְׁמַיָּא וְאִמְרוּ אָמֵן ׃

יְהֵא שְׁלָמָא רַבָּא בֵּן שְׁמַיָּא וְחַיִּים עָלֵינוּ וְעַל כָּל יִשְׂרָ וְאִמְרוּ אָמֵן ׃ עֹשֶׂה

שָׁלוֹם בִּמְרוֹמָיו יְהוּא יַעֲשֶׂה שָׁלוֹם עָלֵינוּ וְעַל כָּל יִשְׂרָאֵל וְאִמְרוּ אָמֵן ׃

בָּרוּךְ אַתָּה יְיָ אֱלֹהֵינוּ מֶלֶךְ הָעוֹלָם אֲשֶׁר קִדְּשָׁנוּ בְּמִצְוֹתָיו וְעִוָּנוּ לִשְׁבּוֹעַ בְּקוֹל שׁוֹפָר ׃ אמן

בָּרוּךְ אַתָּה יְיָ אֱלֹהֵינוּ מֶלֶךְ הָעוֹלָם שֶׁהֶחֱיָנוּ וְקִיְּמָנוּ וְהִגִּיעָנוּ לַזְּמַן הַזֶּה ׃ אמן

תְּרוּעָה	הְקִיעָה	תְּרוּעָה	שְׁבָרִים	תְּקִיעָה		
תְּרוּעָה	הְקִיעָה	תְּרוּעָה	שְׁבָרִים	תְּקִיעָה		
תְּרוּעָה	הְקִיעָה	תְּרוּעָה	שְׁבָרִים	תְּקִיעָה		
	תְּקִיעָה	שְׁבָרִים		תְּקִיעָה		
	תְּקִיעָה	שְׁבָרִים		תְּקִיעָה		
	תְּקִיעָה	שְׁבָרִים		תְּקִיעָה		
תְּקִיעָה	תְּרוּעָה		תְּקִיעָה			
תְּקִיעָה	תְּרוּעָה		תְּקִיעָה			
תְּקִיעָה גְדוֹלָה	תְּרוּעָה		תְּקִיעָה			

אַשְׁרֵי הָעָם יוֹדְעֵי תְרוּעָה יְיָ בְּאוֹר פָּנֶיךָ יְהַלֵּכוּן ׃

אַשְׁרֵי יוֹשְׁבֵי בֵיתֶךָ עוֹד יְהַלְלוּךָ סֶּלָה ׃

יְהַלְלוּ אֶת שֵׁם יְיָ   כִּי נִשְׂגָּב שְׁמוֹ לְבַדּוֹ

לַחֹזֵן

בָּרוּךְ אַתָּה יְיָ אֱלֹהֵינוּ וֵאלֹהֵי אֲבוֹתֵינוּ אֱלֹהֵי אַבְרָהָם אֱלֹהֵי יִצְחָק וֵאלֹהֵי יַעֲקֹב הָאֵל הַגָּדוֹל הַגִּבּוֹר וְהַנּוֹרָא אֵל עֶלְיוֹן גּוֹמֵל חֲסָדִים טוֹבִים וְקוֹנֵה הַכֹּל

וְזוֹכֵר חַסְדֵּי אָבוֹת וּמֵבִיא גֹאֵל לִבְנֵי בְנֵיהֶם לְמַעַן שְׁמוֹ בְּאַהֲבָה

מִסּוֹד חֲכָמִים וּנְבוֹנִים וּמִלֶּמֶד דַּעַת מְבִינִים אֶפְתְּחָה פִי בִּתְפִלָּה

וּבְתַחֲנוּנִים לְחַלּוֹת וּלְחַנֵּן פְּנֵי מֶלֶךְ מָלֵא רַחֲמִים ׃

4. *Mahzor.* Germany. 14th century. Library of the Hungarian Academy of Sciences, Budapest. See Chapter XIII.

diminish. Therefore, hasten to drink me at the banqueting table." For the day is short and the work is great. And the poet took up his refrain and said:

"Place the cup before you in Tishri
And you will blossom and bear fruit in it like a leafy tree.
And if you are disheartened and sad
In your wine you will become strong, hale and glad,
Take joy for a maidservant, take her,
And you shall not have power to sell her to a stranger."[1]

THE DAY OF THE CONCEALED MOON

R. Eleazar said: "This day is called 'the concealing (*keseh*) for the day of our feast,' because the moon is still concealed and does not shine. Through what then will it shine? Through repentance and the sound of the *shofar*, as it is written, *Blessed is the people that know the trumpet sound, because, O Lord, they shall walk in the light of Thy countenance* (Psalms 89.16). On this day the moon is covered, and it does not shine until the tenth day, when Israel turn with a perfect repentance, so that the supernal Mother gives light to her. Hence this day is called the day of atonements (*kippurim*), because two lights are shedding illumination, since the higher lamp is illumining the lower. For on this day the moon receives illumination from the supernal Light and not from the light of the sun." . . .

R. Abba said: "On New Year Adam was created and was brought to trial before his Master and repented and was pardoned by the Almighty. He said to him: Adam, thou shalt be a sign to thy descendants for all generations. On this day they are brought to trial, and if they repent I will pardon them and remove from the Throne of Judgment and sit on the Throne of Mercy and have mercy of them."

Zohar Emor 100b–101a[2]

SHOFAR AND MAN

ISAAC BEN MOSES ARAMA

Such is the nature of man that his inner powers are influenced by exterior factors, as exemplified by Elisha whose spiritual and prophetic sense became sharpened and activated through the playing of musical instruments. As the Bible declares *And it came to pass when the minstrel played, that the hand of the Lord came upon him* (II Kings 3.15). Similarly our sages invented various devices by which the memory of man could be strengthened, thereby indelibly imprinting on his heart things which he saw or heard. The instruments, too, are suited to various moods and the listener may be moved to joy or sadness or to spiritual uplift. Now the principal task of the *shofar* is to arouse spiritual awe in the heart of those who respond to it, as it is said *Shall the* shofar *be blown in the city and the people not tremble?* (Amos 3.6). However, not all the sounds that issue from the *shofar* are the same, for the *tekiah* tends to leave one in a joyful humor, while the *teruah* is a symbol of awe. The call of the *shevarim* lies in between these two sounds. The first note, the *tekiah*, symbolizes the righteous and rejoices in their future when they will receive their reward. The wicked quake and tremble in the fear of the Day of Judgment, whilst the average man is filled with joy, sadness and hope. It is because of this that on Rosh Hashanah these three calls reverberate throughout the Jewish world—*tekiah, shevarim, teruah*.[3]

REASONS FOR SOUNDING THE SHOFAR

SAADIA GAON

There are ten reasons why the Creator, blessed be He, commanded us to sound the *shofar* on Rosh Hashanah.

The first reason: Because this day is the beginning of creation, on which the Holy One, blessed be He, created the world and reigned over it. Just as is with kings at the start of their reign—trumpets and horns are blown in their presence to make it known and to let it be heard in every place—thus it is when we designate the Creator, may He be blessed, as King on this day, for David said: *With trumpets and sound of the horn, shout ye before the King, the Lord* (Psalms 98.6).

The second reason: Because the day of New Year is the first of the ten days of repentance, the *shofar* is sounded on it to announce to us as one warns and says: "Whoever wants to repent—let him repent; and if he does not, let him reproach himself." Thus do the kings: first they warn the people of their decrees; then if one violates a decree after the warning, his excuse is not accepted.

The third reason: To remind us of Mount Sinai, as it is said: *The blare of the horn grew louder and louder* (Exodus 19.19), and that we should accept for ourselves the covenant that our ancestors accepted for themselves, as they said *we will do and obey* (Exodus 24.7).

The fourth reason: To remind us of the words of the prophets that were compared to the sound of the *shofar*, as it is said: *Then whosoever heareth the sound of the horn, and taketh not warning, if the sword come, and taketh him away, his blood shall be upon his own head . . . whereas if he had taken warning, he would have delivered his soul* (Ezekiel 33.4–5).

The fifth reason: To remind us of the destruction of the Temple and the sound of the battle-cries of the enemies, as it is said: *Because thou hast heard, O my soul, the sound of the horn, the alarm of war* (Jeremiah 4.19). When we hear the sound of the *shofar*, we will ask God to rebuild the Temple.

The sixth reason: To remind us of the binding of Isaac who offered his life to Heaven. We also should offer our lives for the sanctification of His Name, and thus we will be remembered for good.

The seventh reason: When we will hear the blowing of the *shofar*, we will be fearful, and we will tremble, and we will humble ourselves before the Creator, for that is the nature of the *shofar*—it causes fear and trembling, as it is written: *Shall the horn be blown in a city and the people not tremble?* (Amos 3.6).

The eighth reason: To recall the day of the great judgment and to be fearful of it, as it is said: *The great day of the Lord is near, it is near and hasteth greatly . . . a day of the horn and alarm* (Zephaniah 1.14–16).

The ninth reason: To remind us of the ingathering of the scattered ones of Israel, that we ardently desire, as it is said: *And it shall come to pass in that day, that a great horn shall be blown; and they shall come that were lost in the land of Assyria . . . and they shall worship the Lord in the holy mountain at Jerusalem* (Isaiah 27.13).

The tenth reason: To remind us of the resurrection of the dead and the belief in it, as it is said: *All ye inhabitants of the world, and ye dwellers on the earth, when an ensign is lifted up on the mountains, see ye; and when the horn is blown, hear ye* (Isaiah 18.3).

Sefer Avudarham, Rosh Hashanah[4]

AN INTRODUCTION TO THE DAY OF THE FAST

MOSES MAIMONIDES

New Year is a day of repentance on which men are aroused from their forgetfulness. Accordingly, the *shofar* is blown. The day is, as it were, an introduction and a beginning to the Day of the Fast, as is common knowledge in the tradition of the nation regarding the ten days between New Year and the Day of Atonement.

Guide for the Perplexed 3.43

JUDGMENT AND MERCY

MOSES NAHMANIDES

Rosh Hashanah is a day of judgment with mercy and Yom Kippur is a day of mercy with judgment.

Ramban, Leviticus 23.24

A SACRED OCCASION

SOLOMON BEN ISAAC

The first day (Rosh Hashanah) *shall be a sacred occasion*: Sanctify it with clean garments and with prayer; and, on the other festivals, with food and drink, with clean garments and with prayer.

Rashi, Leviticus 23.35

THREE PRINCIPLES OF DIVINE LAW

JOSEPH ALBO

It seems to me that the general and essential principles of divine law are three: existence of God, providence in reward and punishment, and divine revelation. . . .

That these three principles are the basis of the faith by which man attains true happiness is proved by the fact that the Men of the Great Synagogue composed three blessings which they incorporated in the Additional Service for New Year, going by the name of "Kingdoms," "Memorials" and "Trumpets." These three blessings correspond to the three principles and are intended to call our attention to the fact that by properly believing in these principles together with the dogmas derived from them we shall win a favorable verdict in the divine judgment.

The blessing known as "Kingdoms" corresponds to the principle of the existence of God. This is proved by the words of the benediction "Therefore do we wait for Thee, O Lord our God, that we may quickly see Thy glorious strength, when the images will be removed from the earth and the idols will be completely cut off, when the world will be established under the Kingdom of the Almighty . . . when all the inhabitants of the world will recognize and know that to Thee shall every knee bend, by Thee every tongue swear . . . and all shall accept the yoke of Thy Kingdom."

The benediction called "Memorials" points to providence and

reward and punishment, as is indicated by its contents: "Thou rememberest the works of the universe, and visitest all the creatures from the beginning; before Thee are all hidden things revealed. . . ."

The benediction called "Trumpets" alludes to the third principle, revelation. Therefore it begins, "Thou didst reveal Thyself in the cloud of Thy glory to Thy holy people and didst speak unto them. From heaven didst Thou cause them to hear Thy voice. . . ." This benediction is called "Trumpets" because at the time of the giving of the Law there was a very loud sound of the trumpet, such as never had been heard before in the world. Thunders and lightning like those seen at Sinai or of the same nature had been heard and seen before, but the sound of a trumpet without a trumpet had never been heard before, and will not be heard again until the time of the redemption. At that time the true law will be made known before the whole world. This is the time that is referred to in the words of the prophet, *And the Lord God will blow the horn* (Zechariah 9.14), according to some authorities.

I have seen a statement that the benediction "Trumpets" bears an allusion to the sacrifice of Isaac. But this is not correct, for if that were the case, we should expect the sacrifice of Isaac to be mentioned in this blessing, whereas mention is made of it in the benediction "Memorials." The origin of this opinion is to be sought in the statement of the Rabbis that the ceremony of blowing the ram's horn on New Year is in memory of the ram which was substituted for Isaac. But this does not justify the opinion. For what the Rabbis mean is that the requirement of a ram's horn is to commemorate the ram of Isaac, not that the command itself to blow an instrument has that meaning, much less does it follow that the benediction "Trumpets" alludes to that event. . . .

Sefer ha-Ikkarim 1.4[5]

ELEMENTS OF REPENTANCE

JOSEPH ALBO

The elements of repentance by which a person may be cleansed of his iniquities and purified of his sin before God are correction of thought, speech and act. Correction of thought means that he should feel regret on account of his sins. Correction of speech signifies that he should confess his transgressions; while correction of act denotes that he should take it upon himself never again to return to his folly, but should do instead such acts as would indicate that the former were done in error and unintentionally. . . .

The things hindering and preventing repentance are three: ignorance of having committed a sin, excusing oneself, and the love of money and glory. It is clear that every one of these hinders repentance. If a man does not recognize or know that he has sinned, he will never regret doing the thing he does, nor repent, as a sick man can not be cured as long as he does not feel or know that he is sick, for he will never seek a cure. So if one does not know that he has sinned, he will never repent. . . .

It is also clear from the thing itself that self-excuse prevents repentance. For if a man thinks that excusing himself for his sin will avail him, he will never regret the doing of it, nor confess his sin. Such a one is called a man "who covers his transgressions," as Solomon says: *He that covereth his transgressions shall not prosper* (Proverbs 28.13). Covering one's sin means to make something else responsible for one's sin. . . .

Love of money and glory prevents repentance. For if a person repents in order to get some financial benefit or honor, his act is not repentance at all. One must undertake not to return again to folly for the love of God and not for any other motive. . . .

Sefer ha-Ikkarim 4.26[6]

FACTORS DETRIMENTAL TO REPENTANCE

BACHYA IBN PAKUDA

Complaisance in sinning means continuance in transgression, persisting in it and delaying its abandonment. As long as this condition continues, there cannot be any repentance. As an old saying put it, "No sin is small, if one persists in it. No sin is great, if one beseeches pardon for its commission." For persistence in sin indicates that the sinner despises the word of God, regards His commandment and prohibition lightly, and so prepares himself for punishment. Of such a person it is said, *But the soul that doth aught presumptuously . . . the same blasphemeth the Lord* (Numbers 15.30). A further consequence of persistence in a sin, however slight it be, is that if it be continued it grows and becomes a great transgression, while a great transgression, if a sinner beseeches pardon for it and abandons it, out of fear of God, gradually diminishes and becomes less and less till it is entirely erased from the record of the sinner's iniquities, and he is cleansed and cleared by repentance.

Observe a silken cord. How strong it becomes when it is doubled over many times, though its origin is the weakest of things—a worm's mucus. Let us note also how a ship's thick cable, when it has been used for a long time, gradually wears out and finally breaks and the material becomes the weakest of the weak. So it is with the grave and light character of transgressions. They become grave if one persists in them, and light if one beseeches forgiveness for them. . . .

Another detriment to repentance is when one assures himself that he will repent toward the close of his life or thinks that he will refrain from transgression when he has attained his desire and gratified his lust. He resembles one who attempts to cheat his God. Of such a person, our teachers, of blessed memory, said "A man who says 'I will sin and repent' will be denied the opportunity for repentance" (Yoma 88b). . . .

Another detriment to repentance is that a penitent repents

of some of his iniquities and persists in committing others. For instance, if a man abandons the transgression of duties to God and repents, but does not renounce transgressions against his fellowmen and commits robbery, fraud, theft and similar crimes. Concerning such conduct, it is said *If iniquity be in thine hand, put it far away* (Job 11.14). . . .

Repentance is more difficult when the offense has been repeated so frequently that the evil deed has become a habit, a second nature, from which the would-be penitent cannot easily separate himself, as it is written, *They have taught their tongues to tell lies; they tire themselves in committing iniquity* (Jeremiah 9.4). Further it is said, *Can the Ethiopian change his skin, or the leopard his spots?* (ibid. 13.23).

Repentance is also difficult if one causes another person loss of property by relaying false information about him to the civil authorities. Repentance in this case will not avail unless the informer endeavors to appease the person he has wronged by making good his monetary loss, or by pacifying him in words and humbly begging him to forgive and pardon the offense, as it is written, *And those who ate the flesh of my people, and did flay their skin from off them . . . they will cry unto the Lord and He will not answer them . . .* (Micah 3.3–4).

Repentance is also difficult when one has accustomed his tongue to tell lies, talk scandalously about people and malign them. He cannot determine the measure of his offenses because of their multitude; in his case these were unlimited, and he has forgotten who the people are against whom he has spoken. It is all held up against him, and recorded in the book of his offenses. Of such a person, it is said, *And if he cometh, it is to spy out; he speaketh vainly; his heart gathereth iniquity unto itself* (Psalms 41.7). . . .

Be ashamed to conduct yourself toward the Creator in a way that you would be ashamed to conduct yourself toward a creature like yourself. You are aware that if you rouse against you the ire of one of the king's officials, even if he be of inferior rank, you will not delay to humble yourself before him and beseech his forgiveness and thus assure for yourself immunity from punishment by him. And you would act thus, even if the servitor had little power in this regard. How much more would you act thus if a lord of high degree were angry with you. And if the king himself were angry with you, you would most surely hasten to beseech his forgiveness, and express your repentance and endeavor to appease him; because you fear that he will speedily punish you. . . .

How then, my brother, shall we not be ashamed in the presence of our Creator who contemplates what is concealed as well as what is visible in all our deeds and thoughts; who neither forgets nor overlooks; whose engagement in one thing does not divert his attention from any other thing; whose judgment none can escape; to whose sovereignty there is no end?[7]

THE PRINCIPLE OF REPENTANCE

JONAH BEN ABRAHAM GERONDI

Among the Blessed One's kindnesses to His creations is having prepared for them the way to rise from the pit of their deeds and to escape the trap of their offenses; to save themselves from destruction and to turn His wrath from them. In His great goodness and uprightness, He has taught and exhorted them to turn to Him upon having sinned against Him, for He knows the inclination of their hearts, as it is said, *Good and upright is the Lord; therefore doth He instruct sinners in the way* (Psalms 25.8). Even if they have offended and rebelled exceedingly, and been utterly faithless, He has not closed the doors of repentance to them, as it is said, *Turn ye unto Him against whom ye have deeply rebelled, O children of Israel* (Isaiah 31.6), and, *Return, ye backsliding children, I will heal your backslidings* (Jeremiah 3.22).

The Torah in many instances exhorts us in relation to repentance. It is shown that penance is accepted even when the sinner repents because of his many troubles, much more so when his repentance proceeds from the fear and love of God, as it is said, *In thy distress, when all these things are come upon thee, in the end of days, thou wilt return to the Lord thy God and hearken to His voice* (Deuteronomy 4.30). And it is clear from the Torah that God assists the penitents when they are limited by their nature, and implants in them a spirit of purity whereby they may attain to the level of loving Him.[8]

LAPSING BACK INTO SIN

SAADIA GAON

The terms of repentance are four in number, to wit: (a) the renunciation of sin, (b) remorse, (c) the quest of forgiveness, and (d) the assumption of the obligation not to relapse into sin. . . .

Now I have no fears, so far as the majority of our people are concerned, in regard to their being remiss in their fulfillment of any of the conditions of repentance except this fourth category—I mean that of lapsing back into sin. For I believe that at the time when they fast and pray, they sincerely mean to abandon their sinful way and experience remorse and seek God's pardon. It seems to me, however, that they are [really] resolved to lapse back into sin.

So I ask myself: "What device is there for eradicating from men's hearts the thought of lapsing back into sin?" My answer is: "Thinking up reasons for holding this world in contempt." Let a person remind himself of his condition of impotence, misery, exertion, and disillusionment, of his eventual death and the decomposition of the parts of his body, of the vermin and the putrefaction that are destined for him, of the accounting he will have to give for his conduct and the torments to which he will be subjected and whatever appertains to any of these matters. The result of such reflection would be contempt for this world, and once all mundane things are held in contempt by him, his sins would be included in the totality of things to be abstained from and his resolve to abandon them would be intensified.

I say, furthermore, that it was precisely for the above-mentioned considerations that I find that the sages of Israel introduced the custom of reciting on the Day of Atonement such liturgical selections as "Thou discernest the thoughts of the heart," "Oh, God, if Thou comest with rebukes," "Lord of all that is done," and the like.

To the four conditions of repentance listed previously should be added the following further aids; namely, more extensive prayer, increased charity, and the endeavor to restore [other] men to the path of virtue.

Let me explain also that if the resolve on the part of a servant of God not to lapse into sin again is sincere, his repentance is accepted, so that if, as a result of temptation, he falls once more, his repentance is not thereby forfeited. What happens is rather that the iniquities he committed before his repentance are canceled, only those committed by him thereafter being charged against him. The same would apply even if this were to occur several times; namely, that he repent and lapse back into sin. Only the wrongs perpetrated by him after his repentance would count against him, that is, provided he has been sincere each time in his resolve not to relapse.

Book of Beliefs and Opinions 5.5[9]

FIVE DEGREES OF REPENTANCE

SAADIA GAON

There are distinguishable five different degrees of repentance, each of which is superior to the next in the order of their enumeration. The first consists of a person's repenting at the epoch and in the locality in which he has committed his sin, and whilst the details of his transgressions are still present before him.

The second degree of repentance is that which is carried out after the epoch in which the sin was committed has passed and the penitent has moved from the scene of his transgression and the details of his sinful conduct are no longer present before him.

The third degree is that which is effected by the sinner only when he is threatened with impending disaster.

The fourth is that which is not undertaken until part of the threatened disaster has already descended upon the sinner.

The fifth degree, finally, is that which is carried out at the moment when the soul passes out. He that repents at that time is also called "penitent."

Book of Beliefs and Opinions 5.6[10]

A KARAITE INTERPRETATION OF REPENTANCE

AARON BEN ELIJAH

Know that the matter of repentance is a great kindness and bounty which the Holy Name has vouchsafed to mankind, so that if a man commit a sin, he might repent, and the Holy Name would forgive his sin and cancel the punishment due him for it, and he might become again one of the community of the meritorious, since the punishment for evil deeds is, in one way, subject to cancellation by the Almighty. . . .

There are twelve aspects to proper repentance. First, the true essence of repentance is regret of one's evil deeds. Second is the abandonment of the evil deed. Third is the hatred of it. Fourth is the submission to repentance with all its conditions. Fifth is confession. Sixth is the condition imposed by the Law as an accompaniment of repentance; while the Temple at Jerusalem was yet standing, this was the duty to offer a sacrifice, but now there remains only the utterance of our lips, as it is written: *So will we render for bullocks the offering of our lips* (Hosea 14.3). Seventh, man must not postpone repentance for long after the feeling of regret—like the one who says, "I will sin now and repent later"—unless he is compelled by circumstances beyond his control to do so. Eighth, he must renounce the evil deed for the sake of its very vileness. Ninth, he must also not do anything like it in the future. Tenth, he must take it upon himself not to do it again at another time. Eleventh, he must do repentance with the intention of can-

celing the punishment for his evil deeds. Twelfth, he must do
repentance because it is a duty, like all other positive ordinances
in the Law.[11]

KINDS OF REPENTANCE

ABRAHAM BAR HIYYA

There are two kinds of repentance—that of the righteous
man, who has erred accidentally, and that of the wicked man
who regrets the sins he has committed wittingly. Another distinction that can be made is between complete and incomplete
repentance. The definition of repentance is the regret of a man
for his evil deeds and sins, the implication being that after he
has committed the transgression, he repents and firmly observes the commandment he has transgressed. This applies
whether it is committed intentionally or unintentionally—but
there is this difference that repentance for an intentional sin
involves confession, and this is not so in the case of the
accidental transgression, which a man does not realize he is
committing and which requires merely repentance and a request for forgiveness. Both types of penitents must believe in
the commandments, which they had transgressed at the time
of transgression; these are the ones principally called repentant.
As to the transgressor who does not believe in the commandment before or during the transgression but only subsequently
—after it has been made known to him—and then he repents
of it, the term "repentant" does not strictly apply and is only
used loosely. He can be called a convert or a seeker of the way
to faith but not a penitent.[12]

A PROPITIATORY PRAYER

SOLOMON IBN GABIROL

We beseech Thee, awaken Thy old love with which thou
didst love the numberless congregation, designated by all en-

dearing terms of love, brotherhood and companionship; for my brethren and companions' sake let me speak, I pray Thee. When Thou didst set foot on the lofty mountain to delight them with the ancient treasure, Thou didst liken them to a kingdom of priests and a holy nation, and didst call them "My son," and they also said "He is my friend, my King, and my Lord." Thou didst cause [the people of Israel] to inherit the delightful heritage, the pleasant portion; they were fastened to Thy glory with festoons of beauty; and now strangers and evil-doers have driven them away, and Thy friends are straying in a land which belongs not to them. Remember, and forget not, hold not Thy peace, and be not still, O God, when Edom and Ishmael design to cut me off; "O Gracious One, Thou knowest all these travails," thus saith Thy friend Israel. From the New Year's day, when Thou dost sit on Thy glorious throne, and look down to examine the hearts of both those who serve Thee and of those who rebel against Thee, exact the debt from all the faithless, and let Thy hand release what Thy brother owes Thee. At the time when the records of the creatures of Thy world are read, decreeing life or death to the rich and poor and in whose temple grace and favor abide, be a surety for Thy servant for good, O Most High, so that Thy brother may live with Thee. Turn to me, and be gracious to me, and set me on high; cause them who provoke Thee to perish in wretchedness and in poverty, but when Thou dealest out to each his appointed supplies for his sustenance, do not shut Thy hand from Thy needy brother. I rose before dawn and cried to Thee, O my Creator; advance Thy kindness, and forgive my transgression and misdeeds; let Thy mercy be extended to me as from one who comforts a mourner; O that Thou were like a brother to me. Turn to the supplication of Thy wretched and to their cry, their soul and spirit are filled with troubles; cast into the depths of the sea all their sins; O we pray Thee, forgive now the trespass of Thy brothers and their sin. Thou wast of old the hope of Israel, and the sword of their excellence; O living God, erect even now, their stature, strengthen their arm, and dwell among them; and see how Thy friends fare, and be a surety for them.[13]

V

ROSH HASHANAH IN JEWISH LAW

The vast corpus of Jewish law embodied in many sources was systematized by Moses ben Maimon (1135–1204), popularly known as Maimonides or Rambam, in his *Mishneh Torah*. Several centuries later, Joseph Karo (1488–1575), recognized as the last great codifier of rabbinical Judaism, prepared the *Shulhan Arukh*, which is still accepted as the basis for traditional practice. The *Kitzur Shulhan Arukh*, an abridged and popular version of Karo's monumental work, was prepared by Solomon Ganzfried (c. 1800–1886).

ARISE FROM YOUR SLUMBER

Moses Maimonides

Even though the sounding of the *shofar* on Rosh Hashanah is a biblical decree, it has an intimation, as if to say: "Arise from your slumber, you who are asleep; wake up from your deep sleep, you who are fast asleep; search your deeds and repent; remember your Creator. Those of you who forget the truth because of passing vanities, indulging throughout the year in the useless things that cannot profit you nor save you, look into your souls, amend your ways and deeds. Let everyone give up his evil way and his bad purpose." Everybody should, therefore, regard himself throughout the year as half innocent and half guilty; so too, he should consider the entire world as half innocent and half guilty. If then he commits one additional sin he presses down the scale of guilt against himself and the entire world, and causes his destruction; if, on the other hand, he performs a good deed he presses down the scale of merit in his favor and that of the entire world, and causes salvation and deliverance to reach him and his fellow men, as it is written: *The just man is the foundation of the world* (Proverbs 10.25); that is, he who justly presses down the scale of merit in favor of the world and saves it. For this reason, the whole house of Israel has formed a custom to engage in the performance of charity and good deeds between Rosh Hashanah and Yom Kippur to a much larger extent than during the entire year. Besides, during these ten days, they are all accustomed to rise in the night and to pray and supplicate in the synagogue until daylight.

Mishneh Torah, Laws of Repentance 3.4[1]

THINGS THAT HINDER REPENTANCE

MOSES MAIMONIDES

Twenty-four things hinder repentance. Four of these are grievous offenses. If one commits any of them, God gives him no opportunity to repent because of the gravity of the offense. Offenders of this type are: 1) he who leads the people to sin; this includes one who prevents them from doing a good deed; 2) he who diverts another from the good to the evil, such as a seducer or enticer; 3) he who sees that his son is falling into bad ways and does not stop him; being under his control, the son would desist if checked by the father; hence, it is as if he actually led him to sin . . . ; 4) he who says: "I will sin and then repent." This includes one who says: "I will sin and Yom Kippur will atone."

Five of the twenty-four misdeeds shut the ways of repentance to those who commit them. They are: 1) he who stands aloof from the community; since he is not among them when they repent, he does not share the merit they attain; 2) he who opposes the rulings of the sages; since his opposition induces him to stand away from them, he remains ignorant of the ways of repentance; 3) he who makes a mockery of the divine precepts; since they are held in contempt by him, he does not eagerly obey them, and if he does not obey how can he attain merit?; 4) he who insults his teachers . . . ; 5) he who hates rebukes, because he leaves himself no way of repentance; for it is reproof that induces repentance. . . . All the prophets rebuked Israel until they repented. It is therefore necessary to engage in every Jewish community a great elderly scholar, God-fearing from his youth and well-liked by the people, to preach to them and lead them to repentance. But he who hates reproof does not come to listen to the preacher; hence he persists in his faults which seem good to him.

Five of the twenty-four misdeeds are of such nature that anyone who commits them cannot attain complete repentance, because they are sins against a fellowman without knowing who it is in order to compensate him and ask his pardon. Offenders of this category are: 1) he who curses the people and not an individual, of whom he might ask to forgive him; 2) he who shares with a thief . . . ; 3) he who finds lost property and does not announce it, that he may restore it to its owner; when he repents after some time, he does not know to whom he should restore it; 4) he who despoils the poor, orphans, and widows; these people are wretched and not well known, they migrate from town to town and have no acquaintance whereby to ascertain how to refund what he has robbed; 5) he who takes bribes to tamper with justice . . . thus encouraging the bribing litigant and leading him to sin.

Five of the twenty-four offenses are such that the person who commits them is not likely to repent, because they are regarded by most people as trivial, with the result that the sinner imagines that it is no sin. Offenders of this class are: 1) he who shares a meal that is insufficient for its owner; since this is a tinge of robbery, he imagines that he has not done any wrong, saying: "I did not eat without his consent"; 2) he who makes use of a poor man's pledge; since a poor man's pledge happens to be only an axe or a plow, and the user says to himself: "The articles have not depreciated, and I have not robbed him"; 3) he who gazes at women lustfully supposes that there is nothing wrong in it, and does not realize that the lustful look is a grave sin, as it is written: *You shall not follow the desires of your heart and your eyes* (Numbers 15.39); 4) he who elevates himself at the expense of another's degradation thinks to himself that this is no sin, since the other person is absent and has not endured shame; nor has he actually shamed him by comparing his own good deeds and wisdom with the other man's deeds or wisdom, implying that he is honorable while the other is contemptible; 5) he who suspects honest men says to himself that it is no sin. "What have I done to him?" he says; "is there anything more in it than a mere suspicion that maybe he has done it and maybe not?" He does not realize that it is sinful to regard a worthy person as a transgressor.

Five of the twenty-four misdeeds are such that anyone who commits them will always be attracted to them, and they are hard to be given up. One should therefore be careful lest he become addicted to them, for they are all extremely obnoxious traits. Here they are: gossip, slander, wrath, evil thought, keeping bad company. . . . In the rules concerning ethical behavior we have explained the traits that all men should ever cultivate, and so much the more one who repents.

All these and similar misdeeds do not prevent repentance, even though they hinder it. If a person is sincerely remorseful over them and repents, he is a repentant indeed and has a share in the world to come.

Mishneh Torah, Laws of Repentance 4.1–6[2]

WAYS OF REPENTANCE

MOSES MAIMONIDES

A man should always consider himself as if he is about to die; he may die when his time is up while still behaving sinfully. He should therefore repent of his sins immediately. Let him not say: "When I grow old I shall repent," since he may die before getting old. Solomon in his wisdom said: *Let your garments be always white* (Ecclesiastes 9.8).

Do not say that repentance is limited to sinful acts, such as fornication, robbery, and theft. Just as a man must repent of these, so he must scan and search his evil traits, repenting of anger, hatred, envy, scoffing, greed, vainglory, excessive desire for food, and so on. One must repent of all these failings. They are worse than sinful acts; when a person is addicted to them, he finds it hard to get rid of them. The prophet says: *Let the guilty man give up his way, and the evil man his thoughts* (Isaiah 55.7).

Let not the repentant person imagine that he is far removed from the merit of the righteous on account of the iniquities and sins he committed. This is not so. He is tenderly loved by the Creator as if he had never sinned. Besides, his reward is great, since he had tasted sin and got rid of it by suppressing his evil impulse. The sages said: "Where repentant sinners stand the thoroughly righteous cannot stand" (Berakhot 34b); that is, their merit is superior to that of persons who never committed a sin, because the repentant had to exert greater effort in suppressing their impulse.

Those who repent should be exceedingly humble in their behavior. If ignorant fools insult them by mentioning their past deeds and say to them: "Last night you were doing this and that; last night you were saying this and that," they should pay no attention to them, but upon hearing this they should rejoice, knowing that this is their merit. As long as they feel ashamed of their past deeds and are disgraced because of them, their merit and worth are enhanced. It is a flagrant sin to say to a repentant person: "Remember your past deeds," or to mention them in his presence so as to embarrass him, or to recall similar incidents that are reminiscent of what he did. All this is forbidden along with all kinds of insulting words against which the Torah warns us, as it is written: *You must not vex one another* (Leviticus 25.17).

Mishneh Torah, Laws of Repentance 7.2–4,8[3]

LAWS FOR THE MONTH OF ELUL

SOLOMON GANZFRIED

The days from Rosh Hodesh Elul until after the Day of Atonement are considered propitious. While the Holy One, blessed be He, accepts repentance throughout the year from those who return to Him with unblemished heart, these days are more decisive for mercy and acceptance. This is because Moses ascended Mount Sinai on Rosh Hodesh Elul to receive the second tablets of the law, tarried there for forty days and descended on the tenth of Tishri, which marked the completion of the atonement. Since then these have been consecrated as days of acceptance and the tenth day of Tishri as the Day of Atonement. . . .

It is customary during this month to sound the *shofar* daily —*tekiah, shevarim, teruah, tekiah*—after the morning service, beginning with the second day of the month. . . . The purpose of sounding the *shofar* during this month is to rouse the people to repentance, since the *shofar* evokes trembling, in keeping with the scriptural verse: *Shall the horn be blown in a city, and the people not tremble?* (Amos 3.6). . . .

From the advent of Elul until the Day of Atonement, when writing to a friend one should mention at the beginning or end of the letter his prayers that the friend shall merit in the coming days being inscribed and sealed in the book of good life. . . .

From the first day of the week preceding Rosh Hashanah, all should rise early for penitential prayers. If Rosh Hashanah

occurs on a Monday or Tuesday, they commence on the Sunday
of the previous week. . . .

Care should be scrupulously exercised to select as congregational representative [cantor] for the penitential services and for the Days of Awe a man respected, erudite in
Torah, and excelling in good deeds, insofar as it is possible
to find such a person. He should be at least thirty years old,
for by then his youthful impulsiveness has subsided. He should
also be married and a parent so that his supplications will
emerge from the depths of his heart. Extreme care should
be taken to select as *shofar*-blower and as reader for the
shofar sounds men erudite in Torah and God-fearing, insofar
as they can be found. However, any Jew is considered qualified for all [these functions] so long as he is acceptable to
the congregation. . . .

It is customary on the day preceding Rosh Hashanah to
visit the cemetery after the morning service, to prostrate oneself on the graves of the righteous and to give alms to the
poor. . . .

It is customary to perform the ceremony of annulling vows
on the eve of Rosh Hashanah. If one is not conversant with
Hebrew, one may recite it in the vernacular he understands.

Kitzur Shulhan Arukh 128

LAWS FOR ROSH HASHANAH

SOLOMON GANZFRIED

On the conclusion of the evening service on the first night of
Rosh Hashanah, it is customary to exchange the greeting:
May you be inscribed and sealed [in the book of life] for a
good year. . . .

The length of the *shofar* sounds should, at the start, be as
follows. The *teruah* is nine short notes. The *shevarim* should
be three consecutive notes, each as long as three short [stac-
cato] sounds of the *teruah*. Thus the *shevarim* will equal the
nine sounds of the *teruah*. One should be very careful not to

prolong the *shevarim* sounds until each one equals nine
sounds, for, if it has been done in this manner, then the obligation is unfulfilled. The *tekiot* are simple sounds. In the series
tekiah-shevarim-teruah-tekiah, each *tekiah* should be as long
as the *shevarim* with the *teruah*, that is, as eighteen sounds. In
the *tekiah-shevarim-tekiah* series, each *tekiah* should be as
long as the *shevarim*, that is, as nine sounds; the same in the
tekiah-teruah-tekiah series. With the *tekiot* preceding the additional service, the *shevarim* with the *teruah* should be
sounded in one breath; therefore, the reader will read without
pause *shevarim-teruah*. The *tekiot* sounded during the repetition of the *Amidah* should be made in two breaths; in any
event, one should not pause between them but they should
sound in immediate succession, and the reader should likewise read both at one time. . . .

When leaving the synagogue one should depart in a cheerful
mood, confident that God has compassionately heard his prayers and the sounds of the *shofar*. One should eat and drink
according to the bounty God provided. One should, however,
avoid eating gluttonously, so that the fear of God will be upon
him. One should study Torah while at the table. Following
the grace after meals one should not sleep but should go to
the synagogue and recite Psalms with the congregation until
the afternoon service. However, if one's head is heavy he may
take a brief nap before going to the synagogue. . . .

Both days of Rosh Hashanah are considered as one long
day possessing equal sanctity. Therefore, the rabbinical authorities differed concerning the propriety of pronouncing the
Sheheheyanu blessing [". . . who hast kept us alive and sus-
tained us and enabled us to reach this season"] with the
Kiddush and the candle blessing on the second night of Rosh
Hashanah, and with sounding the *shofar* on the second day.
Some maintained that since there is the same sanctity for
both days, and since *Sheheheyanu* was already recited on
the first day, there is no need to repeat it on the second.
Therefore, when *Kiddush* is recited on the second night of
Rosh Hashanah a new fruit is customarily placed on the table

so that the *Sheheheyanu* blessing of the *Kiddush* will apply also to that fruit. One may also wear a new garment. However, if one does not have a new fruit or a new garment, it does not preclude his saying *Sheheheyanu* in the *Kiddush*. Likewise the woman when lighting candles on the second night should, if possible, wear a new garment or place a new fruit on the table so that the *Sheheheyanu* blessing will apply to these. If she does not possess them, it does not detract from the fulfillment of her obligation. Likewise, the *shofar*-blower should, if possible, wear a new garment on the second day. If, however the first day falls on the Sabbath, he need not do so because the *Sheheheyanu* blessing was not yet recited on the *shofar* [for it is not sounded on the Sabbath].

Kitzur Shulhan Arukh 129

LAWS OF THE TEN DAYS OF REPENTANCE

SOLOMON GANZFRIED

The name "Ten Days of Repentance" signifies that they should be devoted to penitence. Everyone is obligated to turn with complete repentance to God, blessed be His name, before the advent of the great and awesome Day of Atonement, as it is said, *Before the Lord you shall be clean* (Leviticus 16.30). It is said further, *Seek ye the Lord while He may be found* (Isaiah 55.6). Our rabbis, of blessed memory, said that on these ten days between Rosh Hashanah and Yom Kippur, a man should search his deeds and repent of his evil actions. . . .

On the Sabbath of Repentance [between Rosh Hashanah and Yom Kippur] an eminent member of the community should be called to read the prophetic portion.

Kitzur Shulhan Arukh 130

VI

SELECTED PRAYERS

The sum and substance of Jewish religious thought on God and man is compressed in the liturgy of Rosh Hashanah. The prayers and hymns reflect the spiritual genius of Israel's prophets and psalmists, its Talmud sages and medieval hymnologists. The *Mahzor* for the New Year service comprises prayers created in the days of the Temple, compositions of liturgical poets of the Middle Ages, and, in some editions, modern accretions. Indeed, the prayer books for the Days of Awe are anthologies of selections chosen from the Bible, Talmud, Midrash, and medieval Jewish literature. Notwithstanding the long existence of much of the High Holy Days liturgy, it contains moral postulates and spiritual truths which are as relevant and challenging today as when they were first written.

The dominant and pervasive motif of the *Mahzor* is "the Kingship of God." Since Rosh Hashanah is considered the Day of Judgment for all mankind, the universal themes of

[61

human brotherhood and world unity are echoed and reiterated in the prayers. Emphasis is placed on Divine Providence, revelation, the principle of reward and punishment, and the restoration of the Jewish people to Zion.

As Rosh Hashanah is also "a day when the horn is sounded" (Numbers 29.1), its distinctive ritual is sounding the *shofar*.

Despite the inclusion of many special prayers and *piyyutim*, however, the services are basically the same as those on the Sabbath and the festivals.

This chapter presents selections from the *Mahzor*, followed by commentaries from modern sources which give insights into the origin and significance of the prayers and hymns. Examples of modern prayer-poems that have not been hallowed by traditional usage are also included.

PRAYER FOR ROSH HASHANAH EVE

Heavenly Father! In the twilight of the vanishing year, we lift up our hearts to Thee to thank Thee for all Thy mercies in the past, and to implore Thy guidance and Thy blessing for the future. Thy providence has watched over us and Thy lovingkindness has sustained us. In affliction Thou hast strengthened us; in sorrow Thou hast comforted us. Thou hast brightened our lives with the happiness of home and the joys of friendship. Thou hast blessed us with the satisfaction that comes from performing our daily duties and serving our fellowmen.

As we thank Thee for the joys of life, so we praise Thee for its sorrows. Many burdens have been laid upon us; many tears have furrowed our cheeks; many tender ties have been broken. With a father's love dost Thou discipline us, that we may learn to understand life's holy purpose.

With deep humility we approach Thee, O our God, at this sacred hour. May we listen reverently to its solemn admonition. Give us the will to serve Thee with singleness of heart, so that, as we grow older in years, we may grow stronger in wisdom, broader in charity and more steadfast in faith.

Hidden from our sight are the events of the future. But we trust in Thee and fear not. Open unto us in mercy the portals of the new year, and grant us life and health, contentment, and peace. Amen.

Union Prayer Book[1]

PRAYER FOR ROSH HASHANAH EVE

MAX D. KLEIN

I

Lord, we pray, regard and hear us,
    Thou on whom we all depend;
May Thy love be ever near us,
    As our pleas to Thee ascend.

Many are the tears upwelling,
From full hearts within Thy dwelling,
    On this eve of the New Year.

Israel's sons cry out before Thee,
And with trembling lips implore Thee;
    Bless them in this coming year.

II

Lord, we pray Thee, guard Thou Israel,
    Be with all bowed down in grief;
Hear the sighs of all in travail,
    Hither come to find relief.

All who pray and seek sincerely,
Grant them peace of soul we pray Thee,
    And their pleading voices hear.

May they no more fail or falter,
Stray no longer from Thine altar;
    Bless them in this coming year.

III

Lord, we pray Thee, hear Thy children,
  Gathered in this hallowed place,
As they plead for all their brethren,
  And for all the human race.

Israel's sins and Israel's failings,
Mankind's wrongs and mankind's ailings,
  Lord, to Thee are known and clear.

Unto all grant Thou new power,
Be Thou, Lord, their sheltering tower;
  Bless them in this coming year.[2]

THY STRICKEN DAUGHTER

AHOT KETANNAH

Thy stricken daughter, now, O Lord, prepares
  —Bowed 'neath the rod—
Her songs of fervent praise, her tearful prayers—
  Heal her, O God!
Heal her—deliver her from all her woes—
  A year of sorrows draweth to its close!

The psalmist's lay, the prophet's word sublime,
  To Thee pertain;
And ancient litany and poet's rhyme
  Prolong the strain.
Hide not Thine eyes forever, Lord, but see
Her deep distress, who pours her soul to Thee,
Whilst tyrants scourge her flesh with cruel blows—
  A year of sorrows draweth to its close!

When wilt Thou draw Thy daughter from the pit
  Of misery,
And break her prison-yoke and bid her sit
  With them made free?
Display Thy wonders! From Thy ruined fold,

5. Miscellany. Northern Italy. Circa 1470. The Israel Museum, Jerusalem. See Chapter XIII.

6. *Mahzor*. Germany. 14th century. Biblioteca Palatina, Parma. See Chapter XIII.

7. *Mahzor*. Germany. Early 14th century. University Library, Breslau. See Chapter XIII.

זֹהַר גְבוּרָה ‏ ‏ ‏ גָּדוֹל שִׁמְךָ בְגַב ‏ ‏ ‏ א׳ ‏ ‏ מֶלֶךְ ‏ ‏ ‏ ‏ ‏
מִגְבוּרָה ‏ ‏ לְךָ זְרוֹעַ עִם גְבוּרָתֵךְ"‏ ‏ ‏ ‏ ‏
גָּרִי נָקָם׳ ‏ ‏ ‏ ‏ לְבֵשׁ בְיוֹם נָקָם ‏ ‏ ‏ ב׳ ‏ ‏ מֶלֶךְ ‏ ‏
לְצָרָיו יָשִׁיב ‏ ‏ ‏ ‏ אֶל חֵיקָם"‏ ‏ ‏ ‏ ‏
אוֹת לָבֵשׁ ‏ ‏ ‏ יָמִים מְיַבֵּשׁ׳ ‏ ‏ ג׳ ‏ ‏ מֶלֶךְ ‏ ‏
וְגֵאוּת אֲפִיקִים מְיַבֵּשׁ"‏ ‏ ‏ ‏ ‏
בְּעֶשֶׂרָה לְבוּשִׁים׳ ‏ ‏ הִתְאַזֵּר בְקָדוֹשִׁים׳ ‏ ‏ מֶלֶךְ ‏ ‏
בָּעֲרֵץ בְסוֹד קְדוֹשִׁים ‏ ‏ ‏ ‏ קָדוֹשׁ"‏ ‏ ‏ ‏ ד׳ ‏ ‏ ‏
ר בְּנֶהְדָרָא ‏ ‏ ‏ עִטָּה אַדְרֵךְ׳ ‏ ‏ ד׳ ‏ ‏ מֶלֶךְ ‏ ‏
מִשְׁפָּטֵינוּ יֹדֵיעַ לְאַדְרֵךְ"‏ ‏ ‏ ‏ ‏

8. *Mahzor*. Germany. First half of 14th century. Bodleian Library, Oxford, Ms. Reggio 1, folio 159v. See Chapter XIII.

Drive out the ravening beasts. There, as of old,
Gather Thy scattered sheep and guard from foes—
   A year of sorrows draweth to its close!

Despoiled and mocked, sport of the heathen's wrath,
   But constant still,
The foot of Israel swerves not from Thy path,
   Nor ever will.
Her song is hushed, but all her soul on fire
With frustrate longing; Thou art her desire!
Her breaking heart with love of Thee o'erflows—
   A year of sorrows draweth to its close!

Lead gently, to the bower of blissful rest,
   Her, so long torn
From her Belovèd; bid that anguished breast
   Cease, now, to mourn.
Thy precious vine, whose clusters ruthless men
Have stript, that beasts have trampled, lift again;
Behold! Even now, the buds of hope unclose—
   A year of sorrows draweth to its close!

Be strong, ye faithful, joyously endure,
   For wrong shall cease.
Trust still the Rock; His Covenant is sure,
   His paths are peace.
Yet shall He lead you Zionward, and say:
"Cast up! Cast up! Make firm and broad the way!"
O may the approaching year behold that day!
   Begin, New Year—and bring that joyous day!
                    Translated by Solomon Solis-Cohen[3]

COMMENTARY

This hymn for the eve of the New Year, found in the Se-
phardic liturgy, was composed by Abraham Hazzan Gerondi
of thirteenth-century Spain. His name appears as an acrostic
in the original Hebrew version. Some poetic license was used
by the translator in rendering the title: ahot ketannah means
literally "little sister." This expression is found in Song of Songs

8.8 and according to tradition is interpreted allegorically as the children of Israel.

REMEMBER US UNTO LIFE

ZAKHRENU LE-HAYYIM

Remember us unto life, O King who delightest in life, and inscribe us in the book of life, for Thine own sake, O God of life.

Translated by Ben Zion Bokser[4]

COMMENTARY: *Israel Abrahams*

This prayer, inserted in the daily service from the New Year till the great fast—from the first to the tenth of Tishri, is of uncertain age. Unmentioned in the Talmud, it meets us for the first time in an eighth-century collection of laws. Thus its antiquity is respectable, if not venerable. But the underlying idea is far older, and the metaphor used carries us back to an ancient order of things.

It is plausibly supposed that the "Book of Life" was a spiritual fancy corresponding to a quite material fact. We have several indications that at a fairly early date there was drawn up in Judea a civil list, or register, in which the names of fully qualified citizens were officially entered. Such a practice is attested by statements and allusions in Scripture, and it is probable that the figure of the "Book of Life" was thence derived. To be enrolled in the Book of Life would imply membership of the divine commonwealth; to be blotted out would be to suffer disfranchisement.

From this image the step would be easy to a book containing a record of man's doings. This phase of the conception is found in the Mishnah: "Know what is above thee—a seeing eye and a hearing ear, and all thy deeds written in a book" (AVOT 2.1). These three things—which, as the author of the saying urges, restrain a man from sin—are in essence one, and they convey what is perhaps the leading principle of Judaism as a discipline. Individual responsibility, with the corollary of inevitable retribution; inevitable, that is, unless the wayfarer will divert himself to the road of repentance, prayer, and charity —the path by which the sinner finds a new approach to virtue and life. The moral is enforced in the third chapter of the same collection of Sayings of the Jewish Fathers, *where life is compared to a shop with its open ledger of credit and debit. Here, again, the idea is in germ scriptural. Sin blots man out from the book, virtue sets his name there in indelible ink. . . . . In the day of judgment—in the day wherein God will make a peculiar treasure—He will account as* His *the children who have served their Father, and whose names are inscribed in the book of remembrance. And, on the other hand, just as some things are written in the Book for man's advantage, so are others entered to his disadvantage. . . . Between these two extremes, between good marks for virtue and bad marks for vice, stand entries which cry aloud, not for marks at all, but for mercy. In the 56th Psalm, whose author has been termed "the mouthpiece of oppressed and suffering Israel," the tears of the trusting yet ill-faring people are put into God's bottle. The Psalmist would have man's frailties, his weaknesses, his sorrows, his tears, entered in the Book of Life, as his most eloquent advocates for the pity of the Judge.*[5]

PUT THY AWE UPON ALL

UVEKHEN TEN PAHDEKHA

Lord our God, put Thy awe upon all whom Thou hast made, Thy dread upon all whom Thou hast created; let Thy works revere Thee; let all Thy creatures worship Thee; may they all blend into one brotherhood to do Thy will with a perfect heart. For we know, Lord our God, that Thine is dominion, power and might; Thou art revered above all that Thou hast created.

Now, O Lord, grant honor to Thy people, glory to those who revere Thee, hope to those who seek Thee, free speech to those who yearn for Thee, joy to Thy land and gladness to Thy city, rising strength to David Thy servant, a shining light to the son of Jesse, Thy chosen one, speedily in our days.

May now the righteous see this and rejoice, the upright

exult, and the godly thrill with delight. Iniquity shall shut its mouth, wickedness shall vanish like smoke, when Thou wilt abolish the rule of tyranny on earth.

Thou shalt reign over all whom Thou hast made, Thou alone, O Lord, on Mount Zion the abode of Thy majesty, in Jerusalem Thy holy city, as it is written in Thy holy Scriptures: The Lord shall reign forever, your God, O Zion, for all generations (Psalms 146.10).

Holy art Thou, awe-inspiring is Thy name, and there is no God but Thee, as it is written: The Lord of hosts is exalted through justice, the holy God is sanctified through righteousness (Isaiah 5.16). Blessed art Thou, O Lord, holy King.

Thou didst choose us from among all peoples; Thou didst love and favor us; Thou didst exalt us above all tongues and sanctify us with Thy commandments. Thou, our King, didst draw us near to Thy service and call us by Thy great and holy name.

Thou, Lord our God, hast graciously given us this Day of Remembrance, a day for the blowing of the *shofar*, a holy festival in remembrance of the exodus from Egypt.

Translated by Philip Birnbaum[6]

COMMENTARY: *Max Arzt*

The three Uvekhen *prayers, included in each* Amidah *of the High Holy Days, are ascribed to Rabbi Johanan ben Nuri, who lived during the Hadrianic persecutions, about six decades after the destruction of the Second Temple. The terror and tyranny with which Rome ruled its far-flung empire, and the brutality with which its officials in Palestine pursued the extermination of Judaism, gave rise to these prayers.*

In the oppression practiced by the Roman empire, our sages saw an attempt to unite all mankind by force, exploitation, and ruthlessness. They envisioned and hoped for the time when humanity would be united by man's fear of God rather than by man's fear of man. By the fear of God they meant a universal recognition of the inexorable consequences of the violation of the will of God, which is the moral law. The fear of

*God not only would serve as a deterrent to man's inhumanity,
but would lead to a banding together of all men "to perform
God's will with a perfect heart." . . .*

*With vivid imagery, and reflecting the rabbinic vision of
the messianic hope, the second Uvekhen articulates for us, as
well, the ideal of Eretz Yisrael as an autonomous homeland
for Jews and Judaism, and as a part of a world community
of peoples at peace with one another. There is no conflict
between the ideal of a united humanity and that of the con-
tinuation of the Jews as a distinct entity among the peoples of
the world. Indeed, we can consider the second Uvekhen as
a prayer for the liberation of all peoples, for the Jews have
rightly been characterized as the "barometer of civilization."
"Whenever joy is about to come upon the world, the people of
Israel is the first to feel it; even as when distress is about to
come upon the world, Israel is the first to feel it" (Midrash
Ekhah, ed. Buber, 2.3). . . .*

*This prayer [the third Uvekhen] can serve to remind us that
the ennobling of the individual must be the ultimate goal of
society. Society must develop the conditions wherein its citizens
may become tzaddikim, socially responsible; yesharim, men of
integrity; and hasidim, spirtually dedicated men.*[7]

IN THE BOOK OF LIFE

BE-SEFER HAYYIM

May we and all Israel Thy people be remembered and inscribed before Thee in the book of life and blessing, peace and
prosperity, for a happy life and for peace. Blessed art Thou, O
Lord, Author of peace.

Translated by Philip Birnbaum[8]

COMMENTARY: *Israel Abrahams*

*No doubt one form of the prayer is for temporal life and pros-
perity. It is a modern weakness on the part of Jews to feel it
necessary to apologize for such prayers. Life, earthly and ma-*

terial, is a good thing; prosperity is worth praying for. Judaism could glance at the paradox: "How shall a man die? Let him live. How shall a man live? Let him die." But while accepting the Talmudic paradox as a beautiful expression of the supremacy of the inner over the outer, of spirit over matter, the eternal over the mortal, Judaism did not underrate the value of earthly life because it esteemed more highly the worth of life everlasting. Long life on earth was a blessing, and the Jewish mind did not lose hold of this healthy fact under the fascination of the belief that the less of earth the more of heaven, the shorter life the longer immortality. And yet it did, it must, regard the blessing of life rather as a means than an end. A short life might be full of living; for, as the Rabbi said, some men can qualify themselves for eternity in an hour. A long life was, on the other hand, a fuller preparation, a fuller opportunity. "Rabbi Jacob said, This world is like a vestibule before the world to come; prepare thyself in the vestibule, that thou mayest enter into the hall."

And so in certain passages of Scripture the "Book of Life" transcends earthly existence and identifies itself with the spiritual life with God. The liturgy of the New Year also reproduces this enlarged, spiritualized conception. Another piyyut *runs: "For life eternal may the faithful ones be written, may they behold the pleasantness of the Lord, and find remembrance in His heavenly Temple."*[9]

HE WHO ORDAINS JUDGMENT

LE-EL OREKH DIN
    And thus let all acclaim God as King:

It is He who ordains judgment;
He searches hearts on the Day of Judgment.
He reveals hidden things in judgment;
He ordains righteousness on the Day of Judgment.
He applies knowledge in judgment;
He bestows mercy on the Day of Judgment.

He remembers His covenant in judgment;
He spares His creatures on the Day of Judgment.
He clears His faithful in judgment;
He discerns thoughts on the Day of Judgment.
He curbs wrath on the Day of Judgment;
He is robed in mercy on the Day of Judgment.
He pardons iniquity in judgment;
He is beyond our praises on the Day of Judgment.
He forgives His people in judgment;
He answers His suppliants on the Day of Judgment.
He invokes His compassion in judgment;
He beholds secrets on the Day of Judgment.
He redeems His faithful in judgment;
He loves His people on the Day of Judgment.
He guards His adherents in judgment;
He supports the innocent on the Day of Judgment.

Translated by Ben Zion Bokser[10]

COMMENTARY: *Herman Kieval*

This moving hymn by Eleazer Kallir is one of the best known and most beloved of all the piyyutim in the Ashkenazic Mahzor. The cantor chants it in a pleading melody, standard in most Ashkenazic synagogues.

The theme of the piyyut is stated again and again through the twin refrain: din, *"judgment," and* Yom Din, *"Day of Judgment." The poet enumerates the qualities of judgment associated with the Supreme Arbiter, including His attributes of mercy, compassion, and forgiveness. The portrayal of God as judge is as old as the Hebrew people itself. Abraham challenged "the judge of all the earth" to "do justice" (Genesis 18.25). The Book of Proverbs (16.11) speaks of God as holding in His hand the scales of judgment, and in the Talmud this figure is used repeatedly. Medieval moralists were fond of pointing out that nature herself has designated the first of Tishri as the universal Day of Judgment, since the zodiacal symbol for that month is* Libra, *the scales [of judgment].*[11]

OUR FATHER, OUR KING

AVINU MALKENU

Our Father, our King, we have sinned before Thee.

Our Father, our King, we have no King except Thee.

Our Father, our King, deal kindly with us for Thy name's sake.

Our Father, our King, renew unto us a happy New Year.

Our Father, our King, annul all evil decrees against us.

Our Father, our King, annul the plans of our enemies.

Our Father, our King, frustrate the counsel of our foes.

Our Father, our King, free us of every oppressor and adversary.

Our Father, our King, silence our adversaries and accusers.

Our Father, our King, remove pestilence, sword, famine, captivity, destruction, iniquity, and persecution from the people of Thy covenant.

Our Father, our King, keep the plague from Thy people.

Our Father, our King, forgive and pardon all our iniquities.

Our Father, our King, blot out and remove our transgressions and our trespasses from before Thee.

Our Father, our King, in Thine abundant mercy cancel all the records of our transgressions.

Our Father, our King, bring us back to Thee in wholehearted repentance.

Our Father, our King, send a complete healing to the sick among Thy people.

Our Father, our King, annul the evil decreed against us.

Our Father, our King, remember us favorably.

Our Father, our King, inscribe us in the book of a happy life.

Our Father, our King, inscribe us in the book of redemption and deliverance.

Our Father, our King, inscribe us in the book of sustenance and abundance.

Our Father, our King, inscribe us in the book of merit.

Our Father, our King, inscribe us in the book of pardon and forgiveness.

Our Father, our King, cause our deliverance soon to flourish.

Our Father, our King, raise the strength of Thy people Israel.

Our Father, our King, raise the strength of Thine anointed one.
Our Father, our King, fill our hands with Thy blessings.
Our Father, our King, fill our storehouses with plenty.
Our Father, our King, hear our voice, spare us and have mercy on us.
Our Father, our King, receive our prayer with mercy and favor.
Our Father, our King, be Thou receptive to our prayer.
Our Father, our King, dismiss us not empty-handed from Thy presence.
Our Father, our King, remember that we are but dust.
Our Father, our King, may this hour be an hour of mercy and a time of grace with Thee.
Our Father, our King, have compassion on us, and on our children.
Our Father, our King, act for the sake of those who were slain for Thy holy name.
Our Father, our King, act for the sake of those who were slaughtered for proclaiming Thy unity.
Our Father, our King, act for the sake of those who went through fire and water for the sanctification of Thy name.
Our Father, our King, vindicate the blood of Thy servants shed by tyrants.
Our Father, our King, do it for Thy sake, if not for ours.
Our Father, our King, do it for Thy sake and save us.
Our Father, our King, do it for the sake of Thy abundant mercy.
Our Father, our King, do it for the sake of Thy great, mighty and revered name, by which we are called.
Our Father, our King, be gracious to us and answer us. We can claim nothing by virtue of our deeds. Deal Thou mercifully and graciously with us, and deliver us.

Translated by Ben Zion Bokser[12]

COMMENTARY: *Julius H. Greenstone*

In the liturgy of the Penitential Days and of the Fast Days, the prayer Avinu Malkenu *occupies a prominent, even commanding position. It consists of a number of brief verses, all introduced by the words "Our Father, our King," to whom the* appeal is made. The rabbis related the story that in the time of a great drought, when the customary fast day was held, R. Eliezer ben Hyrcanus chanted the prescribed prayers for such an occasion but no rain came. Then R. Akiba came forward and exclaimed: "Our Father, our King, we have no King except Thee; Our Father, our King, deal kindly with us for Thy name's sake!" and it began to rain immediately. Some inferred from this incident that R. Akiba was the author of the famous prayer, but it is very likely that the formula was much older than R. Akiba, although the number of prayers used with it, or their form, had not been fixed and remained in a fluid state for many generations also subsequent to the period of R. Akiba. Originally it may have had nineteen verses, to correspond to the nineteen benedictions of the Shemoneh Esreh, but already in the time of Amram Gaon (ninth century) the number had been increased to twenty-five. The Sephardic ritual has twenty-five verses, the Ashkenazic thirty-eight, the Polish forty-four, and that of Salonica has fifty-three. Among the Ashkenazic Jews, this prayer is recited every day during the ten Penitential Days.

The idea of the Fatherhood of God is the direct result of the belief in God as the Creator of the world. The term "Fatherhood" was also used by the heathen nations of antiquity, but with them the implication was that the deity was the physical progenitor of the race, while in the Jewish religion it only had a spiritual and moral meaning. . . . While all men, born in the image of God, have the capacity of rising to the stature of God's children in a spiritual sense, Israel, obedient to the Torah and loyal to the destiny assigned to them, are regarded as having reached that stage already. Some of the rabbis, however, would apply the appellation "son of God" only to the pious and upright among the children of Israel. The filial relationship with God is denied to those who stray away from the right path, be they Israelites or Gentiles; and the obverse would be equally true: that all who are conscious of the relationship and manifest it in their lives may designate themselves "the children of the living God." "Have we not all one Father? Hath not one God created us?" is the exclamation of the prophet (Malachi

2.10), *and it has become the slogan of all humanitarians throughout all generations.*

God as King of the Universe is a figure taken from the social and political life of all peoples of antiquity. The king in ancient times was the embodiment of all authority. He was the lawgiver and the judge and to him all the people of his dominion owed unquestioned obedience and loyalty. God as the King of the Universe, who decides the fate of kings and nations, was thus conceived of as the King of kings, although that title was sometimes also claimed by some ambitious earthly rulers, such as the kings of Persia. The meaning assigned to this term in Judaism, in its development during the prophetic period, conveyed the notion of a moral order in the world and stimulated the hope for the ultimate establishment of the Kingdom of God upon earth. Indeed, already at the foot of Mount Sinai, Israel was declared a "kingdom of priests," ruled by the Author of the laws and regulations that would assure the prevalence of righteousness and purity of life among them. The intimacy implied in the figure of God's Fatherhood is enforced by the idea of His sovereignty, maintaining and demanding the strictest loyalty and submission to His laws. . . .

During the ten Penitential Days, the idea of God's sovereignty finds greater emphasis in the liturgy, although God's Fatherhood is often appealed to. On the days of judgment, as these days were conceived to be, God sits on His throne of justice and administers to all their deserts in accordance with their conduct. Justice, however, is stern and rigid, and the author of Avinu Malkenu *prefers to put the appellation of Father ahead of that of King, thus endeavoring to secure for his people the compassion and love of the father for his children, lest justice deal too severely with them.*[13]

THE PRECENTOR'S PRAYER

HINENI

Here am I, deficient in good deeds,
Trembling and terrified,

In dread of You who sit enthroned
Amidst the praises of Israel.
I have come to stand and supplicate before You
For your people Israel who have sent me.

Though I am not worthy or fit for it,
Yet I beseech You, God of Abraham, Isaac and Jacob,
Merciful and gracious Lord,
God of Israel,
Almighty and fearful God.
Prosper my undertaking
In thus standing before You to seek mercy
For myself and for these who have sent me.

Hold them not guilty for my sins
And condemn them not for my transgressions,
For I am a sinner and transgressor.
Let them not be confounded for my transgressions
And let them not be ashamed of me nor I of them.
Accept my prayer as the prayer
Of an old, experienced, righteous, and venerable man
Whose voice is sweet and who is acceptable to his fellow
　　creatures.

Rebuke Satan that he may not accuse us,
Let our omissions be forgiven in love,
And in love cover all our transgressions.
Turn all afflictions and evils
To joy and gladness, life and peace,
For us and for all Israel
That they may love truth and peace,
And may there be in my prayer no manner of impediment.
Translated by Bernard Martin[14]

COMMENTARY: *Bernard Martin*

*Before beginning the Additional Service for Rosh Hashanah
and Yom Kippur, the precentor recites this supplication, composed by an unknown hazzan sometime during the Middle*

Ages. The author, whose deep humility permeates his entire prayer, was obviously aware of the special responsibility that rests, according to tradition, on the person who leads the congregation in this service.. The Talmud (Rosh Hashanah 34b) declares that, while on other occasions only the unlettered among the congregation fulfill their religious obligation by listening to the precentor's repetition of the Amidah, in the case of the Musaf Amidah of Rosh Hashanah and Yom Kippur even the most learned do so, for very few are thoroughly familiar with its special benedictions and insertions.

The author of Hineni was also doubtless aware of the qualifications set forth in the Talmud (Taanit 16a) for the "agent (or emissary) of the congregation" who leads it in prayer. While he need be neither rabbi nor priest, he is to be a man with a pleasant voice, able to chant the prayers melodiously, and possessing a perfect knowledge of all the benedictions and the prescribed biblical readings for all occasions. In addition, he is to be a person whose conduct in youth was unblemished, a hardworking man, and one with a large family to support on a modest income. Such a person, it was believed, would be most apt to pray with thoroughgoing sincerity both for himself and the congregation. Apparently conscious that he does not possess the requisite qualifications, that he—like all other men—is a sinner and transgressor, the author prays that his rendition of the liturgy may be accounted "as the prayer of an old, experienced, righteous, and venerable man whose voice is sweet and who is acceptable to his fellow creatures," and that those on whose behalf he offers prayer may not be held guilty or put to shame by reason of his sins.

The reference to Satan, whom God is asked to rebuke "that he may not accuse us," reflects the popular legend that at the High Holy Day season God holds a court session in heaven at which Satan is the accuser and prosecutor of Israel, while a beneficent angel serves as their defender and advocate.

There is no great artistry in this deeply moving personal supplication, but the authenticity of its religious spirit is obvious.[15]

IT IS OUR DUTY

ALENU

It is our duty to praise the Master of all, to exalt the Creator of the universe, who has not made us like the nations of the world and has not placed us like the families of the earth; who has not designed our destiny to be like theirs, nor our lot like that of all their multitude. We bend the knee and bow and acknowledge before the supreme King of kings, the Holy One, blessed be He, that it is He who stretched forth the heavens and founded the earth. His seat of glory is in the heavens above; His abode of majesty is in the lofty heights. He is our God, there is none else; truly, He is our King, there is none besides Him, as it is written in His Torah: You shall know this day, and reflect in your heart, that it is the Lord who is God in the heavens above and on the earth beneath, there is none else (Deuteronomy 4.39).

We hope therefore, Lord our God, soon to behold Thy majestic glory, when the abominations shall be removed from the earth, and the false gods exterminated; when the world shall be perfected under the reign of the Almighty, and all mankind will call upon Thy name, and all the wicked of the earth will be turned to Thee. May all the inhabitants of the world realize and know that to Thee every knee must bend, every tongue must vow allegiance. May they bend the knee and prostrate themselves before Thee, Lord our God, and give honor to Thy glorious name; may they all accept the yoke of Thy kingdom, and do Thou reign over them speedily forever and ever. For the kingdom is Thine, and to all eternity Thou wilt reign in glory, as it is written in Thy Torah: The Lord shall be King forever and ever (Exodus 15.18). And it is said: The Lord shall be King over all the earth; on that day the Lord shall be One, and his name One (Zechariah 14.9).

Translated by Philip Birnbaum[16]

COMMENTARY: *Sidney B. Hoenig*

Originally the Alenu *prayer was written as an introduction to the* Malkhuyot *(Kingship invocation) of the Rosh Hashanah liturgy. This prayer serves as a fitting prelude to the declaration of the Divine Kingship throughout the entire universe. The first paragraph proclaims Israel's praise of the God of heaven and earth, while the second is an expression of the hope that all mankind will soon recognize His dominion over the universe. Because of its extraordinary appeal, the prayer was carried over from the New Year service to be a stirring conclusion to all the daily services.*

The authorship is attributed varyingly to Joshua, who uttered this prayer upon the entrance of the children of Israel into the promised land, to the men of the Great Assembly, who recognized the Universality of God with the complete demolition of idolatrous worship, or to the congregants in the Temple of the Second Commonwealth, who spontaneously exclaimed these praises when they bowed before the altar together with the priests during the service. Therefore the customs of kneeling in prayer on Rosh Hashanah and Yom Kippur and of bowing the head during the recital of Alenu *are faithfully retained. The composition of* Alenu *as it is today is, however, assigned to Rav, the first great Amoraic teacher in Babylon in the third century.*

An examination of the contents reveals a variation between the wording of the Sephardic ritual and that of the Ashkenazic. The Spanish version includes the following words: "for they bow down to vanity and emptiness and pray to a god that saves not." This passage has been unfortunately a source of misunderstanding between the faiths. It was argued by the Gentiles of the Middle Ages that the Sephardic version vilified Christianity while the rabbis sincerely demonstrated that the entire prayer was directed against idolatry. In fact the prayer was composed long before the rise of Christianity. The particular passage that is attributed as a reference to Christianity is really an excerpt from the words of Isaiah 30.7 and 45.20, which pertained only to the idolatrous practices of his contemporaries. Even at the time of the final composition of the entire prayer by Rav, an idea of abuse could not exist, for he was a Babylonian and in his country there was no practice of Christianity. The omission of these phrases from the reading

*adopted by the Ashkenazim may have been due to the desire
to offset any calumnies or misinterpretations.*¹⁷

THE THREE MUSAF THEMES

THE KINGSHIP OF GOD

MALKHUYOT

Our God and God of our fathers,
Do Thou establish Thy glorious rule over all the world,
Do Thou establish Thy glorious majesty over all the earth,
Let all who inhabit the world behold the grandeur of Thy might,
Let every creature know that Thou didst fashion it,
Let every living thing recognize that Thou didst form it,
Let every creature declare the God of Israel King,
And His dominion extends over all creation.

Our God and God of our fathers, mayest Thou sanctify us by
Thy commandments. Grant that we may have a portion among
those who devote themselves to Thy Torah. Satisfy us with
Thy goodness and cause us to rejoice in Thy deliverance. And
purify our hearts to serve Thee in truth, for Thou art a God
of truth and Thy word is truth and it will endure forever.
Praised be Thou, O Lord, King of all the world, who hallowest
the people of Israel, and the Day of Remembrance. . . .

THE REMEMBRANCE OF GOD

ZIKHRONOT

Thou rememberest the deeds of all the inhabitants of the
world and Thou art mindful of Thy creatures from the beginning of time. All secrets, all things hidden, have always
been known unto Thee. With Thee there is no forgetfulness,
there is no concealment from Thine eyes.

Thou rememberest each deed, and no creature is hidden

from Thee. All things lie exposed before Thee, O Lord our God; Thy discernment embraces all the generations down to the end of time.

Thou hast appointed a time of remembrance for every living being, to bring to judgment the multitude of Thy creations and their countless actions. From the very beginning Thou didst proclaim this as Thy way, and Thou didst make it known since ancient days. This day, when Thy world began, the first day thereof, is a Day of Remembrance. So it is ordained by a statute of Israel, by a decree of the God of Jacob.

Thereon is decreed the fate of countries, which shall know war and which peace; which famine and which plenty. Thereon, too, is decreed the fate of individuals, for life or for death. Who is not judged on this day? Every living thing comes before Thee in judgment, his deeds as well as his purposes, and even the impulses behind his actions. Happy is the man who does not forget Thee and the son of man who seeks his strength in Thee. For those who seek Thee will never stumble, and those who trust in Thee will never be put to shame. . . .

Our God and God of our fathers, remember us for good, ordain for us deliverance and compassion.

Remember Thy covenant with Abraham at Mount Moriah, when he bound his son Isaac and placed him on the altar of sacrifice.

Remember how he heeded Thy call, seeking to do Thy will with a full heart.

Mayest Thou turn away Thine anger from us, renew the glory of Thy people, and of Thy city, Jerusalem.

O Lord our God, fulfill the promise set forth in Thy Torah by Thy servant Moses, as it is written:

I shall remember My covenant with your ancestors whom I freed from Egypt, to be their God. I am the Lord.

Thou rememberest all things past from the beginning of time, with Thee there is no forgetfulness.

Mayest Thou remember the binding of Isaac, and may the merit of his faith evoke mercy upon us, his descendants.

Praised be Thou, O Lord, who rememberest the covenant. . . .

THE REVELATION OF GOD

SHOFAROT

Thou didst reveal Thy glory in a cloud, to speak to Thy holy people. Thou didst cause them to hear Thy heavenly voice and Thou didst manifest Thyself to them in a mist of purity. The entire world trembled before Thee, all creation was in awe of Thee, when Thou, our King, didst manifest Thy presence at Mount Sinai to teach Thy people the Torah and the commandments. Thou didst enable them to hear Thy glorious voice and Thy divine precepts from the midst of the flames of fire. Amidst thunder and lightning didst Thou make Thyself known to them, amidst the sound of the *shofar* Thou didst reveal Thy presence to them.

As it is written in Thy Torah (Exodus 19.16): And it came to pass on the third day, when it was morning, that there were thunders and lightnings and a thick cloud upon the mount, and the voice of the horn (*shofar*) exceeding loud; and all the people that were in the camp trembled. And it is also written (Exodus 19.19): As the sound of the *shofar* grew louder and louder, Moses spoke and God answered him in a clear voice. And it is also written (Exodus 20.15): And all the people perceived the thundering and the lightning and the sound of the *shofar* and the mountain in smoke; and when the people saw it they trembled and stood afar off. . . .

And in the books of Thy prophet it is also written (Isaiah 18.3): All the inhabitants of the world, all the residents on earth, when a banner is raised upon the mountains, see you, and when the *shofar* is sounded, hear you. And it is also written (Isaiah 27.13, Zechariah 9.14–15): And it will come to pass on that day that a great *shofar* will be sounded, and those who were lost in the land of Assyria, and those who were exiled in the land of Egypt will return to worship the Lord upon His holy mountain in Jerusalem. And the Lord will be revealed to them and His arrow will go forth speedily and the Lord God will sound the *shofar*, and He will show His might in the whirlwind of the south. The Lord of hosts will defend them. Even so, mayest Thou protect Thy people Israel, with Thy peace.

Our God and God of our fathers, sound the great *shofar* to herald our freedom and lift a banner for the ingathering of our exiles. Bring together the homeless of our people from among the nations, and assemble them from the farthest places of the earth, under the wings of Thy Presence. And restore us in song to Zion Thy city, and in enduring joy to Jerusalem, the site of Thy sanctuary. There may we yet perform the service of each festival, bringing to Thee our offerings, the tokens of our devotion, as prescribed for us in Thy Torah, given by Thee through Thy servant Moses:

On the day of your gladness, on your festivals and on your new moons, you shall sound the trumpets as you bring the designated offerings, and they shall be a remembrance before your God; I am the Lord.

For Thou hearest the call of the *shofar* and givest heed to its summons; none may be compared to Thee.

Praised be Thou, O Lord, who hearest Thy people Israel as they call to Thee with the sound of the *shofar*.

Translated by Ben Zion Bokser[18]

COMMENTARY: *Max Arzt*

Our liturgy is inspired by the belief that man is held account-able for the mastery of his evil drives and for calling into action the potential good within him. This belief defines man as a morally responsible being, standing under God's judgment. Such a conception expresses a more profound respect for our person than one which would absolve us by attributing man's conduct to hereditary and environmental influences beyond his control. The belief that he is morally irresponsible tends to make a person indeed irresponsible, even as the belief that he is ac-countable for his conduct can serve to heighten his moral sensitivity.

Weary idealists and misanthropes may wonder whether the struggle for human perfection is worth the effort. What can one person accomplish in a vast universe, of which he is but a tiny particle? Against such debilitating speculation, the three-fold division of the Musaf *into the* Malkhuyot, *the* Zikhronot, *and the* Shofarot *suggests some measure of response. Man's brief existence is given perspective and significance, juxtaposed as it is to God's eternity. As God's creatures, we are to acknowledge His sovereignty over the whole universe; as His children we are to see in history the unfolding of His purpose; and as His servants we are to listen to the* shofar *sounds which reassure us of the coming fulfillment of Israel's and the world's redemption. Broad is the vision, deep is the conviction, and deathless is the spirit of the people that expresses all this in the prayers of its liturgy!*

The unique features of this Musaf Amidah *are, first, that it contains nine blessings instead of the usual seven; and second, that it includes three sets of ten verses each: the* Malkhuyot *(Kingship verses), the* Zikhronot *(Remembrance verses), and* Shofarot *(Shofar verses). . . .*

The Kingship of God

The meaning of Judaism's concept of the "Kingdom of God" or, more correctly, the "Kingship of God" is illuminated by this prayer. We pray for the day when all men will acknowledge God as their Maker, accepting His sovereignty. . . .

In the Jewish conception, the "Kingdom" of God is not that which is to be established "at the end of time" or "beyond history" or in an otherworldly existence. The "Kingdom" of God is already here now. God's sovereign will established and maintains the laws of heaven and earth (Jeremiah 33.25), and by His will the destiny of men and nations is decreed. It is therefore not the "Kingdom" of God which man must affirm but His Kingship. Man's moral freedom necessitates his being given the choice of obeying the moral law or of rebelling against it. He must of his own volition "accept the Kingship of God" by ordering his life in accordance with the imperatives and disciplines whereby God's will becomes the rule of man's conduct. In the prayer before us, the hope is expressed that the day would be speeded when God would rule over the whole universe with His glory, and when all mankind would de-clare that the Lord God of Israel is King and His dominion extends over all.

As Israel prays for the day when the Kingship of God would be recognized by all mankind, it is determined to pursue its lonely vocation as it regulates its life under God's sovereignty. In Judaism, mitzvot are the means whereby life can be lived "under God," and whereby it is responsive to that which is holy. For us, the mitzvot are the means whereby we declare that God "not only reigns in the world, but that He also governs our personal lives."

At the conclusion of the present prayer, we supplicate God to purify our hearts to serve Him in truth, and climax that supplication with the ringing declaration that God is King over all the earth and that from Him stems the sanctity of Israel and the sacredness of the Day of Remembrance. . . .

The Remembrance of God

The prelude to the Zikhronot asserts that there appears before God the record of every man's deeds, his works and his ways, his thoughts and his schemes, his plans, and the motives of his acts. It further affirms "Happy is the man who does not forget Thee and the son of man who seeks his strength in Thee." This unquestioning faith enabled the Jew to face the future with courage, in the most trying circumstances. His endurance and strength were derived from the belief that God surveys and sees all that happens to the end of all generations. Rather than presume to sit in judgment over God's government of the world, he chose to subject his own life to God's scrutiny. To know that God did not abdicate His rule once He created the world, nor that God abandoned man to blind fate and random chance, was to him sufficient reason so to live as to merit God's merciful "remembrance." The faith expressed in the prelude to the Zikhronot can be for us, as well, a faith for confident and courageous living. Our inability to plot the curve of retribution and reward in the unfolding of history should not dampen our belief in God's providence. Regardless of the *individual's personal fortunes, God's "remembrance" of our deeds of virtue and valor redeems our life from meaninglessness by validating our struggles for the enthronement of the moral law in the life of all men. . . .*

Envisioning Israel's future redemption, the Zikhronot section reaches a climactic conclusion as it refers to the Akedah, the prototype and the symbol of merit and moral example accumulated for the Jew by the martyred heroes of the past.

The Revelation of God

In the Torah, the first mention of the shofar is in the account of the revelation at Sinai: "And it came to pass, on the third day, when it was morning, that there were thunders and lightnings and a thick cloud upon the mount, and the voice of a horn (shofar) exceeding loud; and all the people that were in the camp trembled" (Exodus 19.16). Since this is the first of the Shofarot verses, the prelude to the Shofarot consists of a stirring retelling of that which transpired at Sinai. The prelude focuses our attention on the extraordinary nature of that revelation. God revealed Himself not to the chosen few, but to an entire people—"to teach Thy people Torah and mitzvot." Yehezkel Kaufmann, in his monumental study of the religion of the Bible, points to the stunning originality of the idea that an entire people was the recipient and vehicle of God's revelation. The concept implies that the moral law is to be regarded not as the doctrine of sages or the dictate of earthly rulers, but as the will of God made known to an entire people consecrated to be "a kingdom of priests, and a holy nation" (Exodus 19.6). Israel is a people not thrown together by accidental circumstances, but drawn together by an indissoluble covenant with God—a covenant that might be defied, but not denied; broken but not annulled. Throughout history this people was haunted by the memory of its corporate commitment, and inwardly plagued by its all too frequent backsliding from provisions of the covenant. . . .

In the three verses from the prophetic books, the shofar sounds are identified with the messianic restoration of the Holy Land. Amidst throngs worshiping in a rebuilt sanctuary at

Jerusalem, a redeemed people will again sound the shofar *on their days of joy, their festivals, and new moons, and win the favor of God who hears "the call of the* shofar *and givest heed to its summons."*[19]

SUPREME KING

MELEKH ELYON

And thus shall God be acclaimed King in Jeshurun:

The Supreme King, whose presence is in the heavens, whose might is revealed in the heavens, who will invoke His might to save, He will be King forever.

The Supreme King, whose power performs all things, who ordains and executes, who bares what is hidden, He will be King forever.

The Supreme King, who speaks in mercy, who is robed in mercy, who heeds entreaty, He will be King forever.

The Supreme King, who remembers our ancestors, who absolves His creatures, who is angry with the wicked, He will be King forever.

The Supreme King, who abides in eternity, whose goodness is everlasting, who spreads forth the endless heavens, He will be King forever.

The Supreme King, who robed Himself with light as a garment, who fashioned the shining stars, who is mighty and glorious, He will be King forever.

The Supreme King, the Sovereign of all worlds, who unravels all hidden things, who gives speech to the speechless, He will be King forever.

The Supreme King, who sustains all, who survives all, who beholds all, He will be King forever.

The Supreme King, who is adorned with power, who will restore His sacred shrine, who redeems and rescues, He will be King forever.

The Supreme King, who commands forces of fire, who directs the waters of the sea, who is near to all who call Him in love, He will be King forever.

The Supreme King, who does not sleep or slumber, who ordained the harmony of the universe, whose praise resounds in the secret places of the universe, He will be King forever.

A mortal king perishes and is laid in the dust; he grows weary and restless. How long is he king?

A mortal king ends his day in sleep; a deep sleep in his final end; the void will swallow him. How long is he king?

But the Supreme King—His might is eternal, His glory is everlasting, His praise is endless, He will be King forever.

Translated by Ben Zion Bokser[20]

COMMENTARY: *Max Arzt*

God, the Supreme King, reigns forever. He knows all and is all-powerful. He fathoms our innermost secrets and outlives all that lives. Infinite in the sway of His power, He is near to those who seek His help. Not so dependable are those lesser beings—the princes and powers of the world—to whom men are wont to offer their allegiance. The human "pauper king," on whom men depend, is powerless. He is destined for the grave. The sleep of death is his end, and into the void he vanishes. But God, the King Most High, His power is everlasting, His glory is eternal, His praise endures forever.[21]

LET US DECLARE THE MIGHTY HOLINESS OF THIS DAY

UNETANNEH TOKEF

KALONYMUS BEN MESHULLAM

Let us declare the mighty holiness of this day, for it is solemn and awesome.

On this day is Thy dominion exalted, Thy throne established in mercy, and Thou judgest thereon in truth.

True it is that Thou judgest and givest reproof, Thou discernest and bearest witness, Thou recordest and sealest, Thou recountest and measurest; Thou rememberest things forgotten.

Thou unfoldest the book of remembrance, and it speaks for itself, for every man's seal is found therein.

The great *shofar* is sounded, and a still small voice is heard. The angelic hosts, seized with fear and trembling, declare: Behold it is the Day of Judgment, when the hosts of heaven are to stand in judgment, for even they are not faultless before Thee.

All who have come into this world, Thou causest to pass before Thee in judgment, as a flock of sheep.

As a shepherd musters his sheep, causing them to pass under his staff, so dost Thou cause every living soul to pass before Thee.

Thou appointest the measure of every creature's life and decreest its destiny.

On Rosh Hashanah it is written,
On Yom Kippur it is sealed,
How many shall pass away,
And how many shall be born,
Who shall live and who shall die,
Who shall complete his years,
And who shall not complete his years,
Who shall die by fire and who by water,
Who by the sword and who by a wild beast,
Who by famine and who by thirst,
Who by earthquake and who by pestilence,
Who by strangling and who by stoning,
Who shall be at rest and who shall wander,
Who shall be serene and who shall be disturbed,
Who shall be at ease and who shall be afflicted,
Who shall be poor and who shall be rich,
Who shall be humbled and who shall be exalted.

But
Teshuvah, Tefillah, and *Tzedakah*
Penitence, Prayer, and Deeds of Mercy
Annul the severity of the judgment.

The praise due Thee is in accordance with Thy renown. Thou art slow to anger and ready to forgive. Thou desirest not the death of the sinner, but that he turn from his evil way and

live; till the day he dies Thou waitest for him, and if he but
return Thou dost readily take him back.

Thou hast fashioned man, and surely Thou knowest the
impulses of his heart. He is but flesh and blood. Man's origin is
dust and his end, dust. He spends his life in the earning of his
bread. He is like a fragile vessel, like the grass that withers, the
flower that fades, the shadow that passes, the cloud that
vanishes, the wind that blows, the dust that scatters, the dream
that flies away.

But Thou, our divine King, art everlasting.

Endless are Thy years and measureless the span of Thy
days. The hosts of Thy creation cannot be fathomed. Thy
mysterious Being eludes our understanding. Thy name befits
Thy glory, and Thy glory is according to Thy name; and Thou
hast linked our name with Thine own.

Translated by Ben Zion Bokser[22]

COMMENTARY: *Max Arzt*

*Because this prayer expresses so dramatically an awareness of
the unpredictability and uncertainty of human life, it has occupied a pre-eminent place among the liturgical preferences
of the Jews. With vivid imagery, the author depicts the heavenly
scene on the Day of Judgment. The shofar is sounded, there
is heard but a still small voice to herald the appearance of the
Divine Judge. The angels are in terror, for judgment is to be
decreed against the habitants of heaven, as well as against
those of earth. In the eyes of God, no being, however angelic,
has perfect purity. One by one, as sheep are counted by the
shepherd, each life passes in review before Him, and its fate
is inscribed in a book of records which contains the seal of
every person's hand. The sense of doom, of almost unrelieved
despair, is heightened in us as we are told that on Rosh
Hashanah the decree is written and that on Yom Kippur it is
sealed.*

*It is not the poet's intention, however, to induce a fatalistic
resignation; but rather the opposite, to deny that man's life is
subject to an irremediable fate. The prayer, in fact, reaches its
climax when it assures us that it is within man's power to annul*

an evil decree, to reopen the future, and to reclaim the initiative it gives. The quantity of man's life is in the hands of God, the quality of his life is in man's hands only. "Everything is in the hands of God except the fear of God" (Berakhot 33b). Everything is foreseen, yet freedom of choice is granted (Avot 3.15). In its climactic declaration, the prayer affirms that man can change the future by changing himself. It suggests a threefold means of annulling "the evil of the decree":

1. Repentance: A courageous break with evil and a "return" to God.
2. Prayer: A re-establishment of our relationship with God.
3. Tzedakah *(deeds of kindness)*: Tangible acts of love and concern for our fellow men. . . .

So pronounced is Judaism's predisposition to direct attention to the quality of man's life on earth, that, in a foreshadowing of the procedure at the "last judgment," Raba (4th century C.E.) suggests that among the questions to be asked of man are the following:

> Did you conduct your business with integrity? Did you set aside fixed times for study of Torah? Did you concern yourself with the duty of raising a family? Did you retain a confident faith in the fulfillment of the prophetic ideals of Israel's redemption and the coming of an era of universal peace? (Shabbat 31a). . . .

The uncertainty, unpredictability, and evanescent nature of human life is depicted here in graphic metaphors equating man with a fragile potsherd, withering grass, a fading flower, a passing shadow, floating dust, and a vanishing dream. This devaluation of human life purports to fortify the belief that God takes cognizance of the inner drives that account for man's lack of mortal constancy and that often disfigure his humanity. No life, however, is irremediably doomed to meaninglessness. The sinner can redeem himself by taking the initial step of repentance towards the reclamation of his worth and dignity as a moral being. Then his life assumes great significance in the eyes of God, for God needs man to sanctify His name on earth, *even as do the inhabitants of the heavens above. Once finite man adopts as his vocation the glorification and hallowing of God's name, his life assumes infinite worth. Israel, the people which in its very name bears the Name of God, is to act and serve as the divinely commissioned vanguard of the terrestrial hosts, expressing the praise of God in thought, word and deed.[23]*

ALL THE WORLD SHALL COME TO SERVE THEE

VEYEETAYU KOL LE-AVDEKHA

All the world shall come to serve Thee
    And bless Thy glorious Name,
And Thy righteousness triumphant
    The islands shall acclaim.
And the peoples shall go seeking
    Who knew Thee not before,
And the ends of earth shall praise Thee,
    And tell Thy greatness o'er.

They shall build for Thee their altars,
    Their idols overthrown,
And their graven gods shall shame them,
    As they turn to Thee alone.
They shall worship Thee at sunrise,
    And feel Thy kingdom's might,
And impart their understanding
    To those astray in night.

With the coming of Thy kingdom
    The hills shall break into song,
And the island laugh exultant
    That they to God belong.
And all their congregations
    So loud Thy praise shall sing,
That the uttermost peoples hearing,
    Shall hail Thee crowned King.

Translated by Israel Zangwill[24]

9. *Mahzor*. Germany. Circa 1320. University Library, Leipzig. See Chapter XIII.

10. White tablecloth with gold brocade appliqué. Oberzell, Germany. 1781. Strauss-Rothschild Collection of the Cluny Museum, Paris. See Chapter XIII.

11. Honey dish for Rosh Hashanah. Silver. By Ilya Schor (1904–1961). Collection of Dr. and Mrs. Abram Kanof, New York. See Chapter XIII.

12. *Kiddush* cup for Rosh Hashanah. Silver. London. 1793–94. See Chapter XIII.

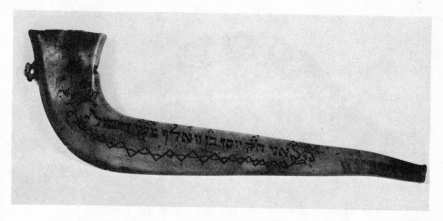

13. *Shofar* with engraved inscription. Dieburg, Germany. 1781–82. The Jewish Museum, New York. See Chapter XIII.

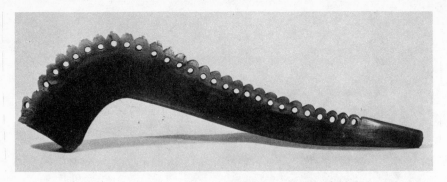

14. *Shofar* with scalloped edge design. Germany. 19th century. Museum of the Hebrew Union College-Jewish Institute of Religion, Cincinnati. See Chapter XIII.

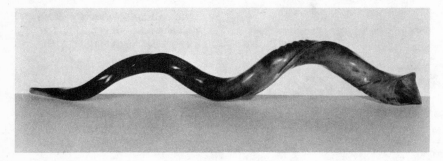

15. Oriental twisted *shofar*. Jonathan David Co. See Chapter XIII.

16. Yemenite twisted *shofar* with Hebrew inscription and floral decorations. Mount Sinai Memorial Park, Los Angeles. See Chapter XIII.

COMMENTARY: *Bernard Martin*

This great hymn, included in the service of the High Holy Days, is probably from the seventh or eighth century. Its authorship is uncertain. . . .

What is most striking about the Veyeetayu *is its exalted universalism, strongly akin to that of the second part of the* Alenu, *of which, indeed, it may be a poetic version. In the early Middle Ages, when fanaticism and intolerance stalked the earth, the author of this poem envisioned the day when all men would be united in the worship of the universal Lord. Here there is no mention of a day of wrath and punishment by a God angry with those who deny him; instead, it is suggested, those who have gone astray and served idolatrous gods will themselves see the error of their ways and turn to the true God. Then, when God's kingdom is established, even nature will be transformed; the prophet's (Isaiah 42) and the psalmists' (Psalms 97, 148) vision of the islands rejoicing and the mountains and hills praising God will be realized.*

Solomon Schechter once wrote:

> How one would like to catch a glimpse of that early hymnologist to whom we owe the well-known *piyyut*, Veyeetayu, which, in its iconoclastic victory over all kinds of idolatries, ancient as well as modern, might best be described as the Marseillaise of the people of the Lord of Hosts—a Marseillaise which is not followed by a Reign of Terror, but by the Kingdom of God on earth, when the upright shall exult and the saints triumphantly rejoice.

"All the World Shall Come to Serve Thee" is particularly appropriate for the New Year's Day service, with its joyous proclamation of God's sovereignty. In the present free poetic version by Israel Zangwill, it has become a favorite hymn in many congregations and, especially in the contemporary liberal synagogue, it is sung on many occasions aside from the High Holy Days.[25]

KADDISH

(A PRAYER CHANTED ON ROSH HASHANAH)

LEVI ISAAC OF BERDITCHEV

Good morning, to You, Almighty God.
I, Levi Yitzhak son of Sarah of Berditchev,
Have come for a judgment against You,
On behalf of Your people Israel.
What do You want of Your people Israel?
Why do You afflict Your people Israel?
The slightest thing, and You say, "Speak to the children of
   Israel,"
The slightest thing and You turn to the children of Israel,
The slightest thing, and you say, "Tell the children of Israel."
Our Father! There are so many nations in the world,
Persians, Babylonians, Edomites.
The Russians, what do they say?
That their Emperor is Emperor.
The Germans, what do they say?
That their Empire is the Empire.
And the English, what do they say?
That their Empire is the Empire.
And I, Levi Yitzhak son of Sarah of Berditchev, say,
"Magnified and sanctified be His great Name!"
And I, Levi Yitzhak son of Sarah of Berditchev, say,
"I shall not stir from this spot,
There must be an end of this,
The exile must end!
Magnified and sanctified be His great Name!"

Translated by Joseph Leftwich[26]

PEACE AND PLENTY

JULES HARLOW

May we see the day when war and bloodshed cease,
When a great and wondrous peace embraces the world,

When one nation shall not threaten another
And we shall not again experience war.
Bless us, O Lord, with peace.
We are greedy for gain, pursuing profit
While soldiers pursue each other far away.
Nations squander their young men's lives on a spree.
Even Abraham was stopped; he did not sacrifice his son.
Help us to seek peace, O Lord, and to pursue it.
Hungry children starve our souls,
Naked children expose us,
Slaughtered children kill our hopes;
We are wretched in their parents' sorrow.
Heal us, O Lord; help us turn to each other.
Let us make no peace with hunger or oppression,
Let us make no peace with hatred or with fear.
Let love and justice flow like a mighty stream,
Let peace fill the earth as the waters fill the sea.
May the curses of the old year end,
May the blessings of the new year begin.
Amen.[27]

VII

THE SCRIPTURAL READINGS

THE TORAH AND *HAFTARAH* PORTIONS

Louis Jacobs

The Torah reading for the first day

The Torah reading for the first day of Rosh Hashanah is the twenty-first chapter of the book of Genesis, dealing with Isaac's birth, his growth to manhood, Abraham's banishment of his son Ishmael, and Abraham's peace treaty with Abimelech. The reason generally given for this choice is the tradition that Isaac was born on Rosh Hashanah. Professor A. Büchler has, however, advanced an ingenious theory to account for the choice. In ancient Palestine it was the custom to read in the synagogue each week smaller portions of the Torah than we do now so that three, instead of one, years elapsed from the beginning of the Torah reading to its completion. Our present practice follows the ancient Babylonian practice of completing the Torah in one year. Now Büchler has shown that in the earlier triennial cycle the portion for Rosh Hashanah was, once every three years, this twenty-first chapter of Genesis. In later ages, though the Babylonian custom was well-nigh universally adopted, the original reading was retained for Rosh Hashanah.

There is the further consideration that this chapter comes immediately before the account of the binding of Isaac, read on the second day of Rosh Hashanah. This is one of the great themes of the festival. As the story of the binding of Isaac was obviously appropriate reading for the day what could be more natural than to choose as supplementary reading the account of Isaac's birth in the previous chapter? (Büchler, on the other hand, suggests that the account of Isaac's binding was read on the second day because it follows, in the Bible, the account of his birth read on the first day!) . . .

There is a significant midrashic comment on the verse: "God heard the voice of the lad where he is." The Midrash imagines the angels protesting: "How can Ishmael be spared in that his descendants will torment Israel?" God replies: "At this moment he is worthy to be saved"; God hears the voice of the lad *where he is*. Man is a creature of moods and cannot live ever on the heights. The firm resolves he makes on Rosh Hashanah may weaken when the days of self-examination are gone. But at least, the Rabbis might have said, let man's purpose be strong on these days that God might hear his voice *where he is*. . . .

The *Maftir* for the first and second days

On both the first and second days of Rosh Hashanah the *maftir* is the portion of the book of Numbers (29.1–6) describing the special offerings of the day. Rosh Hashanah, falling as it does at the beginning of the seventh month, is always, in addition, the New Moon festival. Hence the references in this portion to the New Moon offerings.

The *Haftarah* for the first day

The prophetic reading for the first day is the first part of the book of Samuel (I Samuel 1.1–2.10) describing Hannah's passionate plea for the gift of a son and her hymn of triumph and joy when the prayer was answered. Apart from the tradition that it was on Rosh Hashanah that Hannah's prayer was heard, this portion was chosen because of its link with the Torah reading. Both Sarah and Hannah are blessed with a son when it had seemed that they were destined to be barren. It is a happy coincidence that the mother, who brings the child to birth, should be celebrated in the readings chosen for the festival of creation, the birthday of the world. The tender love of the Jewish mother for her child and her complete, self-sacrificing devotion has been the constant theme of our poets and singers. Even the love of God is, in a memorable passage, described in terms of a mother's love for her child: "Like one whom his mother comforteth, so will I comfort you" (Isaiah 66.13), refuting the allegation that Judaism is a masculine religion which speaks in but halting accents to women. . . .

The Torah reading for the second day

On the second day the twenty-second chapter of Genesis (1–24) is read. This deals mainly with the binding of Isaac. Abraham is commanded by God to take his beloved son, Isaac, in whom are centered all his hopes for the future, and to offer him up as a sacrifice on one of the mountains. Abraham obeys the voice of God. He rises early in the morning, taking the lad with him. Gradually he reveals his dread purpose. Isaac accepts his fate willingly and allows his father to bind him on the altar. Abraham takes the knife in his hand to perform the deed but an angel calls to him from heaven bidding him to stay his hand. A ram is discovered in the thicket and this is substituted for Isaac. God promises Abraham that because he has done this thing his seed will be blessed and be a blessing to mankind.

Such is the story and it has been given two kinds of interpretation. Many have seen the chief value of the story as a dramatic protest against the cruel heathen notion that the wrath of the gods could be averted by child sacrifice. According to this interpretation, the really significant part of the narrative is the angel's call to Abraham that he stay his hand. A new conception of religious worship was given to Abraham, that the true God does not require the death of his followers. It is their lives that he wants.

In modern times, chiefly under the influence of the Danish thinker Kierkegaard, whose doctrine of the need for "commitment" to religious truth has won many adherents, another interpretation, found, too, in many of the Jewish sources, has gained ground. In this view it is not the "happy ending" that is significant but the willingness of Abraham to obey the voice of God even when it appeared to command that which would have the effect of setting at naught all that God's revelation had meant to Abraham. God had promised Abraham that a great nation would spring from Isaac, ready to spread among all men the truth Abraham had recognized. And now Abraham hears the voice of God demanding not alone the complete frustration of this hope but a foul immoral act from which Abraham's noble spirit recoils. Yet despite the anguish of his heart Abraham hastens to obey the call. The test of the strength of a man's religious convictions depends on his preparedness to act on them in offering up his most cherished values in their behalf. Religious faith is not with ease acquired: it is the profound sense of conviction born of the tensions, contradictions, and the very despair of life.

This second interpretation is popular today because man's stresses during the past decades have had the result of making him dissatisfied with an easygoing faith. Many have felt that if the voice of God is to be heard at all today it must be through the bitter struggle of a painful tormented existence. The tendency has been to turn the famous Browning poem upside down, to declare that because all's wrong with the world God's in His Heaven. Only out of the depths can man call upon the Lord.

It would seem that in the best Jewish tradition both interpretations are combined. The anguish of Abraham is vividly depicted in the Rabbinic legend of Satan subtly whispering in his ear: "Yesterday He said: 'For in Isaac shall thy seed be called' and now He says: 'Take now thy son and offer him for a burnt offering.'" The Rabbis speak of the *Akedah* (from the root "to bind") as the greatest "test" to which Abraham was subjected. And the prayers of Rosh Hashanah recall the merit of Abraham who "suppressed his compassion in order to perform Thy will with a perfect heart"—the man renowned for his pity prepared to carry out a pitiless act. But, on the other hand, the "happy ending" is no sentimental afterthought depriving the whole episode of its grandeur. For the God of Israel is the God of life and the whole point of the ending is that He did not, in fact, require the death of Isaac. To emphasize the ending to the exclusion of Abraham's willingness to follow the voice of God wherever it led is to reduce the whole narrative to a rather superficial homily on the sacredness of human life. But to ignore the ending is to invite a jaundiced view of religion which exalts the anti-rational in man's soul and acquires depth at the expense of a healthy, normal outlook on life. . . .

The *Haftarah* for the second day

The *Haftarah* for the second day is taken from the book of Jeremiah (31.2–20). This portion concludes with the verses: "Is Ephraim my dear son? Is he a pleasant child? For as often as I speak against him, I do earnestly remember him still . . . ," a fitting choice of reading for the festival of remembrance.

In this portion, too, the motif of motherly love is found. The matriarch Rachel is described as weeping for her exiled children, to be assured by God that they will be restored to the land of their fathers.[1]

THE SACRIFICE OF ISAAC

Julius H. Greenstone

The reading from the Torah on the two days of Rosh Hashanah is taken from the Book of Genesis, chapters 21 and 22, respectively, which relate the story of the birth and the sacrifice of Isaac. The Hebrew designation for the latter story, *Akedah* (binding), is the more correct, since Isaac was really not sacrificed, but only intended to be offered as a sacrifice. The theme of the story is repeated frequently in the liturgy of the holiday, both in prose and in poetic form, and the entire chapter is recited by pious Jews every morning in their prayers. This manifestation of supreme faith by our father, Abraham, his readiness to comply with what he believed to be a divine behest to bring his son, born to him in the twilight of his life and believed by him to have come in fulfillment of God's promise, as an offering to the same God, is invoked by us to avert the severe judgment that our deeds may merit. We pray that Providence deal with us in kindness and mercy for the sake of our ancestors whose devotion and obedience are so strongly exemplified in the story of the sacrifice of Isaac. . . .

Besides the lesson which the synagogue derived from the story of the sacrifice of Isaac—the lesson of great faith and unquestioning obedience to the divine will—Bible students regard this narrative as a lesson that God does not desire human sacrifice. The custom of offering children to the deity was prevalent not only among the early Semites, but also among the Egyptians and even among the Greeks and Romans. The tragic story of Iphigenia, the daughter of Agamemnon, who was slain to appease a goddess and whose murder led to a series of assassinations in the family, has been immortalized in Greek drama and has served as a theme also for many a modern poet. Abraham in his great zeal for his newly discovered faith may have felt that he should do that which was commonly accepted as the expression of the deepest faith—the sacrifice of a beloved child on the altar of the god. The biblical story seeks to stamp out that notion by telling us how Abraham's intention was frustrated by the intervention of God, thus establishing that the purer idea of God abhors human sacrifice in any form. Later legislators and seers took their cue from this story and denounced such a form of worship as abhorrent to the God of Israel. This was one of the great moral contributions made to mankind by the Jewish conception of God, at the time when idolatry, even in the most advanced countries of antiquity, still exacted its toll of human sacrifices.[2]

THE BIRTHDAY OF THE WORLD

ERNST SIMON

Rosh Hashanah is—in the language of the *Mahzor*, the holiday prayer book—*Yom Harat Olam*, the birthday of the world. . . . [It] bears a universalistic character: it is an acknowledgment of humanity and its unity.

This characteristic of the Jewish New Year is expressed in the excerpts from the Torah and the Prophets that we read by rabbinical prescription on Rosh Hashanah. The first day shows us a very old couple, Sarah and Abraham, who now at last have received their long prayed-for son, Isaac. But Sarah is so jealous of Ishmael, Abraham's son by the Egyptian maid Hagar—whose name points etymologically to *hagira*, hegira, to wandering and flight—that she forces Abraham to drive them forth, and even God gives His consent. But now the suffering and distress of the fleeing mother are depicted, as her son is threatened with death by thirst in the desert. She goes a bowshot's length away from him because she cannot bear to watch him die. But an angel of God comforts her from heaven, and God opens her eyes and shows her a nearby well, "for God heard the voice of the lad where he is" (Genesis 21.17). So God heard the voice of a suffering child then, and leaned down to the heart of a tortured mother, even though she was "only" a fugitive Egyptian.

The prophetic text for the same day, the first chapter of the first Book of Samuel, takes up the same purely human motif of the primal relationship between parents and children and carries it further. Elkanah has two wives, the childless Hannah and Peninnah, the "pearl," the fruitful one. It is Hannah whom he loves more, but she endures one humiliation after another from her fortunate rival, as Hagar, the maid, did from Sarah, the "princess." But whereas in the Torah passage, despite all the sympathy shown to Hagar, the final victory goes to Sarah, in the prophetic text the situation is reversed. We hear no more of Peninnah, but Hannah, whose name is related to *hen*, mercy, finally wins divine mercy by her mute prayer in which "only her lips moved, but her voice was not heard."

However, Eli, the priest, who is the official superintendent of the ritual and the highest representative of "religion," misinterprets Hannah's mute prayer as the behavior of a drunkard, and must learn the truth of her religious intoxication from her. The simple woman conquers the priests' skepticism. . . . And so Judaism begins every new year with this victory of the mother over the institution and its soul-deaf representatives. Hagar the Egyptian, the mother of Ishmael, the ancestor of the Arabs, and Hannah, the mother of the prophet Samuel, join hands as sisters in maternal suffering and maternal consolation.

The second day of the holiday brings a further heightening of the same motif. Abraham must lose Isaac, Isaac, the one of his two sons whom he loves wholly. After the suffering of mothers, passive feminine suffering, comes active masculine suffering; he must inflict it on himself. The paradox of his loyal readiness to sacrifice his son, understandable only as mystery, is rewarded; as God's angel had reserved a well for Ishmael, so God has reserved something better for Isaac: a sacrificial lamb instead of his own sacrifice. The two halfbrothers and foes run the same danger and are saved in similar ways; they too have become brothers, as Hagar and Hannah have become sisters.

But the prophetic text from the thirty-first chapter of Jeremiah lifts one factor in this primally human motif of the day of Rosh Hashanah—and that perhaps the central one—out of the realm of the personal, although it does not destroy its personal meaning. That is the factor of the mother. Rachel weeps for her children and refuses to be comforted, *ki enennu*. The two Hebrew words can be translated in different ways, and next to the customary translation—"because they are not"—one might set the bolder one—"as if they were not." This becomes especially clear when one thinks of the only other biblical parallel in which a man apparently robbed of his child refuses to be comforted: that of Jacob mourning for Joseph (Genesis

37.35). But Joseph is alive, and so are the sons of Rachel, who for Jeremiah's prophetic consciousness was at once mother and ancestress. Thus her children become the temporally lost and eternally safe tribes of Israel.

But the father motif, too, is capable of a further extension. We learn of it in a prayer that belongs exclusively to the "ten days of returning" from the first to the tenth of Tishri, and in which we call God both "our Father" and "our King."

Avinu Malkenu, it is He Who, on the birthday of His world, comforts His children and makes them brothers and sisters, all the loving fathers and mothers and their threatened and rescued children. As it always does, here, too, the thing most individual depends on the universal: the world is reborn in the individual human being.[3]

VIII

THE *SHOFAR*

THE RITUAL HORN OF ISRAEL

MARVIN LOWENTHAL

One of the earliest musical devices of mankind, the primitive ram's horn or *shofar* is the ritual horn of Israel. It was the voice of the *shofar* "exceeding loud" which rang from the thick cloud upon Sinai when Moses "brought forth the people to meet God." The walls of Jericho fell at its sound. It echoed through the hill country of Ephraim the day Ehud slew the thousands of Moab. At En-Harod the *shofar* joined its blast in the night with the crash of pitchers and the battle cry of the valiant hundred, "The sword for the Lord and for Gideon!" Throughout biblical times it resounded on the festival of the New Moon and on the First Day of Tishri, called "the memorial of blowing," as well as on other solemn occasions. It gave the alarm in case of siege, flood, or pressing danger and figured, perhaps magically, in rain-making ceremonies. The

Romans, it is easy to understand, were bewildered by its frequent blowing and suspected its treasonable intent in a land of rebels. Later, other rebels, in the bitter moment of excommunication, trembled at its note.

Although the Jews, as befitted a race of music-lovers, made no scruples in adapting and modifying their other instruments, they clung stubbornly to the primitive *shofar*. To this day it keeps its ancient form and use; and the traditional notes, the deep *tekiah* and the shrill *teruah* usher in the New Year and dismiss Israel after the repentant hours of Atonement. Unlike the cornucopia of the Gentiles brimming with earthly fruits, the *shofar* is big with the dooms of the future. A day shall come when, as on Sinai, it will throb again beneath an awful breath. "The Lord God will blow the *shofar* and will go with the whirlwinds of the earth" (Zechariah 9.14). On that day promised of the prophets and become the hope of Zion, "a great *shofar* shall be blown, and they shall come that have been lost in the land of Assyria and dispersed in the land of Egypt, and they shall worship the Lord in the holy mountain of Jerusalem" (Isaiah 27.13).[1]

"A PRAYER WITHOUT WORDS"

Max Arzt

Professor Saul Lieberman characterizes the *shofar* sounds as "a prayer without words." The sounds induce in us a range of emotions that surge in the heart, of thoughts that race through the mind. We think of the situation of man, "his works and his ways, his thoughts and his schemes," as the introduction to the *Zikhronot* expresses it; we are awakened by the awesome *tekiah* sounds to the multiple dangers that threaten human life and make it so precarious. The weird, plaintive *shevarim-teruah* notes which follow serve to remind us that the fears that we fear often come upon us, that human life is frequently the bearer of tragedy and frustration. But not for long are we allowed to wander in despondency. We are lifted to the heights of a bright hope as we hear the *tekiah gedolah*, the prolonged concluding blast. This hope is one of redemption—the redemption of man from the inner and outer "drives" that threaten to efface the divine image in which he is made, the redemption of Israel from the yoke of exile, and the liberation of all mankind from exploitation and tyranny.[2]

THE PIERCING SUMMONS

SAMSON RAPHAEL HIRSCH

With the sound of the *shofar*, God once called us together on Sinai, with it He will once again gather us together. The sound of the *shofar* used to call the slave to freedom, the poor man to his property, the dispossessed to his home. Even so the sound of the *shofar* at every Tishri calls us all to God, it calls the slave of sensuality to Divine freedom, it calls poor and rich to true riches, it calls the most distant wanderer to his own home, it calls every heart and spirit to a glorious jubilee.

The *tekiah* blast used to summon our fathers to the leader; the piercing *teruah* was the signal for striking tents and for war; while the concluding *tekiah* blast bade them go forth to the new goal where God was awaiting them, and to which the cloud of His grace and the ark of His covenant were already advancing. Even so, the *tekiah* of Tishri calls us back to the Shepherd whom we have deserted; the *teruah* summons us to leap up and fight, to break away from every position, every connection on which the blessing of God does not rest, and to fight against everything which interposes itself between us and our God. While once again the *tekiah* beckons us to the spot where the Divine Law is ensconced under the protecting and beneficent cloud of the Divine Majesty.

The basic note of the day is, however, *teruah*, the piercing summons to strike tents and fight. In vain do you present yourself at its call before your God and your Leader if you are too weak to follow His *teruah*, if it does not shake you out of the sleep in which you lie dreaming on the edge of the abyss. In vain it calls you if, bewitched by the Sodom flowers which bloom by the abyss, you fail to hear the warning voice which seeks to save you, so that you do not tear yourself from the bonds of the transitory which you adore, and have not the courage to shake yourself free from your favorite thoughts, plans, resolves, connections, conditions, ties, advantages, and pleasures in which God does not dwell; if you have not the courage to fight against habits, passions, and impulses which fasten on you the yoke of this world; if you have not the courage to fight for God against the world, though you have the courage to fight for the world against God. Alas for you if your God, to whom the *tekiah* summons you, is only a far-off potentate to whom you would like to show yourself just once in the year, concerning Whom you feel that at least you ought to pay your respects on New Year. Alas for you if you fail to give ear to His warning *teruah*, with which He demands your whole being, your whole lifetime, your whole strength, the whole range of your thoughts, feelings, enjoyments, words, and actions, with which He penetrates into all recesses of your whole being, seeks to transform and reshape everything.[3]

THE *SHOFAR* OF ROSH HASHANAH

Samson Raphael Hirsch

For the *shofar* of Rosh Hashanah, whose purpose it is to rouse the purely Divine in man, no artificially constructed piece of work may be sounded. It must be an instrument in its natural form (naturally hollow), with life given to it by the breath of man, speaking to the spirit of man. For you cannot attain to God by artificial means or by artifice. And no sound which charms the senses, but which does not appeal to man's better self, can raise you to God—indeed, you might surrender yourself again to your low, base way of living. The pure, unaffected sound of the natural *shofar* should stir your heart and mind and attune them to the significance and call of its tones.

All naturally hollow horns of clean animals are valid for the *shofar* of Rosh Hashanah except the horn of the bull, which is linked with the memory, sad for our nation, of the sin of the Golden Calf and which in fact is not called *shofar*. One should

take, if possible, the bent horn of a ram—bent, in conformity
with the contrite mood of the day evoked by the *teruah*; of a
ram, because it preserves the noble memory of Abraham's
sacrifice, the prototype in history of the subservience of self to
God.[4]

THE *SHOFAR* MAKER

PAUL RADER

From the tender manner with which he cradled the object
in his left arm one might suppose it was a baby that Meir
Bar-Sheshet was bent over. Such an impression, too, might be
furthered by the low, crooning melody that softly flowed from
his lips as he industriously rocked back and forth in his Haifa
workshop.

But it was no infant Bar-Sheshet held in his arm. It was a
curved ram's horn, easily a foot long, a horn he gently caressed
with the fingers of his right hand as he paused now and then in
his labors. Bar-Sheshet—scion of the 16th-century Spanish sage
"Haribash," Rav Yitzhak Bar-Sheshet—was fashioning a *shofar*
from the horns of a prize Australian merino.

"You know," said a recent visitor to his *shofar* workshop in
Haifa, "there was a fascinating story in the paper the other day.
The Bible tells us that seven priests circled the walls of Jericho
for seven days, sounding blasts on seven *shofarot*. On the
seventh day, the walls of Jericho crumbled. Our archaeologists
have been busily studying the ground at Jericho where the walls
once stood and they've come up with a new theory."

Bar-Sheshet continued to hone away at the horn, scarcely
pausing in his song, but listening intently.

"Our archaeologists now believe that Joshua's engineers un-
dermined the foundations, which had been poorly constructed.
So Joshua had the priests parade around the ramparts for seven
days as a diversionary tactic while at night the engineers were
busily digging and weakening the fortifications."

Was that a shadow of a smile on Bar-Sheshet's face as he
rummaged through an assortment of files and picked a narrow,

pointed one? One might suppose he was saying to himself, "Joshua had his secrets and I have mine."

Secrets there are in *shofar*-making and perhaps the Bar-Sheshet family is unique in this respect. He is the only commercial *shofar* maker in all Israel, for this is a select art that has been handed down in his family from generation to generation, going back 400 years. His ancestor of that era had emigrated from Spain to Algiers, where he served as *dayyan*, a judge of a rabbinical court. Finding no proper *shofarot* available, he began to make them himself. The calling was thus passed down from father to son, each elder son succeeding to the post.

In the course of time, two closely guarded secrets have become part of the Bar-Sheshet lore: how to make the horn elastic enough so that the *shofar* can be shaped according to the wishes of the congregation, and how to give it the "proper tone."

"It's simple to bore a hole into a straight *shofar*," he said, "but try to do it with one of these curled ones. That's a Bar-Sheshet secret.

"There are three 'Bar-Sheshet' tones," the artisan went on.

"First, there is the deep, bass note, preferred by the Yemenites. For this tone, which follows the biblical phrase, 'and the big *shofar* shall be sounded,' an antelope's horn is used—giant-sized ones, too. They are the most expensive.

"Then comes the Sephardic *shofar*—a low and ceremonial note. Finally, there is the Ashkenazic—a high, supplicating note.". . .

A careful worker, Bar-Sheshet turns out around 400 *shofarot* a year, at the rate of one to three a day, depending on the size and the curvatures desired. . . . He obtains the rams' horns from Australia in a consignment weighing one ton, containing enough material for approximately 800 horns. However, about half arrive unfit—with holes or split—or are spoiled during manufacture and become rejects. . . .

Each *shofar* carries his family trademark and the legend: "Made in the City of Elijah the Prophet," referring to Elijah's sojourn on Mt. Carmel.[5]

IX

THE SYMBOLIC CEREMONY
OF *TASHLIKH*

Julius H. Greenstone

On the first day of Rosh Hashanah, a little before sunset, observant Jews congregate at the edge of a body of running water and recite the last verses of the Book of Micah, concluding with the sentence: "And Thou wilt cast all their iniquities into the depths of the sea." The seashore, a river or flowing brook, or even a well of spring water, may serve the purpose, but not a pool or any stagnant water. The later rabbis required that the water should have fish, which serve the purpose of reminding us that we are like the fish caught in the net, weak, helpless, and subject to the many ills that beset us in life. After the lines from Micah and some additional prayers composed in more recent years have been recited, it is customary to shake the skirts of one's garments over the water, as if physically transferring the sins, which are figuratively supposed to cleave to one's garments, to the river or ocean so that they may be carried away and not be remembered. If the first day of Rosh Hashanah falls on a Sabbath, the ceremony is performed on the second day.

[119

The symbolic nature of the ceremony is quite obvious. The consciousness of sin becomes very keen on the Day of Memorial and the regret for the commission of the sins rankles in the heart of every pious Jew. He hopes and prays that in deciding his fate for the coming year God will overlook his shortcomings and failings during the past year, which might stand in his way. By sending his sins away on the bosom of the ocean or the flowing stream, he figuratively expresses his desire that they might disappear from the sight of God and might not serve as a deterrent in the way of his gaining the favor of Providence. We find occasional references in the Bible to the custom of holding prayer meetings at the waterside, and these references are multiplied in postbiblical literature. According to Philo, the shore of a river is a most appropriate spot for prayer, since this is the "purest place." Josephus quotes a decree which permitted the Jews of Halicarnassus "to have their places of prayer by the seaside, according to the custom of their forefathers." More pointed is the remark found in the *Zohar*, a cabbalistic work of the thirteenth century, which says that "whatever falls into the deep is lost forever; it acts like the scapegoat for the absolution of sins." It is doubtful, however, whether the custom of *Tashlikh* existed before the fourteenth century, as there is no mention of it in the Talmud or in any of the subsequent works to the time of the German rabbi Jacob Molin, who lived at the end of the fourteenth century. In his compilation of the *Minhagim* (customs) of his generation and his land, Jacob Molin mentions the custom of *Tashlikh* and refers to the midrashic legend concerning the attempted sacrifice of Isaac. According to the legend, Satan, intent on thwarting Abraham's plan to follow the command of God and sacrifice his son, placed himself in front of Abraham in the form of a deep stream. Abraham and Isaac nevertheless plunged into the river and prayed for aid, whereupon the stream disappeared. While the sacrifice of Isaac is frequently alluded to in the prayers for Rosh Hashanah, the connection of *Tashlikh* with this legend seems far-fetched. Nor are the various explanations offered by later authorities more convincing.

Purely symbolic in its origin, the ceremony has been given mystical meanings, and several superstitions have become associated with it. The custom of casting small pieces of bread upon the waters as food for the fish is already mentioned by Molin, who strove to discourage it. In the added prayers arranged for the occasion, reference is made to evil spirits (*kelippot*) created by the sins of the individual, which cling to one's garments and which should be shaken from them into the water. It was mainly due to these mystical elements of the ceremony that many have been opposed to its practice altogether and others tried to find in it traces of heathen superstitions. . . . There is no doubt that the ceremony of *Tashlikh*, observed mainly by the Ashkenazic Jews, has no such superstitious notions connected with it. It is rather a symbolic act emphasizing concretely the yearning to be cleared of sin and the hope that one may be forgiven.[1]

X

ROSH HASHANAH PARABLES

ALEXANDER ALAN STEINBACH

The parable (*mashal*) in Jewish literature is *sui generis*. Its function extends somewhat beyond the dictionary definition: "A short, allegorical story, designed to convey some truth or moral lesson." The added component converts the *mashal* into an ideational as well as moral aid, analogous to book illustrations that serve as visual aids for a graphic understanding of the textual material. Another comparable example is the poet's recourse to imagery and symbolism in order to illumine a truth he seeks to articulate.

The pragmatic role of the *mashal* has a further analog in the contemporary role assigned to *myth* (not to be equated with the absurd phantasm characteristic of classical mythology, which Judaism has always opposed). The dictionary definition of myth as "a traditional or legendary story" seems to focus on fable, fairy tale, or *babe maaseh* invented by the imagination. These by their very nature play havoc with credulity; they fade into naive fancies when subjected to criteria of reason and common sense.

A highly respected coterie of modern writers and thinkers have, however, advanced a contrary theory that regards myth, not as a denial of reality, but rather as an affirmation of an idea, speculation, or doctrine too profound for reason alone to apprehend. It speaks in a tongue that offers an amendment to an idea, or a concept, or a truth hidden beneath the deepest layer of ratiocinative activity. Goethe said, "The beautiful is a manifestation of secret laws of nature which, except for this appearance, had been forever concealed from us." The myth, likewise, penetrates into terrain to extract concealed "ore" that can be reached by no other instrument.

The ethical viability of a myth is adumbrated in Jewish literature. Rabbi Eliezer in the Talmud claimed that the world was created in Tishri, but according to a Jewish legend the Creation was completed on Rosh Hashanah with the formation of Adam. Beyond and above the belief that Rosh Hashanah memorializes man's and the world's birthday is a majestic verity. The beginning of the world cannot be dissociated from the beginning every Tishri of man's own world—the renewal of himself, adding a spiritual layer that will enrich his existence.

The Rosh Hashanah *meshalim* to be presented in the ensuing pages will, it is hoped, demonstrate the deeper motivations that undergird the Jewish New Year. They are to be viewed as amendments purposing to clarify and reinforce the spiritual, ethical, and moral values the solemn High Holy Days require us to contemplate and renew during the ten-day penitential season. This specific genre of Jewish literature was employed by itinerant *maggidim* (preachers) who spiced their sermons with parables as they traveled from town to town in Eastern Europe and harangued their listeners to amend their sinful ways. Foremost among these preachers was Jacob ben Wolf Kranz (1741–1804), better known as the Dubner Maggid, since he resided for many years in Dubno, Russia. His homiletic interpretations of the Bible and his ingenious parables attained wide popularity, so that numerous *maggidim* embellished their discourses with *meshalim* originated by him. Some of them will be among the following parables, rendered in free translations. His homilies have been recorded in *Ohel Yaakov* (Jozefow, 1830) and in other works.

SEARCHING FOR THE RIGHT WAY

Before commencing the *Selihot* service the Baal Shem Tov related the following parable.

A man lost in a forest wandered for several days trying to find a way out. He felt greatly enheartened when, suddenly looking up, he saw a man walking toward him. "Now," he bethought himself, "I'll learn how to get out of here," and he asked when the man approached, "I've been lost in this forest for some days, can you show me the way out?"

The stranger replied, "I'm lost myself and don't know my way back. But I can tell you that the road you're on now isn't the right one; let's try together to find a way out."

"So it is with us," the Baal Shem Tov went on. "I know that the road we've traveled thus far will only lead us astray. Let us join together to discover the right way."

OUR LONE ARROW

The Dubner Maggid (Jacob Kranz) delivered himself of the following parable as an admonition to the *shofar*-blower (*baal tokea*).

A man, lost in a forest denizened by wild animals, was naturally terribly frightened with only a bow and arrows to defend himself. As he wandered through the thicket, whatever he saw at a distance was conjured up in his imagination as a bear or lion or wolf, at which he discharged his arrows. When he neared the target at which he had aimed, he discovered it was only a tree or a crag or some similar object. Now, with only one arrow remaining in his quiver, he realized he had to be more careful, since he was in a perilous situation and might need that arrow to keep from being mangled.

This parable bears a special relevance. When we Jews lived

in our Holy Land, numerous avenues of redemption were available to us: the Holy Temple, the altar, the sacrifices, the High Priest. But in our own day, none of these sacramental instrumentalities is open to us except this lowly *shofar*.

Therefore, my dear *shofar*-blower, open your eyes and attune your heart to the performance of your sacred task so that the sounds of the *shofar* will reach the target at which you are aiming.

SOUNDING AN ALARM

The Maggid of Dubno, in keeping with the injunction in *Mishnah Abot* 2.13, "Do not let your prayers become per- functory," frequently exhorted his hearers to perform their devotions on the High Holy Days with understanding and rever- ance, and not by rote. He reminded them that fulfilling the rituals was a means to a higher end, namely, to achieve an inner purification.

To dramatize the nobler objective, he related this graphic parable:

A naive villager, born and reared in an obscure rural environ- ment, came to a big city for the first time and obtained lodging at an inn. Awakened in the middle of the night by the loud beating of drums, he inquired drowsily, "What's this all about?" Informed that a fire had broken out and that the drum beating was the city's fire alarm, he turned over and went back to sleep.

On his return home he reported to the village authorities: "They have a wonderful system in the big city; when a fire breaks out the people beat their drums and before long the fire burns out." All excited, they ordered a supply of drums and distributed them to the population. When a fire broke out later, there was a deafening explosion of beating of drums, and while the people waited expectantly for the flames to subside, a num- ber of their homes burned to the ground.

A sophisticated visitor passing through that village, when

told the reason for the ear-splitting din, derided the simplistic natives: "Idiots! Do you think a fire can be put out by beating drums? They only sound an alarm for the people to wake up and take measures to extinguish the fire."

This parable, said the Maggid of Dubno, applies to those of us who believe that beating the breast during the *Al Het* (confessional), raising our voices during worship, and blowing the *shofar* will put out the fires of sin and evil that burn in us. They are only an alarm, a warning to wake up and resort to *heshbon ha-nefesh* (soul-searching), so that we may merit the favor of God. The Maggid probably had in mind Maimonides' interpretation of the *shofar* sounds as urging: "Awake all ye who sleep, rouse yourselves all ye who slumber and search your deeds and repent; remember your Creator."

PUNISHMENT TO FIT THE CRIME

The following parable is a commentary on the Jewish doctrine of reward and punishment based on Psalms 62.13: "Unto Thee, O Lord, belongeth mercy; for Thou renderest to every man according to his deeds."

This is comparable to a king who owned a menorah that had no equal in all the world. Studded with many precious stones and pearls, it hung in the king's palace suspended by ropes. A dullard who happened to be in the palace coveted the ropes, cut and stole them. Naturally, the menorah fell and crashed to pieces. The king, being a compassionate person, judged him culpable only for the sin of stealing the ropes because he was not competent, due to his moronic intellect, to realize that his act would result in demolishing the menorah unparalleled in beauty and in worth.

In this wise, the Almighty holds each individual responsible for his personal deeds, and not for the widespread ignorance and defection extant in our world.

SOUL-SEARCHING

This simple but highly suggestive parable was spoken by the Maggid of Dubno in relation to the need for self-examination.

A prince assigned to a group of workmen the gigantic project of constructing imposing buildings and a spacious palace, among other edifices. Before turning the completed structures over to their owner, they carefully inspected every nook and cranny to make certain that nothing was overlooked and that the prince would find nothing lacking.

At this solemn season it is fitting for us, too, to search our ways and to take stock of our behavior. On Rosh Hashanah it is incumbent upon us to inquire into and evaluate in retrospect our dealings during the past year so that we may repent lest God find that our performance was incomplete.

THE HUMBLE REQUEST

One of the Dubner Maggid's *meshalim* equates a significant prayer in the High Holy Days *mahzor* with humility as a desideratum in man's behavior pattern.

The following question was propounded to the Maggid of Dubno. Why is it that in the group of *Avinu Malkenu* petitions all are recited in a loud voice except the concluding verses: "Our Father, our King, be gracious and answer us; though we plead no merit, deal with us according to Thy mercy and loving-kindness and help us"? This one is rendered softly, in an undertone.

The Dubner Maggid replied with this *mashal*. A retailer came to a certain wholesale dealer to purchase merchandise. Entering with proud bearing, he would announce his order loudly: "I want so many yards of velvet and pure silk, so many yards of linen," etc.

On hearing the retailer's order, the wholesaler instructed his employees to prepare it for delivery. This accomplished, the retailer whispered to the wholesaler, "I regret I have no ready cash; please be good enough to accept my note for this merchandise."

"We are in the same predicament," the Dubner Maggid continued. "On the Ten Days of Repentance we present ourselves to our Father and King, and supplicate Him with firm voices to supply our long list of requisites in the new year: a life of happiness, sustenance and maintenance, redemption and salvation, complete healing, pardon and forgiveness, inscription in the Book of Merit, and so forth. After registering this lengthy list of entreaties, we approach Him humbly and tremulously and whisper the final prayer almost inaudibly, "Our Father, our King, be gracious and answer us; though we plead no merit, deal with us according to Thy mercy and loving-kindness and help us. We come as poor suppliants, beseeching Thee to accept our promissory note for all these benefactions.""

DAILY REPENTANCE

While the parables cited above were originated some two centuries ago, it should be pointed out that rabbinical literature tracing back two millennia abounds in the use of the *mashal*. Not infrequently the *mashal* is introduced by *mashal le-melekh*, "it is comparable to a king. . . ." Whether consciously or unconsciously, the Jewish psyche was attuned to the metaphorical juxtaposition of God (the King of kings) and a human king. One of the three sections in the Rosh Hashanah *shofar* liturgy is *Malkhuyot*, glorifying the sovereignty of God. One of the long liturgical pieces recited in unison by the reader and the congregation on Rosh Hashanah stresses the theme: "The Lord is King, the Lord was King, the Lord will reign forever." The *Avinu Malkenu* group was alluded to above.

The following parable, found in the Talmud (*Shabbat* 153a), is in keeping with the central role assigned to a human king.

A king invited his subjects to dine with him, without designating the date. The prudent among them kept themselves well dressed to honor the king when his call should arrive and

17.   Torah shield. Silver. Breslau, Germany. Late 17th century. See
Chapter XIII.

18. Rosh Hashanah scenes. From *Kirchliche Verfassung der heutigen Juden*, by Johann C.G. Bodenschatz, Erlangen, 1748. See Chapter XIII.

19. Sounding the *shofar*. From *Juedisches Ceremoniel*, by Paul C. Kirchner, Nuremberg, 1726. See Chapter XIII.

זיכר הופֿפֿט עמוסיך · בֿיזֿ־אֿן קרית משוש · לֿאֿנֿ זֿאֿנֿג

20. Sounding the *shofar*. Woodcut. From *Sefer Minhagim*, Amsterdam, 1662. See Chapter XIII.

21. Sounding of the *shofar* in the Amsterdam Synagogue. From *Cérémonies et coutumes religieuses*, by Bernard Picart, Amsterdam, 1723. See Chapter XIII.

waited at the palace gate. The stupid subjects paid no attention to the royal invitation and continued wearing their old
clothes. Quite unexpectedly, the king summoned the people to
his palace. He rejoiced with the wise but was angry at the
fools. He ordered the well-dressed subjects to be seated and to
eat and drink, and the others to stand and watch.

The lesson this parable teaches is that when an upright person dies, he enters blissfully into God's presence. But un-
repentant evildoers will not know such future bliss when they
expire. Since nobody can foretell his day of death, everyone
should repent every day.

THE PURCHASE PRICE

"Let us search and try our ways, and return to the Lord"
(Lamentations 3.40). This biblical verse inspired the following
parable.

Two merchants, one alert and the other rather dull, traveled
together to a market to purchase merchandise, each carrying
a considerable sum of money. Feeling weary, they stopped at an
inn to lodge and placed their money under their pillows. They
awoke at daybreak and hastened on their way, forgetting to
take their money with them. When they discovered their loss,
the simplistic merchant suggested, "Let's hurry on because it
will soon be market day." His sophisticated companion replied,
"You stupid fool, what good will it do for us to hurry now
that we are empty-handed? The most sensible thing is to turn
back and search for our money on every road we took; after
we find the money we'll travel to the market."

The parable is quite clear. On Rosh Hashanah it is incumbent
upon us to wend our journey into the precincts of the Eternal
One and to acquire the necessary spiritual merchandise for
the whole year. But all of us must bring a bundle of money,
namely, repentance and good deeds. Because of our numerous
iniquities during the year, we were in a sort of torpor. We
strayed from the path of rectitude and pursued a crooked road,

and as a result we have nothing with which we may hope to merit God's favor.

Foolish people say: "Come, let's hurry to the synagogue on the Holy Day and seek to garner all our needs." But those who are prudent say, "How can we present ourselves before the Almighty empty-handed? We must first search out the ways that led us astray and expiate our guilt. Only then can we 'return to the Lord.'"

A FIRE ALARM

Someone asked the Maggid of Dubno whether or not it was presumptuous of him to rebuke his congregation on the High Holy Days, since among those present were persons perhaps more meritorious than he. He replied, "Let me cite a parable appropriate for these days.

"Once, about midnight, a lame man, who was unable to walk by himself, woke up suddenly out of his sleep and saw a raging fire not only in his own home, but also in other homes whose occupants were fast asleep. He awakened them with lusty shouts: 'Help! Fire! Get up! Save yourselves and save me also!'" The Dubner Maggid then continued: "So it is with me. I am fully aware of my backslidings, but alone I am devoid of strength to salvage myself from the inroads of evil. These Days of Awe come like a flaming furnace to purge us of sin, and perhaps in our common worship and repentance, I as well as you will be saved from the fire and will merit forgiveness."

"HEAR OUR VOICE"

Before reciting the prayer "Hear Our Voice" in the penitential collection captioned *Zekhor Brit* ("Remember the Covenant"), Rabbi Meshullam Issakhar ha-Levi Horwitz of Stanislav related with tearful supplications before the open ark:

A king, blessed with an only son, reared him lovingly from tender childhood in the path of rectitude and rejoiced in witnessing his sacred wedlock. His fondest aspiration was to have his son cultivate a life-pattern of integrity and virtue; but he was doomed to bitter disappointment. The young man became a wastrel, a good-for-nothing prodigal, like the desolate vine to which the prophet had compared sinful Israel: "And he looked that it should bring forth grapes, and it brought forth wild grapes" (Isaiah 5.2.).

The son made a shambles of the ideals and the noble standards his regal father had sought to inculcate in him. He deserted his young wife and attached himself to an alien slut. This wanton behavior converted the father's love into hostility which prompted him to banish his errant, miscreant son.

For many years the young man wandered from city to city, from village to village. His clothes were worn to shreds. His features became haggard beyond recognition. Finally, weary and surfeited with wandering, he recalled his father and the palace and the circumstances that led to his banishment. A poignant yearning to return to his former status and to make amends possessed him more and more each day.

At long last he wended his way back to the palace, threw himself at his father's feet, and implored for forgiveness. But the king did not recognize his son because of the withering metamorphosis that had scarred his features. "Father, father," he cried out in anguish, "if you do not recognize my face, surely you must remember my voice, which has not changed." At that moment the king perceived it was truly his son, and after a tearful reconciliation he was restored to the royal household.

"So it is with us," Rabbi Meshullam continued. "We are children of the King of kings, the Holy One blessed be He, who in His love has selected and exalted us above all peoples. He entrusted unto us the sacred Torah that brings spiritual enrichment to man and leads to the pathway of righteousness and truth. But we have strayed from this pathway He set before us. We departed from His commandments; we were removed from our land; our iniquities distorted and corrupted all these things. As a result, our whole appearance has been altered; our glory has been mutilated into a destructive void.

"And now, with the advent of our Holy Days, we become remorseful over our misdeeds. We cry out to Him, 'Hear our voice! If you do not recognize our appearance, at least You must remember our voice; for we are Your children. Be gracious unto us and receive our prayer with merciful favor.'"

XI

HASIDIC TALES AND TEACHINGS

Numberless are the tales of the hasidic rabbis that have been told and retold for generations since the days of Rabbi Israel Baal Shem Tov (1700–1760), founder of the movement. He and his disciples employed the story or anecdote to inspire their followers with the love of God and man. They succeeded in implanting faith and confidence, righteousness and hope, joy and gaiety in the hearts of despondent and poverty-stricken Jews throughout Eastern Europe. The *hasidim* cultivated an intimate relationship with God. During the High Holy Days they not only prayed to Him for atonement but actually demanded that He remit their sins; they even brought their complaints before Him. The compassionate hasidic master Rabbi Levi Isaac of Berditchev (1740–1809) was known as an eloquent defender of his people who saw only the good in man and evinced deep sympathy for the widow, the orphan, the rejected, and the downtrodden. On Rosh Hashanah and Yom Kippur, the Berditchever composed original invocations and intercessions which reflect his saintly character and reveal his ecstatic devotion to God. Many of his tales and teachings, as well as those of other hasidic rabbis, teem with profound insight into the spiritual significance of these Days of Awe.[1]

REPENTANT JEWS

As Rabbi Levi Isaac of Berditchev and his sexton were going to the synagogue for the *Selihot* services on the eve of Rosh Hashanah, a sudden downpour made them seek shelter under the awning of a tavern. The sexton peered through one of the windows and saw a group of Jews feasting, drinking, and reveling. He impatiently urged Levi Isaac to see for himself how these Jews were behaving when they should be in the synagogue praying to God for forgiveness for their sins.

Disregarding the sexton's urging, the rabbi chided him:

"It is forbidden to derogate the children of Israel. They are surely reciting the benedictions for food and drink. May God bless these loyal Jews."

The disillusioned sexton continued to peep into the tavern and to eavesdrop.

"Woe to us, rabbi!" the sexton exclaimed. "I just heard two of the Jews telling each other of thefts they committed."

"If that be so, they are truly observant Jews," Levi Isaac rejoicingly admonished his sexton. "They are confessing their sins before Rosh Hashanah. As you know, no one is more righteous than he who repents."

PENITENTIAL PRAYERS

During a penitential season, Rabbi Levi Isaac was ill. As he lay in bed, he prayed:

"Merciful Lord! I am old and weak; I do not have the strength to arise and recite the lengthy *Selihot* prayers of forgiveness.

But You are powerful and mighty and Your penitential prayer is so brief: 'I have forgiven.' Therefore, You recite the *Selihot* for me and say: 'I have forgiven.'"

DISTURBANCE BY A *SHOFAR*

The saintly Abraham Isaac Kook, late chief rabbi of Israel, lay critically ill in the hospital. When the month of Elul began, he asked that the *shofar* be sounded each morning so that he might fulfill the commandment of hearing the trumpet sounds during this month preceding Rosh Hashanah. The doctor, reluctant to comply with this request lest the blasts have an adverse effect on the rabbi, vainly tried to dissuade his patient. The rabbi insisted that the *shofar* be blown.

Finally one of Rabbi Kook's pupils discreetly suggested:

"If the *shofar* is sounded in the hospital, wouldn't the other patients be disturbed?"

The pious sage immediately said:

"Maybe you are right. If that be so, do not blow the *shofar*."

WHEN REPENTANCE COMMENCES

Rabbi Israel Lipkin Salanter once said:

"Most people repent during the *Selihot* week preceding Rosh Hashanah; the more pious during the month of Elul preceding Rosh Hashanah; but I say that one should begin to repent immediately after Yom Kippur."

THE MORE SEVERE SIN

Rabbi Israel Lipkin Salanter was wont to say: "Sometimes people, in their zeal to fulfill a commandment that applies between man and God, trespass a more severe commandment that applies between man and man. For example, a man who rises very early during the days preceding Rosh Hashanah, so that he may go to the synagogue to recite *Selihot*, may cause grief to the maid in his home, who is generally a poor orphan. She will also feel obliged to rise early to prepare hot tea for her master before he leaves for the synagogue. Thus, the sin of oppressing an orphan outweighs the duty of reciting *Selihot*."

VIRTUES OF A CANTOR

A wealthy Jew came to Rabbi Meier of Premishlan magnanimously offering his services as cantor for the High Holy Days. Aware of the man's questionable merits, the rabbi frankly said to him:

"In the Book of Psalms there are three prayers: the Prayer of Moses (Psalm 90), the Prayer of David (Psalm 17), and the Prayer of a Poor Man (Psalm 102). If one is as righteous as Moses, even though he has difficulty in speech and is unable to sing, his prayer is acceptable to God. If one has a voice as sweet as David, even though he may not be so righteous, his prayer too is acceptable. If one is poor and prays with a chastened and contrite heart, even though he may not be so righteous as Moses nor possess a voice as sweet as David's, his prayer is also acceptable."

The rabbi paused and then continued:

"But you unfortunately do not possess any of these three virtues. You do not perform righteous deeds, your voice is not sweet, and you do not have the merit of being poor."

A REQUIRED EXAMINATION

On the eve of Rosh Hashanah Mordecai of Nadvorna, a nineteenth-century sage, stopped a cantor who was obviously in a great hurry.

"Why are you rushing so?" the rabbi asked.

The cantor politely replied:

"I must examine the *mahzor* and put the Rosh Hashanah prayers in the proper order."

Mordecai paused momentarily and said with a smile:

"You know well that the *mahzor* has not changed since last year. Better examine your heart and your deeds of the past year and try to put yourself in proper order."

THE BURDEN

One New Year eve as Rabbi Menahem Mendel of Rimanov entered the synagogue, he was impressed by the large congregation.

"A beautiful assemblage," he told them. "However, I think you should know that I alone cannot carry all of you on my shoulders. Do not depend on me; each one of you must exercise his own repentance, prayer, and charity."

CHOOSING A *SHOFAR*-BLOWER

Rabbi Levi Isaac was interrogating a number of candidates for the blowing of the *shofar* on Rosh Hashanah. He asked each one:

"What will be your thoughts while you blow the *shofar*?"

The Berditchever rabbi was dissatisfied with the variety of pious sentiments voiced by the candidates until one of them said:

"Rabbi, I'm a simple, poor Jew. I have four daughters who have long ago reached the marriage age but I am unable to provide dowries for them. When I will blow the *shofar*, I will bear my daughters in mind. I will think: 'Merciful One! I am fulfilling the commandments You have ordained. Give ear to the *shofar* sound beseeching You to fulfill your obligation of providing dowries for my daughters.'"

The straightforward, sincere honesty of this Jew appealed to Levi Isaac and he engaged him to sound the *shofar*.

UNDERSTANDING PRAYER

Rabbi Levi Isaac of Berditchev was accustomed to preach to his congregation before *shofar*-blowing on Rosh Hashanah. One year he told the following incident to strengthen his congregants' faith in the efficacy of their prayers:

"Once I was lodging in an inn where many Jews had come for the market day. I rose early to join in the morning service with my fellow Jews who were there for business. I was shocked to observe how they rushed through the prayers, mispronouncing half of the words and swallowing the other half. At the conclusion of the service I began to speak thus to these merchants: 'Ba . . . me . . . be. . . .' They naturally stared at me in astonishment, undoubtedly wondering if I had lost my reason. I explained to them:

"'The manner in which I have just spoken to you was very similar to the way you spoke to God. I could not understand a word.'

"One of the businessmen replied:

"'A baby in his cradle utters syllables that are completely meaningless even to sages. Yet the mother and father know their infant and understand his every utterance. Even if you, rabbi, did not comprehend our prayers, I have every confidence that the Almighty knows our thoughts and intentions.'

"This merchant was right," concluded the rabbi. "He evinced more faith in God than I did. Therefore, my friends, know that on this sacred day even the prayers of those who are unable to worship properly will be answered."

COMPOSING PRAYERS

Levi Isaac stood by the reader's table prepared to sound the *shofar*. The congregation waited patiently for him to commence. After a long interval, the sexton hesitatingly approached Levi Isaac and asked the cause for the delay.

The rabbi whispered to the sexton:

"A stranger is seated near the door of the synagogue. Reared among non-Jews, he never learned to pray. However, he has just said to God:

"'Lord of the universe, You understand the true meaning of prayers and You know those that are most acceptable. Since I know only the letters of the alphabet, I shall repeat them and

You can compose from them the prayers I should recite on this sacred day.'

"The Almighty is now preoccupied with composing prayers from the letters. Therefore, we must wait."

THE REASON A JEW PRAYS FOR PROSPERITY

During the Rosh Hashanah services Levi Isaac, in his own inimitable manner, addressed the King of kings:

"Almighty One, blessed be Thy Name! Why does a Jew pray for a year of sustenance and plenty? Why does a Jew need money? When a Jew has the means he gives charity to the poor, provides for the education of his children, purchases a choice *etrog* for Sukkot, buys beautiful clothing and tasty food to honor Your Sabbath; he also uses money to fulfill other laws that You have commanded him. If you want the children of Israel to continue to obey Your commandments during the coming year, You must grant them an abundance of wealth."

ROSH HASHANAH OF THE SABBATH

On a Rosh Hashanah that coincided with the Sabbath, Rabbi Levi Isaac made this appeal to God:

"Master of the Universe! Today is the New Year when You inscribe the Jews either in the Book of Life or in the Book of Death. Today is also the Sabbath. As it is forbidden to write on the Sabbath, how will it be possible for You to inscribe the Jewish people for the coming year? There is only one course open to You. If You will inscribe them for a year of life, it will be permissible for You to write, as 'the obligation of saving a life supersedes the Sabbath laws.'"

A FAIR EXCHANGE

During the Rosh Hashanah services the Berditchever rabbi paused in the middle of a prayer and presented a claim to God: "Master of the Universe, You must remember that at one time

You went with Your Law from nation to nation like a peddler with rotten apples, and not one nation was willing to accept it from You. No one would even look at You. Then we, the children of Israel, took the Law from You. Now I want to make You a proposition. We have a heap of sins and transgressions; You have an abundance of forgiveness and atonement; therefore, let us exchange. However, should You consider the exchange unfair, let me ask: If we did not have sins, what would You do with your pardons? Moreover, I desire a commission for handling this transaction: I demand that You also grant the children of Israel life and sustenance in the ensuing year."

FILLED WITH SINS AND MERCY

When Levi Isaac came to the passage in the *mahzor*, "We are filled with sins and You with mercy," he said: "It is true that we are 'filled with sins,' yet how big is Levi Isaac and how many sins can he possibly amass? But You who are 'filled with mercy,' You are Infinite and there is no limit to Your mercy."

A WONDER

Rabbi Leib, the "Grandfather" of Shpola, paused before the blowing of the *shofar*, lifted his eyes to heaven, and said: "Master of the Universe, how can You have any complaint against Your people Israel? No people has endured the trials and tribulations that have been the fate of the Jews. They have suffered a long and bitter exile. Therefore, I believe Israel is indeed a holy people. If I did not see with my own eyes that they obey Your commandments and perform good deeds, I would not believe it. It is a wonder that they have strength to fulfill even one of Your commandments."

PREPARATION FOR BLOWING THE *SHOFAR*

Rabbi David of Lelov was the regular *shofar*-blower at the synagogue of Rabbi Jacob Isaac, the Seer of Lublin. One Rosh

Hashanah when the time arrived for the blowing of the *shofar* Rabbi David was not in the synagogue. The Seer of Lublin, who thought Rabbi David must be concentrating on solemn meditations for the *tekiot*, sent a disciple to look for him. After a wide search he found Rabbi David in the marketplace feeding horses. The disciple angrily said, "What's wrong with you? The Rabbi is waiting for you a long time and here you are feeding the horses!"

Rabbi David retorted, "I know that the Jewish wagon drivers are in the synagogue and they have undoubtedly forgotten to give fodder to their horses. So I went to feed them. After all, it is a duty to prevent cruelty to animals."

He then returned to the synagogue and blew the *shofar*. After he had finished the Seer of Lublin remarked, "Today Rabbi David entertained lofty sentiments before sounding the *shofar*."

THE REWARD OF A MITZVAH

Rabbi Simhah Bunam was once told a story about Rabbi Eleazar Rokeach of Amsterdam, who was on a sea journey when, on the eve of Rosh Hashanah, the ship sprang a leak endangering the lives of all the passengers. Throughout the night water poured into the boat and hourly the situation became precarious. In the morning Rabbi Eleazar assembled his disciples on deck and blew the *shofar*, to fulfill the *mitzvah* on Rosh Hashanah. No sooner was the *shofar* sounded than the leak was found and repaired. The ship's passengers were deeply grateful to the rabbi for the miracle they thought he had wrought.

Rabbi Bunam commented that Rabbi Eleazar's purpose in blowing the *shofar* was not to salvage the boat but to perform a final *mitzvah* before he died. Had he anticipated a miracle by blowing the *shofar*, it would not have availed. The reward of fulfilling the commandment of the *shofar* saved the ship and its passengers.

APPRECIATION OF THE CANTOR

At the synagogue of Rabbi Velvel, the *maggid* of Wilna, a cantor was wont to display his vocal talents at the Rosh Hashanah services. He sang the prayers, repeating the words many times, thereby prolonging the service until late into the afternoon.

At the conclusion of the service, the cantor approached Rabbi Velvel to extend New Year greetings and to be complimented for the manner in which he led the congregation in prayer.

The rabbi returned his greeting and added:

"It is written in the *Ethics of the Fathers*: 'The world is based on three things—Torah, prayer, and deeds of kindness.' Blessed is our congregation which fulfills these three requisites. I teach them the Torah; you pray for them; and they perform deeds of kindness by listening to both of us."

CONFUSING SATAN

Rabbi Tzvi Hirsh Levin of Berlin had been known as a precocious child. Once his father discovered him eating before the *shofar*-blowing on Rosh Hashanah. He rebukingly reminded his son that it was forbidden to eat until after the *shofar* was sounded.

The boy justified his action:

"Father, I ate intentionally to confuse Satan, who surely knows it is not permissible to eat until the *shofar* sounds are heard. Now that Satan has seen me eating he will think we have concluded the services, and will make no attempt to confound the sounding of the *shofar*. Thus, we can be assured of a good year."

GATHERING IN SINS

Rabbi Jacob Isaac, the Seer of Lublin, and his former pupil, Rabbi Naphtali Tzvi of Ropshitz, were standing on a riverbank reciting the *Tashlikh* service on Rosh Hashanah. When the teacher emptied his pockets as symbolically casting off his sins, his modest pupil motioned with his hands as if gathering them up.

When Rabbi Jacob Isaac looked quizzically at his pupil, Rabbi Naphtali explained:

"My teacher and master, I am gathering up your sins, certain that those you may have committed will be reckoned as good deeds for me."

UNWARRANTED HUMILIATION

On the Sabbath of Repentance a visiting *maggid* preached a sermon in the synagogue of Rabbi Meir Hurwitz of Tiktin, renowned for his piety. The preacher castigated the congregants for their sins and admonished them to repent. When the severe tongue-lashing was over, Rabbi Meir, tears rolling down his cheeks, said to the *maggid*:

"I was deeply moved by your stirring words and I will surely repent for my transgressions. However, I am sorely distressed that you found it necessary to put me to shame before my entire congregation. Do I really merit such treatment from you?"

Abashed, the preacher replied:

"I would never humiliate you in public. I was not referring to you at all for you are well known for your piety."

Unappeased, Rabbi Meir retorted:

"My congregants are all pious and only I could be guilty of sin."

CONCERN FOR BODY AND SOUL

Rabbi Israel Lipkin Salanter preached a sermon on the Sabbath of Repentance in which he observed:

"It is usual for a man to express concern for his own body and for his neighbor's soul. He doesn't worry about his own soul nor about his neighbor's body. The reverse should obtain if man is to repent and earn his share in the world to come. Man should disregard his own body and pay attention to his soul. He need not concern himself about the soul of his neighbor, but rather make certain to provide for his mundane needs."

A PLETHORA OF WORDS

The Ropshitzer Rabbi once said: "There is a good rationale for the practice of rabbis to deliver lengthy sermons on the Sabbath of Repentance. Some truly pious and virtuous rabbis have no sins to expiate and seek forgiveness on the Day of Atonement. In order to have cause for repentance and to keep their atonement prayers from being in vain, they preach at length on the Sabbath of Repentance, for it is written in the Book of Proverbs, 'In the multitude of words there wanteth not transgressions.'"

RECEPTIVITY TO REPENTANCE

Rabbi Moses of Kobrin commented: "In Psalm 90.3 we read: 'Thou turnest man to contrition and sayest: Repent, ye children of men.' However, I say, 'If you, Almighty, turn man to despair, You cannot expect him to repent. Grant him his needs and then his heart and mind will be receptive to return to You.'"

AN ACCOUNTING

A tourist visited Rabbi Abraham Isaac Kook during the Ten Days of Repentance. The rabbi cordially inquired of the visitor the country of his origin and his occupation. The guest replied that he was an accountant from America.

"Then, surely," Rabbi Kook said with a smile on his lips, "you must know how to make an accounting of your soul during these Days of Awe."

XII

ROSH HASHANAH IN
MODERN PROSE

▼▼▼▼▼▼▼▼▼▼▼▼▼▼▼▼▼▼▼▼▼▼▼▼▼▼▼▼▼▼▼▼▼▼▼

THE JEWISH NEW YEAR

JOSEPH H. HERTZ

The New Year festival is far other than the mere opening day, according to the olden Jewish reckoning, of another
year in the flight of time. Unlike the New Year celebrations of
many ancient and modern nations, the Jewish New Year is not
a time of revelry. It is a solemn season of self-examination and
self-judgment in the life of the Jew. Scripture prescribes a
special symbolic rite for this day, the sounding of the ram's
horn, the *shofar*. Whoever has once heard during the New
Year service the shrill notes of this oldest of wind instruments
will never forget them. And the meaning of this ceremony to
the worshipers who listen to these notes in solemn awe is as
stirring as the sounds themselves. Since days immemorial, the
sounding of the ram's horn on the New Year has been interpreted in Israel as the clarion call to repentance and spiritual

renewal, saying: "Awake, ye sleepers! Be not of those who miss realities in their hunt after shadows. Consider your deeds; purify your hearts. There is an Eye that seeth all things; there is an Ear that heareth all things. There is a heavenly Judge with whom is no unrighteousness, nor forgetfulness, nor respect of persons."

And on the High Festivals the Jew thinks not only of himself, but of peace and blessedness for all mankind. In the most ancient and solemn part of the services, both of the New Year and of the Day of Atonement, he prays God to hasten the time when the mighty shall be just and the just mighty; when all the children of men shall form one band of brotherhood; when national arrogance and oppression shall have passed away, like so much smoke from the earth.[1]

THE DAY OF MEMORIAL AND OF BLOWING THE TRUMPET

MORRIS JOSEPH

An impressive significance has clung to the New Year festival for centuries past. The Day of Memorial reminds us that the one way of making our peace with God is to remove the causes that have estranged us from Him. If we would have Him mercifully and forgivingly mindful of us, we must be mindful of our responsibilities to Him and to our higher nature. So that the Day of Memorial is a day for human as well as Divine memories. It should bring us face to face with ourselves; it should help us to understand our true moral position; it should set us asking: "What am I doing with my life?" It should spur us to the task of self-recollection, self-scrutiny. . . .

New Year's Day joins its appeal to that of the Day of Blowing the Trumpet. For no one can realize that another chapter of his life has closed without chastened feelings. Even the most worldly and frivolous—those who are wont to live only for the passing hour—are sobered by the thought. That life is both fleeting and uncertain is a truth that presses upon the mind with especial force as the old year ends and the new begins.

Time speeds on, and we go with it, and though we have seen the old year close we can never be sure of seeing the end of the new. We are utterly in God's hands. And so we are led to turn our thoughts to Him, to remember that He has given us our lives in trust, to use in His service. But since life is so fleeting and frail, we must needs begin this right, this serious use of it at once, and begin it by entering upon the task of self-examination and self-ennoblement which is its essential preliminary. New Year, say the rabbis, should inaugurate a new life. Thus the voices of the festival blend themselves into one message. The admonitions of the Day of Memorial are interpreted by the note of *shofar*—interpreted to every heart, so that he that runs may read—and the impressive associations of New Year's Day lend them additional solemnity. The momentous duties of introspection and penitence could not be preached at a more congenial season.

New Year's Day, then, is a solemn occasion, though not a mournful one. Unlike the ordinary New Moon it is not marked by the recital of the joyous Hallel; but, on the other hand, the prayers with which we mark its advent have little in them that is sad. A day of chastened memories, a day for reflecting upon our frailty of frame and character—that is the aspect in which the prayer book presents it to us. But beneath this somber sense of weakness, both physical and moral, there lies in the worshiper's heart the serene certitude of God's justice and mercy. If we pass away, He will redeem us; if we have sinned, He will help our resolve to sin no more. We are not morbidly to fix our thoughts upon ourselves alone; we are bidden to turn them also to God. Our littleness, but His greatness too, is to be the theme of our meditations. And so among the most impressive, as well as the most ancient, passages of the New Year liturgy are those which celebrate the Divine majesty, which tell of the kingdom of Heaven to be established on earth in the messianic time, of God, the Omniscient Searcher of hearts, of the great Sovereign who has revealed His will to mankind. Sublime conceptions all of them, and they clothe both the liturgy and the day with grandeur.[2]

THE JUDGMENT DAY

Franz Rosenzweig

The horn blown on New Year's Day at the peak of the festival stamps the day as a "day of judgment." The judgment usually thought of as the end of time is here placed in the immediate present. And so it cannot be the world that is being judged— for where could the world be at this very present! It is the individual who faces judgment. Every individual is meted out his destiny according to his actions. The verdict for the past and the coming year is written on New Year's Day, and it is sealed on the Day of Atonement, when the last reprieve constituted by these ten days of penitence and turning to God is over. The year becomes representative of eternity, in complete representation. In the annual return of this day of judgment, eternity is stripped of every trace of the beyond, of every vestige of remoteness; it is actually there, within the grasp of every individual and holding every individual close in its strong grasp. He is no longer part of the eternal history of the eternal people, nor is he part of the eternally changing history of the world. There is no more waiting, no more hiding behind history. The individual confronts judgment without any intermediary factor. He stands in the congregation. He says "We." But the "We" of this day are not the "We" of the people in history; the sin for which we crave forgiveness is not the sin of transgression of laws which separates this people from the other peoples of the world. On these days, the individual in all his naked individuality stands immediately before God.[3]

UTILIZATION OF EMOTION

Joshua Loth Liebman

The older forms of the Jewish religion intuitively understood the part played by emotion in the collective life of Israel. The builders of Judaism utilized emotion in order to sublimate the passions, the angers, the dreams of the people. Let us look for a moment at the great holy days and festivals of Judaism: how artistically they arranged for the expression of feeling and the harnessing of emotion. The New Year and the Day of Atonement were occasions for the collective expression of sin and guilt; the participation of the entire group in this verbalization did bring cleansing and inner peace. Jews expressed, rather than repressed, their shortcomings and inadequacies and sins.[4]

AN ETHICAL-HUMANIST VIEW OF ROSH HASHANAH

ISRAEL KNOX

According to tradition Rosh Hashanah and Yom Kippur are *yamim noraim*, days of awe, solemn days. Rosh Hashanah marks the beginning of a period of penitence and Yom Kippur completes it.

The Jew who labels himself "secularist" or "agnostic" is baffled by these holidays. He has not been able to cope with them as he has, for example, with Passover, by extracting their historical, poetic, and cultural elements, and just bypassing their religious content. . . .

The basic trouble is that the very terminology of the Holy Days—sin, repentance, forgiveness, Kingship of God—sounds alien to the secularist. It is at best an echo out of his remote past. And the fact is that for many in the synagogue too these words are no longer meaningful and do not correspond to genuine experience. But if there is an ethical-humanist dimension to Rosh Hashanah and Yom Kippur, then it should be possible to invest this terminology with contemporary significance and provide a reason for regarding these Holy Days as a common possession of all Jews.

There is a wonderful Hebrew-Yiddish phrase, *heshbon ha-nefesh*. The phrase connotes a taking stock of one's soul, an inner accounting, a sitting-in-judgment upon oneself. As we make our *heshbon ha-nefesh* we confess our failure to span the gap between conscience and conduct, between the standards we profess and the actions we perform. We remember what we should have done and did not do. This chasm between *believing* and *living* may or may not always be surmountable, but the refusal to try to span it is *sin* and the will to bridge it, at least to narrow it, is *atonement* and *redemption*. Sin is the gap between our promise and our conduct, between our standards and our actions.

The linkage of religion and righteousness, the insistence upon their inseparability, represented the most exalted and radical advance in the long history of religion, and perhaps in the whole of human thought. And this was the singular accomplishment of the prophets of Israel. These men were mountain peaks in the history of religion and their message was plain and direct. God is the God of righteousness and He abhors injustice. God's law is a summons to holiness—to help the widow, the orphan, the stranger in the gate, and above all, to love one's neighbor as oneself. And *neighbor* was everybody: all who were in need, who were victims of injustice, who were hungry and destitute. For the prophets, faith was not exhausted in lip service to dogma or a creed; faith was *faithfulness* to a covenant of righteousness. And sin was falling away from this covenant, or circumventing it, or corrupting it, or even externalizing it in rites and ceremonies without embodying it in conduct.

The prophets did not reject rites and ceremonies as an enhancement of life, as a crystallization of tradition, and as a concretization of collective memory. And they discerned their symbolic value as an expression of man's reaching out to something or to someone transcendent—something so near, because in our own groping toward the ideal there is an ineffable quality, and something so far, because so much of the ideal eludes us as we seek to attain it. Sin was now defined as social and ethical; it was located in the community and it involved the diminution of dignity through poverty and ignorance and man's inhumanity to man. . . .

The Hebrew-Yiddish word for repentance is *teshuvah*, and it means a turning and a returning: a *turning* from the wrong path and a *returning* to the right one. Sin is falling away from the covenant, from the law of righteousness, and repentance is both a subjective change of heart and an objective change of social relations and conditions in community through right action. Atonement is not private and introspective only, but also public and outgoing. It is *at-one-ment* with humanity and history and with the God of history, or, if you will, with that which is highest and best in history, in the universe.

The social and ethical aspect of sin is never lost sight of in Judaism, and the Talmud informs us that while all sins against God are forgiven on Yom Kippur, the transgressions against one's fellowman are outside of God's jurisdiction and can be forgiven only by the one who was wronged. . . .

Rosh Hashanah stresses the universalist motif. The prayers are not for Israel alone but for the entire world—for its redemption in righteousness and truth. There is the poignant plea in them for the establishment of the Kingdom of God. This Kingdom is to be one of righteousness and truth, in the spirit of brotherhood and neighborliness, and the annihilation of tyranny and inequality. The Kingdom is the ideal, the aim and object of the messianic expectancy and is in the future. But like the messianic tension within us, it is already a component of the present, pointing toward the road before us. The going and the goal are one. *Kingdom* and *kingship* have an archaic ring for us, since they come to us from another epoch, but we ought not to regard such words literally.

The Kingship of God is noteworthy for its negations, its flaming *no* to idolatry, whether it be of man or of things. Idolatry is the ultimate and absolute loyalty to the *part* rather than to the *whole*. The Kingship of God was for ancient Judea what parliaments are for us today. It was a check upon the unbridled whims of the ruler; it was the voice of social justice; it was a constant reminder of the supremacy of the law of righteousness. Nowhere else did such a check prevail, and there was no appeal from the total authority and ruthlessness of the tyrant. Nor was it always effective in Judea, but there the ruler could at least be branded as one who did evil in the sight of God.

Our world is in crisis, and with Hamlet we repine that the

time is out of joint. How are we to resolve this crisis? What is the remedy for our ills? It is incumbent upon us to realize that loyalty to a fragment, to a part, must merge into the comprehensive loyalty to the whole. The *one* must not swallow up the *many*, but the *many* must not stand in opposition to the *one*. The orchestration of the *many* into a *whole*, without impairing the uniqueness and distinctiveness of those who compose the *many*—that must be our immediate enterprise, if there is to be deliverance for humanity. Some of the prayers in the liturgy of Rosh Hashanah and Yom Kippur are for the disappearance of idolatry from the world and for the consummation of the Kingship of God. Never was this as urgent as it is today when mankind stands upon the very edge of a precipice with the abyss stretching before it.

The Kingdom of God is symbolic of oneness of mankind in freedom, righteousness and dignity. And if God is what is best and highest in *us*, reaching out to that which is best and highest in the *universe*, then God is not in Heaven, but is a power in the world and in us for transforming ourselves and the world in preparation for the Kingdom.[5]

WE ALL NEED *TESHUVAH*

Samson Raphael Hirsch

We all stand in need of *teshuvah*; for who can say that he has never departed from the path of the law, that his life has been a flawless realization in practice of the model presented in the Torah—who can say that he has never sinned? We all need *teshuvah*; the one means for rehabilitating our communal life in the future is *teshuvah*, nothing but *teshuvah*. *Teshuvah* is the goal of our thousand years of suffering and trial among the nations, that at last Israel should return to God and to itself, and should not, through aiming at something other than the real goal, make it a matter of chance how far this path leading elsewhere coincides with walking with God; but that at last great and small in Israel should learn to look upon walking with God as the highest and supreme goal for everyone, to which everything else should be subordinated. We all need *teshuvah*. Therefore we cling to one another in order that the path to return which is trodden by one may stimulate another by its example. (This is also one of the reasons why our confession of sin is pronounced in the plural, collectively.) Let us hold converse with scholars in order that their words may admonish us and strengthen us to mend our ways. Let us never even in jest mock at that which should be holy to us in actual life, in order that its holiness may not become cheap to us. Let us respect our teachers in order that they may show us the way of goodness and lead us along it. Let us love instruction and not be ashamed to let ourselves be taught and corrected even by the humblest; and let every community in Israel see that there lives in its midst a man who himself can present the example of a blameless life, dedicated to the law of God, filled with the fear of God and love of mankind, and who shall keep an eye on their conduct and their ideas where he thinks he sees anything reprehensible. These are helps to self-improvement which our Sages recommend to us; and they add, beware particularly of such sins as are not sins in the eyes of most people, for it is not easy to take the first step in freeing yourself from such sins—which consists in our recognition of the sin; also of those which come your way only too frequently and may easily become a habit, for with them the last and greatest step in self-purification is difficult—genuine reform for the future.

Translated by I. Grunfeld[6]

LIGHTS OF REPENTANCE

Abraham Isaac Kook

For a long period of time I have been involved in an intense inner struggle and a strong spirit impels me to speak on the subject of repentance, and all my thoughts are centered on this theme. Repentance encompasses the major part of Torah and life; upon it are based all the hopes of individual man as well as the community. It is the commandment of God that, on the one hand, is the simplest to perform, for the slightest thought of repentance is in itself repentance. Yet in another sense, repentance is the most difficult of all commandments to fulfill, for indeed it has not been fully actualized in the world and in human life. . . .

Without the thought of repentance, its tranquility and assurance, man would be unable to find rest, and spiritual life would be unable to develop in the world. The ethical sense demands of man righteousness and virtue—perfection. How remote from man is the realization of ethical perfection in terms of actuality! How feeble is his ability to make his deeds correspond to the purity of the ideal of absolute righteousness! How then shall he strive for that which is not at all within the realm of his ability? If man is constantly prone to stumble, to impugn righteousness and morality, since the primary basis of his perfection is the yearning and firm desire toward perfection, this desire itself is the basis of repentance, which constantly triumphs over his way of life and truly perfects him. . . .

All melancholy comes as a result of sin; repentance illumines the soul and transforms the melancholy into joy. The general melancholy in the world has its source in the "collective coarse substance" to be found in the universe, from the sins of society and individuals and from the concealed sin of the earth which emerged to actuality with the sin of man; the righteous who sustain the world, and the Messiah, particularly, return in repentance for the nature of this sin and transform it to joy. . . .

Every perfect repentance must inevitably achieve two contradictory effects upon the soul: on the one hand, trembling and sorrow for the sin and evil within him; and on the other hand, trust and joy for the virtue, since it is impossible that man should not discover within himself some share of virtue. Even if at times his reckoning is so beclouded that he can find no vestige of virtue, the very fact that trembling and sorrow encompass him as a result of his awareness of the sin and evil within him—this fact in itself possesses great virtue. And immediately he must rejoice, trustful and filled with strength and might, even for this virtue, till he shall find himself constantly, even amidst the greatest oppression, involved in the emotions of repentance, abounding with spirit of life, fortified with the very basis of achievement and action with joy of life and preparation for their blessings.

Translated by Alter B. Z. Metzger[7]

A UNIQUELY JEWISH CONCEPT

ELIEZER BERKOVITS

Teshuvah, a uniquely Jewish concept, means literally "response" or "return." Repentance and "renewal" of faith are only one phase of *teshuvah*. Isaiah said: "Let the wicked forsake his way, and the man of iniquity his thoughts; and let him return unto the Eternal and He will have compassion on him, and to our God, for He will abundantly pardon" (Isaiah 55.7). The return to God is not merely "a change of heart," but a change in one's way of life. Ezekiel deals with *teshuvah* by declaring: "As I live, saith the Lord God, I have no pleasure in the death of the wicked, but that the wicked turn from his way and live; turn ye, turn ye from your evil ways, for why will ye die, O house of Israel?" (Ezekiel 33.11). *Teshuvah* is a turning away and a turning toward—a matter of believing and of altering one's daily living.

The turning away begins with a realization of having sinned. At times, that realization and confession of sin are enough to bring God's forgiveness. When King David confesses to the prophet Nathan, "I have sinned against the Eternal One," the prophet reassures him: "The Eternal hath put away thy sin; thou shalt not die" (II Samuel 12.13). David demonstrates his greatness by renouncing royal dignity and pride in his confession of sin.

But realization of guilt is not enough. The sinner must also forsake his way. "He that covereth his transgressions shall not prosper; but whoso confesseth and forsaketh them shall obtain mercy" (Proverbs 28.13).

Jewish tradition recognizes four conditions necessary for

teshuvah: regret for the past, desisting from objectionable conduct, confession, and the firm resolution never to backslide.
Repentance is the first phase and regeneration the second. The
first is only the preliminary condition necessary for leading a
man up to the second, the turning toward God. Every sin
undermines the spiritual strength of the sinner; his regeneration is required. . . .

The Talmud draws a sharp distinction between those moti-
vated by *teshuvah me-yirah*, "return out of fear" (of punishment), and *teshuvah me-ahavah*, "return out of love" (of God).
Of the former it is said that their intentional sins are accounted
as if they were unintentional; of those who return out of love,
their intentional transgressions become like merits. At the source
is a concept of the human personality as dynamic, spontaneous,
and capable of regeneration and renewal.

Teshuvah is thus an experience of personality transformation.
When performed out of fear, it lessens the burden of sin but
does not remove it; intentional transgressions become unintentional ones. *Teshuvah* undertaken out of love accomplishes
a fundamental transformation, in which healing and purification are complete. Intentional sins of the past function almost
as meritorious deeds in their impact and significance for the
new personality. Past failures may serve as new sources of spiritual strength and security for the *baal teshuvah*, "the man who
returned."[8]

GOD THE ACCUSED

Elie Wiesel

On the eve of Rosh Hashanah, the last day of that accursed
year, the whole camp [Buna] was electric with the tension
which was in all our hearts. In spite of everything, this day was
different from any other. The last day of the year. The word
"last" rang very strangely. What if it were indeed the last day?

They gave us our evening meal, a very thick soup, but no
one touched it. We wanted to wait until after prayers. At the

place of assembly, surrounded by the electrified barbed wire, thousands of silent Jews gathered, their faces stricken.

Night was falling. Other prisoners continued to crowd in, from every block, able suddenly to conquer time and space and submit both to their will.

"What are You, my God," I thought angrily, "compared to this afflicted crowd, proclaiming to You their faith, their anger, their revolt? What does Your greatness mean, Lord of the Universe, in the face of all this weakness, this decomposition and this decay? Why do You still trouble their sick minds, their crippled bodies?"

Ten thousand men had come to attend the solemn service, heads of the blocks, Kapos, functionaries of death.

"Bless the Eternal. . . ."

The voice of the officiant had just made itself heard. I thought at first it was the wind.

"Blessed be the Name of the Eternal!"

Thousands of voices repeated the benediction; thousands of men prostrated themselves like trees before a tempest.

"Blessed be the Name of the Eternal!"

Why, but why should I bless Him? In every fiber I rebelled. Because He had had thousands of children burned in His pits? Because He kept six crematoria working night and day, on Sundays and feast days? Because in His great might He had created Auschwitz, Birkenau, Buna, and so many factories of death? How could I say to Him: "Blessed art Thou, Eternal, Master of the Universe, who chose us from amongst the races to be tortured day and night, to see our fathers, our mothers, our brothers, end in the crematorium? Praised be Thy Holy Name, Thou who has chosen us to be butchered on Thine altar?"

I heard the voice of the officiant rising up, powerful yet at the same time broken, amid the tears, the sobs, the sighs of the whole congregation:

"All the earth and the universe are God's!"

He kept stopping every moment, as though he did not have the strength to find the meaning beneath the words. The melody choked in his throat.

And I, mystic that I had been, I thought:

"Yes, man is very strong, greater than God. When You were deceived by Adam and Eve, You drove them out of paradise. When Noah's generation displeased You, You brought down the Flood. When Sodom no longer found favor in Your eyes, You made the sky rain down fire and sulphur. But these men here, whom You have betrayed, whom You have allowed to be tortured, butchered, gassed, burned, what do they do? They pray before You! They praise Your Name!"

"All creation bears witness to the greatness of God!"

Once, New Year's Day had dominated my life. I knew that my sins grieved the Eternal; I implored His forgiveness. Once, I had believed profoundly that upon one solitary deed of mine, one solitary prayer, depended the salvation of the world.

This day, I had ceased to plead. I was no longer capable of lamentation. On the contrary, I felt very strong, I was the accuser, God the accused. My eyes were open and I was alone —terribly alone in a world without God and without man. Without love or mercy. I had ceased to be anything but ashes, yet I felt myself to be stronger than the Almighty, to whom my life had been tied for so long. I stood amid that praying congregation, observing it like a stranger.

The service ended with the *Kaddish*. Everyone recited the *Kaddish* over his parents, over his children, over his brothers, and over himself.

We stayed for a long time at the assembly place. No one dared to drag himself away from this mirage. Then it was time to go to bed and slowly the prisoners made their way over to their blocks. I heard people wishing one another a Happy New Year!

Translated by Stella Rodway[9]

A SEARCH FOR THE HOLY SPIRIT

Mordecai Zeev Feierberg

The Holy Days approach. He prepares to follow out instructions in every detail, so that he may not, God forbid, spoil his chances. He is aware of the vigorous care that must be exercised in such holy matters. He reviews his conduct and is inclined to be penitent. Perhaps some sin may, God forbid, stand in his way; his plans will have no effect. He reads continually in "ethical books" that tell you just how to behave during these Holy Days. Since he heard the first sounds of the *shofar*, at the beginning of the month of Elul, he has come to believe that rigorous rules prevail. The air is filled with fear and terror. The dread of the Law fills every heart with trembling. Nahman is nevertheless confident. He feels, too, that this eternal warfare is now more intense. He is filled with a kind of longing and strange faithfulness. "The Lord is the stronghold of my life; of whom shall I be afraid? When evildoers come upon me, my adversaries, my foes, they stumble and fall; though a host should encamp against me, my heart will not fear; though war should rise up against me, even then will I be confident. . . . Be strong and let thy heart take courage; yea, wait thou for the Lord."

He prays each day even more than the necessary concentration. He recites Psalms and reads in the famous book of Horowitz. He rises at the traditional watches every night to recite *Selihot* with the community, and then he hides behind the stove in the *bet ha-midrash* and meditates penitently. Even at *heder* and at home, he is always respectful and humble, like a sinner who sits on the bench of the guilty. He breaks his bread in sorrow, fearful lest, God forbid, he violate the commandment that warns against gluttony, lest he forget, God forbid, that he may eat only so much as will be necessary to enable him to serve God, lest he may turn epicure, become greedy for the pleasures of the world, lest he neglect the washing of his hands or grace after meals. For surely every Jew is obliged to be mindful at all times that his table is an altar. He who eats is priest, the food is a sacrifice, and whoever eats sanctified food uncleanly is worthy to be destroyed by God. Nahman takes the ritual bath each day. The eve of Rosh Hashanah, he prays all day, reciting Psalms, reading books, getting himself accustomed to real piety.

On Rosh Hashanah, he rises early; night has been very long.

With eyes strained he waits long for the first peep of dawn. Very meekly he makes his way to the synagogue. Humbly, with bowed head, he looks at no one; he speaks to no one lest he fall into committing slander, falsehood, lest he even speak unnecessarily.

Now the cantor is reciting the *Kedushah*; his heart beats rapidly, his feelings overwhelm him, his knees are weak from fear and hope, his hair is standing on end. He is trembling. Just another moment—there, the cantor is now singing "Where is His glorious place. . . ." How he concentrates upon the necessary thoughts and seeks the Holy Spirit!

The thoughts come to him easily. He has done everything as he planned. His eyes glisten, his heart is light.

Translated by Ira Eisenstein[10]

XIII

ROSH HASHANAH IN ART

Joseph Gutmann

Only from the late thirteenth century on do we find illustrations of the most significant lessons of Rosh Hashanah in medieval Hebrew manuscripts, especially in the German *mahzor*. Prior to that time, no illustrations of the Rosh Hashanah celebration or its symbolism are known.

We note, for instance, in a fourteenth-century German *mahzor*, the word *"melekh"* in bold, square Ashkenazic letters —the *piyyut* beginning "O King, Your word stands steadfast from of yore," recited in the morning service of the second day of Rosh Hashanah. To the left of the Hebrew letters, a hand is emerging from schematized clouds holding a scale wherein the merits, the good deeds, and demerits, the evil deeds, of man are weighed. A little devil is desperately trying to weight down the pan of demerits (fig. 1). As the zodiacal sign for the month of Tishri is the balance, it is an appropriate symbol to express the rabbinic idea that the deeds of man are weighed on the scales of judgment during that month. The

Musaf service of the first day of Rosh Hashanah clearly expresses this theme: "This day has been ordained of old as a day of reckoning, when the deeds of man are weighed and judged."

A beautiful manuscript page from late fifteenth-century northern Italy shows a man wrapped in a *tallit*, standing in a pavilion and blowing the *shofar*, while seated and standing men ardently listen to the plaintive notes (fig. 2). Below the blessings for the *shofar* service of Rosh Hashanah of another fifteenth-century Italian manuscript, a small figure stands before a lectern sounding the *shofar*, as four figures seated in their pew with open prayer books before them listen. Two of the men, in a contrite gesture, have placed their hands on their hearts (fig. 3). To make the Jew aware of the awesomeness of the day, the *shofar* is blown. It sounds the alarm to the slumbering conscience of man, appealing to him to repent and search his heart.

In a German *mahzor* of the fourteenth century, we see next to the notes for the *shofar* a man with medieval Jew's hat blowing the *shofar*, his left foot resting on a three-legged footstool, while a monstrous horned and winged figure is running away on the left side of the page (fig. 4). This figure is intended to be Satan, who was to be confounded by the blasts of the *shofar*—one of many popular beliefs was that blowing the *shofar* prevented Satan from bringing before God accusations against Jews. The three-legged footstool probably had magical connotations and may have been intended to further placate and confuse Satan. It may have constituted a barrier between the man blowing the *shofar* and the ground where the devils and evil spirits reside and are able to maintain their powers and destructive influence.

"Remember us unto life, O King who delightest in life and inscribe us in the Book of Life" is a major theme of the High Holy Days. This pious wish is decorated in many medieval manuscripts. In a late fifteenth-century north Italian manuscript, the cantor intones this phrase before the lectern on the right. To the left can be seen the bold lettering of the opening word, "*zakhrenu*," surrounded by splendid Renaissance floral and animal decoration (fig. 5).[1]

A German manuscript of the fourteenth century has the typical Gothic animal decoration, so popular during this period, within the Hebrew letters and even reveals the main characters of the *Akedah* story placed within separate panels, above the Hebrew word "*zakhrenu*" (fig. 6). The *Akedah* plays an important role on Rosh Hashanah because rabbinic tradition saw in the *Akedah* an instrument of vicarious atonement whereby God forgives Israel's sins because of the merit of Abraham and Isaac. The linking of the sacrifice of Isaac with the blowing of the *shofar* alludes to the belief that the sacrifice of Isaac occurred on Rosh Hashanah and that the blowing of the ram's horn is intended to remind us of the ram sacrificed in place of Isaac. In the morning service recited on the second day of the New Year, the Jew appeals to God to "account to His people the sacrifice of Isaac according to Your oath, and reverse [Your decree] from stern judgment to mercy." An early fourteenth-century German *mahzor* illustrates this passage. To the left, we see Abraham lovingly guiding his son to the scene of the sacrifice. Isaac is bound upon the altar, his eyes shielded from the sight of the sword by Abraham's left hand. In his right hand, Abraham holds the mighty sword, which is dramatically intercepted by a winged angel, who points to the ram standing in a bush. Below the sacrifice are the two servants with the ass (fig. 7).

The *Akedah* also appears in *mahzorim* to introduce the *piyyut* found in the morning service of the first day of Rosh Hashanah —"O King, girt with power," stressing the sovereignty of God over man and nature. In a fourteenth-century *mahzor*, we see Isaac kneeling on the altar and Abraham, with uplifted knife, standing next to him. A winged angel in the upper left-hand corner points to Abraham with one hand and to the ram, centered above the word "King," with the other. In the upper right-hand corner, a man is blowing a *shofar* (fig. 8). A somewhat abbreviated version of the scene is found in another early fourteenth-century *mahzor*. We simply observe a crown above the word "King," a man blowing a *shofar* on the left, and a ram standing next to a tree in the right margin of the page (fig. 9).[2] To the medieval German Jew, the memory of the event on Mt. Moriah was very much alive; it was the model for the many who followed martyrdom (*kiddush ha-Shem*, sanctification of the Name) to escape baptism or cruel butchery. For the sake of *kiddush ha-Shem*, many offered their sons exactly as Abraham offered up his son Isaac. A twelfth-century poem by Rabbi Ephraim of Bonn emphasizes this point: "Recall to our credit the many *Akedahs*, the saints, men and women, slain for Thy sake."[3]

Not many ceremonial objects are associated with the Rosh Hashanah holiday and none antedate the seventeenth century.

For home use, a very rare white tablecloth with gold brocade appliqué from Oberzell, Germany, dated 1781, has survived. In the center is a *shofar* with the inscription "Shofar for Rosh Hashanah." Around the borders are inscriptions from Lamentations 3.20, Ecclesiastes 12.7, Psalms 69.32, and from rabbinic sources (fig. 10).

Prior to the festival meal, it is customary in many homes to dip bread in honey and recite "May it be Your will to renew unto us a good and sweet year." A contemporary craftsman, the late Ilya Schor (1904–61), fashioned a handsome honey dish especially for this occasion. It carries in the center the inscription "a land flowing with milk and honey" (fig. 11). For the *Kiddush*, special wine cups were sometimes made, such as the silver one from London, dating from 1793/94. Two men blowing a *shofar* are depicted on the cup itself (fig. 12).

The most important ceremonial object linked with Rosh Hashanah is, of course, the *shofar*. In keeping with Jewish legal proscription, the *shofar* is usually plain, although some have a simple decoration or a biblical text etched on the surface. An unusual *shofar*, dating from 1781/82, carries the inscription: "I, the humble Joseph, the son of Wolf of the city of Dieburg" (fig. 13). Others simply have circles and scalloped edge designs, such as the nineteenth-century specimen from Germany (fig. 14). Although rabbis generally frowned on such practices, some rabbis, such as Israel Isserlein of fifteenth-century Vienna, tolerated it.

Torah shields often carry interchangeable holiday plates to

indicate the Torah scroll which contains the portion of the Torah to be read on a specific holiday. A silver Torah shield, made in Breslau in the late seventeenth century, reveals the Rosh Hashanah plate. It has twisted columns, surmounted by crowns, and has the relief figure of Moses to the left and Aaron to the right. In the center are the Tablets of the Law (fig. 17).[4]

Books on Jewish customs and holiday observance, written by Jews and non-Jews, from the fifteenth century on depict both the preparations for and the celebration of Rosh Hashanah. The custom of bathing in a cold stream in the afternoon before Rosh Hashanah, to be pure and clean before God, is illustrated in the lower left-hand corner of an eighteenth-century etching. We note the figures immersing themselves three times, as prescribed, in the presence of witnesses (fig. 18).

The blowing of the *shofar* is a common theme in seventeenth- and eighteenth-century illustrations. In Paul C. Kirchner's *Jüdisches Ceremoniel*, Jews are dressed in the prescribed *kittel* (or *sargenes*) and the customary Jewish ruff of the period. From the *bimah*, an enclosed, raised structure, the *shofar* is being sounded. The Torah scrolls are being taken from the ark and carried in procession around the synagogue (fig. 19). Another illustration from a late seventeenth-century woodcut from an Amsterdam *Minhagim* book, also from an Ashkenazi synagogue, simply shows the *shofar* being blown before the *bimah*, on which is an open prayer book. Several Jews stand behind the *shofar*-blower (fig. 20). Bernard Picart (1673–1733) captures for us the Rosh Hashanah services of the Sefardi Jews in the famous Spanish-Portuguese synagogue in Amsterdam. The scene depicts the blowing of the *shofar* at the *tevah* (*bimah*). The men seated on the benches around the *tevah* are wrapped in a *tallit* and wear the three-cornered hat and fashionable wig of the day. The women can be seen behind the grillwork of the balcony (fig. 21).

One of the most interesting customs of Rosh Hashanah, a custom which arose in Germany in the late Middle Ages, is the ceremony of *Tashlikh*. The earliest depiction is an early sixteenth-century woodcut, where men and women stand on

separate bridges and shake out their garments to the waiting
fish below. On Rosh Hashanah afternoon, everyone goes to a
stream, preferably one with running water and fish. The clothes
are taken by the seam and shaken over the water in the firm
belief that the fish will take away the sins so cast in the water
(fig. 22). The biblical prooftext for this custom was based on
Micah 7.19: "He will again have compassion on us, He will
subdue our iniquities and You will cast all their sins into the
depths of the sea." Samuel Hirszenberg (1865–1908), a painter
who achieved fame for his patriotic and historical canvases,
also did Jewish genre compositions, such as his version of
"Tashlikh" (fig. 23). With a minimum of pathos, he paints
several Polish Jews closely huddled together before a body of
water to perform the ceremony. Marc Chagall, in a drawing
done for Burning Lights, utilizes a few lines to capture the
essence of the ceremony as performed in a world gone by. A
little child and his elders stand with prayer books before a
river to perform the ceremony of Tashlikh (fig. 24).[5]

At a time when hallowed, sacred traditions and customs are
in danger of being forgotten, the precious artistic remnant here
discussed allows us to experience and relive the Rosh Hashanah
celebration of our ancestors.

XIV

THE MUSIC OF
THE ROSH HASHANAH LITURGY

MAX WOHLBERG

The music of the synagogue comprises four distinct elements: 1) the cantillation system that governs the chanting of the various books of the Bible; 2) the musical modes in which larger sections of the service are recited; 3) the *Misinai*[1] tunes applicable to specific texts of the liturgy; and 4) free recitatives and compositions (for solo, choir, and congregation) that may or may not be based on the above elements.

Thanks to a propitious tradition, melodic variations of these elements correspond to the various holidays and seasons. The specific holiday tunes enhance immeasurably the emotional experience and musical effectiveness of the synagogue service.

The general quality of the High Holy Days music reflects solemnity and hopeful determination. Its overall effect is forthright and impassioned rather than sad and despairing.

Rosh Hashanah is ushered in by the evening service sung to a robust major tune[2] in conjunction with traditional motifs also used elsewhere (example 1*).

* The musical examples follow this article.

[171

The *Kiddush* is followed by a *Yigdal* melody (example 2) exclusive to the High Holy Days. Other *Yigdal* and *Adon Olam* melodies (example 3) are limited to the morning service. The latter is, in at least its preliminary section, dominated by the *Barukh she-amár* tune (example 4).

As the Kingdom of God is a major theme of the Rosh Hashanah liturgy, every mention of the word *Melekh* (King) is given special dynamic emphasis. The *baal shahrit* (precentor chanting the first major section of the service) commences with the word *Ha-Melekh* (The King), which he sings to a prolonged, melismatic tune (example 5).

For a thousand years (from approximately the sixth to sixteenth century) poets have composed *piyyutim* (liturgical poems) which have become incorporated into the *siddur* and into the *mahzor*. Many of these *piyyutim* have their own *Misinai* tunes. Over fifty such tunes, together with their variations, are associated with the Rosh Hashanah liturgy. Typical of these are *Tair vetaria* and *Adonai Melekh* (examples 6 and 7) whose themes are, respectively, the sounds of the *shofar* and God the Eternal.

In order to emphasize the special significance of this day, the basic passages of the daily liturgy are supplied with elaborate musical settings. Such a one is *Avot* (introductory paragraph of the *Amidah*) (example 8).

While the German *nusah*[3] may contain melodic elements absent in the Polish *nusah*, the mode designated for the recitation of the *Amidah* (example 9) is used by all branches of Ashkenazic Jewry. Characteristic also is the High Holy Days cadence reserved for concluding benedictions (example 10).

An ingratiating melody (example 11) became associated with the *Avinu Malkenu*. This melody, formerly also utilized elsewhere, has unfortunately become less popular in our day. A familiar folksong (example 12) set for the last verse of the prayer has, of late, come into favor.

The *Shema*, as would be expected, is on the High Holy Days supplied with a festive setting (example 13).[4] Likewise, a distinctive version of the cantillating mode is provided for these

solemn days (example 14) and is reflected in the Torah benedictions chanted on this day.[5]

A high point of the service is undoubtedly the sounding of
the *shofar*. The rabbi (as a rule) calls out for the *baal tekiah*
each of the three notes (or motifs) to be sounded: *tekiah*,
shevarim, and *teruah* arranged in three groups. Actually, only
three notes are involved. The *tekiah* consists of a prolonged
note preceded by a short (upbeat) note and concluded by a
short (octave) note. The *shevarim* represents the division of
the prolonged note into three parts. The *teruah* in turn divides
each of the *shevarim* notes into three parts, producing nine
short staccato blasts (example 15). The stentorian *shofar*
sounds, in sharp contrast to the mellow human voice, are likely
to make a strong emotional impact on the worshiper.

An altogether different effect is intended in the poignant
cantorial *Hineni* prayer, which serves as a prelude to the *Musaf*
service. In this prayer the *hazzan* humbly avows his shortcomings (traditionally sung *sotto voce*) and with mounting fervor
pleads for divine help in the successful conduct of his awesome
assignment in leading the congregation.

Musically, the zenith of the service is reached with the
Unetanneh Tokef. This majestic prayer, profuse in vivid
imagery, dramatic intensity, and passages of acute pathos,
intrigued most of our synagogue composers. Its three paragraphs were cast in numerous ambitious musical settings. Well
known are those of Moses Milner, Salomon Sulzer, and Eliezer
Gerowitch. Those of Nisi Blumenthal and especially of Louis
Lewandowsky (example 16) achieved great popularity.

Among the best known *Misinai* tunes is that associated with
the *Kedushah* (example 17) recited at the repetition of the
Amidah.

On other days of the year, the *Alenu* concludes each of the
three daily synagogue services with a simple chant. On this
day, however, affirming as it does the sovereignty of God, the
Alenu is solemnly intoned with a majestic melody (example
18) in front of the open ark, accompanied by ceremonious
genuflection and kneeling.

The three sections of the *Musaf* service employ—with liberal allowances for modulations to other modes—the major *Adonai Malakh* mode[6] for *Malkhuyot* and *Shofarot*, and a minor mode—related to the *Magen Avot* and *Selihah* modes—for *Zikhronot*.

It is noteworthy that the *Kaddish* has a special tune for each of the following occasions: the evening service (example 19), the morning *Barkhu* (example 20), the conclusion of the *Amidah* (example 21), the Torah service (example 22), and before *Musaf* (example 23).

At the turn of the century the High Holy Days music of Sigmund Schlesinger and Edward Stark was the common fare of the modern American synagogue. This was later supplanted by the works of Max Graumann and Lazare Saminsky. Within recent decades Abraham W. Binder, Herbert Fromm, Eric Werner, and particularly Gershon Ephros contributed substantial elements to the standard High Holy Days repertoire.

The Orthodox synagogue, largely untouched by these works, retained elements of the classic Salomon Sulzer, Louis Lewandowsky, and Samuel Naumburg music, as well as its preference for the "traditional" East European composers. In this category belong, among others, Salomon Weintraub, Eliezer Gerowitch, Nissan Belzer, Abraham M. Bernstein, Nissan Blumenthal, Osias J. Abrass, Baruch Schorr, Wolf Shestapol, and David Nowakowsky.

Their American successors, particularly in the creation of an extensive repertoire of cantorial recitatives, were Samuel Weisser, Jacob L. Wassilkowsky, Jacob Rapaport, Herman Semiatin, Samuel Kavetsky, Adolph Katchko, and Yisrael Alter.

The Conservative synagogue, depending on the orientation of the particular congregation and on the background of its *hazzan*, utilized music from all available sources. While the congregational tunes vary from congregation to congregation, a number of these have achieved fairly wide acceptance.[7]

It may justly be said that the music of the Rosh Hashanah service invests the festival with an unmistakable emotional quality that is stronger than any of its other ingredients, a quality capable of arousing in the worshiper a mood of devotion and profound spiritual involvement.

To the average worshiper these tunes and modes are a link to his people and to his history. Through them he is united with his ancestors. In these chants he hears the prayers of the venerable congregations of Mainz, Seville, Amsterdam, and Warsaw. With them the universal congregation of Israel approaches the Almighty as it once did in the Temple that stood in Jerusalem.

Example 1   L. LEWANDOWSKY

Bar - khu et A-do-nai ham - vo-rakh.

Example 2   I. GOLDFARB

Yig-dal E - lo-him hai___ v'-yish - ta - bah, nim-

tza v'-en et el m'-tzi - u - to. E-had v'-en ya-hid k'

yi - hu-do ne - lam v'-gam en sof l'-ah - du - to.

Example 3A   A. BAER

Yig - dal___ E- lo-him___ hai v'-yish- ta -

bah nim-tza v' - en et el m'-tzi- u - to. E-had v'-

en ya-hid k'-yi-hu-do ne-lam v'gam en sof l'-ah-du - to.

Example 3B   A. BAER

A- don o - lam   a- sher ma - lakh   b'- te- rem

kol y'- tzir niv - ra   l' - et na- a- sa v'- hef -

tzo__ kol   a - zai____ me-lekh   sh'- mo nik-ro.

Example 4   A. BAER

Ba - rukh she- a- mar v'- ha - ya__ ha - o - lam,   ba-

rukh hu ba-rukh o - se___ v' re - shit, ba-rukh o-mer v'-o-se ba-

rukh go-zer u- m' ka-yem, ba-rukh m'-ra-hem al ha-a-retz, ba-

rukh m'- ra- hem _____ al hab- ri - yot.

Example 8   M. WOHLBERG

Ba-rukh a-ta— A-do-nai E-lo-he - nu ve-lo.he____ a-vo-

te - nu, E-lo-he _____ Av - ra - ham,

E - lo - he— Yitz -

ḥak _____ ve-lo-he _____ Ya-a-kov.__ *etc.*

Example 9   J. HELLER

U - v'-khen ten paḥ - d'-kha A - do-nai E - lo-

he-nu al kol ma-a-se-kha v'-e-ma-t'-kha al kol ma she-ba-ra-

etc.

ta V'-shi-m-'kha no-ra_____ al kol ma she-ba-ra - ta.

Example 10   A. FRIEDMANN

Ba - 'rukh a - ta— A-do-nai ma - gen Av-ra - ham.

Example 11   After M. GRAUMAN

A - vi -   nu mal-ke -

- nu kat-ve - nu   b'- se-fer ha-yim to - vim.— A -

vi - nu mal-ke-nu kat - ve- nu b'-se-fer g'-u - la— vi-shu-

a.— A - vi - nu mal-ke-nu kat - ve- nu b'-se-fer par-na-

sa v'- khal-ka - la.   A - vi - nu mal - ke - nu kat-

ve - nu b' - se - fer   b'- se- fer za-khu - yot.

Example 12

A - vi - nu mal - ke - nu___ ḥa - ne-nu va-ne-nu

ki en ba-nu ma-a-sim.___ A-se i-ma-nu___ tz'-da-ka va-ḥe-

sed,___ a-se i-ma-nu tz'-da-ka va-ḥe-sed v'-ho-shi - e - nu.___

Example 13

Sh' ma___ Yis-ra-el___ Ado-nai E-lo-ḥe-nu Ado-nai E-ḥad.

Example 14   M. WODAK

Va-do-nai___ pa-kad et Sa-ra ka-a-sḥer a-mar   va-ya-mal

Av-ra-ḥam et Yitz-ḥak b'-no___ ben sh'mo-nat ya-mim ka-a-sher___

___ tzi-va o-to___ E-lo-him.___

Example 15

T'- ki - a. Sh'- va - rim.   T'- ru-a. _____   T'- ki - a.

Example 16

Un'- ta - ne   to -kef   k'- du - shat   ha-yom,   ki   hu _____

no - ra v'- a - yom.   U - vo   ti - na - se mal-

khu - te - kha,   v' - yi - kon b' - he - sed ___ kis - e -

kha,   v' - te -shev   a - lav ___   be - e - met.   *etc.*

Example 17

Arr. M. WOHLBERG

K'vo - do ___ ma - le _____   o - lam ___ m'shar-

tav ___ sho-a-lim ___ ze la-ze a - ye ___ m'- kom ___ k'- vo -

do___ l'-u-ma-tam___ ba-rukh yo-me - ru.

Example 18   S. SULZER

A - le - nu l'sha-be - ah la - a - don___ ha-kol la-tet g'du-

la_____ l'yo - tzer_ b' - re - shit she-lo a-

sa - nu k'go-ye _____ ha- a - ra - tzot v'- lo sa-

ma-nu k'-mish-p'-hot_ha - a-da-ma_ she - lo sam hel-ke - nu ka-

hem_____ v'-go-ra-le-nu k' khol ha-mo-nam.

Example 19

Yit-ga-dal___ v' yit-ka-dash _____ sh'-me ra-ba__ *etc.*

Example 20   M. WOHLBERG

Yit- ga - dal v' yit-ka-dash sh'-me ra - ba —— b' ol-ma div-ra khir-u-te v'-yam-

likh — mal - khu - te,   b'- ha-ye-khon uv- yo-me- khon— uv -ha. *etc.*

Example 21   A. BAER

Yit - ga - dal v'yit - ka - dash sh'- me ra - ba *etc.*

Example 22

Yit - ga-dal v'yit-ka- dash _____ sh'-me_ra-ba *etc.*

Example 23

Yit-ga-dal— v'yit-ka-dash_____ sh'me ra-ba b'ol - ma *etc.*

XV

ROSH HASHANAH IN MANY LANDS

DAYS OF AWE IN AN EAST EUROPEAN TOWN

HAYYIM SCHAUSS

The Days of Awe do not arrive suddenly and unexpectedly; people start preparing for them a long time in advance. The attitude during the entire month of Elul is already an earnest and sober one, and all feel that soon the solemn days, the days of penitence, will begin.

But undercurrents of the coming holidays are felt even earlier, are felt on the Sabbath at which the blessing for the coming New Moon, that of Elul, is recited. Every Sabbath before a New Moon is a special Sabbath in the synagogue. But the Sabbath before Elul is exalted above all the other pre-New Moon Sabbaths. One knows that very soon, in just a few days, the call of the *shofar* will be heard and when the cantor, holding the Torah scroll, calls out "*Rosh Hodesh Elul*," the ring of his voice is far different from the tone he uses on other Sabbaths on which he announces *Rosh Hodesh*.

The first real sign that the Days of Awe are nearing appears on the day before the New Moon of Elul. The day before each New Moon is called a minor day of atonement. There are no more than three or four very pious old Jews in town who observe all these minor days of atonement. But the day before Elul is different. Many Jews fast on that day, and there is a big congregation present for the afternoon prayers, to recite *Selihot*, prayers of supplication and confessions; it really feels like Yom Kippur.

On the second day of *Rosh Hodesh*, the first of Elul, at the end of the morning services the blowing of the *shofar* begins, after which Psalms 27 is recited. The *shofar* call is a signal that the time of penitence is approaching, and sober earnestness descends on all.

The life of the town goes on as ordinarily. But it is easy to see that the Jews are deliberately more pious. Certain petty sins, common the year round, are now guarded against. People pray more carefully and with greater fervor, and those with ample time remain in the *bet ha-midrash*, the house of study, to recite Psalms, to study a chapter of Mishnah, or other religious and devotional books. For these are days, it is said, when the very fish in the stream shiver with foreboding.

The solemnity of the month of Elul is more in evidence in the cemetery than anywhere else, for these are the days on which one visits the graves of his ancestors. Women, for the most part, come and weep and bare their hearts to those who were once near and dear to them, and who now lie between markers of stone and wood. Some stand at the headstones and weep silently; others, however, moan and howl hysterically and are heard far afield. There is a special book of prayers written for this occasion, but most of the women lack the education to pick out the appropriate ones. There are, however, a couple of learned women in town and they recite these prayers at the cemetery with the mourning women. It is understood that they are to be paid for their trouble. Some of the women are not content just to mourn at the cemetery. They "measure the field." That is, they pace about the cemetery with a spool of cotton which they unroll and with which they span the ground. This cotton is then taken to the candle-maker, who uses it as wicks for candles, which the women donate to the synagogue.

For the children it is, in many ways, a very pleasant period. For the days from the middle of Elul till after Sukkot are vacation days between the summer and fall semesters, and school is open only half-days. But they do not get much satisfaction from their freedom. The sober air of penitence that rules over the adults has its influence on them. Their conscience forbids them to frolic and joy. The children also know that life hangs in the balance now, and the time is coming when the fate of every man will be judged and inscribed in heaven.

The awesome atmosphere becomes even more pronounced, and still more circumspect becomes the attitude of the townspeople during the week of *Selihot* (supplications) which begins on the Sunday before Rosh Hashanah. On that day all rise early, while it is still pitch dark outside. Since the hour of arising is much earlier than usual, the beadle goes about the town with a lantern in his hand, knocking on windows with a wooden mallet, waking the Jews for *Selihot*. There are some pious people in town, women as well as men, who fast on this day.

Even the school boys, the older ones, rise early to attend the *Selihot* services in the House of Study. They attend only on the first day's services and not on the succeeding days, with the exception of the day before Rosh Hashanah. . . .

In the synagogue the atmosphere is festive for the evening services, but the prayers are chanted with the intonation associated with the Days of Awe, which induces a highly religious attitude. After the service all wish one another "A Festive Holiday," and add, in Hebrew, "May you be inscribed and sealed for a good year"; but everyone does not know Hebrew well and the words are difficult to pronounce, so many content themselves with just saying simply, "A good year."

The table is festively arrayed when the worshipers arrive home from the synagogue. On the table is a small jar filled with honey, an omen for a sweet year; this is spread on the first slice of bread eaten. In many homes some new fruit of the season is served. This fruit is generally grapes, for all other fruits have been tasted in the course of the summer. But grapes come from distant, warm countries and are expensive, so not all can afford to partake of this luxury. Pious Jews, therefore, deny themselves one certain fruit all summer long, in order to be able to make the special blessing over it at the Rosh Hashanah table on the second evening.

Rosh Hashanah is not a home festival. Meals are eaten in the home, but the entire observance and ceremonial is in the synagogue. For this reason the cantor plays the chief role in the festival, and the better his voice, the more involved his trills and arpeggios, the greater is the satisfaction one receives from the festival.

Services start very early in the morning and do not end till after midday. All the prayers are recited and chanted with pious fervor. But there are, in addition, certain exalted moments when the spirit that fills all hearts on the Days of Awe expands and religious feelings are raised to the highest pitch. Such an exalted moment comes at the blowing of the *shofar*. Psalms 47 is recited seven times; then all quiets down. The hearts of the worshipers beat fast; and when the trumpeter calls out "Blessed be," the beginning of the benediction, a tremor of awe and fear passes through the congregation.

The greatest and most exalted moment of the service comes when the ark of the Torah is opened and the chant of *Unetanneh Tokef* begins. An unnatural fear grips the hearts of the worshipers. They pull their prayer shawls over their heads and recite the words in a loud voice, with tears and sobs. The sobbing and weeping is much louder in the women's section. The women weep oceans of tears as they read the simple, yet expressive words that tell how God judges the world on that fearful and solemn day.

The moans die down and the congregation calms itself somewhat at the words: "But Repentance, Prayer, and Charity avert the evil decree."

There is no sleeping or promenading after the midday meal. As soon as dinner is finished, the worshipers return to the synagogue to recite Psalms and conduct the afternoon services. And after that comes the *Tashlikh* custom. The entire town, young and old, dressed in festive array, goes out to a nearby stream, men and women at different points on the river, and recite the *Tashlikh* prayers, so named from the passage in Micah read there which begins with the word, *ve-tashlikh* (and Thou wilt cast [all their sins into the depths of the sea]).

There is a slight respite after this ceremony, during which tea is served, and a festive feeling rules. But then people rush back to the synagogue and chant Psalms again, until it is time for evening prayers.

With the exception of the *Tashlikh* ceremony, the entire ritual of the day is repeated on the morrow.

Translated by Samuel Jaffe[1]

THE DAYS OF PENITENCE IN A LITHUANIAN VILLAGE

LEON KOBRIN

Shortly before the Solemn Days, even as decade upon decade before, the heavens hung gray and gloomy over the forest, and out of grayness at times came the long-drawn, angry caw of a crow; the village was redolent of the gathering produce of the surrounding fields—of ripe apples from the neighboring orchards, of fruit for the local gentile neighbors, of the heavy depression that came to all the Jews there with New Year's Day and the Day of Atonement.

And upon the countenances of the men and women shopkeepers would fall a preoccupied earnestness; every heart would turn to God's mercy, entreating a prosperous new year to be written down against their name, and sealed, and every heart trembled before the Lord's wrath.

Not a curse could be heard, nor any scolding. Folks were afraid to curse when heaven was astir with preparations to write and seal the fates of all, and the earth bustled with purification from sin. All did their utmost to bury their evil feelings toward their neighbor until the awe-inspiring days should pass. . . .

The older children, too, became more pious during this season; they were more fervent in the recitation of their prayers and shunned all transgressions. Particularly did they avoid such transgressions as were punishable by having their years cut off in their prime.

A youngster is standing in prayer. Into the lower windows of the house peers a gray, cloudy morning. The child is about ten, pale and thin, wearing patched trousers through which hangs the grimy tail of his shirt. In his hands is a prayer book, and he recites with deep fervor, in a loud voice. His mother enters from without, exhausted, bearing a small basket; she is likewise pale, of small build, and still young; a shawl is thrown over her shoulders and a kerchief over her head, completely hiding her hair. She deposits the basket upon the table and begins to extract cookies from its depths, counting them in a whisper. The reckoning concluded, she replaces the cookies in the basket and glances about uneasily at her younger children, who are still asleep: one in a crib and two upon a couch. She must hurry to the marketplace and set up her little stand. All the shopkeepers are already in their places and she finds it impossible to tear away from the house, for the children must be dressed and given their meal. Her husband is away in the village of Kalyeda and will probably return today or tomorrow with a little produce. At any other time she would burst into cries and curses against her children, because they snooze so and do not allow her to get away. Today, however, so near to the New Year holidays, she fears to be angry, and however much she is tortured by the thought that she is probably losing business by this delay, she masters her indignation, approaches the slumbering children, caresses them, and wakes them with a voice that throbs with tenderness.

"Get up, children! A good, good year to you, my fledglings, I'm late on account of you!"

And while she is occupied there with her younger offspring, who have now awakened, and washes their faces with a moist towel, reciting "I confess" with them, the little ten-year-old continues saying his prayers from the devotionary and every moment glances furtively at the cookies in the basket. The contents fascinate him and confuse his thoughts. In his little heart the Evil Spirit contends with the Good.

"How sweet they smell! Steal one!" urges the Evil One.

"You mustn't. That's theft. Such a sin on the very eve of New Year and the Day of Atonement!" admonishes the Spirit of Good. And the youngster turns his back upon the tempting morsels, shuts his eyes, and prays in a voice louder than ever.

"You can tell your mother afterwards and ask her forgiveness. How tasty, how sweet!" persists the Spirit of Evil. He recalls the cookie that he furtively abstracted from the basket several weeks before and can still taste its sweetness. At length he reaches a decision: he will take it only this once and then he'll confess to his mother and beg her forgiveness.

He steals backwards to the table, his eyes distended in fearful surveillance of his mother, sticks his hand behind him and fumbles around for the basket, thrusts in his fingers, withdraws them cautiously with a cookie, and quickly conceals it under his fringed garment, next to his bare bosom. Then he resumes his praying, but in a confused manner, no longer as ardently as before.

His mother has left with the basket. The youngster has finished his prayers and has gone into the street with his cookie. He is on his way to the *heder* and can feel that the stolen sweet has fallen down to his abdomen, where it has been caught in his fringed garment. As he proceeds, he debates with himself: To eat or not to eat? Yes, eat! No, not eat! It tastes so nice! But it's such a sin! Just in spite of the Evil Spirit he'll not eat it! Just in spite! But how sweet it tastes! "I'll tell mama: 'Mama, I took a cake.' Took? Stole! Stole!" he begins to scold himself in his thoughts. "That is theft! Fie! On the eve of New Year and the Day of Atonement you've committed a robbery!"

All at once he catches sight of a playmate on the way to the same *heder*—little Shlayme, "the wild creature," Mirke's little rat, a child of the same age with a scratched face, a torn cap on his head, barefoot, and a grimy shirttail likewise flapping out of his trousers. And the said Shlayme is really a wild creature. . . . Now, however, just before the Solemn Days, Shlayme has reformed and has become as meek as a dove.

He accosts Shlayme.

"Shlaymekele, I've got a cookie!"

"Where?"

"Right here."

He taps his belly.

"Give us a piece!"

"I mustn't. . . ."

"Why?"

". . . Mustn't. . . ."

"Mustn't share a cookie? Why?"

"'Cause I mustn't. . . . I took it on the quiet."

"Ooh!" cries Shlayme, with a start. "Before New Year's! Thief! . . ."

"Not from a stranger. From my mother."

"You're a thief just the same. . . . You mustn't. You die early for doing that. Just ask the rabbi and you'll see. Hurry, give it back!"

"I was ready to go myself and give it back. That's just why I told you I mustn't share."

"A big cake?" asks Shlayme suddenly. "Your mouth is watering to eat it. Let's have a look at it!"

"I mustn't," and the speaker shakes his head, breaking into a beeline dash for the marketplace.

His mother is already at her place beside her stand, which is laden with cookies, candies, and kvass.

He rushes over to her and halts briskly, brings forth from under his garment the cookie, which is warm from contact with his body, and hands it to his mother without looking at her.

"Where did you get it?" she asks, after the cookie is already in her hand.

22. *Tashlikh.* Woodcut. From *Eyn buchlijn der Judenbeicht,* by Johannes Pfefferkorn, Cologne, 1508. Spencer Collection, New York Public Library. See Chapter XIII.

23. *Tashlikh.* Pastel on canvas. By Samuel Hirszenberg (1865–1908). Tel Aviv Museum. See Chapter XIII.

194]

24. *Tashlikh*. By Marc Chagall. From *Burning Lights*, by Bella
Chagall, New York, 1946. See Chapter XIII.

25. G.I. Rosh Hashanah services on the high seas. National Jewish Welfare Board.

26. G.I. Rosh Hashanah services in Vietnam, 1965. National Jewish Welfare Board.

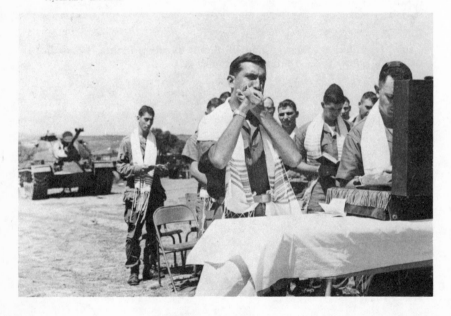

"Took it," he stammers, bringing his slender arm to his face, rubbing his nose against it and commencing to sob.

"What are you crying for?"

"I took it from your little basket," he continues to sob, while his arm has already reached his forehead; from behind it he eyes his mother with a twitching face, awaiting the slap.

But today his mother does not slap him. At any other time she would have flayed him alive, heaping curses upon him, crying: "The idea! Such a bloodsucker! With what labor she earns a kopek." Today, however, she merely says:

"It isn't nice, my son; it's a sin—on the eve of New Year. . . . I would have given it to you myself."

And this kindly speech, instead of the blow he expected, upsets him entirely and he cries more than ever, with deep contrition, with genuine repentance and all his heart. . . .

Then his mother caresses both his cheeks. "Hush, hush, you won't do it again." She wipes his nose with a corner of her skirt, presses the cookie into his hand and says:

"There, now; go to school, a sweet year to you!"

He leaves her with sparkling eyes. He is no thief; his years will not be cut off in the middle; and he has the cookie, anyway! . . .

For sheer joy he begins to kick about like a calf, and the soiled tail of his shirt dances after him. . . .

The shopkeepers sit now before their booths deeply absorbed in thought.

A peasant woman and a maiden pass by, the former with a brass kerosene vessel in her hand and the latter with an empty sack. Both wear upon their heads white linen kerchiefs and bast shoes upon their feet. The shopkeepers, however, do not stir from their places. They do not pull the prospective customers from one another, do not contend for them, but are content to call to them from where they sit, so softly and abjectly, as is possible only on the eve of New Year and the Day of Atonement. And when the peasant woman and the gentile maiden walk into Mottel's, the men and women shopkeepers say to one another:

"Well, he's a Jew as well as we. . . . May God send all Jews a happy New Year."

And Mirke, the serpent's tongue, adds with an upright, pious mien:

"Amen, Lord of the Universe, amen!"

And thus in this season, until the Day of Atonement has passed, do these Jews and their wives and children strive to be better and more pious, even as their forebears decades upon decades ago; they cleanse and scour their souls of sin, just as they do their houses and their cooking utensils for Passover, and the strange mood of the approaching Solemn Days, so mysterious and awe-inspiring, so majestic and pregnant with God's presence, grows more powerful daily, in and about them.

Translated by Isaac Goldberg[2]

NEW YEAR IN SVISLOVITZ

SHMARYA LEVIN

The week before New Year we were told not to be terrified if, in the middle of the night, we heard a knocking at the window. It would be the wakers for the night prayers which usher in the New Year. These prayers were only for the grown-ups, but I had scarcely become a *heder* boy before I begged to be taken along, and my wish was granted. That night I did not close my eyes for fear of sleeping through the call. I heard it, leaped into my clothes, and went into the living room. The samovar already stood on the table, and my father, my mother, my older brother, and I took glasses of tea before going to the synagogue.

The night was cool and clear, and in the deep blue heavens the stars shone, countless and bright. In my mind, as in the mind of every other Jewish child with my upbringing, there was not the slightest doubt that there, above, behind the stars, God sat. Our God, of course, for there was no other. He looked down between the stars and watched the Jews rising so early to go to night prayers. I was happy that I was there among the older people passing in review before Him.

The *Selihot,* or penitential prayers, made an even deeper impression on me than the Lamentations of Tishah be-Av. I saw
a synagogue packed in the dead of night; no Nebuchadnezzar
or Titus the wicked was mentioned. There was only God enthroned above the stars and toward Him our prayers streamed;
and all that was mystic in me woke in response.

On Rosh Hashanah, New Year's Day, the *yishuvniks* came to
town. There is no word for *yishuvnik* in English, for the type
is known only to us. The *yishuvniks* were the Jews who lived
abandoned in the midst of some gentile village or settlement,
alien figures in a world not their own. Months might pass
without their seeing the face of another Jew. We did our best
to make them feel at home, gave up to them our nicest rooms,
and in the synagogue assigned to them the place of honor. We
children received the children from the backwoods with all
friendliness. Some of them were wild creatures, terrified by
the vast crowds of Svislovitz. The elders took special pains with
them; my father would take some of them on his knee, caress
and comfort them, and we would teach them some of our games.

Thus the New Year would have been a jolly festival if it had
not been drummed into us that the Day of Judgment was at
hand. God sat enthroned in the midst of His cohorts of angels,
and one after another the tremendous account books were laid
before Him, with their debit and credit columns of bad and good
deeds; and God decided who should live out the next year and
who should die, who among the living should be sick, and who
well; and the prayers went into such details that my soul
trembled. Young as we were, our elders already had breathed
into us the terrors of death and had broken up the pure peace
that had been in our minds. We were spiritually careworn in
days which should have been utterly carefree. I was scarcely
more than a baby when I lay awake the night of the New Year
and implored God for mercy on my father and mother.

There was something of a relief in the *Tashlikh* ceremony,
when we went down to the river to shake our sins into it.
The place we chose was the spot behind the Castle Hill, where
the Svislo falls into the Beresina. It seemed to me like a first-
class idea. The usual ceremony was to flap the skirts of our

garments over the water; but in an excess of piety many of us turned our pockets inside out. I do not know what my sins were, but I shook my coattails and my pockets mightily, and when I left the river brink with my father I felt I had been relieved of a great weight.

Translated by Maurice Samuel[3]

ROSH HASHANAH IN VITEBSK, RUSSIA

BELLA CHAGALL

The fearful days have come, and our whole house is in an uproar. Each holiday brings with it its own savor, each is steeped in its own atmosphere. A clear, joyful, purified air, as after a rain—this is the air of Rosh Hashanah.

After the black nights of the *Selihot* prayers a bright, sunny day dawns for the New Year. The week of *Selihot* is the most restless week. Father wakes up in the middle of the night, rouses my brothers, and all of them dress quietly and go off like thieves slinking through the door.

What are they looking for in the cold, in the dark streets? It is so warm in bed! And what if they don't come back at all —how mother and I would weep and weep! I am almost beginning to cry even now, and I wrap myself closer in my blankets.

In the morning when father drinks his tea his face is pale and fagged. But the bustle of the holiday eve dispels everyone's weariness.

The shop is closed at an early hour. Everybody makes ready to go to *shul*. There are more preparations than ever before, as if it were the first time they were going there. Each one puts on something new—one a fresh, light-colored hat, another a new necktie, still another a new garment.

Mother dons a white silken blouse; she seems refurbished, she has a new soul, and she is eager to go to *shul*.

One of my elder brothers opens the thick prayer book for her and creases down the pages from which she must pray. They are marked with notations made by grandfather's hand many years ago: "Say this."

Mother recognizes the lines over which she wept last year. A trembling comes over her and her eyes dim with tears. She is in a hurry to go to *shul* to weep over the words, as if she were reading them for the first time.

A stack of books has been prepared for her. She wraps them in a large kerchief and takes them all with her. Must she not pray for a good year for the whole family?

As for father's books and *tallit*, the *shammash* came to fetch them to the *shul* during the day.

I remain behind, alone. The house is empty, and I too feel emptied. The old year, like a thing forlorn, drags itself away somewhere outside. The coming year must be a clear one, a bright one. I want to sleep through the night as quickly as possible.

On the following day in the morning I too go to *shul*. I too wear new garments from tip to toe. The sun is shining, the air is clear and alive. My new shoes give a dry tap. I walk faster. The New Year must be already arrived in *shul*. The *shofar* must be sounding there; even now it echoes in my ears. I fancy that the sky itself has come down lower and hurries to *shul* together with me. I run to the women's section, I push open the door. A whiff of heat comes from there, as from an oven. The heavy air stifles my breath. The *shul* is packed full. The high lecterns are piled with books. Old women sit bent, sunk in their chairs. Girls stand almost on the heads of the grandmothers. Children tumble underfoot.

I want to elbow my way to mother. But she is sitting so far off, all the way up at the front, next to the window that opens into the men's section. As soon as I try to move, a woman turns around to me, a weeping face gives me an angry look.

"Oh! Oh!" She breathes wrath at me.

I am pushed from behind; I am suddenly freed, and thrown to the handrail.

My mother signals to me with her eyes. She is glad that I am near her. But where is the *shofar*? Where is the New Year?

I look at the walls of the men's section. The ark of the Torah is closed, its curtains drawn. Silently and calmly the two embroidered lions guard it. The congregation is in a tumult, as though busy with something else. Have I come too early or too late?

Suddenly from under a *tallit* a hand holding a *shofar* stretches out and remains suspended in the air. The *shofar* blares out; everyone is awakened. They are all very still. They wait. The *shofar* gives another blast. The sound is chopped off, as though the horn were out of breath.

People exchange glances. The *shofar* trumpets hoarsely. A murmur ripples through the *shul*.

What manner of *shofar*-blowing is that? He lacks strength. Perhaps another man should be called up.

And then suddenly, as though the trumpet-blower had pushed out the evil spirit that was clogging the *shofar*, there comes a pure, long sound. Like a summons it runs through the whole *shul*, sounding into every corner. The congregation is relieved: one gives a sigh, another nods his head. The sound rises upward. The walls are touched by it. It reaches me and my handrail. It throbs up to the ceiling, pushes the thick air, fills every empty space. It booms into my ears, my mouth, I even feel an ache in my stomach. When will the *shofar* finish trumpeting? What does the New Year want of us?

I recall all my sins. God knows what will happen to me: so much has accumulated during the year!

I can hardly wait for afternoon. I am eager to go with mother to the rite of *Tashlikh*, to shake off all my sins, cast them into our big river. Other women and men are on their way. All of them walk down the little street that leads to the river bank. All of them are dressed in black; they might be going, God forbid, to a funeral. The air is sharp. From the high river bank, from the big city park, a wind is blowing; leaves are falling, yellow, red-yellow, like butterflies; they whirl in the air, turn over, scatter on the ground. Do our sins fly in the same way? The leaves rustle, stick to my shoes. I drag them along. Having them, it is less fearsome to go through the *Tashlikh*.

"Why do you stop all the time?" Mother pulls me by the hand. "Let the leaves alone!"

Soon everyone stops. The street seems suddenly to end; the deep, cool waters seem to be flowing up to our feet.

On the river bank dark clusters of people have gathered. The men, with their heads thrust out and their beards swaying, bend down to the water, as though they wanted to see the very bottom. Suddenly they turn their pockets inside out; little crumbs, scraps, detach themselves from the linings. The men recite a prayer aloud and throw their crumbs, together with the sins, into the water. But how shall I shake off my sins? I have no crumbs in my pockets—I do not even have pockets.

I stand next to mother, shivering from the cold wind that lifts our skirts. Mother tells me the ritual words that I have to say, and the prayers together with the sins fall from my mouth straight into the water. I fancy that the river is swollen with all our sins, and it rolls along with its waters suddenly turned black.

My burden eased away, I return home. Mother at once sits down to read Psalms. She wants still to make use of the day to obtain something more from God. A humming fills the dark room. The air becomes clouded, like mother's spectacles. Mother is weeping, silently shaking her head.

What shall I do?

I fancy that from the closely printed lines of the Psalms our grandfathers and grandmothers come gently out to us. Their shadows sway, they draw themselves out like threads, encircle me. I am afraid to turn around. Perhaps someone is standing at my back and wants to seize me in his arms.

"Mother!" I cannot contain myself, I shake her by the sleeve.

She raises her head, blows her nose, and ceases weeping. She kisses the psalter and closes it.

"Bashke," she says, "I'm going to *shul*. We'll be back soon, all of us. Will you set the table, my child?"

"Mother, is it for the *Sheheheyanu*?"

As she goes out I open the cupboards. I drag out the tall paper bags filled with fruit and spread all of it out on the table.

As in a great garden, thick green melons roll on the table. Beside them lie clusters of grapes, white and red. Big, juicy pears have turned over on their little heads. There are sweet yellow apples that have a golden gleam—they look as if they had been dipped in honey. Plums, dark red, scatter all over the table.

Over what shall we offer the benediction of first fruits? Haven't we eaten of all these things all year long?

I notice that from another bag there protrudes, like a fir tree, a pineapple, a new, unfamiliar fruit.

"Sasha, do you know where pineapples grow?"

"Who knows?" She spreads her hands. "I've got other things to think about!"

No one knows whence the pineapple comes. With its scaly skin it looks like a strange fish. But its tail stands up at the top like an open fan. I touch its stuffed belly, and it trembles from top to bottom. It is not a casual matter to touch the pineapple; it behaves somewhat like an emperor. I reserve the center of the table for it.

Sasha slices it pitilessly. The pineapple groans under her sharp knife like a live fish. Its juice, like white blood, trickles onto my fingers. I lick them. It is a tart-sweet taste.

Is this the taste of the New Year?

"Dear God," I whisper hurriedly, "before they all come back from *shul*, give a thought to us! Father and mother pray Thee all day long in *shul* to grant them a good year. And father always thinks of Thee. And mother remembers Thy Name at every step! Thou knowest how toilworn they are, how care-ridden. Dear God, Thou canst do everything! Make it so that we have a sweet, good year!"

I quickly sprinkled powdered sugar on the pineapple.

"*Gut yom-tov! Gut yom-tov!*" My brothers run in, trying to outshout one another.

They are followed immediately by father and mother, who look pale and tired.

"May you be inscribed for a happy year!"

My heart leaps up. I imagine that God himself is speaking through their mouths.

Translated by Norbert Guterman[4]

IN A RURAL COMMUNITY IN GERMANY

HERMANN SCHWAB

The month of Elul with the sound of *shofar* and the *Selihot* days filled the hearts of the village community with solemn devotion.

The service on *Selihot* days started in the small hours of the morning, at four or five o'clock. From all parts of the village the families arrived at the synagogue, led by the father who carried the stable lantern. Generally there were also visitors from villages in the neighborhood who came on foot, by carriage, or on horseback. Autumn was approaching, and rough winds were blowing in the mountainous districts at night. Arriving before dawn, the visitors were the guests of the *parnas* or teacher for a hot drink, before the commencement of the service and the fast which was the rule on the first *Selihot* day. After the conclusion of the service the guests sat together with their hosts for an hour to discuss Jewish affairs, local events, and business matters. The political scene also appeared in their talks together with their hopes and fears for the future.

An important requisite for the High Holy Days was the *mahzor*. The *mahzorim* of old were mighty folios, bound in leather and often fitted with a metal clasp. The *mahzor* was treated with great respect. On the eve of Rosh Hashanah it was solemnly taken to the synagogue.

"May you be inscribed for a happy year" were the words of felicitation going round the synagogue after the conclusion of the service on the eve of Rosh Hashanah. In the early morning men and women returned to the synagogue to stay there until noon. When the *shofar* sounded through the windows, and the mighty voice reached the houses of the non-Jews, they paused for a moment and listened to a message which they could not understand. In the afternoon the congregation went to the nearest brook or river to say *Tashlikh*. The Gentiles were very familiar with this custom; they used to say: "The Jews are throwing their sins into the river."[5]

NEW YEAR IN MARSEILLES

ISRAEL COHEN

Being the solemn day of New Year, we wended our way to the synagogue. It is a modern and imposing building, standing back a little from the narrow street in which it is situated, the space between the entrance and the tall railings forming a convenient exercise-ground for the little knots of worshipers who came out in quest of fresh air. The French flag fluttered aloft from either gate in honor of the great day, and a policeman was on duty to see that fervor of devotion did not bubble over perchance into some emotional outburst. Within there was a large and animated congregation, which showed that though Jewish life was decaying in the interior of Provence it was still fairly vigorous in what the medieval traveler Benjamin of Tudela described as "a city of princely and wise citizens." Not only the body of the shrine but the two women's galleries were filled, and as the day was warm and few windows were open, the air was oppressive. The men presented a strange contrast to their co-religionists in any English synagogue, not so much in appearance—although there were many Algerians and Tunisians among them—as in attire, for among the whole of the devout assembly there was not a single silk hat. There were all kinds of other headgear—bowlers of London pattern, trilbies of different hue, straw hats, cloth caps, even the peaked hats of two or three Jewish soldiers and the quaint cylinders of the cantors, but though I scanned every row of worshipers from the entrance doors to the ark my eye did not light upon the sheen of a single top hat. Even the president, who occupied an elevated pew near the ark, bravely sported a circular hat of straw!

The most distinguished-looking hats of all were those on the heads of the beadles. They were magnificent structures, shaped like the cocked hats of a Lord Lieutenant and adorned with a white and red cockade, whilst the rest of the attire of these functionaries was in keeping, consisting of black coattails, white tie, and a silver shield on the breast suspended by a chain round the neck. Not even the Marshal of the City of London could have stalked with a prouder bearing than the senior beadle, as he headed the procession of the cantors and the scrolls of the Torah through the thronged aisles to the ark, which was draped, not with a curtain of symbolic white, as in England, but with a brocade of palish brown. And the rabbi, clad from head to foot exactly like a padre, must have felt a little thrill of pride as he saw the flock crowding round the scrolls, which they were so eagerly anxious to touch, if not with their lips, with the corner of their *tallit*, whilst the women high above, many of them with a dark lace mantilla over the head, threw out their hands in an imaginary caress and kissed the tips of their fingers.[6]

HOW AFGHAN JEWS CELEBRATE ROSH HASHANAH

REUBEN KASHANI

For Afghans as well as other Jews, the High Holy Days really start with the month of Elul, a time of heart-searching and repentance. Afghans lay particular stress on Torah study and alms-giving during that month, and their nightly recitations of *Selihot* at synagogue are attended *en masse*, even by young children.

A salient feature of the eve of Rosh Hashanah service is the Remission of Vows, at which, for some reason, Afghan women make a particular point of being present. Nor will they leave for home until they have heard the thrice-uttered solemn formulas, "You are absolved," "You are released." After this ceremony, a sheep is slaughtered. The meat is then distributed to the poor—except the head, which is served up at the table on Rosh Hashanah night for a benediction to be recited over it in remembrance of the ram that was sacrificed in place of Isaac.

On the afternoon preceding Rosh Hashanah, the worshipers meet for the actual reception of the New Year. The prayer-leader, usually a venerable old man, chants the prayers and *piyyutim*, in part amid tears and in heartbroken tones, while the congregation responds with refrains such as "Let a year and its curses end" up to the final "Let a year and its blessings begin."

While in some Afghan synagogues the service is conducted by the rabbi (known as *mulla*) alone, in most of them respected laymen take turns as prayer-leaders or assistant prayer-leaders. The latter (called *somkhim*, "supporters") are required, *inter alia*, to recite aloud the *Amidah* prayer—usually said *sotto voce*—to allow for the fact that not all congregants possess prayer books. None expects a material reward for his labors.

In contrast to the tense, awesome mood at synagogue, the atmosphere at home on Rosh Hashanah night is one of relaxed cheerfulness, in keeping with the belief that he who is happy that night is assured of happiness throughout the year. All the members of the family sit on the floor, on carpets and cushions, around the well-laid table.

After *Kiddush*, they each lift an apple coated with honey and the oldest member of the party prays "that we may be granted a good and sweet new year." Next, pieces of the aforementioned sheep's head are touched "that we may be head and not tail." Then come pieces of the lung, "that our sins may be light as the lung." Other benedictions are over the beet (*selek*): "that all our enemies may go away" (*yistalku*); the carrot (*gezer*): "tear up the harsh sentence [*gezar din*] imposed on us"; the pomegranates: "may we be full as the pomegranate of meritorious deeds"; and so on. The benedictions are followed by reading of the *Mishnah* and the cabbalistic *Zohar*. Part of the proceedings are translated into the vernacular for the benefit of any present who do not understand Hebrew.

Next morning, the scene shifts again to the synagogue, where the prayers lead to the climax of the day's service, the blowing of the *shofar*. Again, there are moving recitations of *piyyutim* by the prayer-leaders and their assistants; the rabbi proclaims the thirteen attributes of the Almighty; the portion of the Law is read.

Finally, the *shofar*-blower mounts the dais. With growing tension, the congregation hears him chant the songs preliminary to the blowing, sometimes drawing out a note or trill as long as his breath allows, sometimes pausing to heighten the effect of some passage of magical import.

Eventually, he recites "the *shofar*-blower's prayer," humbly declaring his utter unworthiness of the high office entrusted to him. And then, amidst reverent silence in the congregation, he sounds the thirty blasts, each announced by a *somekh* standing beside him. The service continues into the afternoon, though the children go home to eat after hearing the *shofar*.

At home on Rosh Hashanah, most of the time is devoted to sacred study. The father sings and translates to the members of his family portions of the Bible and other texts. Study is continued after dinner, the post-prandial nap being out of order for once. On Rosh Hashanah, old and young try to read through the Book of Psalms twice, since the number of its chapters multiplied by two—300—is the numerical value of the Hebrew word for pardon, *kaper*.[7]

NAVIACHA SAN OF THE BENE-ISRAEL

Haeem Samuel Kehimkar

Elul is a month specially dedicated to the preparation for the approaching days of judgment and expiation. Israelites therefore daily offer propitiatory prayers early in the morning at four o'clock called *Selihot*. The devout Bene-Israel fast, taking only one meal every day in the evening during the month, except on Sabbath, when they do not observe the fast. At the time of the propitiatory prayers the *shofar* is blown in the synagogue thrice at every time of prayer. On the last day of this month, the *shofar* is not blown, but when the morning service is over, the congregation divides into two parties facing each other. One party stands, while the other sits. Those standing read the *Hattarah,* or the prayer of forgiveness. Those sitting say, "As we forgive you, so may you be forgiven from on High." Then those that are standing sit down, and those that are sitting stand up, and in their turn ask and receive forgiveness. This having been done, they kiss one another's hands and return home, where children kiss the hands of the mothers and sisters. During this month new clothes are made and houses are whitewashed.

Tishri is the most important of all the months on account of its sacred days. The first and second of this month are kept as New Year's days, and have been always solemnized as a great feast since the religious revival, but previous to that day, only one New Year day was observed by the Bene-Israel. This holiday was called by them *Naviacha San,* which answers to New Year. . . .

During the dark ages, the Bene-Israel knew nothing more than that they were tried on this day by the Judge of the whole earth, and that on the day of *Kippur* or Atonement, which falls on the tenth of this month, they were either condemned or pardoned.

On the first night of this holiday after services, *Kiddush* is first recited, and before the supper is served grace is said over apples, dates, pumpkins, honey, fish, and a sheep's head. On the first and second day of this holy day many Bene-Israel repair to the synagogue for the morning, noon, and evening services. They also go to the seashore for *Tashlikh.*[8]

THE NEW YEAR IN COCHIN

DAVID G. MANDELBAUM

My stay in Cochin extended from Rosh Hashanah to Simhat Torah and I was able to participate in the celebration of the High Holy Days with the white Jews. On the eve of Rosh Hashanah, the entire community is to be found within the synagogue. All are in their best clothes, the young and middle-aged men in European suits, the elders in loose white trousers and knee-length shirts with a brightly colored kaftan over all. Every male, down to the youngest, wears the prayer shawl at morning services, but not usually at evening prayers. Women wear blouses and waistcloths of the usual style, but their synagogue blouses must have a strip of braid at the neck and at the sleeves, and two strips down the front. A veil attached at the waist is drawn over the head.

As the service opened, the eldest man uttered the word "*kabod.*" He was too feeble to conduct the prayers himself and he thus indicated that he passed his privilege to the next eldest man. Others took up the cry as a salutation of respect to the elder who now rose to lead the service. Everyone joined in the prayers and the pace was slow because the "i" and "a" vowels were lovingly protracted into trills and runs and arpeggios.

The evening service on this day coincided with the evening *puja*, the worship of the Hindu deity, in the Raja's temple just over the synagogue wall. From the temple there resounded the clang of a large bell, interspersed with periodic reports from what may have been a small cannon or a large firecracker. But the Hebrew service went serenely along, and at one place was fittingly combined, by an appropriate coincidence, with the Hindu worship. The prayers, in English translation, at that point were, "Praise ye the Lord. Praise him with the sound of trumpet (bang from the cannon); praise him with the psaltery and harp (bong from the bell). Praise him (bang bang) with timbrel and reed pipe. Praise him with harmonious cymbals (bang bang bang). Let everything (bong) that hath (bong) breath (bong) praise the Lord (bang bang bang bong). Hallelujah." As soon as the last prayer was said, the boys rushed forward to kiss the curtains of the ark. Whenever the scrolls are taken out of the ark to be read, men and boys press close to kiss the holy books as they are being carried.

During the services on the day of Rosh Hashanah, the *hazzan* is flanked by two young men on each side who help him chant the liturgy. It is a coveted honor to participate in this choir and the young men vie to attain it. An elder takes precedence over a younger man; those junior in age wheedle and coax their seniors to relinquish the right to them. Synagogue prerogatives are assigned largely according to age—a youth eagerly looks forward to the time when his years will entitle him to the coveted honors. For it is primarily in the synagogue that the individual may rise and shine, and there he has the opportunity of standing out from among his fellows.

The blowing of the *shofar* delighted the children. When it was taken down from the balcony to be sounded for the last time (it had previously been blown from the upper lectern), the boys crowded around to observe the technique of its use with minute attention. For hours thereafter, blasts from the thirty-inch spiral erupted from every house in which there was a *shofar*, as the boys practiced on the instrument.[9]

ROSH HASHANAH IN PERSIA, 1944

H. Z. HIRSCHBERG

Only a Spanish Marrano, I am sure, could ever appreciate the profound spiritual experience we felt when, for the first time in two and a quarter years, we prayed in a synagogue furnished with an *Aron Kodesh* and a *Sefer Torah*. For twenty-seven months we had not heard the Torah read from the scroll, for all public prayer had been eyed askance and held almost a crime against the state. Now I could walk through the streets with a *tallit* in my hand and observe the multitude, festively clad, streaming toward the New Synagogue in the wealthy quarter. The very procession lent a solemnity to the occasion. In the evening we prayed in the Little Synagogue set aside for the Ashkenazim—that is, the Jews hailing from the various European countries. Here, too, the refugees, who by now felt themselves members of a large family, prayed. After the prayers we returned home with our host, Reb Hiya.

It was the first time I found myself in the home of an Oriental Jew. Some twenty-five people were seated about the table, including the master of the house, his wife and children, and ourselves, refugees. We, who were as yet not accustomed to the usage of our Oriental brethren, gained the impression that the table had been laid for the Passover *seder* and not for Rosh Hashanah eve. There was a huge platter laden with various vegetables, roast beef, a sheep's head, and unleavened bread closely resembling the *matzot* we had baked in Russia. The newcomers sat open-mouthed, silently expectant of what was to follow. The customary *Kiddush* was pronounced. But after *Kiddush* there was no washing of the hands and blessing of the bread. Instead, they proceeded with *Seder Rosh Hashanah*. The Persian Jews have a special little book containing all the Rosh Hashanah customs, explained in the Judeo-Persian vernacular, resembling in its lingual structure Spaniolish or Yiddish and printed in Hebrew characters. In this "Haggadah" the origins and significance of the various customs are set forth, and the blessings with the corresponding *"Yehi ratzon"* printed in simple language, so that even a person not versed in the religious precepts cannot err.

The blessings began.

In the intervals, quinces, aromatic grasses, and herbs were passed round and all inhaled their fragrance while pronouncing the requisite benediction. In the meantime the master of the household and his sons recited by heart chapters from the *Zohar* and *piyyutim* (liturgical poems in Judeo-Persian, composed during the Middle Ages). I gained the impression that we exceeded the prescribed daily one hundred benedictions before we washed our hands and blessed the bread.

In the middle of the meal there were again *piyyutim*, somewhat like our own *zemirot,* all by heart. Our host told me that at one time a current custom in Persia had been to examine every eligible young man before marriage to see whether he knew by heart at least sixty to seventy chapters of the *Zohar*, and a similar number of liturgical poems; otherwise he had no prospect whatever of securing a bride of good family. Now, however, he added ruefully, Torah was being forgotten and a generation completely ignorant was arising.

The meal lasted about four hours and it was already past midnight when we went to sleep on the carpets that had been spread on the terraces in the garden.

In the morning we rose early to go to the synagogue. Out of respect for our host we went to the synagogue of the Persian Jews. Here the custom of appointed prayer-leaders is unknown, a number of notables going to the *bimah* and praying alternately in a loud voice. When one becomes tired, another continues. Nor do the Jews of Persia read the Torah with the traditional chant; they have a peculiar melody of their own. Many of those called up to the Torah read the portion themselves. The second day of the holy day fell on Sunday, but they did not restrict themselves to the prescribed number of portions, some twenty people being called up to the reading, and they continued to read and reread the portion as we do on Simhat Torah.

Tashlikh is a custom highly honored and scrupulously observed among the Persian Jews. They gather at the fish ponds with which every house is equipped, choosing one in which, at the moment, the water is running. Pockets are meticulously emptied, and the little goldfish darting rapidly up to swallow the crumbs cause them extreme gratification, for it is reckoned a good omen for the worshipers.[10]

IN THE JEWISH GHETTO OF YEMEN

S. ERNST

Not everywhere is Rosh Hashanah celebrated in the same way. Each section of the Diaspora has its own special prayers, its own rites, its own melodies.

The Yemenite Jews are in all respects a unique branch of the Jewish tree. . . . The service of the Creator permeates their every day; but never is the fear of God more present than in the season of the *Yamim Noraim*.

The fear of the Day of Judgment begins already to be felt during the week preceding Rosh Hashanah. Observance of religious practice is stricter than ever; there is an atmosphere of heightened awareness. From every corner resounds the *shofar*, blown with a force that is unimaginable for a mere European. As Tishri draws nearer, the *Selihot* are said more loudly and more intensely. The rabbi and the members of the *Bet Din* make the rounds of all the synagogues at the time of the morning prayer, carrying leaflets that contain exhortations and warnings for the Days of Repentance. The leaflets are asked for eagerly, read by all, read with eyes atremble for fear of the terrible day which is so near at hand.

On the eve of Rosh Hashanah the whole community visits the cemetery. Dense crowds offer prayers of intercession on the graves of the saintly men of olden days. Their laments are counterpointed by the faraway voice of a muezzin who calls upon the faithful to praise Allah and his true prophet Mohammed.

Evening falls. All assemble in the synagogues and squat on the rugs spread for them. Torches flame, little oil lamps spread their flickering light over the slender, brown-skinned Jews of Yemen, who know of no cantors and choirs. A venerable ancient takes his place at the prayer stand and hoarsely intones the prayers of Rosh Hashanah in a Yemenite tune. The whole congregation accompanies the *hazzan*, shouting and gesticulating, moving about and singing each at his own pitch, in the sincere belief that their prayers are the first to reach the Throne of Mercy: for are they not the most persecuted, the lowliest, the most heavily oppressed of all children of Israel?

Old and young rock their spent bodies, outshouting each other, as if they are competitors for heavenly favors. For the Yemenites actually believe that the louder one shouts, the sooner his prayer reaches Heaven and "he who shouts loudest is praiseworthy" . . . but the shouting carries an undertone, the Jewish voice that comes straight from the heart, straight from the afflicted Jewish soul.

During the whole two days of the feast the mood of fear of the Day of Judgment holds sway. All make haste to wish friends a happy year. In the synagogue everyone is absorbed in his prayers; in vain one would seek for such a silence and attention in any *shul* elsewhere. The rabbi is wholly clad in white; wears a large *tallit* with a heavy silver collar-piece. Before the reading from the Torah he recites a special hymn. The melody is unfamiliar. His throaty voice reminds one of the desert's drought. But more than its strangeness one feels its sincerity. And when his eyes go over the people they are starry and moist with love. . . . . The scrolls of the Law are decked with beautiful ornaments; the crowd presses around them to kiss them before they are read.

I have stood listening for a whole day, listening to the prayer-tunes of the Yemenites, those dusky-skinned brothers of ours from hot Arabia. And I came to see that they have the old, familiar faces; that they pray the same prayers that I have known at home; that they use the same texts; that they have the same Jewish heart as millions of Jews all over the world.

On the afternoon of the second day the atmosphere becomes more relaxed. Old and young stroll through the lanes of Sana, the women a glory of color in their exotic dresses. The quiet faces and contemplative eyes of the Yemenites remind us of those Nazarites of olden days about whom we used to learn.

At the end of the feast the rabbi preaches to the assembled community. His sermon is full of exhortations for the coming Ten Days of Repentance, of legends and allegories which often remind one of "The Thousand and One Nights."

After the evening prayer we went home, wishing each other a good year and a long life.[11]

HOLY DAYS IN THE HOLY CITY

Rahel Yanait Ben-Zvi

The High Holy Days approached. The chants of *Selihot* prayers rose all around us in the nights. The poor quarters glowed with a second and sublimer soul. Jerusalem wore its holiday face.

The eve of the New Year. Everyone grew ready for the great day. At sundown we went out, looking into synagogues through the iron grates of the windows. Voices rose in prayer in the traditional chant. We went from one synagogue to the next, standing outside and listening. Somehow we did not dare to enter, perhaps because we did not have holiday clothes. I was melancholy and the face of Avner* was covered with sadness. Was this nostalgia for the tradition of our childhood days?

The next morning we rose early and made our way to the Old City. We went down the steps of the Street of David. The covered marketplace was bustling and noisy as always. The narrow lanes smelled of fruit and vegetables, fresh and rotten. Crowds of *fellahin* and *bedouin*, with their overladen asses, jostled with Jews in their holiday finery: Ashkenazim in black silk *kapotes* or colorful velvet robes with hairy *streimels* on their heads, Sephardim in their many-colored gowns. All of them had the same expression on their faces—the look of sanctity. As if walking in some higher sphere, they passed by the traders and hurried to the synagogue, to the Wall. We, too, hastened.

Stooping, we passed under the low arch and came into the courtyard of the Hurvah Synagogue of Rabbi Yehudah the Pious. I tried to follow Joseph and Avner inside, but the angry looks of the gatekeeper warned me off. With a wave of his hand he directed me to the women's gallery, and I climbed the narrow wooden staircase. I was later to become better acquainted with this courtyard—in the days of Haganah. I climbed hesitantly and sat myself near the door. There were many women at prayer. I could almost have been back in my hometown synagogue. Here were the same spotlessly white silk kerchiefs on the women's heads, the mothers and the grandmothers grasping the familiar prayer book. I peered through the partition which separated the women's gallery from the men praying below. The chant was exactly like that of my

* The political alias of Isaac Ben-Zvi, late president of the State of Israel.

old home. When the reading of the Law was reached, I saw that Avner and Joseph were making their way out, and I hurried down the steps to join them.

Opposite the Hurvah towered the minaret of a mosque. There the muezzin summoned the faithful to prayer. His call rang out as if in challenge to the sounds of Hebrew prayer. We moved on to the synagogue of the Karaites in a nearby courtyard paved with smooth stones. The ceiling was low and domed, and the two barred windows looked out to an inner court. The building was shabby and dilapidated, but in the corners of the yard geraniums grew and ivy clung to the wall. This New Year Day was no festival for the Karaites, whose calendar differed from that of other Jews. I was depressed by the workday atmosphere and by the breach between us and these brothers of ours. This Karaite synagogue contained a treasure: a *Keter Torah*, one of the most ancient bound manuscripts of the Bible. Avner bent over it. Every word, every phrase excited his attention. Years later, in 1957, he was to bring it back to Israel from exile. [When the Arabs captured the Old City of Jerusalem and looted its synagogues, they got hold of the *Keter Torah* (Crown of the Law) and sold it to a Swedish dealer. In 1957, on the initiative of President Ben-Zvi, the Hebrew University acquired it from the dealer.]

In low spirits we left the Karaites and went on to the Sephardi synagogue of Rabbi Yohanan Ben Zaccai. A few steps led down into a dimly lit hall which echoed to the sounds of prayer. I had never heard the Sephardi ritual before. The worshipers were seated on low, narrow benches covered with straw mats, and they held sprigs of fragrant herbs. A mystic emotion welled up in me. Here we stood at the very source of Hebrew melody. This was the atmosphere I was looking for with all my heart in Jerusalem. We sat there entranced by the prayers, then wandered from room to room, the dimness accentuating the sense of antiquity.

Avner turned to the hall at the bottom of the court. I followed him and stood by the door. The strains of a familiar psalm floated up to us: "From the depths I called upon thee,

O Lord." I remembered it from childhood, from the time before I knew the meaning of the words. The cry seemed to be directed to us, perplexed as we were, striving for guidance in our land.

Translated by
David Harris and Julian Meltzer[12]

SECRET SERVICES IN WARSAW

CHAIM A. KAPLAN

October 2, 1940
The Eve of the New Year, 5701

We have no public worship, even on the High Holy Days. There is darkness in our synagogues, for there are no worshipers—silence and desolation within and sorrow looking on from without. Even for the High Holy Days there was no permission for communal worship. I don't know whether the *Judenrat* made any attempt to obtain it, but if it didn't try it was only because everyone knew in advance that the request would be turned down. Even in the darkest days of our exile we were not tested with this trial. Never before was there a government so evil that it would forbid an entire people to pray. But never before in our history, drenched in tears and blood, did we have so cruel and barbaric an enemy.

Everything is forbidden to us. The wonder is that we are still alive and that we do everything. And this is true of public prayer, too. Secret *minyanim* by the hundreds throughout Warsaw organize services and do not skip over even the most difficult hymns in the liturgy. There is not even a shortage of sermons. Everything is in accordance with the ancient customs of Israel. When there is no informer at work, the enemy doesn't know what is going on, and we can assume that no Jewish man, even if he is a Jew born in Poland, would inform on Jews standing before their Maker in prayer.

They pick some inside room whose windows look out onto the courtyard and pour out their supplications before the God of Israel in whispers. This time there are no cantors and choirs, only whispered prayers. But the prayers are heartfelt; it is possible to weep in secret, too, and the gates of tears are not locked.

And so we give praise to the God of Israel "who kept us alive and supported us and brought us unto this season." During the year many individuals drank the cup of hemlock; many have gone to their graves. The community has been debased and impoverished. But it still exists.

Translated by Abraham I. Katsh[13]

IN THE WARSAW GHETTO

Henry Shoskes

Once more the Jewish New Year [1941] had come. The Nazis finally gave their permission to reopen a few synagogues, but at the same time let it be known that the Jews would do better not to assemble for prayer, otherwise there might be incidents. But the Jews could not be frightened off. They went to their places of worship and they prayed:

"We celebrate the mighty holiness of this day, for it is one of awe and terror. Thereon is Thy dominion exalted and Thy throne established in mercy, and Thou sittest thereon in truth. Verily it is Thou alone who art Judge and Arbiter, who knowest and art witness. Thou writest down and settest the seal, Thou recordest and tellest. Yea, Thou rememberest the things forgotten. Thou unfoldest the records and the deeds therein inscribed proclaim themselves; for lo! the seal of every man's hand is set thereto!"

The Jews never believed, not for one moment, that God would forget them. But the world, they were certain, had forgotten them. Nobody was coming to their help. Nobody was trying to liberate them from their prison. The world was going to let them perish.

And just then they were given proof that the world had not forgotten them. Some of the Jews still had radios hidden away somewhere which they sometimes tuned in after they had locked the doors. That night they heard a secret Polish station broadcasting a New Year's greeting to the Jews in the Warsaw Ghetto.

"We Poles of whatever party or religion are mourning together with you Jews in this, the darkest hour of our history. We are waiting for the time when our and your tragedy will have finished and a new Poland will rise from the ashes. We see the sun rising for a better morning—even for you, within the walls of the ghetto. Together we will destroy our common enemy, the Nazis."

During the same night a group of Polish workers approached the walls of the ghetto near Chlodna Street and threw flowers over the wall. There was a little card, too, which said that this was a New Year's greeting from the Polish workers of the Wola factories.[14]

TASHLIKH IN THE WARSAW GHETTO

JOHN HERSEY

Yesterday was Rosh Hashanah, the first day of a new Jewish year [1942]. How relentless the calendar is! While we had all been assembled at the bakery, the night before, talking about Stefan and Symka, Reb Yehiel Mazur had expressed the wish that he could get to the banks of the Vistula the following day, in order to pronounce, at the side of a body of water moving toward the sea, the customary New Year's prayer for the washing away of sins. Wladislaw Jablonski, overhearing, said jokingly that he could lead Reb Yehiel Mazur to a passable place for saying this prayer: the culvert of the sewer where he had hidden during the last days of the "registration." Reb Yehiel took the joke seriously: he said he thought that would be all right—the sewer ran into the Vistula, and the Vistula into the sea. He really wanted to go; he became insistent. Wladislaw agreed at last to take him.

Early yesterday morning, before it was time to go to work,

Wladislaw led Reb Yehiel Mazur to an apartment house on Mila Street, and took him down to the cellar under one of the staircases, and there he lit a carbide lamp and took a shovel into a coal bin and moved some of the coal within to one side. A barrelhead was exposed. Wladislaw took the barrelhead away from the wall, and this uncovered the mouth of a small tunnel. Through this tunnel, which sloped downward about four meters, Wladislaw, holding the lamp, led Reb Yehiel Mazur. The smell there was evil. The two came to the big concrete pipe of the sewer. A hole had been chiseled through from the tunnel. The sewer pipe was about a meter high. Wladislaw, who wanted to stay in the tunnel, let Reb Yehiel Mazur wriggle past and the older man went down into the tube. A foul, watery stream, apparently not much more than ankle-deep, ran along the drainage-way. Reb Yehiel Mazur crouched all doubled over, with a foot on each side of the pipe above the stream. Wladislaw, the Jewish boy who had been brought up to be a Catholic, held the light down through the jagged, chiseled hole, as the voice of Reb Yehiel Mazur echoed and echoed in the arched conduit.

". . . And Thou wilt cast all their sins into the depths of the sea. Oh, mayest Thou cast all the sins of Thy people, the house of Israel, into a place where they shall be no more remembered or visited, or even again come to mind. Thou wilt show faithfulness to Jacob, and lovingkindness to Abraham, as Thou hast sworn unto our fathers from days of old."

Reb Yehiel Mazur raised his head, sighed, and said he was ready to go back. Wladislaw says that in the light of the carbide lamp the elderly man's face, bent down over the stream, during the prayer, had had a look of repugnance, as if the noisome waters of this ghetto stream did in fact contain all the sins of Israel.[15]

RESCUE IN DENMARK ON ROSH HASHANAH

HAROLD FLENDER

On the morning of Wednesday, September 29, 1943, Rabbi Marcus Melchior stood before the Holy Ark of the 110-year-old Copenhagen synagogue.

It was the day before Rosh Hashanah, the Jewish New Year. About 150 members of the congregation were present. They were puzzled by the fact that Rabbi Melchior was not in his rabbinical robes.

"There will be no service this morning," said Rabbi Melchior. "Instead, I have very important news to tell you. Last night I received word that tomorrow the Germans plan to raid Jewish homes throughout Copenhagen to arrest all the Danish Jews for shipment to concentration camps. They know that tomorrow is Rosh Hashanah and our families will be home. The situation is very serious. We must take action immediately. You must leave the synagogue now and contact all relatives, friends, and neighbors you know are Jewish and tell them what I have told you. You must tell them to pass the word on to everyone they know is Jewish. You must also speak to all your Christian friends and tell them to warn the Jews. You must do this immediately, within the next few minutes, so that two or three hours from now everyone will know what is happening. By nightfall tonight we must all be in hiding.". . .

Rabbi Melchior's warning to his congregation of the planned German raid stunned them into silence. When he exhorted them to leave immediately to spread the word throughout Copenhagen, a few were too shocked to move.

"You must do what I tell you!" Melchior shouted and those who had lingered behind departed, leaving the rabbi alone in the deserted prayer hall.

Melchior was forty-six years old. He and his wife had five children. He wondered whom he could call upon to give refuge to his large family. He wondered about the holy objects of the synagogue—the scrolls of the Torah, silver candelabra, prayer

books—where could they be safely hidden? He decided to call
his friend Pastor Hans Kildeby, Lutheran minister at the church
of Ørslev, sixty miles south of Copenhagen. Pastor Kildeby told
Rabbi Melchior to set out with his family to Ørslev as soon as
possible. . . .

Before leaving with his family for Ørslev, Melchior contacted
another Lutheran minister he knew—the pastor of the church
down the street from the Copenhagen synagogue. The pastor
agreed to hide all of the synagogue's holy objects in the cellar
of his church.

Word of the planned German raid spread quickly. Following
Melchior's instructions, those who had attended the early morning service at the synagogue pointed out to everyone they knew
the importance of going into hiding. . . .

Magnus Ruben, a young Orthodox Jew and a lawyer, had
planned to leave his office early in the afternoon to help his
wife prepare for Rosh Hashanah. Just before departing, he
decided to call his friend Erik Hertz to wish him a happy New
Year.

"I'm afraid," said Hertz, "it won't be a very happy New Year
for us."

"Why?"

"I'm not feeling well."

"Are you sick?"

"No, it's just that I'm not feeling well, my wife Ruth is not
feeling well, my whole family is not feeling well, and you are
not feeling well, too. I cannot say any more over the telephone.
Do you understand?"

"I think so."

"We are supposed to receive guests this evening," said Hertz,
"but we don't plan to be home. You shouldn't plan to be home
either.". . .

Ruben went home and found his wife washing dishes that
had been left over from lunch. He told her why they had to
leave immediately.

"All right," said his young wife. "We'll leave as soon as I
finish the dishes."

27. Sounding the *shofar*. Ministry for Foreign Affairs, State of Israel.

28. Sounding the *shofar*. Israel Information Services, New York.

29. *Tashlikh* around a well in the courtyard of a synagogue in Jerusalem. Ministry for Foreign Affairs, State of Israel. See Chapter XX.

30. *Tashlikh* on the shores of the Mediterranean. Ministry for Foreign Affairs, State of Israel.

"There's no time to finish the dishes," said Ruben. "The Germans may be here any minute."

"But," asked Mrs. Ruben, "how will it look for them to find dirty dishes in the sink?"

Ruben had to employ force to get her to leave the dishes. . . .

Thanks to the spontaneous, willing, and effective cooperation of Jew and non-Jew, Rabbi Melchior's wish that within a matter of hours every Jew in Denmark know the danger that faced him was largely fulfilled. Word was gotten to almost everyone directly concerned, except the Germans.

Shortly before midnight, September 29, 1943, two German transport vessels, including the large *Wartheland*, dropped anchor in Copenhagen harbor. Several hours later, after midnight, the Germans struck. Trucks filled with Gestapo commandos and special German police raced through the streets to arrest the eight thousand Jews living in Denmark. . . .

Throughout the long night, the Gestapo, armed with address lists, raided the residences of Denmark's eight thousand Jews.

They were not at home.[16]

REVIVAL IN SICILY

Samuel Teitelbaum

My first overseas assignment was with the organization that came to be known as the Island Base Section (IBS) of Sicily. We landed in Palermo on August 7, 1943, after crossing the Mediterranean from Bizerte, Tunis, in LSTs. The city had fallen into American hands only a few days earlier.

The number of Jews on the entire island, even prior to the war, had been insignificant; perhaps 50 to 75 families, many of them intermarried and few, except the children, native. Only 15 to 25 Jewish families survived by the time we were disembarked in Sicily.

Chaplain Earl S. Stone of 7th Army Headquarters had arrived in Sicily some days earlier. The religious services he

instituted for Jewish military personnel in Palermo were the
first organized Jewish services on the island probably since the
days of the Inquisition. After my arrival, Chaplain Stone and I
alternated covering the occupied areas of the island to bring
religion to as many Jewish servicemen as possible. A sprinkling
of Sicilian Jewish civilians occasionally appeared at these
services.

We were in a particularly bad fix as the High Holy Days
approached. We had practically no equipment, not even JWB
prayer books. The promised shipment had not arrived. And
we had no place to worship.

I investigated a Methodist church, which, like all Protestant
churches in this part of the world, was a rarity. It was usable,
even though it had been damaged severely and lacked windows,
seats, and other appurtenances. I drove out to Santa Flavia,
about 12 miles from Palermo, to contact the pastor and secure
his permission to use the church for Jewish worship (it had
not been used for some time). The pastor, a kindly old man,
readily agreed. I, in turn, promised to have the building refurbished and to obtain contributions from my men for the
maintenance of the church.

Thus we did establish our "Methodist *shul*"! It was spic-and-
span for the *Yamim Noraim*. Headquarters cooperated mag-
nificently and our Rosh Hashanah services (September 29–30,
1943) were more than awe-inspiring. All the seats were occupied by soldiers, including some British, and a few civilians.
Men stood in the aisles, in the corridors and vestibules, and
even outside on the broken sidewalk and street. They joined
heartily and heartfully in the praying and chanting. The
hazzanim, all GIs—especially my assistant, Corporal Irving
Fishman—were in excellent voice. We had no *shofar*; a bugler
sounded the traditional notes on a bugle. We had no *Sefer
Torah*; we cantillated from a *Humash* I had managed to scrape
up. The one *mahzor* we had was lent to us by a civilian and
served for the cantor and myself, while the congregation
listened attentively.

These were the first organized High Holy Day services in

Sicily in several hundred years. I had a number of signs painted and posted to direct the men to our *"shul."* What a transformation! In a city where organized Jewish services were virtually unknown, where Judaism had not been recognized since the Spanish Inquisition, where, indeed, our faith and culture had been almost proscribed, where the Fascist regime had cruelly persecuted the few Jews who lived on the island and the Nazis had nearly succeeded in exterminating them, we were now able to announce publicly in bold, red letters: "JEWISH SERVICES."[17]

XVI

ROSH HASHANAH IN POETRY

ROSH HASHANAH

PENINA MOISE

Into the tomb of ages past
Another year hath now been cast;
Shall time unheeded take its flight,
Nor leave one ray of higher light,
That on man's pilgrimage may shine
And lead his soul to spheres divine?

Ah! which of us, if self-reviewed,
Can boast unfailing rectitude?
Who can declare his wayward will
More prone to righteous deed than ill?
Or, in his retrospect of life,
No traces find of passion's strife?

With firm resolve your bosom nerve
The God of right alone to serve;

Speech, thought, and act to regulate,
By what His perfect laws dictate;
Nor from His holy precepts stray,
By worldly idols lured away.

Peace to the house of Israel!
May joy within it ever dwell!
May sorrow on the opening year,
Forgetting its accustomed tear,
With smiles again fond kindred meet.
With hopes revived the festal greet![1]

THE NEW YEAR

ROSH HASHANAH, 1882

EMMA LAZARUS

Not while the snow-shroud round dead earth is rolled,
    And naked branches point to frozen skies—
When orchards burn their lamps of fiery gold,
    The grape glows like a jewel, and the corn
A sea of beauty and abundance lies,
        Then the new year is born.

Look where the mother of the months uplifts
    In the green clearness of the unsunned West,
Her ivory horn of plenty, dropping gifts,
    Cool, harvest-feeding dews, fine-winnowed light;
Tired labor with fruition, joy and rest
        Profusely to requite.

Blow, Israel, the sacred cornet! Call
    Back to thy courts whatever faint heart throb
With thine ancestral blood, thy need craves all.
    The red, dark year is dead, the year just born
Leads on from anguish wrought by priest and mob,
        To what undreamed-of morn?

For never yet, since on the holy height,
    The Temple's marble walls of white and green

Carved like the sea-waves, fell, and the world's light
Went out in darkness—never was the year
Greater with portent and with promise seen,
    Than this eve now and here.

Even as the Prophet promised, so your tent
    Hath been enlarged unto earth's farthest rim.
To snow-capped Sierras from vast steppes ye went,
    Through fire and blood and tempest-tossing wave,
For freedom to proclaim and worship Him,
    Mighty to slay and save.

High above flood and fire ye held the scroll,
    Out of the depths ye published still the Word.
No bodily pang had power to swerve your soul:
    Ye, in a cynic age of crumbling faiths,
Lived to bear witness to the living Lord,
    Or died a thousand deaths.

In two divided streams the exiles part,
    One rolling homeward to its ancient source,
One rushing sunward with fresh will, new heart.
    By each the truth is spread, the law unfurled,
Each separate soul contains the nation's force,
    And both embrace the world.

Kindle the silver candle's seven rays,
    Offer the first fruits of the clustered bowers,
The garnered spoil of bees. With prayer and praise
    Rejoice that once more tried, once more we prove
How strength of supreme suffering still is ours
    For Truth and Law and Love.[2]

THAT WE BE REBORN

HILLEL ZEITLIN

Father of all that are born,
Thou createst Thy world anew every moment.

Wouldst Thou but for a moment withhold Thy creative love,
The whole universe would come to an end
  But Thou pourest out Thy blessings on Thy creatures every
  instant.

So the morning stars renew their song of love to Thee;
The sun in its might keeps singing its songs of strength to Thee.
  The angels chant over and over their song of holiness to Thee;
  The souls of mortals repeat the song of their thirst for Thee.

The blades of grass take up the tune of their yearning for Thee;
The birds keep chirping and twittering their carols of joy to
  Thee.
  The trees wrap themselves in their *tallit* of leaves and offer
  their worship to Thee;
  The fountains in whispered cadences murmur their prayer
  to Thee.

And the voice of one, poor and crushed, pours forth his plaint
  to Thee.
And lo, the soul of his prayer cleaves a path through the heavens
  to Thee;
  And, though bent his back 'neath the weight of awe at Thy
  majesty,
  His soul is uplifted to Thee.

Turn on me but one ray of Thy light and, lo, I am steeped
  in light;
Let but one word issue from Thee and I rise resurrected;
  But one throb of Thy life eternal and I am drenched in the
  dew of youth.

Dost Thou not continually renew Thy creation, O my Father?
Take me Thy child and make me over.
  Breathe Thy spirit into me that I may live, that I may start
  life afresh
  With childhood's unbounded promise.

                              Translated by Eugene Kohn[3]

SHOFAROT*

SHIN SHALOM

In grandfather's house, Atonement Day drew near.
The sacred trumpet blew so loud, so much,
The pregnant women would come at dusk to hear,
And smooth my bedclothes with an absent touch.

Their eyes knew secrets, brimming with a tear
As they smoothed down my sheet. I did not see:
What has this gentle hand that draws so near
To do with sorrow none can remedy?

An amulet lay on my breast: they'd bend
To press soft lips there, shuddering painfully.
And then I prayed that this would never end,
For sweet and soft their lips were, touching me.

So smooth their cheeks were, drawn across my cheek,
I wanted more; my mouth was moved to ask.
But all the sacred trumpets would suddenly speak
And every face would turn to a white mask.

Translated by Dom Moraes[4]

PIYYUT FOR ROSH HASHANAH

HAYYIM GURI

For this is not the road against which stand enemy lines, or
    foreign languages
Or muteness.
Neither I nor my voice is tied by the conditions set on these
    distances.
I walk and I am not murdered.
I come at last to the house. I stop. I knock at the door.

All men who forgive say. What has been has been. I repeat.
All women who forgive stand on the porches sooner or later.

* All rights reserved by the author.

There is a window which is not black. There is a letter which is
not lost on the way.
And if it did not arrive yesterday it will certainly arrive
tomorrow.

All the cities are open tonight. None is besieged or embalmed.
Guests will arrive tonight and I am one of them.
In all the windows branches of regret are opening one after
the other.
Many words come up in pilgrimage from lands of silence and
death.

The curtains billow and the doors move on their hinges.

Translated by Ruth Finer Mintz[5]

IN PRAISE OF ANOTHER YEAR

JOANNE GREENBERG

In heaven and on earth,
In a clap of thunder, in a whisper of the soul,
In praise on yellowed parchment in an ancient tongue,
In yearning of the heart, in a child not yet born,
Blessed be He.

Taste of tears and wine, sight of starry skies,
Old men's voices warping the chant, children singing,
Scientists asking, artists proclaiming,
Blessed be He.

All the web of creation shining in His bright sunlight.
The dew that has gathered in darkness
Transfixes the light of day.
Blessed be He.

I am afraid of my suffering, and ashamed,
But He made it. May I be worthy of His bitter gifts.
Who but the living can know its agonies?
The aged draw breath slowly from long-drawn pain.
Blessed be He.

Children extinguished, futures lost as broken promises;
But to have lived one moment is that much glory.
God's warm sun, God's soul-searching fire,
And moments when our only pride
Is that we have turned from nothing.

Blessed be He.

Inform us in self-knowledge, Lord Creator,
One and together;
Inform us in the hunger for peace
Between men and nations.

Grant us another year in the Book of Life,
With its peril, injustice
And the good daylight.

Amen, Amen[6]

SOUND OF THE TRUMPET

FANIA KRUGER

The *shofar*, symbol of the new year, blows;
The tone resounds, and hopeful mankind knows
It is the call of peace that's yet to be
A long-drawn note of all humanity.[7]

SELIHOT

RUTH F. BRIN

In darkening shade
lies city street
in deepening shadow
wood and meadow,
and barren and shallow
our thoughts tonight

Through blackened window
through tight closed door

no wind can wander
no light can enter,
empty our hearts
and fallow and blight

Now do we ask of Thee
deep in Thy universe
far in Thy wanderings,
Maker so merciful,
Open Thy cloudbanks
to moon full and bright

Let moonlight
illumine us,
night winds
come brushing us,
breath of Thy presence
be felt in our souls.[8]

THE *SHOFAR* CALLS

RUTH F. BRIN

The *shofar* calls: *Tekiah*
Arise! Awake! come from your beds, your homes
to the blast that calls you,
the siren that warns you:
seek shelter for your spirit
enter now the opening gates

The ram's horn cries: *Shevarim*
Worship in truth, pray together
in confidence and trust,
determined that promises shall be kept
oaths fulfilled, words spoken thoughtfully
in honor and truth

The shrill notes tremble: *Teruah*
Listen to the cries of the ancient martyrs,

Sense the unbearable silence of the dead,
Contemplate in reverence and awe
all those who died "Kiddush ha-Shem"

The *shofar* blasts: *Tekiah gedolah*
Remember! Recall the ages of our people,
Dwell on your own life in the year that has passed,
Call up from the darkness the mistakes, the errors,
the evil deeds that you must deal with now

Three times three the great horn blows: *Tekiah, shevarim,
teruah*
Return! Return to God Who made you
Arise to prayer, awake to memory, achieve repentance
Return to God Who loves you,
Now while the days of awe are passing,
before the closing of the gates.[9]

IN THE DAYS OF AWE

RUTH F. BRIN

Dangling from a leather sling in the oak,
the tree trimmer, high in the swaying tree,
reaches out to saw away a branch.
It leaves a staring eye when it drops,
a round white eye on the tree trunk.
Cautiously, with rope and saw,
tools swinging from his belt,
he crawls upward, seeking limbs to cut.

Now I too slash away unnecessary branches,
opening eyes to the sky.
Imperiled, dangling, lacking skill to choose
the limbs that stifle growth, I pray
to Thee Whose marks I bear within
like rings of trees.
I pray Thee guide my hand,
I, the tree trimmer, I the tree.[10]

XVII

ROSH HASHANAH IN
THE SHORT STORY

IF NOT HIGHER

I. L. Peretz

Early every Friday morning, at the time of the Penitential Prayers, the Rabbi of Nemirov would vanish.

He was nowhere to be seen—neither in the synagogue nor in the two houses of study nor at a *minyan*. And he was certainly not at home. His door stood open; whoever wished could go in and out; no one would steal from the rabbi. But not a living creature was within.

Where could the rabbi be? Where should he be? In heaven, no doubt. A rabbi has plenty of business to take care of just before the Days of Awe. Jews, God bless them, need livelihood, peace, health, and good matches. They want to be pious and good, but our sins are so great, and Satan of the thousand eyes watches the whole earth from one end to the other. What he sees he reports; he denounces, informs. Who can help us if not the rabbi!

That's what the people thought.

But once a Litvak came, and he laughed. You know the Litvaks. They think little of the Holy Books but stuff themselves with Talmud and law. So this Litvak points to a passage in the *Gemara*—it sticks in your eyes—where it is written that even Moses, our teacher, did not ascend to heaven during his lifetime but remained suspended two-and-a-half feet below. Go argue with a Litvak!

So where can the rabbi be?

"That's not my business," said the Litvak, shrugging. Yet all the while—what a Litvak can do—he is scheming to find out.

That same night, right after the evening prayers, the Litvak steals into the rabbi's room, slides under the rabbi's bed, and waits. He'll watch all night and discover where the rabbi vanishes and what he does during the Penitential Prayers.

Someone else might have got drowsy and fallen asleep, but a Litvak is never at a loss; he recites a whole tractate of the Talmud by heart.

At dawn he hears the call to prayers.

The rabbi has already been awake for a long time. The Litvak has heard him groaning for a whole hour.

Whoever has heard the Rabbi of Nemirov groan knows how much sorrow for all Israel, how much suffering, lies in each groan. A man's heart might break, hearing it. But a Litvak is made of iron; he listens and remains where he is. The rabbi, long life to him, lies on the bed, and the Litvak under the bed.

Then the Litvak hears the beds in the house begin to creak; he hears people jumping out of their beds, mumbling a few Jewish words, pouring water on their fingernails, banging doors. Everyone has left. It is again quiet and dark; a bit of light from the moon shines through the shutters.

(Afterward the Litvak admitted that when he found himself alone with the rabbi a great fear took hold of him. Goose pimples spread across his skin, and the roots of his earlocks pricked him like needles. A trifle: to be alone with the rabbi at the time of the Penitential Prayers! But a Litvak is stubborn. So he quivered like a fish in water and remained where he was.)

Finally the rabbi, long life to him, arises. First he does what befits a Jew. Then he goes to the clothes closet and takes out a bundle of peasant clothes: linen trousers, high boots, a coat, a big felt hat, and a long wide leather belt studded with brass nails. The rabbi gets dressed. From his coat pocket dangles the end of a heavy peasant rope.

The rabbi goes out, and the Litvak follows him.

On the way the rabbi stops in the kitchen, bends down, takes an ax from under the bed, puts it in his belt, and leaves the house. The Litvak trembles but continues to follow.

The hushed dread of the Days of Awe hangs over the dark streets. Every once in awhile a cry rises from some *minyan* reciting the Penitential Prayers or from a sickbed. The rabbi hugs the side of the streets, keeping to the shade of the houses. He glides from house to house, and the Litvak after him. The Litvak hears the sound of his heartbeats mingling with the sound of the rabbi's heavy steps. But he keeps on going and follows the rabbi to the outskirts of the town.

A small wood stands behind the town.

The rabbi, long life to him, enters the wood. He takes thirty or forty steps and stops by a small tree. The Litvak, overcome with amazement, watches the rabbi take the ax out of his belt and strike the tree. He hears the tree creak and fall. The rabbi chops the tree into logs and the logs into sticks. Then he makes a bundle of the wood and ties it with the rope in his pocket. He puts the bundle of wood on his back, shoves the ax back into his belt, and returns to the town.

He stops at a back street beside a small broken-down shack and knocks at the window.

"Who is there?" asks a frightened voice. The Litvak recognizes it as the voice of a sick Jewish woman.

"I," answers the rabbi in the accent of a peasant.

"Who is I?"

Again the rabbi answers in Russian. "Vassil."

"Who is Vassil, and what do you want?"

"I have wood to sell, very cheap." And not waiting for the woman's reply, he goes into the house.

The Litvak steals in after him. In the gray light of early

morning he sees a poor room with broken, miserable furnishings. A sick woman, wrapped in rags, lies on the bed. She complains bitterly, "Buy? How can I buy? Where will a poor widow get money?"

"I'll lend it to you," answers the supposed Vassil. "It's only six cents."

"And how will I ever pay you back?" says the poor woman, groaning.

"Foolish one," says the rabbi reproachfully. "See, you are a poor sick Jew, and I am ready to trust you with a little wood. I am sure you'll pay. While you, you have such a great and mighty God and you don't trust Him for six cents."

"And who will kindle the fire?" says the widow. "Have I the strength to get up? My son is at work."

"I'll kindle the fire," answers the rabbi.

As the rabbi puts the wood into the oven he recites, in a groan, the first portion of the Penitential Prayers.

As he kindles the fire and the wood burns brightly, he recites, a bit more joyously, the second portion of the Penitential Prayers. When the fire is set he recites the third portion, and then he shuts the stove.

The Litvak who saw all this became a disciple of the rabbi.

And ever after, when another disciple tells how the Rabbi of Nemirov ascends to heaven at the time of the Penitential Prayers, the Litvak does not laugh. He only adds quietly, "If not higher."

Translated by Marie Syrkin[1]

THE MOUSE AND THE COCK

SHMUEL YOSEF AGNON

There was a cock that lived with a Jew. He made an easy living and lacked for nothing. Nonetheless he was troubled and worried and never a smile would you catch on his face. When the month of Elul came round at the end of the summer his troubles were doubled, and he'd never crow without bursting into tears. Now a mouse lived there as well. The mouse asked the cock, Choicest of poultry, why dost thou sorrow so? If it be by reason of thy sustenance, 'tis always awaiting thee; and if it be thy dwelling, thou dwellest with human beings; yet despite all this thou'rt grieved and terrified and quivering and crestfallen like to a helpless and weary cock.

Said he, Hath not Jeremiah said, "Curst be the cock that trusteth in man," while Elihu hath told Job, "Is there an angel over him, a single counselor, one among a thousand, to tell his uprightness to Man?"; all the good things of thy speech are as nought to me when I see the master of the house taking his prayer book in hand. And why? By reason of a certain prayer, in the Order of Prayers, called "Sons of Man"; when he readeth this prayer on the appointed Eve of Atonement he taketh a cock, whirleth it about his head, saith, This cock shall go to death, and handeth it over to the slaughterer. Of me did Jeremiah lament, "I am the cock that hath seen affliction."

Said the mouse to the cock, Yet King David, may he rest in peace, hath said in the Psalms, "Which cock shall live and not see death?"; and Job likewise saith, "And cock shall die and waste away." How be it, so long as thy time is not come to be rid of the world, by thy life thou'rt not yet dead; therefore gird up thy loins as a cock and trust in the Lord; as it is said in Jeremiah, "Blest is the cock that trusteth in the Lord," and in Psalms, "Blessed be the cock who hath set his trust in the Lord," and in thee shall be fulfilled the verse of Job, "Thy years as the years of the cock." And if thou dost set thy trust in me, I shall deliver thee from the pitfalls of Mankind, as is written in Job elsewhere, "Deliver him from going down to the pit; I have found a ransom." Said the cock, And how canst thou deliver me from the hand of Man?

Said the mouse, Hast never in thy days heard what my father did to the lion who was bound and captive among Mankind? Father gnawed the ropes and freed the lion. What father did for the king of beasts I can do for thy cockyness, strongest of birds. But of thee I require that thou shouldst hearken unto me, as Job hath said, "Let a wise cock hearken unto me."

Said the cock to himself, Let the miracle come whence it will, I shall hearken to that which is in his mouth; and to the mouse he said, And how wilt thou act to deliver me?

Said he, Choicest of poultry, the days of the Night Prayers of Penitence that precede the New Year do approach, when men arise betimes to the synagogues; I shall go and eat up the prayer book so that not so much as a single letter shall be left. Said the cock, For Thy salvation have I hoped, O Lord. And when the nights of the Prayers of Penitence came round, the household all went off to the synagogue and left the house without a human being. Out came the mouse from his hole to eat the prayer book, and thereupon the cat on the watch fell upon him and consumed him.

Translated by I. M. Lask[2]

THE MARTYRDOM OF RABBI AMNON OF MAYENCE

Once upon a time there lived a rabbi called R. Amnon. He was held in high esteem by the bishop of Mayence, for he was a great man in every way. He was rich, learned, wise, of distinguished family—in short, he had all the good qualities which a good Jew ought to possess, and therefore he was respected and loved by nobles and princes and counts and lords, who loved him very much and delighted in his company, and yet there was none like him in piety.

One day, as he was visiting the bishop in his palace, the nobles said to him: "Master Amnon, if you would only embrace Christianity, our gracious prince would make you his chief counselor, for he is very fond of you. We have often spoken to the prince about you and asked him to give you an honorable post, and he replied that if you would accept his faith, he would give you a post of great honor. Therefore we ask you to embrace the Christian faith." But R. Amnon refused to listen. One day the bishop himself asked him to join the Christian church, but he declined. This went on day after day, but he refused to listen to them. One day the bishop importuned him urgently to embrace Christianity, and R. Amnon replied: "I will

consider the matter, and in three days I will give your lord-
ship a reply." He did this merely in order to put the bishop
off so as to have respite. When he had left the bishop, he
realized what he had done in that he had told the bishop that
he would consider his proposal, as if he had the remotest notion
of embracing Christianity and (Heaven forbid!) deny his own
God. This weighed heavily upon his heart, and he went home
sad and despondent and would not be comforted. His wife
asked him what he had done or what had happened to him,
for it was not usual for him to be sad, but he would not tell
his family anything, and said to himself: "I cannot rest until
I have expiated the sin, or I will go down in sorrow to the
grave."

On the third day, the bishop sent for him to hear his decision. R. Amnon replied that he would not go and that he
would have nothing to do with him. The bishop sent for him
twice again, but he refused to go. Then the bishop ordered
him to be brought to him by force. And when he came, the
bishop said to him: "What do you mean by refusing to come
after I had sent for you three times? You promised to give me
an answer to my proposal in three days. I therefore want your
answer now." The pious man replied: "I can give you no
answer to the question you asked me or are asking now. My
thoughtless remark that I would take three days to consider
your proposal was tantamount to a denial of my God. I will
therefore suggest my own punishment. My tongue, which
uttered the words, 'I will consider,' shall be cut off." R. Amnon
was anxious to do penance and to sanctify the name of God.
Then the wicked bishop replied: "The punishment which you
suggest does not appeal to me, for it is by far too light. The
tongue which spoke those words, spoke nothing but the truth;
but the feet, which refused to come to me, shall be cut off and
the other members of your body shall also be tortured." And he
ordered R. Amnon's hands and feet to be cut off, and every
time they cut off a limb, they asked him whether he still refused to be converted, and R. Amnon always replied, "I do."
And he said: "Make your torture more severe, for I deserve

it all for the words which I have spoken." When the wicked man
had accomplished his will and had tortured R. Amnon cruelly,
he ordered him to be put into a bed, his severed limbs by his
side, and carried to his house. When his wife and children
saw him in this state, they raised a pitiful wail, and one can
easily imagine how they felt. But R. Amnon said to his wife
and children: "My dear wife, I have fully deserved what was
done to me, for I was on the point of denying the Lord, but I
hope to God that He will let me expiate my sin in this world
that I may have a share in the world to come."

When New Year's Day arrived, he asked to be carried in
his bed to the synagogue and to be placed close to the reader.
When the reader was about to begin the *Kedushah* of the *Musaf*
prayer, the saint said to him: "Wait, I want to sanctify the
name of God before I die." And he began the hymn, *Uvkhen
Lekha Ta'aleh Kedushah*, which we still say every year on New
Year's Day and the Day of Atonement. Then he recited the
hymn, *Unetanneh Tokef Kedushat ha-Yom*. When he had
finished it, he disappeared and no one ever saw him again, for
the Lord took him to the other pious men in paradise.

On the third night after that event, he appeared in a dream
to his teacher, R. Kalonymos son of R. Meshullam, and asked
him to make a copy of the *Unetanneh Tokef* hymn, which he
had composed on that occasion, and to send it to all the communities where Jews dwelt. We still intone the *Unetanneh Tokef*
on New Year's Day and on the Day of Atonement for his sake.
May the Lord grant us the benefit of this saint.

Ma'aseh Book
Translated by Moses Gaster[3]

ECSTASY ON THE NEW YEAR

MAURICE SAMUEL

BASED ON THE STORY BY I. L. PERETZ

"As you know," a *hasid* reminds us, "we *hasidim* make a
happy occasion of the services of the New Year. We aren't like

other Jews, the *mitnagdim*, who are terrified by the approaching judgment. We know that we are not being hailed before a foreign potentate. It is our own Father in heaven who is going to judge us; and so, after prayers, we take a couple of glasses of brandy, and we dance."

But on this New Year of which he tells, something quite out of the ordinary happened and made it the most memorable New Year in the annals of that hasidic group.

The rabbi stood before the congregation, leading it in prayer. And what a prayer-leader he was! All day long his voice poured out supplication and praise; for on the New Year he permitted no one to take his place. And who would have wanted to? Who would have dared? As he stood there, the messenger of Israel to the Throne, his voice was like a pathway from earth to heaven. It stretched from prayer to prayer, broad and unbroken, bearing the hopes of his people.

And then, suddenly, a dreadful pause, a break. He had reached the prayer that begins: "To God who prepareth judgment." The words rang out clearly. But those which followed: "To Him that searcheth heart, to Him that uncovereth the deeps," were uttered uncertainly. And when he came to the words: "To Him that buyeth His slaves in the day of judgment," his voice broke completely, and a frightful silence followed.

One second, two seconds, three—and every second an eternity. Terror spreads through the congregation; up in the gallery women fall down, fainting.

And then the rabbi comes to. A shudder passes through his body, and the tense and terrified silence is broken by a joyous cry: "Who taketh mercy on His people on the day of judgment." And the rabbi prolongs the words in happy turns and roulades, while his feet begin to move, as of themselves, in a jubilant dance. And the rest of the morning prayers continue with renewed strength.

Between the first and the second morning prayers the rabbi explained what had happened. A very trifling matter, you would imagine; but wait.

As we know, when a man reads from the prayer book, the

eyes run ahead of the lips. The lips say "uncovereth the deeps," the eyes are already at "buyeth His slaves in the day of judgment." And thus it happened with the rabbi that morning of the New Year service. But there and then it occurred to him that the words made no sense! He simply did not understand them, had never understood them. What possible interpretation could one put upon these words, which declared that "God bought His slaves in the day of judgment"? And in the utter confusion of that moment the rabbi suspended his prayer and became silent.

As you may well imagine, the break was noted at once in the Upper Circles. Our rabbi's prayer suspended! A calamity! Not to be endured! Immediately the decision was made to reveal to him, in a vision, the meaning of the words, so that he might continue with the prayer.

And as the rabbi closed his eyes in perplexity, the heavens were cleft before him. This is what he saw:

The chamber of the heavenly court. It is still empty. The prosecuting attorney, counsel for the defense, the judges, all are yet to arrive. The rabbi looks around. The chamber has five doors: one in the right wall, with the sign: "Counsel for the Defense"; one in the left wall: "Prosecuting Attorney"; three doors at the back, in the eastern wall, and in front of them the table and the scales. The middle door at the back, which is closed, bears the legend: "Hosts of the Blessed"; the other two doors at the back are open. Through the one on the right the rabbi sees the garden plots of paradise. There the patriarchs and the sainted ones are seated, steeped in the effulgence of the Divine Light, studying the Torah. Their crowned heads are bent over the sacred texts: for them there is no judgment day. Through the door to the left the rabbi sees the labyrinths of hell. Hell is empty and silent; on a holy day the souls in hell are given respite, there is no torment and no punishment. The fires still burn—it is "the everlasting fire which shall not be extinguished"—but the demons are occupied with a special task.

And now the door in the right wall opens, and counsel for the defense enters, carrying under his arm the records of

the good deeds of mankind for the past year. Alas, a very
small sheaf. A poor year it has been for good deeds. Counsel
for the defense observes that the door opposite is still closed.
A bad sign, that. It is taking them too long to collect *their*
records. The harvest of mankind's misdeeds fill the granaries
of hell. Counsel for the defense drops into a seat and closes his
eyes sadly.

The door in the left wall opens, and two demons enter,
staggering under the load of the first bundle. The rabbi hears
their bones creaking under the burden. They throw down the
bundle and sing out loudly: "That isn't even a tithe of the
harvest. The demons are still collecting—whole treasuries are
yet to come."

Counsel for the defense covers his face and groans. He apparently feels that no one hears him. The court is not yet
assembled, the residents of paradise are busy with the Torah,
hell is empty.

Counsel for the defense is mistaken! Among the residents of
paradise there is the beloved, the unforgettable hasidic Rabbi
Reb Levi Yitzhak of Berditchev, the Compassionate One. *He*
hears the groan of anguish that bursts from the lips of counsel
for the defense. He alone among the children of bliss has not
forgotten those who dwell in darkness and the shadow of
death; he alone remembers that for *them*, on earth below,
there is still a judgment day. And if someone groans in heaven,
it is undoubtedly for them. Reb Levi Yitzhak interrupts his
studies, looks up, and through the open door perceives the
crushed figure of counsel for the defense.

Levi Yitzhak of Berditchev, tenderest of all Jews, most vigilant
in defense of his sinful people, rebuker of the Almighty for
His severity toward mortals, Levi Yitzhak of Berditchev steals
into the chamber and understands at once what is toward: he
sees the slender sheaf under counsel's arm, the vast bundle
on the table. It takes Reb Levi Yitzhak just one instant to
decide. He bends down and, straining himself to the utmost,
picks up the bundle of adverse records; he flings it through the
door at the left, down into the flames of hell.

Again two demons enter, bent double under a load of records.

The moment they leave, Reb Levi Yitzhak deals with this bundle as he dealt with the first. And so with the third and the fourth and the rest.

Finally it is the Ashmedai himself, Asmodeus, the Devil and prosecuting attorney, who enters, a broad grin on his face. What is this? Help! The records! Not a sign of that opulent harvest. He looks around, sees the last bundle burning in hell; looks around again, and sees Reb Levi Yitzhak sneaking back toward paradise. He runs over, grabs him by the arm, and yells: "Stop, thief!"

The cry resounds through all the seven heavens. Patriarchs and saints start up from their studies and rush into the chamber. The center door at the back opens and the members of the court file in. Counsel for the defense starts up.

"What is it?"

Before this heavenly assembly the Devil declares how he caught Reb Levi Yitzhak red-handed. He points to the fires of hell, where the last bundle—it was the heaviest of all—is still smoldering.

Truth is truth! Reb Levi Yitzhak confesses. Justice is justice! The Devil is asked what sentence he demands. He too decides on the instant. He quotes the Scriptures—he would!—"The thief shall be sold for his theft." Let Reb Levi Yitzhak be sold as a slave publicly, to the highest bidder. The Devil will of course join in the bidding. And no matter what it costs him, he intimates, he will find it worthwhile.

This is the law, and there is no appeal from it. Let the auction begin!

So they stand facing one another, the Devil on one side, the children of bliss on the other, Reb Levi Yitzhak between them. The members of the court take their seats; the bidding opens.

Father Abraham makes his offer: his heavenly credit for the priceless gem of the Covenant, the first Jewish commandment; and he adds as bonus his credit for his famous hospitality. After him comes Isaac, whose contribution is almost as large: the credits for his readiness to be sacrificed on the altar by his father. Jacob follows; his possessions are his simplicity, his devotion to learning in the days when his brutish brother, Esau, went hunting in the fields. Then comes Rachel, with *her* special distinction, the love-mandrakes; and after her the other matriarchs, each contributing her own glory. And row upon row the saints follow, each putting up, for the purchase of Reb Levi Yitzhak, whatever reward he had garnered during his sojourn on earth.

But it is the Devil himself against whom they are bidding, and he has treasures beyond computation. For every addition to the right scale he throws a corresponding price into the left scale. He ransacks the earth, brings out forgotten wealth from beyond the hills of darkness, till the eyes are dazzled by the display. The saints have exhausted their stocks, the two scales stand level, and in a last flourish the Devil takes the crown off his head and flings it into the auction. He must have Reb Levi Yitzhak at any price. The scale on the left begins to sink; it falls lower, lower.

Counsel for the defense advances and throws in on the right the meager records of the year's good deeds. In vain. They are not substantial enough to arrest the downward flight of the scale on the left.

A crooked and vindictive grin spreads over the Devil's lips, and triumph flickers in his eyes. Oh, what a catch, what a haul, what a victory for hell! Reb Levi Yitzhak of Berditchev, perhaps the most glorious figure in the hasidic world after the founder himself, the Master of the Name! Before the scale has touched bottom the Devil places a hand on Reb Levi Yitzhak's shoulder and points significantly to the door on the left, the door opening on hell. "This way, please."

Horror runs through the ranks of the blessed. What! Reb Levi Yitzhak lost? It cannot be! And yet—what is to be done?

The horror and confusion increase—until they are suddenly stilled by a Voice. It is the Voice from the Throne of Glory. "*I* buy him!"

And again through the deathly silence: "I raise the bid! 'For Mine is the earth and the fullness thereof'—and I give the whole world for Reb Levi Yitzhak."

The Devil's face became black as thunder.

Gleefully the *hasid* finishes the story:
"That's what the rabbi told us in the pause between first and second prayers that New Year's morning. And you, you non-*hasidim*, you *mitnagdim*, you unbelievers, can you understand what happiness was ours that New Year?

"First, there was the record of our sins destroyed—which means a happy and prosperous New Year as good as in our pockets. Second, Reb Levi Yitzhak redeemed. And third, to top it all, and the best of all, the secret of a text at last revealed. 'To Him that buyeth His slaves in the day of judgment!' "[4]

THE *SHOFAR*

I. L. PERETZ

"You must have something precious under your arm, Reb Simeon! You press it to your breast with a trembling hand, and your old eyes shine with joy!"

"Yes!" says Reb Simeon, "it's my *shofar*, my festival *shofar!*"

"Festival *shofar?*"

"Yes! You see, it's my custom on an ordinary weekday in Elul to blow on an ordinary *shofar*. This one is for the festival, a beautiful, precious *shofar.*"

He took it out from under his arm and eyed it fondly. A little *shofar*, ash-gray, thin, but lovely to look at, bent like every other *shofar*, but bent charmingly, like a child's attractive waywardness. He stroked it with quivering fingers, lifted it to his beard and fondled it against the long, fine silver hair. And both holinesses mingled—the holy ash-gray *shofar* and the holy silver beard. The old eyes lightened up with childlike happiness. They looked so youthful!

"You love this *shofar!*"

"Like my life! I love blowing the *shofar*. My father, peace to his memory, was a farmer. We lived in the village, and—I was a boy—I envied the shepherd with his pipe. He piped, and at the sound the sheep gathered round him, lay down round

him, and looked into his eyes. But a *shofar* is something higher
—it gathers souls, Jewish Mount Sinai souls! They listen! I
love blowing the *shofar*!

"Not always," he corrected himself. "Not the *tekiah gedolah*
on Yom Kippur! I put the *shofar* to my lips, and already half
the congregation lies prostrate on the floor, under the benches.
I look round, and it is like a field after a storm, three-quarters
of the corn bowed to the ground—and there is the *tekiah
gedolah* still to come! It isn't right!

"And blowing the *shofar* all through Elul isn't the same thing!
Why? It's a weekday congregation, small and scattered, one in,
one out. The market keeps breaking in through the open windows. The women stallholders shout their wares; the peasants
talk loudly. The youngsters play in the synagogue courtyard.
It's terribly confusing! It's not right!

"Rosh Hashanah is utterly different! The whole congregation
stands, wrapped in their *tallitot*! They are the sons of kings!
They sway like the green stalks in the blessed fields, and there
is a rustling as in a forest or like the rushing of a stream."

"You can't get the village out of your mind, Reb Simeon?"

"It was a good time! Forest and stream, and an old mill by
the stream. When there was a wind and the forest rustled and
the stream rushed past, I used to think—foolish lad that I
was!—that they were singing praises to God, and that heaven
was going to blow the *shofar*! . . . In those old days . . ."

"And today, Reb Simeon?"

"Today, when I have to go to the village before Passover, to
kasher the mill, and the forest rustles and the stream runs
by, I think they are angry, I think they are annoyed with
me! They growl: 'What brings you here? Weren't you chased
out of here!' But in the holy synagogue, when the congregation
sways and shakes, I see the old good kindly forest before my
eyes, and I hear the old good kindly stream. It roars louder
and louder till it bursts out like a flame, like a sea of fire, and
breaks through the walls, and rises up and breaks through the
ceiling—it goes out into the world, up to heaven, this flame,
this burning, boiling psalm of praise!

"Then suddenly it stops! It disappears! Everything is quiet, utterly quiet! The congregation holds its breath. You hear the candles on the reading desk burning and hissing in the holy heat.

"The congregation is waiting for my prayer, for my blessing! I put the *shofar* to my lips. The *dayyan* calls out the notes, and I sound the *shofar—tekiah, shevarim, teruah!* Sounds clear as water, silver sounds, pure. . . ."

His eyes light up with childlike happiness.

"You're wonderful, Reb Simeon, at your age!"

"Yes," he says, "ordinarily I am a fly. But when I sound the *shofar*, I soar!"

"Like an eagle! You are like a lion!"

"Yes, indeed, like an eagle, like a lion!"

"And you always get the right note?"

"Always? No, not always! Sometimes there are obstacles."

"What obstacles? Satan gets in your way?"

"Worse than that! We have ways of dealing with Satan! Tried and sure ways. If not, you do what the Berditchever did —let Ivan sound the *shofar!*"

"Then what is the obstacle?"

"I'll give you an instance—Satan comes along, and I start coughing. An old cough. I've had it for forty years. It dates back to *Tashlikh* that year. The police chief had issued an order not to throw any Jewish crumbs in the stream. 'When you are in Jerusalem,' he said, 'you can do what you like! Not here!'

"Well now, if the police chief says no, we've got to find a way of getting round it. So each of us goes to the stream separately, one by one, but we all meet there, all together. If we are seen, we run! We get hot running, and we cool off in the water of the *mikveh*. With my poor constitution, I got pneumonia! Thank God, I got over it, but it left me with this cough, as a reminder. Once it catches me, it tears me to bits. And just then it caught me, immediately after the blessing!

"What could I do! The *shofar* trembled in my hand, like a fish out of water, and wouldn't go to my lips! When it finally did it knocked against my teeth! In those days I still had my teeth!

31. Rosh Hashanah greeting cards on sale in a Tel Aviv street. Ministry for Foreign Affairs, State of Israel. See Chapter XVIII.

אם חדש עלינו שנה טובה ..

אַשְׁרֵי מַשְׂכִּיל אֶל דָל
בְּיוֹם רָעָה יְמַלְּטֵהוּ יְיָ :
יְיָ יִשְׁמְרֵהוּ וִיחַיֵּהוּ

וואהל דעם / דער פיר דען אַרמֶן זאָרגט!
נוּר אונגליקסצייט עררעטעט איהן דער העררה
דער עוויגע טיצע דיך / בעוואהרעט דיין לעבן :

אַל תַּשְׁלִיכֵנִי לְעֵת זִקְנָה
כִּכְלוֹת כֹּחִי אַל תַּעַזְבֵנִי :

פֿערווירף מיך נור אים אַלטער ניכט /פֿערלאָם מיך
ניכֿט וואן מייֻנע קרעֿפֿֿטע פֿֿערֿגעהֿט ❖

32. Greeting card.
Germany. 1837. Manuscript.
See Chapter XVIII.

בעז"ה

וְאֵל שַׁדַּי יְבָרֵךְ אוֹתָךְ · וְיִתֵּן לָךְ
חַיִּים טוֹבִים אֲרוּכִים וְשָׁלוֹם ❖

גאָט דער אַלמעכטיגע זעגענע דיך · אוּנד
ערלייהע דיר גֶענהֿר הֶיעלֶע / אוּנד גוּטע ·
יאָהרע · מיט פֿֿרֿידֶען · אָמֵן ❖

לְשָׁנָה טוֹבָה תִּכָּתֵב וְתֵחָתֵם ·
לְאַלְתָּר לְחַיִּים
❖

תרל"ב לפ"ק

33. Greeting card.
Germany. 1841. Manuscript.
See Chapter XVIII.

258]

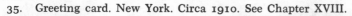

34. Greeting card. England. Circa 1900. See Chapter XVIII.

35. Greeting card. New York. Circa 1910. See Chapter XVIII.

וּבְשׁוֹפָר גָּדוֹל יִתָּקַע, וְקוֹל דְּמָמָה
דַקָּה יִשָּׁמַע וּמַלְ... אֵלָיִם
יֵחָפֵזוּן וְחִיל וּרְעָדָה יֹאחֵזוּן
וְיֹאמְרוּ הִנֵּה יוֹם הַדִּי
וּתְשׁוּבָה וּתְפִלָּה וּצְדָקָה
מַעֲבִירִין אֶת רֹעַ הַגְּזֵרָה
כְּתִיבָה וַחֲתִימָה טוֹבָה מָרְדֳּכַי בִּירְנְהַא אלץ

36. Greeting card. By Uriel Birnbaum, Holland. Circa 1935. See
Chapter XVIII.

"Or something like this happens. There is a Christian living across the way, who keeps a dog. And this dog takes it into his head to bark just at that moment. You've got to wait until he stops. Sometimes, as though a *dybbuk* had got into him, he goes on barking for an hour or more!

"Or just on Rosh Hashanah the military maneuvers start. The army comes marching along the street, bands playing, brass bands; it deafens you! The ground rocks under their feet. The houses shake, the windows rattle. Try blowing the *shofar* in that din!

"A few years ago there was a big fire in one of the back streets. I was just going to sound *teruah*. I had the *shofar* to my lips when the fire engine dashed past! Do you think the congregation didn't rush out to see the fire! I was left alone, with the *dayyan*, he with the prayer book, and I with the *shofar*!

"Something much worse happened a few years before that! I was sounding *shevarim*. I tell you it was a real broken *shevarim*, a *shevarim* with all the fear of heaven in it! Suddenly there was a lot of loud whistling in the street, shouting, bells ringing! The pogromists arrived in the marketplace! God in heaven, what a panic there was! The people tried to rush out, to escape. They ran to the doors, to the windows! The old rabbi, blessings on his memory, was still alive. A short, thin little man—but he was a rabbi!

"He jumped up on a chair, and cried: 'Stay where you are!' and they all stayed where they were.

" 'Shut all the doors and windows!' It was done. It made the synagogue pitch black! The few candles on the reading desk only threw black shadows! We were all terror-stricken! But not the rabbi! 'Sound the *shofar*!' he cried.

"I sounded the *shofar*! I put my whole soul into the *tekiot*!

"I may have conquered Satan," he added, smiling ruefully, "but not the pogromists! They laid the town in ruins!

"Who can conquer them? Unless it is the *shofar* of Messiah!"

Translated by Joseph Leftwich[5]

THE *SHOFAR* BLOWER OF LAPINISHOK

AARON D. OGUS

This happened in the days when the Polish nobility was all-powerful, when each played the role of kinglet over his own town and village.

Count Jarszhevski, the *paritz* [squire] of Lapinishok, was an eccentric fellow, capricious and quite mad besides, like all other wealthy landowners of the time. If he suddenly got an idea about something, it had to take place right away. As soon as he uttered something with his *trefeneh* lips nothing in the world could change it. Many of the townspeople suffered greatly from his crazy caprices, although, to give the devil his due, there were not a few who did very well by him.

He would, for instance, on a whim order Berel, the water-carrier to dance a *kazatske* right in the middle of the street and for the amusement that it gave him he'd throw him a ruble. Mendle the bagel-baker often used to leave the palace court-yard with a fine fat coin and all because he had come to entertain the count, wearing a garland of bagel around his neck and singing *Ma Yafet* from the Sabbath liturgy. If anybody dared oppose the count's will he'd drive him out of his house or order him whipped. Such a *meshuggener* that was!

Take, for instance, Moishe-Yossel the *melamed*. He was one pious, upright Jew! In fact, one might even say a pure-hearted, unworldly *tzaddik*. He was also a pauper whose poverty had no limit. He had three grown-up wenches to provide dowries for and half a *minyan* of smaller fry to feed, but his earnings were never enough for that. So he lived in great want all his days and never could make ends meet. His luck was that he, Moishe-Yossel himself, and his wife used to fast every Monday and Thursday. If not for that they wouldn't have had a crust of dry bread for the children.

It was this Moishe-Yossel who on all the holy days used to sing the entire *Shahrit* prayers before the congregation in the Great Synagogue. He also blew the *shofar*. He had held sole right to this honor for many years.

Moishe-Yossel was already past sixty at the time, but his singing of the prayers and his blowing on the *shofar* were still as good as in his best days. Especially celebrated was he for his performance on the *shofar*. His intonation of the prayer *Lamnatzeah*, his *Barkhu*, his *Sheheheyanu* were exquisite, but his *shofar*-blowing was really something to hear! He never faltered or broke in the middle of a note, never made an error by substituting one tone cluster in the triad for another. The notes from his *shofar* issued so clearly, so smoothly that it was a pleasure to hear. And when finally he sounded the long, deep blast, the walls of the synagogue literally shook.

True enough, it often happened that he blew into the *shofar* so hard that, when he was through, he'd start spitting blood. But a Jew like Moishe-Yossel couldn't be bothered with such trifles. *Nu*, so what if he bled a little! Have you any idea how much blood a person has?

And although everybody was delighted with his singing and with his *shofar* blowing, it never occurred to the communal authorities to provide Moishe-Yossel with the necessary expense for the holy days. They didn't even make him a gift of a bottle of wine or brandy, with which to recite the benediction. People in Lapinishok did not bother themselves with such things, nor was Moishe-Yossel the kind of person to make demands on the community.

This was nothing unusual. The rabbi, the rabbinical judge, and the *hazzan*, whom the community was definitely obligated to support, were themselves three-story paupers. Take the rabbi: he wore a *kapote* with threadbare sleeves; the rabbinical judge never owned a sound pair of boots; and as for the *hazzan*, he didn't make enough to buy himself a *yarmulka*.

This neglect by the community was a favorite peeve of Moishe-Yossel.

"There's no lot as wretched as that of us synagogue officials," he used to complain. "Now take the *goyim*. Among them the priests and the choir singers live like princes. They dwell in fine houses, eat well, and ride around in handsome carriages drawn by first-class horses. But just take a look at our rabbi, our rabbinical judge, and our *hazzan*! They can't even make ends meet. Furthermore, *goyim* feel reverence for their religious officials. But Jews take them in a matter-of-fact way. It's all so dull, so workaday!" And he often used to say jokingly: "If you have to take a religious post, by all means choose it among the *goyim*."

Once—it happened to be the first day of Rosh Hashanah—Count Jarszhevski suddenly got a crazy idea to visit the Great Synagogue and watch Jews at their prayers. He entered just before *shofar*-blowing time, when Moishe-Yossel began intoning *Lamnatzeah*. The *paritz* went forward to the east wall and stood next to the rabbi.

It happened that at this time Moishe-Yossel's heart was full of woe. The season had been a bad one, and most of his pupils in his *heder* hadn't paid their fees. Also a child was ailing, and on top of that his goat had gone and died. That's why, when he intoned *Lamnatzeah*, it was with such deep emotion that he could have melted a stone. The *paritz* himself was so moved by it that he stood motionless, holding his breath.

Finally, when the time came for Moishe-Yossel to blow the *shofar*, a holy silence fell on all, on the count as well as on the worshipers.

Moishe-Yossel took his place in the pulpit. He was dressed awesomely in his white *kittel*, the pious man's shroud, and his *tallit* was wrapped around his head. And, when he pronounced the benediction, *Lishmoa kol shofar*, the candelabra on the ceiling literally trembled.

Then he began to blow the *shofar*, winding up every brief declamatory statement with a piercing blast, so that it sounded as though the Heavenly Hosts were singing "Hosanna."

The *paritz* was enchanted by this Jewish ceremony. He stood with mouth agape until after the last tone, which Moishe-Yossel produced so flawlessly and sustained so long that the count was simply amazed. He ran up to the pulpit and said to Moishe-Yossel: "Moshke, tomorrow at noon I want you to come to my palace, in the same clothes you're wearing now and with your *shofar*! I want you to perform this ceremony, exactly as you did it just now, for my family and the guests."

Everybody was thunderstruck by the count's command.

Moishe-Yossel stood stunned, unable to move a limb. All the
worshipers in the synagogue were pale and trembling and
looked mutely at Moishe-Yossel. Such an outrageous blasphemy
hadn't been heard of since the destruction of the Temple in
Jerusalem by Titus—to use the Heavenly Mysteries for enter-
tainment, and on Rosh Hashanah too!

The *paritz* left the synagogue, entered his carriage, and rode
off. Immediately a wild tumult broke out in the synagogue.
But the rabbi rose up sternly and ordered that the recitation
of the *Musaf* prayers be begun. After the service they'd hold a
meeting and then decide what to do about it.

During the *Musaf* prayers, Moishe-Yossel was dissolved in
tears, imploring Heaven for aid. He was so spent and broken
at the end that they had to half carry him home.

The service over, all the dignitaries went to confer with the
rabbi at his house. But they couldn't find any means by which
to make the count withdraw his decree: everybody knew that
he never changed his mind in such matters. And, inasmuch
as they were certain that were Moishe-Yossel to fail to make
his appearance at the palace the count would order him to be
whipped and he might, God forbid, die yet, therefore the rabbi
gave Moishe-Yossel rabbinical sanction to blow the *shofar* for
the *paritz*, everything being permitted when life itself is en-
dangered.

Before noon the following morning on the second day of
Rosh Hashanah, Moishe-Yossel started out for the count's palace
dressed in his *kittel* and *tallit* with the *shofar* under his arm.
Before he left, the rabbi blessed him in the synagogue.

"Reb Moishe-Yossel," he said, "you are now like one of the
Ten Martyrs whom they led before the Roman tyrant. Go, and
may God be with you!"

The sound of lamentation arose in the synagogue, and the
cries of Moishe-Yossel himself pierced the Seventh Heaven.

Almost the entire town accompanied Moishe-Yossel to the
gates of the palace and stood there waiting for him to come
out again. Most of the pious were afraid that, because of his
fright and grief, Moishe-Yossel wouldn't be able to blow the
shofar properly, and God forbid, that dog of dogs, the *paritz*,

might have him whipped. So they stood in a nearby field, intoned the Psalms, and prayed to God for Moishe-Yossel's protection.

The poor *melamed* was led into the great hall where the *paritz*, his family, and his invited guests, were assembled. Then the *paritz* ordered him to sing the prayers and blow the *shofar* exactly the way he did the day before in the synagogue.

With a broken heart, crushed and meek, Moishe-Yossel intoned *Lamnatzeah*. He fervently uttered the blessing recited before blowing the *shofar*, and because he felt certain that he was treading the martyr way to "Glorify His Name," he blew upon the *shofar* as he had never blown before—in one breath, so to speak.

When he had finished, the count and all the assembled cried, "Bravo!" and applauded him.

When Moishe-Yossel left the palace, his fellow townsmen saw him come out weeping. His wife and children ran toward him with outcries of joy just as if he were coming back from the other world.

"Moishe-Yossel! . . . *Tattele*!" they cried and threw themselves on his neck.

Moishe-Yossel drew his wife to his breast and sobbed like a child.

"What are you crying for?" asked his wife. "*Narrele*, better thank Him who endures forever that you came through that ordeal unhurt."

"*Narrele* yourself! It's for joy I'm crying. I thank and praise the Almighty for it."

And thus saying, he put his hand into his pocket and took out a bag of money.

"Look at this, wife!" said he tearfully. "For forty years I led the prayers and blew the *shofar* for the Jews, and what did I get out of it? Nothing! And here, just once, for a few minutes I blew *shofar* for a *goy*, and what does he do but give me three hundred rubles! Enough for the dowries for our three daughters! What did I always tell you? If you've got to blow the *shofar* blow it for the *goyim*!"

Translated by Nathan Ausubel[6]

TASHLIKH

Isaac Bashevis Singer

Aaron the watchmaker did not live on our street, but when I climbed to the highest branch of the lime tree that grew in our garden, I could see his house clearly; it was the only one in the village that had a small lawn in front of it. The shutters of Aaron's house were painted green; flowerpots stood in the windows; there were sunflowers in the garden. Aaron and his family lived on the ground floor, that is with the exception of his daughter, Feigele; she had a room in the attic. At night a lamp burned in Feigele's window long after the lights downstairs had been extinguished. Occasionally I caught a glimpse of her shadow passing across the curtain. Mottel, Feigele's younger brother, had built a dovecote on the roof and often stood on the top of the building chasing pigeons with a long stick. Leon, the older boy, who was studying at a polytechnic in Cracow, rode around the village on a horse when he came home on vacation. There was nothing that that emancipated family did not possess: they had a parrot, canaries, a dog. Aaron played the zither; his wife owned a piano—she came from Lublin and didn't wear a wig. Aaron the watchmaker, who was also both goldsmith and jeweler, was the only man in the village with a telephone in his house; he could speak directly to Zamosc. . . .

I was not a native of that hamlet. I had been brought up in Warsaw, but when the war came, my parents left the city and went to live with my grandfather the rabbi. There we were stuck in a village which was on no railroad and was surrounded by pine forests. My father was appointed assistant rabbi. I never stopped longing for Warsaw, its streets, its trolley cars, its illuminated show windows, and its tall balconied residences. Aaron the watchmaker and his family represented for me a fragment of the metropolis. Aaron had a library containing books written in several languages. In his store one could put on earphones and listen to the radio. He sub-

scribed to two Warsaw newspapers, one in Polish and one in
Yiddish, and was always hunting for a chess partner. Feigele
had attended the gymnasium in Lublin, boarding with an aunt
while she was away from home; but now having received her
diploma, she had returned to her parents.

Aaron the watchmaker had been a student of my grandfather's and had been considered a religious prodigy until
he had been caught reading the Bible in German translation,
a sure sign of heresy. Like Mendelssohn, Aaron was a hunch-
back. Although he had not been officially excommunicated, it
was almost as if he had been. He had a high forehead, a
mangy-looking goatee, and large black eyes. There was something ancient and half forgotten in his gaze for which I knew
no name and which made me think of Spinoza and Uriel
Acosta. When he sat at the window of his store studying some
mechanism through a watch glass, he seemed to be reading
the wheels like a fortune teller does his crystal. All day his
sad smile enunciated over and over again, "Vanity of vanities."
Feigele had inherited her father's eyes. She kept to herself, was
always to be seen strolling alone, a tall, thin girl with a long,
pale face and thin nose and lips. She always carried two books
under her arm, one thick and one thin. A strange gentleness
emanated from her. By this time the fashionable girls cut their
hair au garçon, but Feigele wore hers in a bun. She always
took the road to the Russian cemetery. Once I saw her reading
the inscriptions in the graveyard. . . .

I was too shy to talk to her, wasn't even sure she knew who
I was, since she had a way of looking over people's heads.
But I knew that, like me, she was living in exile. She didn't
seem to ever stop meditating, would pause to examine trees
and would reflectively stare down well shafts. I kept trying to
meet her but couldn't think of a plan. Moreover, I was ashamed
of my appearance, decked out as I was in a velvet cap, a long
gabardine, and red earlocks. I knew that I must seem to her
just another hasidic boy. How could she guess that I was
reading Knut Hamsun and Strindberg on the sly and studying
Spinoza's Ethics in a Hebrew translation? In addition, I owned

a work of Flammarion and was dabbling in the Cabbala. In the evening, when I perched on the highest branch of the lime tree, I gazed up at the moon and the stars like an astronomer. Feigele's window was also visible to me and just as inaccessible as the sky. I had already been matched with the daughter of a rabbi. Every day my father read me a lesson from the *Shulhan Arukh* on how to become a rabbi. The villagers watched me constantly to make sure that I committed no transgressions. My father complained that my frivolity jeopardized his livelihood. All I needed was to be caught talking to a girl, particularly Aaron the watchmaker's daughter.

But when I sat in my tree at night watching Feigele's window I knew indubitably that my longing for her must someday bring a response. I already believed in telepathy, clairvoyance, mesmerism. I would narrow my eyes until the light from Feigele's lamp became thin, fiery filaments. My psychic messages would speed across the blackness to her, for I was seeking to emulate Joseph de la Reina, who by using the powers of Holy Names had brought the Grand Vizier's daughter in a trance to his bed. I called out to Feigele, trying to invade both her waking thoughts and dreams. I wrapped a phantom net around her like some sorcerer from "The Thousand and One Nights." My incantations must inevitably kindle love in her heart and make her desire me passionately. In return I would give her caresses such as no woman had ever received before. . . .

I would adorn her with jewels dug from the moon. We would fly together to other planets and she would dwell a queen in supernal palaces. For reasons which I was unable to explain I became convinced that the beginning of our friendship would date from the reading of the *Tashlikh* prayer on Rosh Hashanah afternoon. This premonition was totally illogical. Probably an enlightened girl like Feigele would not even attend the ceremony. But the idea had entered into me like a *dybbuk*. I kept counting the days and hours until the holiday, formulated plans, conceived of the words I would say to her. Two or three times, perching among the leaves and branches, I noticed Feigele standing at the window looking out. I could not see her

eyes but knew that she had heard my call and was searching
for me in the darkness. It was the month of Elul and every
day the ram's horn was blown in the study house to drive
away Satan. Spider webs drifted through the air; cold winds
blew from the Arctic ice cap. So bright was the moon that
night and day were nearly indistinguishable. Crows, awakened
by the light, croaked. The grasshoppers were singing their final
songs; shadows scampered across the fields surrounding the
village. The river wound through the meadows like a silver
snake. . . .

It was Rosh Hashanah, and I put on the new gabardine and
new shoes I had been given and brushed my sidelocks behind
my ears. What more could a young *hasid* do to look modern?
In the late afternoon I started to loiter on Bridge Street, watching the townspeople file by on their way to the *Tashlikh* ceremony. The day was sunny, the sky as blue and transparent
as it is in midsummer. Cool breezes mingled with the warmth
exuded by the earth. First came the *hasidim,* marching together as a group, all dressed in fur hats and satin coats. They
hurried along as if they were rushing from their womenfolk
and temptation. I had been raised among these people, but now
I found their dishevelled beards, their ill-fitting clothes, and
their insistent clannishness odd. They ran from the Evil One
like sheep from a wolf.

After the *hasidim* came the ordinary Jews, and after them
the women and girls. Most of the older women wore capes and
gowns which dated from the time of King Sobieski; they had
tiaras and bonnets with ribbons on their heads. Their jewelry
consisted of gold head chains, long earrings so weighty they
almost tore the lobes of their ears, and brooches inherited
from grandmothers and great-grandmothers that vibrated as the
women walked. My mother had on a gold silk dress and a
pelerine decorated with rhinestones. But the younger women
had studied the fashion magazines (which always showed up
in the village a year or two after they had been issued) and
were dressed in what they considered to be the latest style.
Some of them wore narrow skirts that scarcely covered their

knees and even bobbed their hair. The ladies' tailors stood to one side commenting on the dress of the women. They contrasted their handiwork with that of their competitors and not only ridiculed each other's designs but the clients who wore them. I kept looking in vain for Feigele. My sorcery had failed and I walked with downcast eyes among the stragglers. Some of the townspeople stood on the wooden bridge reciting the *Tashlikh*; others lined the river's banks. Young women took out their hankerchiefs and shook out their sins. Boys playfully emptied their pockets to be sure that no transgression remained. The village wits made the traditional *Tashlikh* jokes. "Girls, shake as hard as you want, but a few sins will remain." "The fish will get fat feeding on so many errors."

I made no attempt to say the prayer but stood under a willow watching a huge red sun which was split in half by a wisp of cloud sinking in the west. Flocks of birds dipped toward the water, their wings one instant silver, the next leaden black. The color of the river turned from green to rose. I had lost everything that mattered here on earth, but still found comfort in the sky. Several of the smaller clouds seemed to be on fire and sailed across the heavens like ships with burning sails. I gaped at the sun as if I were seeing it for the first time. I had learned from Flammarion that this star was a million and a half times as large as the earth and had a temperature of six thousand degrees centigrade on its surface and hundreds of thousands in its interior. Everything came from it—light, warmth, the wood for the oven, and the food in the pot. Even life and suffering were impossible without it. But what was the sun? Where did it come from? Whence did it travel, moving in the Milky Way and also with the Galaxy? . . .

Suddenly I understood why the pagans had worshiped it as a god. I had a desire to kneel and bow down myself. Well, and could one be certain that it lacked consciousness? *The Guide to the Perplexed* said that the heavenly bodies possess souls and were driven in their orbits by Ideas emitting a divine music as they circled. The music of the spheres now seemed to mingle with the twittering of the birds, the sound of the coursing river, and the murmur of the praying multitude. Then a greenish-blue shimmer appeared on the horizon, the first star, a brilliant miniature sun. I knew that it had taken years for the rays from this fixed star to reach my eyes. But what were rays? I was seized by a sort of cosmic yearning. I wanted to cease existing and return to my sources, be once again a part of the universe. I muttered a prayer to the sun. "Gather me to you. I am weary of being myself."

Suddenly I felt a tug at my sleeve. I turned and trembled. Feigele stood next to me. So great was my amazement that I forgot to marvel. She wore a black suit, a black beret, and a white collar. Her face lit by the setting sun shone with a Rosh Hashanah purity. "Excuse me," she said. "Can you locate the *Tashlikh* for me? I can't seem to find the place." Her smile seemed to be saying, "Well, this was the best pretext available." In her gaze there were both pride and humility. I, like Joseph de la Reina, had summoned my beloved from the Grand Vizier's palace. . . .

She held in her hand a prayer book which had covers stamped in gold. I took one cover of the book and she grasped the other. I started to turn the pages. On one side of the page was Hebrew and on the other Polish. I kept turning the leaves but couldn't find the prayer either. The crowd had already begun to disperse, and heads kept turning in our direction. I started to thumb through the book more quickly. The *Tashlikh* prayer just could not have been omitted. But where was it? Feigele glanced at me in wonder and her eyes seemed to be saying, "Don't get yourself so wrought up. It's nothing but a stratagem." The letters tumbled before my eyes; the prayer book trembled as though it were living. Inadvertently Feigele's elbow and mine touched and we begged each other's pardon. The prayer seemed to have flown from the book. But I knew that it was there and that my eyes had been bewitched. I was just about to give up looking when I saw the word "*Tashlikh*" printed in big bold letters. "Here it is," I cried out, and my heart seemed to stop.

"What? Thank you."

"I haven't recited the *Tashlikh* myself," I said.

"Well, suppose we say it together."

"Can you read Hebrew script?"

"Of course."

"This prayer symbolizes the casting of one's sins into the ocean."

"Naturally."

We stood muttering the prayer together as the crowd slowly moved off. Boys threw mocking glances at us; women scowled; girls winked. I knew that this encounter was going to get me into a great deal of trouble at home. But for the moment I reveled in my triumph, a sorcerer whose charms and incantations had worked. The look of religious devotion on Feigele's face made her appear even gentler. The sun had already disappeared behind the trees and in the distance the forest looked blue and like mountains. Suddenly I felt that I had experienced this moment before. Had it been in a dream or in a former life? The air was alive with sound: the croaking of birds, the buzzing of insects, a ringing as if from bells. The frogs began their evening conversation. A herd of cows passed nearby, their hooves pounding the ground. It was a miracle that the animals did not drive us into the river. No longer did the book tremble in our hands. I heard Feigele murmur:

"The Lord looketh from Heaven. He beholdeth all the sons of men . . . He fashioneth all their hearts alike. He considereth all their works . . ."

Translated by the author and Cecil Hemley[7]

XVIII

ROSH HASHANAH
GREETING CARDS

The Rosh Hashanah custom of wishing one another *Le-shanah tovah tikatev ve-tehatem* ("May you be inscribed and sealed for a good year") probably originated in Germany in the Middle Ages. The wording of the greeting derives from the Talmudic passage, "Three books are open on Rosh Hashanah: one for the wholly righteous, one for the wholly wicked, and one for the intermediate. The wholly righteous are immediately inscribed in the Book of Life; the wholly wicked are immediately inscribed and sealed in the Book of Death; and the fate of the intermediate is held in abeyance from Rosh Hashanah until Yom Kippur."[1]

This custom was first mentioned in the work of Rabbi Jacob Molin (c. 1360–1427), known as Maharil. There it is stated that with the advent of the month of Elul one should extend good wishes to his friend in this manner: "May you be inscribed and sealed in a good year." He further advocated the practice of his teacher, Rabbi Shalom ben Isaac of Vienna, of appending a fitting salutation to all one's letters during the month preceding Rosh Hashanah.[2] This was the general Jewish practice until printed greeting cards became the vogue. There are, however, extant in manuscript special greeting cards made in Germany in the first half of the nineteenth century. One, on a double sheet of white paper and dated 1841, bears the text in Hebrew and Yiddish embellished with a golden decorative border (fig. 33). Another, drawn on a greenish paper and dated 1837, employs the same languages, which were common among German Jews, and has a border of musical instruments (fig. 32).[3]

In the course of time, with the popularization of printing, greeting cards for the Jewish New Year were printed. The commercial card was probably first produced in Eastern Europe in the late nineteenth century.[4] Rosh Hashanah cards tracing back to the first decade of this century are extant. Their illustrations often depict scenes of Jewish life, particularly those related to the High Holy Days and Sukkot, such as blowing of the *shofar*, *Tashlikh*, the *sukkah*. Others portray a bride and bridegroom under the wedding canopy, a dove bearing a letter in her bill, or baskets of flowers.

In addition to the traditional Hebrew wish mentioned above, to which the *hasidim* added "immediately for life," there was often a rubric in Yiddish. Many cards bore tender sentiments; others included excerpts from the Rosh Hashanah prayer book. One card depicts a family gathered around a table, and contains the following prayer in Yiddish:

> O God, O God, Almighty!
> Forgive the sins, forgive!
> Erase not from the Book of Life
> Any member of my household.

Some greetings were in the form of checks drawn on the "Bank of Heaven," promising "120 happy years will be granted by the Creator of the world with health, sustenance, blessing and success, wealth and honor."

In Eastern Europe at the end of the nineteenth century, the synagogue sextons and their assistants delivered the Rosh Hashanah cards in cities and towns. Up to the rise of Hitler, the exchange of greeting cards was widespread in Russia and Poland, where a great variety of cards were printed.[5]

Zionist and other Jewish organizations found New Year cards useful as fund-raising devices. In 1894 a source of income for a Zionist group was a poem for a Rosh Hashanah card written at the request of Rabbi Isaac Nissenbaum by Hayyim Nahman Bialik, the eminent Hebrew poet.[6]

With the introduction of printing in Jerusalem in the latter half of the nineteenth century, the head of the local *yeshivot* ordered Jewish calendars for distribution to their supporters in America and other communities. These calendars carried a typical New Year greeting. Large sheets of paper were used later, with illustrations of the Western Wall, the Temple site, and the Tower of David, among other holy and historic places in Jerusalem, as well as pictures of the *yeshivah* buildings. In more recent years, Israel has become a major source for the supply of New Year cards for Jewish communities throughout the world. Many are attractively designed; some reproduce paintings by such noted Israeli artists as Nahum Gutman, Abel Pann, Jacob Pins, and Reuben Rubin. Hundreds of diversified cards are displayed for sale on stalls set up in the streets of Israeli cities and towns during the weeks before Rosh Hashanah (fig. 31). The Rosh Hashanah card's significance is enhanced in Israel by the fact that the government sends one to every citizen.[7]

In England at the turn of the century Jewish New Year cards were printed by the publishing firm founded by Raphael Tuck, which subsequently became "Art Publishers to Their Majesties the King and Queen." In 1866 Tuck, an Orthodox Jew, started printing commercial Christmas cards in London which were highly regarded for their artistic character. His sons Gustave and Adolph continued the business. The former was president of the Jewish Historical Society of England; Adolph was made a baronet in 1910 in recognition of his production of Christmas cards for the royal family. Some of the Rosh Hashanah cards of the Tuck firm featured baskets overflowing with flowers and such legends as "A Bright and Happy New Year" and "All Good Wishes for the New Year" (fig. 34).[8]

In 1903 the London *Jewish Chronicle* stated: "Staid Jewry has been, and still is, afflicted with the prevalent craze for pictorial postcards, and in the form of these artistic and convenient souvenirs, the dawn of the New Year will be heralded extensively. . . . One gathers that the humorous Jewish picture postcard is in great vogue as a souvenir of 5664, and that its popularity is but of recent growth. One cannot fail to notice that the most comical are of Teutonic origin; and on glancing through them it is impossible to mistake the humor, which is essentially and undeniably Jewish." Besides humorous New Year cards, the correspondent reported also a varied assortment of greeting cards with biblical scenes, portraits of Herzl and Nordau, views of the Holy City, as well as "the old-fashioned cards, the 'hardy annuals' to all appearance just a trifle weary, but seemingly content at their contact with the more frolicsome representatives of their kind."[9]

More recent cards from England frequently express a twofold wish: "A Happy New Year and Well Over the Fast." The last phrase constitutes British Jewry's addition to the customary greeting.[10]

The earliest Rosh Hashanah cards produced in America reflected the American environment. They appear to be adaptations of cards for the secular New Year with an imprint in Hebrew and "A Happy New Year" in English (fig. 35). Prior to World War I, Jewish New Year cards were imported from Germany in large numbers. Among them were numerous types, including three-dimensional cards. When unfolded, these depict a Rosh Hashanah synagogue service, a wedding ceremony, and other popular scenes of Jewish life.

Most unusual are the New Year greetings created during World War II for Jewish personnel in the armed forces of the United States stationed overseas. To expedite the dispatch of mail the government instituted V-Mail Service, in which messages written on special forms were photographed in reduced size before being sent to the United States. Jewish chaplains engaged local artists, usually servicemen, to draw appropriate illustrations and New Year messages on these special forms. These were reproduced and distributed to Jewish soldiers for use as New Year cards. One from North Africa depicts a soldier who is blowing a *shofar*; "Peace, peace, to him who is far off and him who is near" (Isaiah 57.19) is the legend on a form from Guam (fig. 38). Through these attractive and meaningful cards, Jewish servicemen in foreign parts were enabled to extend the traditional greetings to their families and friends.

With the approach of the High Holy Days in America, tens of thousands of New Year cards are distributed to members and donors year in and year out by American Jewish organizations of every type. The *yeshivot* and other institutions in Israel do the same thing. Many eleemosynary agencies sell cards in bulk as a profitable fund-raising project. The Jewish National Fund sells many thousands annually. Even UNICEF (United Nations Children's Emergency Fund) sells, among its cards for various occasions, one for Rosh Hashanah, with greetings in Hebrew and English and a primitive drawing entitled "Birds and Trees," by Shalom of Safed. The annual flood of Rosh Hashanah greetings that pours into the post offices in Israel as well as in the cities of the United States with large Jewish populations creates a problem of no small proportions for the postal services. Senders are reminded to "mail early." In Israel new stamps are issued in honor of Rosh Hashanah with the legend "Festivals for Rejoicing." Most of these—fourteen million were printed in one year—are used to mail New Year cards.[11]

The popularity of Jewish New Year cards is so extensive that their production and sale have become big business. Tiffany & Co. of New York has been selling these cards at fifty-six dollars per hundred. Although available in a profusion of shapes, designs, and colors with a diversity of illustrations and inscriptions, a good many of the Rosh Hashanah cards are hackneyed and unesthetic. Despite the wide selection on the market, many persons are dissatisfied with the conventional commercial cards and have personalized ones designed by printers or artists for their own use. Many graphic arts media—wood cutting, linoleum cutting, etching—are employed to create sophisticated works of art to convey the New Year greetings. Uriel Birnbaum, the noted Dutch Jewish artist, drew a New Year card for Marcos Birnholz of Vienna which features an angel blowing a horn (fig. 36). The New York stage designer Samuel Leve created his own Rosh Hashanah card by writing the text of the poignant prayer *Unetanneh Tokef* and other passages to form the words *hatimah tovah* (a good seal or inscription) (fig. 37). Stan Brod of Cincinnati designed an unusual card—a collage of torn Yiddish newspapers shaped into the likeness of a bird. The New Year greetings are contained in a small paper scroll attached to the bird's foot (fig. 39).

Many foremost Jewish artists have designed Rosh Hashanah cards for themselves as well as for individuals and printers, thus creating a distinctive phase of Jewish folk art.[12]

XIX

THE CULINARY ART
OF ROSH HASHANAH

A number of symbolic customs were prescribed to enhance the significance of Rosh Hashanah meals. According to
some writers, their original motivation may have been a belief
that these customs would be omens of good luck, a concept
many rabbis condemned as an exercise in superstition. As they
evolved, however, they served to induce a festive holiday atmosphere and to inspire faith and confidence that God's mercy
would be ever present in the new year.

The custom of feasting on Rosh Hashanah is adumbrated
biblically in the Book of Nehemiah (8.10). After Ezra the scribe
had read from the book of the Law on the first day of the
seventh month (Tishri), the assembled people burst into weeping. Whereupon Nehemiah said to them: "Go your way, eat
the fat and drink the sweet, and send portions unto him
for whom nothing is prepared, for this day is holy unto the
Lord. . . ." This passage also reminds the Jew of his obligation
to provide food for the poor. Thus it is customary to invite
the needy for the Rosh Hashanah meals.

The Culinary Art of Rosh Hashanah [281

The *hallot* (loaves of bread) for the New Year meals are usually baked in different shapes, each with a symbolic meaning. Some are shaped like a ladder or topped with a ladder, in keeping with the midrashic assertion that on Rosh Hashanah, "The Holy One, blessed be He, sits and erects ladders; on them He lowers one person and elevates another . . . that is to say, God judges those who will descend and those who will ascend."[1] The interpretation is clear: He decrees who will rise on the ladder of prosperity and who will be reduced to poverty.

Bread is also baked in the form of a bird, which is tender imagery for God's protection as suggested in Isaiah 31.5: "As birds hovering [over their fledglings] so will the Lord of hosts protect Jerusalem." Lithuanian Jews bake *hallot* topped with a crown, in accordance with the *piyyut* by Eleazar Kalir: "And thus let all crown God." To signify the desire for a long span of life, circular loaves of bread are usually served.

At the evening meal, after the *Kiddush* over wine is chanted and the benediction for bread is pronounced, a piece of *hallah* is dipped in a dish of honey and eaten. Then the blessing for fruit is said over a slice of apple dipped in honey, and the following formula is recited: "May it be Thy will to renew unto us a good and sweet year." Some continue eating apples with honey until the conclusion of Sukkot. Rabbi Jacob Molin, "Maharil" (c. 1360–1427), cites this custom of eating an apple dipped in honey as a long-established tradition based on Nehemiah 8.10, and indicates that in Jewish mysticism special meaning is ascribed to it.[2]

The Maharil also points out that the head of a lamb is eaten at the evening meal in remembrance of the ram sacrificed by Abraham as a substitute for his son Isaac. The eating of a head was believed to presage that one would become a head, a leader, rather than a tail, a follower.[3] In modern practice the head of a fish is served, and he who eats it says: "May it be Thy will that we become like a head [*le-rosh*] and not a tail." Some hold that fish are eaten because they are so prolific; when eating the fish they recite: "May it be Thy will that we will be fruitful and multiply like fish." Others avidly sought a certain fish called *kerat*, meaning "destroy" in Hebrew, which they ate to signify the hoped-for destruction of their enemies.

Many Sephardi Jewish families eat a series of special foods preceding the meal, in observance of the Talmudic tradition: "Abaye said, if you maintain that symbols are meaningful, every man should acquire the habit of eating pumpkin, fenugreek, leek, beet, and dates on Rosh Hashanah."[4] As these foods grow rapidly, they are considered symbolic of fertility, abundance, and prosperity.

It appears that the attempt to find symbolic meanings for foods was always popular. In France in the twelfth century, according to *Mahzor Vitry* (no. 323), it was the custom on Rosh Hashanah "to eat red apples; in Provence they ate white grapes, white figs, and a calf's head, or any new food easily digestible and tasty, as an omen of good luck to all Israel."

A favorite Ashkenazic dish is carrot *tzimmes*—the Yiddish for carrot is *mehren*, which also means "increase." The eating of carrot *tzimmes* is accompanied by the expression: "May it be Thy will that our merits will be increased." Carrots were also cooked whole and then sliced into circles, resembling coins in color and shape. This patently alluded to a yearning for a prosperous year.

Sweet cakes have long been considered appropriate fare for Rosh Hashanah, a custom said to be traceable to King David. The Bible relates: "So David and all the house of Israel brought up the ark of the Lord with shouting, and with the sound of the horn [*shofar*]. . . . And he dealt among all the people . . . to every one a cake of bread, and a cake made in a pan, and a sweet cake" (II Samuel 6.15,19).[5] The "sweet cake" is identified as a raisin cake (Hosea 3.1). Honey cake and *teiglach* have long been popular among many Jews.

Sour or bitter foods are not eaten on Rosh Hashanah. It is customary not to eat nuts, for the following reason. The numerical equivalent of the Hebrew letters for "nut" (*egoz*) is 17, the same as for "sin" (*het*) when the silent vowel is dropped. To avoid the possibility of suggesting sin, the eating of nuts is frowned upon.

Notwithstanding the general avoidance of sour foods, in France and in Jerusalem bitter pickled olives were distributed to the worshipers as they departed from the synagogue on the night of Rosh Hashanah. This was a reminder to have faith in God, as asserted in the Talmud: "Let my sustenance be as bitter as the olive in Thy Divine charge, rather than sweet as honey in the charge of flesh and blood."[6]

An innovation is introduced on the second night of Rosh Hashanah. Since the two days of Rosh Hashanah are regarded as a single "long day," doubt arises about the necessity to pronounce the *Sheheheyanu* blessing on the second night. In order to avoid the possibility of reciting a *berakhah le-vatalah* (a blessing in vain), a new seasonal fruit is placed on the table or a new garment is worn when the *Kiddush* is recited. Thus, the *Sheheheyanu* will be on the fruit or on the garment, either of which requires this benediction.

▼▼▼▼▼▼▼▼▼▼▼▼▼▼▼▼▼▼▼▼▼▼▼▼▼▼▼▼▼▼▼▼▼▼▼▼▼▼

ROSH HASHANAH DISHES

HANNA GOODMAN

ROUND HALLAH

1 package (¼ ounce) active
dry yeast
1 cup warm water (105°–
115°)
¼ cup sugar
1 teaspoon salt
2 tablespoons margarine,
softened

1 egg, beaten
3½ cups flour, sifted
⅓ cup raisins
1 egg yolk
poppy seeds or sesame seeds

In a large mixing bowl, dissolve the yeast in the warm water. Stir in the sugar, salt, margarine, beaten egg, and 2 cups of the flour. Beat with a wooden spoon or by hand until smooth. Add the remaining flour and the raisins and work in until it is easy to handle and the dough is not sticky. Knead for a few minutes.

Grease a bowl and place the dough in it. Turn the dough over so that the greased part is on top, to prevent drying. Cover tightly with foil and refrigerate overnight, or up to five days.

Divide the dough in half. On a floured board roll the dough into a rope 16″ long, tapering the ends. Coil the rope tightly and tuck the end under. Lay the *hallah* on a greased pan.

Repeat this procedure with the second piece of dough. (See below for directions on decorating the *hallot*.) Cover the shaped *hallot* with a clean towel and allow to rise in a warm place (85°) for 2 hours or until double in size.

Beat the egg yolk with 1 teaspoon of water. Brush the tops of the *hallah* with the egg yolk mixture and sprinkle with the poppy seeds or sesame seeds.

Bake for 25–30 minutes in a 375° oven or until the *hallah* sounds hollow when tapped on the bottom. The yield will be two medium size *hallot*.

To decorate a *hallah* with the traditional symbol of a ladder, reserve a piece of dough for each *hallah*. For each ladder, form dough into two pencil-thin 4″ strips for the 2 sides and 4 pencil-thin 2″ strips for the rungs. Brush the strips with the egg yolk mixture and place on the *hallah* to form a ladder. Small pieces of dough may be shaped into little birds or wings to symbolize angels.

GEFILTE FISH

3 pounds fish fillets (white, pike, and carp)	salt
	white pepper
fish heads	2 teaspoons sugar
fish bones	4 beaten eggs
5 onions	⅓ cup *matzah* meal
3 carrots	4½ cups water

When buying the fish, request all the bones and heads of the fish purchased.

Wash and dry the fish fillets, heads, and bones; place in a bowl. Sprinkle with salt and let stand overnight or for a few hours in the refrigerator. Do not wash the salt off.

To make the broth, put all the bones, except the fish heads, into a pot and cover with 4 cups of cold water. Bring to a boil, lower the heat, and simmer for 30 minutes. Strain the broth, discarding the bones. Return the broth to the pot. Add 3 sliced onions, carrots, salt, pepper, and sugar.

While the broth is cooking, make the stuffing. Put the fish fillets and 2 onions through the grinder twice. Add the beaten eggs, *matzah* meal, salt, pepper, and the remaining ½ cup of water. Mix well. Taste the fish and add more salt or pepper, if necessary.

Wet your hands with cold water; then take some of the fish mixture, form a ball for each reserved fish head, and stuff the heads. Put the stuffed fish heads on top of the onions and carrots in the broth. Continue to form balls with the rest of the fish mixture, wetting hands with water, and place the balls in the pot.

Cover the pot, bring to a boil, lower the flame, and cook for 1 hour. Shake the pot occasionally so the fish will not stick to the bottom of the pot. Lift the cover, taste the broth for seasoning, and add more water if needed. Continue to cook the fish covered for another hour. Let the fish cool in the pot before removing the fish balls. When cold, remove the fish to a bowl. Remove the carrots and cut into slices. Strain the broth into another bowl or, if preferred, pour over the fish. Refrigerate the fish and the broth. Serve the fish with a slice of carrot and some of the jellied broth. A stuffed fish head is served to the head of the family. Yields approximately 12 servings.

CARROT TZIMMES WITH MEAT

2 pounds carrots	½ cup honey
3 pounds brisket	1 teaspoon cinnamon
1 onion, chopped	2 tablespoons lemon juice
salt	1½ tablespoons flour

Scrape the carrots and slice into rounds. Put the meat, carrots, onion, and salt in a pot. Cover with water and bring to a boil. Lower the heat and cook until the meat is tender. Add the honey, cinnamon, and lemon juice. Correct the seasoning to taste.

Mix the flour with some of the broth from the pot, then slowly add it to the rest of the ingredients. Continue to cook for 20 more minutes.

The *tzimmes* can also be baked in a 325° oven. Yields 6 servings.

CARROT TZIMMES

1 pound carrots	salt
¼ cup margarine	1 teaspoon ginger
½ cup brown sugar	orange juice

Scrape the carrots and slice into rounds. Place in a pot with the margarine, brown sugar, salt, and ginger. Add orange juice to cover and bring to a boil. Lower the heat and continue to cook until the carrots are soft and glazed. Yields 4 servings.

LEEK PANCAKES

2 large leeks	salt
1 egg	pepper
¼ cup bread crumbs	oil for frying

Wash the leeks thoroughly in cold water to remove all sand from the leaves. Cut off the discolored parts and discard. Cut the clean leeks into small pieces and place in a pot. Cover with water and cook for 10 minutes. Remove the leeks from the water and drain well.

Chop up the leeks. Mix the chopped leeks with the rest of the ingredients, except the oil.

Heat the oil in a frying pan, and drop the leek mixture by tablespoons into the hot oil. Fry on both sides until light brown. Serve hot. Yields 4 servings.

PUMPKIN WITH DUMPLINGS

3 pounds pumpkin
1 teaspoon salt
1 cup brown sugar
4 tablespoons margarine

½ teaspoon cinnamon
¼ teaspoon nutmeg
¼ teaspoon allspice
¼ teaspoon ginger

Peel the pumpkin and scrape out the seeds. Wash and cut in 2″ pieces. Place the pumpkin in a pot and add the salt, brown sugar, and margarine. Sauté over very low heat until the pumpkin is soft. Add the spices and ½ cup of water. Transfer to a casserole, and bake the pumpkin in a 350° oven for ½ hour. Add the cooked dumplings (recipe follows) and continue to bake for 15 minutes. Serve hot. Yields 6 servings.

DUMPLINGS

½ cup farina
¼ cup *matzah* meal
1 teaspoon salt

2 eggs, beaten
4 tablespoons margarine, melted

Mix the farina with the *matzah* meal and salt.

Beat the eggs and add the melted margarine. Beat into the dry ingredients and mix well. Cover and refrigerate for a few hours or overnight.

In a big pot with a cover, bring 2 quarts of water to a boil. Add a little salt to the water. Wet hands and form dumplings the size of a walnut. Drop the dumplings into the boiling water. Cover the pot and cook the dumplings for 45 minutes. Do not remove the cover, but shake the pot so dumplings will not stick to the bottom of the pot.

Drain the dumplings and add to the casserole, placing them in the syrup. Bake for 15 minutes.

PINEAPPLE PUDDING

1 pound 14 ounce can crushed pineapple
3 tablespoons flour
4 eggs

1½ tablespoons margarine
½ teaspoon salt
juice of 1 lemon

Mix the flour with some of the pineapple juice, and stir the flour into the crushed pineapple. Beat the eggs well and add to the crushed pineapple. Add the margarine, salt, and lemon juice and mix well. Pour into a greased baking dish and bake for 45 minutes in a 350° oven. Serve as a pudding or as a side dish with chicken or meat. Yields 6 servings.

RAISIN CAKE

1 cup raisins	½ teaspoon baking soda
1 cup water	1 teaspoon cinnamon
1 cup brown sugar	1 egg, beaten
½ cup margarine	grated peel of 1 lemon
2 cups flour	juice of 1 lemon
2 teaspoons baking powder	confectioners sugar

Put the raisins, water, brown sugar, and margarine in a saucepan and bring to a boil. Lower the heat and simmer for 5 minutes. Allow to cool.

Sift the flour together with the baking powder, baking soda, and cinnamon. Add the dry ingredients to the cooled raisin mixture together with the the beaten egg, lemon peel, and lemon juice and mix well.

Pour the batter into a 9 x 9″ greased pan. Bake in a 350° oven for 1 hour.

Sift confectioners sugar over the top of the cake when cooled.

HONEY CAKE

4 cups flour	1½ cups sugar
1 teaspoon baking soda	2 tablespoons brown sugar
2½ teaspoons baking powder	½ cup margarine
1 teaspoon cinnamon	4 eggs
½ teaspoon ginger	1 pound honey
½ teaspoon allspice	¾ cup strong coffee
½ teaspoon nutmeg	

Sift the flour together with the baking soda, baking powder, and the spices.

A HAPPY NEW YEAR

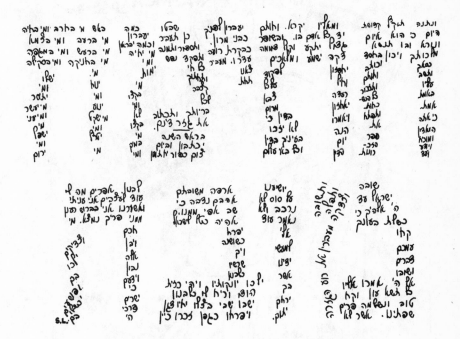

37. Greeting card. By Samuel Leve, New York. 1940. See Chapter
XVIII.

Print the complete address in plain block letters in the panel below, and your return address in the space
provided. Use typewriter, dark ink, or pencil. Write plainly. Very small writing is not suitable.

No.

(CENSOR'S STAMP)

To

From

(Sender's name)

(Sender's address)

(Date)

5704 NORTH J.W.B. AFRICA 1943-44

לשנה טובה תכתבו ותהתמו

A Happy New Year

V---MAIL

☆ U. S. GOVERNMENT PRINTING OFFICE 1 1943 16—36162-6

290]

38. V-mail greetings. North Africa, 1943, and Guam, 1944. See
Chapter XVIII.

39.   Greeting card. By Stan Brod, Cincinnati. 1966. See Chapter
XVIII.

Cream the sugars with the margarine until fluffy. Add the eggs one at a time, mixing well. Add the honey.

Stir the dry ingredients and the coffee into the honey mixture. Mix well.

Pour the batter into a greased and floured 9 x 12" pan. Bake the cake in a 350° oven for 15 minutes. Reduce the oven temperature to 325° and continue to bake for 45 minutes longer or until done.

TEIGLACH

3 eggs
1 tablespoon sugar
3 tablespoons margarine
2 cups flour
2 teaspoons ginger

1 cup broken walnuts
Syrup
1 cup honey
1 cup sugar

Cream the eggs with the sugar and margarine. Add the flour and mix together to form a soft but not sticky dough. If the dough is sticky, use a little more flour.

Divide the dough into several batches. On a floured board, roll out each batch of the dough into a long rope. Cut into half-inch pieces.

Make the syrup in a deep pot by bringing the sugar and honey to a boil. Drop the pieces of dough into the syrup. Cover the pot, lower the flame, and cook for 30 minutes. Shake the pot a few times while cooking so that the *teiglach* will not stick to the bottom of the pot. After cooking for 30 minutes, remove the cover and stir the *teiglach* with a wooden spoon to bring the top pieces into the syrup and the bottom ones to the top. Stir gently in order not to break the *teiglach*. Add the ginger to taste and the walnuts. (Those who adhere to the custom of not eating nuts on Rosh Hashanah can omit the walnuts.) Cover and continue to cook until all the pieces are browned. The *teiglach* are done when they are dry inside and not doughy.

Pour the *teiglach* on a flat wet board, and with wet hands

flatten them out. Sprinkle with more ginger if desired. When cold, cut in squares. *Teiglach* are best made on a dry rather than a humid day.

STUFFED DATES

1 cup ground almonds
6 tablespoons honey

10 ounces pitted dates
1 cup coconut

Mix the ground almonds with two tablespoons of the honey. Stuff each date with some of the almond filling.

Put the rest of the honey in a dish. Dip each date into the honey and then roll in the coconut. Place the dates on a foil-covered dish. Cover with Saran and refrigerate until served.

APPLE AND HONEY COMPOTE

2 pounds baking apples
1 cup honey
¼ cup white wine or orange
  juice

2 tablespoons lemon juice
¼ teaspoon nutmeg

Cut the apples into quarters and place them in a baking dish. Mix the honey, wine, lemon juice, and nutmeg, and pour the mixture over the apples. Bake uncovered in a 375° oven for 45 minutes, basting the apples a few times during the baking. Yields 6 servings.

X X

ROSH HASHANAH MISCELLANY

NAMES

The term Rosh Hashanah, literally "head (or beginning) of the year," is found only once throughout the Bible (Ezekiel 40.1), and even there it does not appear to refer to the first day of the year. In the Bible it is denominated *Zikhron Teruah*— "a memorial of the sounding (of the *shofar*)" (Leviticus 23.24) and *Yom Teruah*—"a day of blowing (the horn)" (Numbers 29.1).

The designation commonly used is clearly enunciated in the Mishnah: "The first day of Tishri is Rosh Hashanah (New Year) for [the reckoning of] years."[1]

Yom ha-Din ("Day of Judgment"), denoting the period when men are divinely judged for their deeds of the past year, is the talmudic designation used in the liturgy.[2] Another name for the holy day in the Talmud and popular in the Rosh Hashanah liturgy is *Yom ha-Zikkaron*—"Day of Remembrance."

It has a dual meaning: the day on which God remembers His creatures and shows them mercy, and the day on which the children of Israel remember their Heavenly Father by doing penitence.[3]

The Talmud also refers to Rosh Hashanah as *Yom ha-Keseh* ("Day of Concealment"), this being the only festival which falls at the beginning of the month when the new moon may still be concealed.[4]

According to Philo of Alexandria, "Trumpet Feast" is another appellation by which Rosh Hashanah was known.[5]

ROSH HASHANAH IN HISTORY

It is appropriate for Rosh Hashanah to be known as *Yom ha-Zikkaron*, "Day of Memorial," for in Jewish tradition it commemorates the many events purported to have occurred on this day or on other days in the month of Tishri. We shall briefly describe a number of these events.

Rabbi Eliezer claimed in the Talmud that the world was created in Tishri,[6] but according to a Jewish legend the Creation was completed on Rosh Hashanah with the formation of Adam. Evidence for this was adduced by medieval writers from the letters of the word *bereshit* ("in the beginning"), which begins the Genesis account of Creation. Its letters may be transposed to read *aleph be-tishri* ("on the first of Tishri").[7] The modern Rosh Hashanah liturgy iterates and reiterates that "Today is the birthday of the world."

Cain and Abel offered their sacrifices on Rosh Hashanah.[8]

Some authorities have held that the patriarchs Abraham and Jacob were born and died in Tishri.[9]

The *Akedah*, the binding of Isaac as a sacrifice, is said to have occurred on Rosh Hashanah. Because the ram was sacrificed in lieu of Isaac, its horn is used for the New Year *shofar*.[10] The biblical account of the *Akedah* (Genesis 22.1–24) is the Torah reading on the second day of the festival.

On the New Year Jacob arrived at Beth-El, where he built an altar.[11]

The matriarchs Sarah and Rachel and the prophetess Hannah, all of whom had been childless, were remembered by God on Rosh Hashanah. He answered their prayers, and subsequently they conceived and gave birth.[12] Hence the scriptural portions read on Rosh Hashanah center around three mothers in Israel: Genesis 21.1–34 regarding Sarah and I Samuel 1.1–2.10 regarding Hannah on the first day; Jeremiah 31.1–20 about Rachel on the second day.

On Rosh Hashanah Joseph was liberated from an Egyptian prison. This is deduced from the verses, "Blow the *shofar* on the new moon, on the day of the concealment for our festival. . . . He appointed it for Joseph for a testimony when He went forth against the land of Egypt" (Psalms 81.4–6).[13]

On Rosh Hashanah the children of Israel were emancipated from Egyptian bondage, although their exodus was delayed until Passover. In Tishri they will attain their future redemption.[14]

The dedication of the First Temple, built by King Solomon, took place in Tishri (I Kings 8.2).

On Rosh Hashanah of 444 B.C.E., Nehemiah and Ezra convened a great assembly of the returnees from Babylonian captivity in the Temple court, where Ezra read from the Torah (Nehemiah 8).

In the Middle Ages rivalry between leaders of the Jewish communities in Palestine and Babylonia resulted in an acrimonious controversy about the calendar regulations. As a result, in 922 C.E. Rosh Hashanah was observed on a Tuesday in Palestine and on a Thursday in Babylonia.[15]

A similar dispute in the eleventh century between Rabbanites and Karaites led to the observance of Rosh Hashanah by the Karaites one month after the Rabbanites.[16]

In 1280 Abraham Abulafia, one of the early cabbalists, boldly planned to convert Pope Nicholas III to Judaism on the day preceding Rosh Hashanah, so that he might participate with all Jewry in the New Year services. When the pope heard about Abulafia's audacious intention, he condemned him to be burned on the stake. But the pope died suddenly, and Abulafia was imprisoned instead.[17]

When several converts from Judaism denounced the Talmud
as blasphemous in 1533, Pope Julius III decreed that all copies
must be burned. Officers raided the Jewish homes in Rome
and confiscated all copies of the Talmud and other Jewish
books. The book *auto-da-fé* took place on Rosh Hashanah on
the Campo dei Fiori in Rome.[18]

On New Year of 1665, the cabbalist pseudo-messiah Sabbatai
Zevi publicly proclaimed himself to be the expected "messiah"
with the sounding of horns, while the congregation in Smyrna
exclaimed, "Long live the king, our messiah."[19]

THE TWO-DAY NEW YEAR

Only Rosh Hashanah is observed for two days both in the
Diaspora and in Israel; the other festivals are celebrated by
traditional Jews one day in Israel and two days in all other
countries. Reform Jews observe only one day of the festivals,
although some observe Rosh Hashanah for two days. The
traditional practice stems from the period of the Talmud. The
beginning of the month, which was determined by the sighting
of the new moon, was officially proclaimed by the court authorities in Jerusalem. They informed the Jewish communities
in Palestine and Babylonia of the precise time by signal fires on
mountains or by couriers. Since tidings about the start of the
new month were frequently delayed, Jews outside Palestine
were often in doubt as to the exact day and therefore observed
each festival for two days.

There was uncertainty regarding Rosh Hashanah even in
Palestine, for this is the only festival that occurs on the first
day of the month. Often witnesses to the appearance of the
new moon failed to testify promptly, or they appeared late in
the afternoon of the thirtieth day of Elul and occasionally not
until the next day. Hence, the last day of the sixth month (Elul)
and the first day of the seventh (Tishri), known as *Yom
Arikhata*—"one long day," were celebrated as Rosh Hashanah.

At the end of the second century, however, Rosh Hashanah
was generally observed in Palestine for only one day—on the

thirtieth of Elul. When the calendar was fixed and there was no longer a need for a proclamation by a court, Diaspora Jews continued to observe two days. The two-day observance of Rosh Hashanah was reintroduced in Palestine by Provençal Jewish scholars settling there in the twelfth century who preferred to maintain their former Diaspora practice.[20]

THE CALENDRICAL FORMULATION

As a result of the ingenuity of the rabbis, the first day of Rosh Hashanah can never fall on a Sunday, Wednesday, or Friday. This was arranged so that Yom Kippur would neither immediately precede nor follow the Sabbath. The rationale for this formulation was to eliminate the possibility of having two consecutive days on which it is forbidden to prepare food and to bury the dead. This system also provides that Hoshanna Rabba will not occur on a Sabbath, on which the traditional practice of beating the willow twigs at the religious service would be forbidden.[21]

"WAKE UP FOR THE SERVICE OF THE CREATOR"

During Elul, the month preceding the Days of Awe, *Selihot* (penitential prayers) are recited in the synagogue either after midnight or before dawn. In small East European Jewish communities and in some other countries, it was customary for the *shammash* (beadle) to go from house to house and awaken villagers to attend the *Selihot* services. Knocking on the doors or windows of the Jewish homes, the beadle chanted in a mixture of Hebrew and Yiddish such exhortations as:

"Wake up for the service of the Creator as you were created for this purpose."

"Israel, holy people, wake up, little Jews, for the service of the Creator. Judah ben Tema used to say: 'Be strong as a leopard, swift as an eagle, fleet as a deer, and mighty as a lion, to do the will of your Heavenly Father.'"[22]

"Wake up, wake up for the service of the Creator, hasten to

the synagogue. Fathers, mothers, boys and girls, wake up and come to serve the Creator."

"The hour has arrived, day is dawning, arise grandchildren of King David and recite Psalms" (an allusion to the tradition that David authored the Book of Psalms).[23]

Some sextons were the proud possessors of special hammers with which they knocked on the windows or doors. Some hammers, especially designed for the purpose, were carved out of wood in the shape of a *shofar*. On one side an eagle was etched and on the other a deer, to symbolize the admonition of Judah ben Tema.[24]

In Kurdistan the *shammash* went through the Jewish quarters before midnight, knocking on the doors and summoning each person by name to attend *Selihot* services. The children would urge each other to get up, and if one was slow to awaken, water was poured over him. The Jews' Moslem neighbors, believing that to rise during these nights brought good fortune, would pay the beadle to awaken them also at midnight.[25]

The Jewish children of Yemen, eager to participate in the *Selihot* service, would tie a string to their feet and hang one end out the window. When the beadle made his rounds at midnight he pulled the string to waken the youngsters, who would then accompany him with small *shofarot* and join in waking the sleeping population. They did not hesitate to blast their *shofarot* in the windows of the houses and even encouraged the dogs in the street to add to the racket by barking.[26]

VARIATIONS OF *TASHLIKH*

In the Galician village of Bolehov the *hasidim* would march to the river in a procession for *Tashlikh*, carrying lighted candles. By the time they had recited the prescribed prayers, the setting sun's last rays intermingled with the light of the candles, whereupon they ignited small bundles of straw with their candles and placed these floating "boats" on the water. When darkness fell, there was the spectacular scene of fire and water on the river, bringing joy and excitation to the *hasidim.* They believed that they were now purged of all their sins—that the waters swept them away and that the fires burned them.²⁷

The nineteenth-century Jewish traveler Israel ben Joseph Benjamin reported a very strange custom he witnessed among the Jews of Kurdistan. "On Rosh Hashanah all of them went to the river flowing at the foot of the mountain and said the *Tashlikh* prayer. Then they jumped into the water and swam among the waves like the fish of the sea, instead of only shaking the corners of their garments on the bank of the river, as is done by Jews in Europe. When I inquired of them the reason for this strange custom, they replied that by this action they will be cleansed of all their sins, for the waters of the river will cleanse them of all the sins they committed during the previous year."²⁸

In Israeli cities and towns where there are no rivers or lakes, *Tashlikh* is said alongside wells or cisterns containing water (fig. 29). In Safed the *hasidim* go to the roofs of their homes, where they can see Lake Kinneret in the distance. In some Oriental Jewish communities *Tashlikh* was recited in the synagogue around a basin of water into which live fish were placed.

The custom of *Tashlikh* was responsible for yet another false accusation against Jews in some European communities—anti-Semites claimed they went to poison the rivers.²⁹

AN EXEMPTION

Rabbi Shlomoh Goren, chief of chaplains of the Israel Defense Forces, advised soldiers near enemy bases that they were exempt from listening to the sounds of the *shofar*, so that their locations might not be betrayed.³⁰

GEMATRIA–NUMERICAL EQUIVALENTS

The numerical equivalent of the Hebrew letters for Elul is 67, the same as for *binah*, understanding. Thus it is deduced that understanding is propitious for repentance during the month of Elul. Furthermore, the prophet said, "and understanding with their heart, return, and be healed" (Isaiah 6.10).

The awe-inspiring *Unetanneh Tokef* prayer admonishes that "Repentance [*teshuvah*], prayer [*tefilah*], and charity [*tzedakah*] avert the evil decree." In some festival prayer books there appear in small letters, above these three avenues to salvation, the words *tzom* (fast, i.e., repentance), *kol* (voice, i.e., prayer) and *mamon* (money, i.e., charity). The Hebrew letters of each of these three words equal 136, or a total of 408 for the trio.

Mystical commentators note that the value of *sulam* (ladder) is also 136, suggesting that the ladder to heaven can be ascended on the rungs of repentance, prayer, and charity.

The word *zot* (this) is also equivalent to 408. Hence, when the Bible states "With this (in this manner) Aaron shall enter the holy place" (Leviticus 16.3), it implies that the high priest must perform repentance, prayer, and charity to be able to enter the shrine.

A ZODIACAL SIGN

Scales are the zodiacal sign for the month of Tishri, the period when man's deeds are weighed in the balance. A hasidic teacher noted that, just as the first of Tishri, Rosh Hashanah, is the middle of the year, so if a person's conduct during the first six months has been average, the balance of the scale is level.

THE HIGH HOLY DAYS IN WARTIME

While London was under air attack during World War II, Chief Rabbi Joseph H. Hertz and the *Bet Din*, following consultation with government authorities, issued the following instructions regarding the 1939 High Holy Days services:

> The services on the eve of New Year, as well as *all* Synagogue evening services throughout the War, must conclude half an hour before the time of the official blackout.

There will be *no* service in the Synagogue on the Eve of the Day of Atonement (Kol Nidre).

On the mornings of New Year, the service should begin at 8:30 and must conclude not later than 10:30. This can be done, including a sermon of a quarter of an hour's length, by omitting all *piyyutim* and replacing *hazzanut* by plain chanting. . . .

On the Day of Atonement, services will be held as follows: 11:30 to 1, Reading of the Law, Sermon, and Musaph; 5:15 to 6:30, Sermon and Neilah. The *Shofar* is not to be sounded at the end of Neilah, as *the Fast does not end till* 7:37 *p.m.* (in London).

In case of air raids during a service, the Minister is to advise those living within a few minutes' walk to return to their homes, and announce to the others the locality of the nearest air shelters. . . .

For obvious reasons, old men, women, and children should say their prayers at home on High Festivals.[31]

ROSH HASHANAH IN THE *KIBBUTZ*

New forms for observing the Jewish holidays, many based on traditional practices, are emerging in the nonreligious Israeli *kibbutzim* (collective settlements), despite their secular ideology. Until about a decade ago Rosh Hashanah and Yom Kippur played practically no role in the life of the average nonreligious collective settlement. In many *kibbutzim* the High Holy Days were completely ignored.

However, although the secular settlements were reluctant to observe Rosh Hashanah in the traditional manner of "weeping and praying for divine mercy," it was evident even before the establishment of the State of Israel that the holy day cannot be abolished. One writer suggested that the *shofar* be blown as a symbol of freedom and that a communal assembly be convened to discuss the improvement of society and to receive a report in depth on the *kibbutz*. He further suggested the participation of a chorus and readings from ancient and modern literature which might eventualy develop into a uniform pattern of observance.[32]

Gradually *kibbutzim* began to take cognizance of the Jewish New Year. One authority on the *kibbutz* movement reported in 1956 that he observed in a settlement the celebration of Rosh Hashanah as a secular New Year. The dining hall, adorned with greenery, paintings, and slogans, was the setting for a festive evening meal with the tables laden with an unusual abundance of food. The special program included a piano recital, a report on the economic status of the *kibbutz*, songs by youth groups, and humorous skits by local talent. It was, however, termed "an observable failure" because many in the audience left before it was over. This led the observer to conclude that the *kibbutz* "is still struggling with the problem of the 'religious' holidays."[33]

While some *kibbutzim* still mark Rosh Hashanah with outings, picnics, family visiting, and elaborate meals,[34] recent years have witnessed what might be termed an upsurge of interest in tradition and the development of uniform practices.

A publication issued by the *Ihud ha-Kevutzot veha-Kibbutzim*, the major national association of collective settlements, records *kibbutz* "customs" for the observances of Rosh Hashanah. A few days preceding the holiday an atmosphere of anticipation is created by advance preparations, and on Rosh Hashanah eve a bottle of wine, pomegranates, a jar of honey, and a gift are distributed to the members' rooms. Greeting cards or postcards with photographs of the *kibbutz* are also made available. In Bet ha-Shitah the children act as "messengers of good deeds" by distributing the refreshments and the gifts.

The dining hall is decorated with symbols of the festivals, the signs of the zodiac for the month of Tishri prominently displayed, an abundance of flowers and foliage, a selection of newspaper clippings on the outstanding events of the preceding year, and photographs of the settlement. Banners bear such legends as "For a blessing and not for a curse," "For plenty and not for scarcity," "For life and not for death,"[35] and "A good year." The tables for the festive meal are set with white cloths, wine, honey, and apples. In Bet ha-Shitah each person receives a portion of pomegranate seeds dipped in honey. This symbolizes, according to tradition, a sweet and fruitful year. The special menu includes fish and *kreplach*.

The most unexpected development in the Rosh Hashanah observance of *kibbutzim* is the publication of pamphlets, either mimeographed or photo-offset, entitled *Festival Readings for Rosh Hashanah, Tractate Rosh Hashanah*, and the like. By 1966 at least thirty-five *kibbutzim* had issued such booklets within a period of a few years.[36] These pamphlets are used at "services," generally on the first night of the holiday. A comparison of two illustrated pamphlets, issued in 1962 and in 1967 respectively—the first mimeographed and the second by photo-offset—in the kibbutz Neveh-Etan, reveals evidence of a groping for an acceptable format and contents. Indeed, many of these booklets, consisting of six to sixteen pages, appear to be experimental in character.

A typical *"mahzor"* includes appropriate Rosh Hashanah selections from the Bible, the Talmud, midrash, and liturgy; also modern Jewish literature and songs for community singing. The service may open with the kindling of the festival candles and the *Kiddush* over wine or conclude with the blessing over wine and with grace after the meal. A children's or adult choir generally participates. The liturgical portions include *Unetanneh Tokef, Atah Zokher Maaseh Olam, Atah Bahartanu, Yehi Ratzon she-Tehe ha-Shanah ha-Zot*, and other prayers. The songs most frequently rendered by a choir or used for community singing are *Mah Tovu Ohalekha Yaakov, Ve-Taher Libenu, Avinu Malkenu, Shanah Tovah, Torat Emet, Halleluyah, Yibane ha-Mikdash*—all reflecting a religious emphasis. Likewise, many of the poems selected for reading convey a religious message. Rosh Hashanah of 1967 saw the insertion of passages referring to the Six-Day War.

On the first day of Rosh Hashanah in 1967, kibbutz Hatzerim instituted a prayer service that was attended by fifty members.[37] The question may now be asked: Do these innovations portend a reversion to "weeping and praying for divine mercy" rejected a score of years ago?

XXI

CHILDREN'S STORIES FOR ROSH HASHANAH

▼▼▼▼▼▼▼▼▼▼▼▼▼▼▼▼▼▼▼▼▼▼▼▼▼▼▼▼▼▼▼▼▼▼▼▼▼

HAPPY BIRTHDAY, WORLD!

SADIE ROSE WEILERSTEIN

(age level five to eight)

Ruth and Debby were getting ready for a birthday. It wasn't Ruth's birthday or Debby's. It wasn't Danny's birthday or Judith's or Mother's or Daddy's. It wasn't even George Washington's birthday or Abraham Lincoln's. It was the WORLD'S birthday. It was Rosh Hashanah, the New Year.

"How old will the world be today?" Ruthie asked Mother.

"Ever so old," said Mother.

She was spreading their nicest white cloth on the table and Ruth and Debby were helping her.

"A hundred years old?" asked Ruthie.

"A thousand years old?" asked Debby.

"More than five thousand years old," said Mother.

"There ought to be a birthday cake for the world," said
Ruthie, "with candles."

"Goodness," said Mother. "Where could we get a cake big
enough? But we'll have our holiday candles and lots and lots
of good things. Come and help me put them on the table."

So Ruth and Debby helped. There were two round loaves,
hallahs, at Daddy's place. They weren't twisted, like the Sabbath loaves. They were round, for a good round year. And there
was honey for a sweet year, and sticky little round honey cakes.
Mm! Ruth and Debby could hardly wait to taste them. There
were shining red apples to dip in the honey.

Ruth and Debby danced round and round the table. They
were so happy, they made up a little song. Ruth began it.

> Everything is NEW on Rosh Hashanah!
>> Our shoes are new,
>> Our dresses are new,
>> Our ribbons are, too,
> Everything is NEW on Rosh Hashanah
> For a Happy NEW Year!

Then Debby sang.

> Everything is ROUND on Rosh Hashanah!
>> The apples are round,
>> And the cakes are round,
>> And the *hallahs* are round and round!
> Everything is ROUND on Rosh Hashanah
> For a good ROUND year.

"Now it's your turn, Mother," said Ruth and Debby. So
Mother sang too.

> Everything is SWEET on Rosh Hashanah!
>> Daddy's flowers are sweet,
>> And the cakes are sweet,

And the honey is sweet,
And my children are VERY sweet!
Everything is SWEET on Rosh Hashanah
For a good SWEET year.

But still Ruth and Debby wished there could be a birthday cake with candles. They didn't say anything about it, because just then Daddy came in from synagogue. Ruth and Debby flew across the room to meet him.

"Le-shanah tovah! Happy New Year, Daddy," they cried.

After that there were so many things to do. There was Daddy's Kiddush to listen to. They stood very still and quiet while he thanked God for the New Year. Then Daddy cut one of the big round loaves and each one dipped a bit of bread in honey.

"Le-shanah tovah u-metukah," they said. "For a good sweet year."

They dipped apple in honey, too. Apple is very good when you dip it in honey. Mother's candles blinked brightly, and Daddy sang songs, and it was past their bedtime but they didn't have to go to bed, and the food was so good! But still Ruth and Debby wished there could be a birthday cake with candles.

They told Daddy about it.

"Hm," Daddy said. "A birthday cake for the world's birthday! Do you know how big it would have to be? If all the wheat fields were one wheat field, and all the scythes were one scythe, and all the mills were one mill; if all the mixing bowls were one mixing bowl, and all the baking pans one baking pan, all the ovens one oven—"

"And all the bowls of frosting one bowl of frosting," Ruthie helped him.

"Of course," said Daddy. "We mustn't forget the frosting. If all the men were one man, one great giant man! If the great giant man took the great big scythe and cut down the great big field of grain; if he ground the grain in the great big mill, and gave the great sack of flour to his great giant wife, and she mixed it in the great big bowl and baked it in the great big pan—"

"And frosted it with the great big bowl of frosting," said Ruthie.

"Then MAYBE," said Daddy, "that great big cake would be big enough to hold the world's birthday candles."

Ruth and Debby laughed. They liked Daddy's stories. But still they wished they could see those candles.

"There ought to be birthday candles on a birthday," said Debby.

Then what do you suppose happened? Daddy whispered something to Mother. Mother nodded her head.

"Maybe we can find those candles," said Daddy.

The next minute Mother was slipping on Ruth's and Debby's coats and they were all out of doors—out at night, long past their bedtime.

It was very still and shadowy in the garden.

"Look up," said Daddy. "Do you see the candles?"

Ruth and Debby threw back their heads and raised their eyes to the sky. It was dark and velvety—and it was filled with stars. There were hundreds and hundreds of them, blinking and twinkling like birthday candles.

"The stars are the world's birthday candles," said Debby softly. Her eyes were shining.

Mother and Daddy nodded.

Ruth and Debby looked up at the sky with its twinkling stars, at the new moon, the Tishri moon, like a silver cradle. They looked at the grass under their feet, at the elm tree lifting its dark boughs to heaven.

"Happy birthday, world," they said.

"Happy New Year!"[1]

HOW K'TONTON DROVE SATAN OUT OF THE *SHOFAR*

SADIE ROSE WEILERSTEIN

(age level four to seven)

K'tonton [a little Jewish Tom Thumb] was talking to Sammy, the sexton's boy. He often talked to Sammy in the synagogue between the afternoon and evening prayers. Sammy would sprawl on a bench and K'tonton would sit on a reading stand looking down at him.

"So you'd better watch out, K'tonton," Sammy was saying. "If you commit the tiniest little sin, Satan will pick it up and carry it straight to God. He watches especially near Rosh Hashanah."

K'tonton glanced toward the shadows gathering in the corner. "But Sammy," he said, "how do you know?"

"How do I know? My father told me, that's how I know."

"Oh!" said K'tonton. If Sammy's father had told him, there was nothing more to say. Wasn't it Sammy's father who blew the shofar, the ram's horn, on Rosh Hashanah?

Sammy had once told him about the shofar. "Do you know why you blow the shofar so loud, K'tonton?" he had asked. "To confound Satan! There is Satan before God's throne telling all the sins of Israel. All of a sudden there comes a great sound. Tekiah-ah teruah-ah, tekiah-ah!" Sammy imitated the notes exactly. "Satan is so upset he forgets everything he was going to say and begins to stutter. So what does Satan do next time? He goes down to earth and tries to crawl inside the shofar to stop the sound."

"Did he ever really stop it?" asked K'tonton.

"I don't remember," said Sammy, "but he might. If it weren't for Satan, we would be in Eretz Yisrael already. The messiah would have come long ago."

K'tonton thought about what Sammy had said as he lay awake in the dark that night. He thought of it the first thing he opened his eyes in the morning.

"Mother," he said, "could Satan get inside a shofar?"

"Stop troubling your little head about Satan," said his mother, "and come and try on your new suit."

K'tonton went to his father.

"Father," he said, "do you suppose that Satan could get inside our shofar?"

Father was reading the paper.

"He has gotten into too many shofars already," he answered without looking up.

All that day K'tonton went about worrying whether Satan could get into the *shofar*. After that he forgot all about him. There were too many pleasant things to do. New Year's greetings to write out, rosy apples to shine, the big *hallahs* to sniff as they came out of the oven. And then it was Rosh Hashanah night. K'tonton got into his brand new suit and hat and shoes, to "renew the year" you know. He went to synagogue and wished everyone *Le-shanah Tovah*, Happy New Year! He sat at the table before Mother's shining candles and dipped apple in honey for a sweet year.

It was not until next morning in the synagogue when the *shofar* was blown that K'tonton remembered Satan again. Then he gave him no more than a thought. He was too busy counting the blasts. Father had said there would be one hundred *shofar* blasts and K'tonton was counting to see whether he was right.

"*Tekiah-ah, shevarim teruah, tekiah!*" called the rabbi.

"*Tekiah-ah, t-t-t-t-t-t-t-too, tekiah-ah!*" answered the *shofar* now clear and ringing, now broken like a sigh, now bold and clear again.

All morning K'tonton counted the notes carefully on his fingers; thirty after the reading of the Torah, ten and ten and ten again during the additional prayers, more of them toward the end of the service. "Seventy, eighty, ninety," counted K'tonton; then "ninety-five, ninety-six, ninety-seven, ninety-eight, ninety-nine."

It was time for the final note, the great triumphant blast, the *tekiah gedolah*. K'tonton sat up tense and waiting. But no sound came—nothing but a muffled "pf, pf, pf." Sammy's father shifted the *shofar* sidewise to his lips. He blew again. He puffed and panted. His face grew red with the exertion. All that came was a broken, stuttering t-t-t-t.

A buzzing and whispering rose in the synagogue. People leaned over the benches and whispered to one another. Someone behind K'tonton was speaking quiet loudly.

"Satan has gotten into the *shofar*!"

Satan! Satan in the *shofar*! Sammy had said he sometimes got inside, but K'tonton had not thought he would really do it, not in their *shofar* at least. Suppose he stayed there! Suppose he stayed the whole Rosh Hashanah. Suppose they couldn't blow the *shofar* at all! How would the people be forgiven? How could they be written down for a good year?

Suddenly a thought came into K'tonton's head. It grew and grew until it was so big it filled his whole mind. HE, K'TONTON, WOULD GET INSIDE THE *SHOFAR* AND DRIVE SATAN OUT.

K'tonton hardly knew what was happening during the rest of the service. His mind was so busy with his plans. Services were over at last. Father folded his prayer shawl and carried it to the little back room. On a table near a pile of prayer books lay the ram's horn. K'tonton slipped from his father's arm and hid. Father walked out of the synagogue not even noticing that K'tonton had been left behind.

The last footsteps passed. Voices died away. K'tonton was alone.

Cautiously he crept from behind the prayer books and approached the *shofar*.

He stooped and peered into its deep mouth. Somewhere among those shadows Satan was lurking—Satan the adversary, the enemy. Who was he, K'tonton, to fight the dread angel? He trembled, but he did not turn back. Firmly he stepped into the mouth of the *shofar* and groped his way. The darkness grew; the walls drew closer. He stopped and stretched out his hand. He could scarcely see it in the blackness. Suddenly something clutched his arm. He felt his shoulders held fast. The enemy!

"*Shema Yisrael!*" K'tonton called wrenching himself free. He stepped back. He struck out against the enemy. He gave blow upon blow fiercely without stopping.

"*Kera Satan!* Rend Satan," he cried.

Steps were approaching in the room outside. A voice spoke. "Sammy," it said, "I'd better try the *shofar* and see what's wrong."

The *shofar* was lifted.

But K'tonton inside the *shofar* was so absorbed in the struggle he neither heard nor felt. He knew nothing until suddenly through the narrow end of the horn came a blast like a whirl-wind. It lifted K'tonton up. It shot him out of the *shofar*, across the room, out through the open window. He landed on some-thing soft. It was his father's shoulder.

"K'tonton," said his father, "what have you been up to? I've been all the way home and back."

K'tonton smiled and shut his mouth tight.

Next morning at services the *shofar* rang out so clear and bold, everyone remarked about the difference. Anxiously K'ton-ton listened to each blast, lest some sign of Satan appear. But no! Each note came clearer than the one before. At the end, the *tekiah gedolah* rang out so loud and held so long, the people gasped with wonder.

"K'tonton," said Sammy after the services as K'tonton sat waiting for his father, "do you remember what I told you about Satan getting into the *shofar*? Yesterday I saw him. I was in the back room with my father. He shot out of the *shofar* like a rocket. I saw him with my own eyes."

K'tonton nodded and smiled. He didn't tell Sammy who it was who had driven Satan out of the *shofar*.[2]

THE *SHOFAR'S* MESSAGE

MORRIS EPSTEIN

(age level five to eight)

Susan and Billy were as proud as a pair of haughty peacocks.

Their faces were scrubbed and gleaming. Susan wore a new blouse with pretty lace ruffles, and Billy's new shoes squeaked gaily as he tried to keep up with Father's quick pace.

The twins had good reason to be proud. This was the first year that Father had arranged for them to have seats for themselves in the synagogue on Rosh Hashanah and Yom Kippur. They were *really* grown-up!

"Squeak! Squeak!" said Billy's shoes as the family marched toward the synagogue on Rosh Hashanah eve.

"Goodness!" said Mother. "You'd better stand still during the services, Billy. If you move, those shoes of yours will be heard above the *shofar*!"

"Does the *shofar* squeak, too?" asked Billy.

"No, indeed!" laughed Father. "When it is blown properly it sounds like the call of a mighty trumpet."

"Is it a trumpet?" asked Susan.

"No, it isn't," said Father. "A trumpet is usually made of metal. A *shofar* is always a ram's horn. It has no pushbuttons, or reeds, or anything else added to it.

"The *shofar* is a symbol. It reminds us of days long, long ago. Many centuries before Columbus discovered America, the Jewish people used the *shofar*. They used it in many ways. In wartime, a blast of the *shofar* called the army together. There was no telephone or radio, so the *shofar* was used to announce important events. For instance, when a new king took his place on the throne, the *shofar* was blown. In our own time, in the State of Israel, the *shofar* is blown on Fridays before sundown, to announce that Shabbat will soon arrive. And, when a new President was chosen after Dr. Chaim Weizmann died, the call of the *shofar* welcomed him into the *Knesset*, or parliament."

"But why did our people always use the *shofar*?" asked Susan.

"Daddy said it was a symbol," replied Mother.

"Yes," nodded Father. "It was and still is a symbol to remind us of a story in the Bible. When Abraham wanted to show his love for God by giving up his son, Isaac, God showed *His* love for Abraham by refusing to take Isaac away. Then Abraham presented a ram to God instead. And since that time we have used the *shofar*, the horn of a ram, in the ways I have mentioned.

"Today we use the *shofar* only in the synagogue. Its mighty, rolling sounds fill the house of worship. The *shofar* says: 'Te-ki-ah! Come to prayer! Happy New Year! Te-ru-ah! Let us

ask God for a sweet year, for us and for all people in every
corner of the world.'

"That is what we pray for on Rosh Hashanah. And that is
what the call of the *shofar* means."

When the family reached the brightly-lit, freshly-cleaned
synagogue, many men and women were already there. Holding
on to their parents' hands Susan and Billy proudly marched in
and took their seats, their very own seats.

And no one seemed to notice that Billy walked very carefully,
almost on tip-toe. Little Billy was making sure that his new
shoes would not drown out the sound of the *shofar*![3]

THE BOY'S PRAYER

MORRIS EPSTEIN

(age level six to nine)

The days before Rosh Hashanah were busy ones for Gita and
Jerry. They helped Mother with her shopping. Mother had a
list and Gita checked off the items. The list included rosy
autumn apples to munch on, and sweet honey for father to
dip bread into and say:

"May the New Year be as sweet as this honey."

Gita loved Rosh Hashanah, the Jewish New Year. The house
was full of fragrant flowers and the table was set with the
best linen and silver. The synagogue, too, looked scrubbed and
fresh and more holy than ever. The ark was covered with a
white silk curtain instead of the usual dark one. And the *shofar*,
the curved ram's horn, was brought out of its velvet bag, ready
to be used for the long, loud blasts blown on the New Year.

Outside, the red and purple fall leaves had begun to flutter
to the ground. It was a brisk Sunday afternoon just before
Rosh Hashanah and Gita was carefully writing New Year cards
to her relatives and friends. Father had written out a sample
for her. She slowly copied it, her tongue peeking out of the
corner of her mouth. Jerry was very busy too. He licked each

envelope, put the New Year card into it, and sealed it. Then
he placed a stamp on the envelope and made certain that it
was pasted tight.

Gita wrote: *Le-shanah tovah tikatevu,* and the English translation, "May you be inscribed for a happy year."

Suddenly Gita turned to Father, who was enjoying the Sunday
paper.

"What does 'inscribed' mean, Daddy?"

"It means 'written,'" said Father.

"Written in—in what?" Gita kept on.

"In the Book of Life," answered Father, rustling his newspaper a little.

"What Book of Life?" asked Gita. She was not to be put off
that easily.

Father gave up. He put the newspaper down and said, "The
Book of Life contains all the names of those who do good deeds
and who will enjoy good health during the coming year.

"In the synagogue on Rosh Hashanah we pray to God and
ask Him to grant us a good year of life and happiness. And
on Yom Kippur, the Day of Atonement, it is decided in Heaven
who shall live and who shall be happy. Yom Kippur falls about
a week after Rosh Hashanah and is the most solemn holy
day of the whole year."

"But Daddy," said Gita, a quiver in her voice, "I can only
say *some* of the prayers. And Jerry, why, he's only *six.* What
about us, Daddy?"

Father held back a smile. He pulled Gita and Jerry close to
him.

"Children," he said, "your few prayers are just as important
as anyone's. Why, once there was a little boy who had a
whistle, and. . . ."

"A story!" cried Gita, and clapped her hands.

"A story!" echoed Jerry gleefully.

"Very well, a story it shall be," said Father with a grin.

"There once was a great rabbi named the Baal Shem Tov,
the Master of the Good Name. He was known for his kindness
to all living beings, human and animal alike. One year, on the

eve of Yom Kippur, all the townspeople gathered in the synagogue. The Baal Shem Tov, whom everyone called the Besht
for short, stood near the ark. Slowly he chanted *Kol Nidre*, the
beautiful prayer said only on Yom Kippur eve. . . .

"In the meantime, a Jew from the village and his little son
had entered the synagogue. They stood in the back. The man
was ashamed of himself because he had never taken the trouble
to teach the boy any Hebrew, and the boy could not pray.

"But the boy wanted *so much* to pray. He wanted to tell God
how unhappy he was because he was different from the other
boys in the synagogue.

"Again and again he opened his mouth, but not a word of
prayer came out. Suddenly, the boy pulled a reed whistle out
of his pocket. His father said, 'Put that away. One must not
whistle in a holy place.'

"The boy pleaded with his eyes. His father swallowed the
lump that was in his throat and looked away, blinking. He
felt sorry for his son. Then the boy put the whistle to his lips.
In the hushed synagogue, he blew long and hard upon his
whistle.

"The congregation grew very angry. Several men rushed up.
They wanted to chase the boy out. At that moment, the Besht
raised his hand for silence and said:

"'All evening I have prayed hard so that our sins might be
forgiven. But I felt that my prayers were not being heard. When
this little boy blew on his whistle, a strange thing happened.
I knew at once that he had caused our prayers to be accepted
by God. Because of this boy who has never wronged anyone,
we shall all be inscribed in the Book of Life.'"

Father paused and looked at Gita and Jerry. "You see, children," he said, "*how* we pray is not most important. What *is*
important is that we pray as best we can. We must have a pure
heart and a clean soul. Always remember the story of that
little boy. Especially on Rosh Hashanah and Yom Kippur."

Gita straightened Father's tie and looked right into his eyes.
"Daddy," she said, "would you please take me to the public
library tomorrow?"

"Certainly," Father replied with a look of surprise. "Is there any book in particular you want to read?"

"Yes, Daddy," said Gita. "I'd like to read the Book of Life."[4]

YOW CELEBRATES ROSH HASHANAH IN HIS OWN WAY

ALTHEA O. SILVERMAN

(age level seven to ten)

Yow, Habibi's little black spaniel, was too young to understand everything his master told him. He could not understand, for instance, how the world could have a birthday. The world was not like a boy or a girl or a lady or a man.

Yet, that's just what Habibi had told him when he returned from the synagogue with his parents and Uncle Peter on Rosh Hashanah day.

"*Shanah Tovah!* Happy New Year!" Habibi had called in his cheeriest voice.

The little dog did not know what *Shanah Tovah* meant, so Habibi proceeded at once to explain.

"Today is the world's birthday," he said. "Instead of 'Happy Birthday!' we say 'Happy New Year!'"

Habibi could see by the expression in Yow's eyes that the little spaniel still did not understand, so he sat Yow on a high, high stool and he repeated the words that the rabbi had spoken after the *shofar* was sounded that morning.

"This day the world was created," Habibi said. "On this day all stand before God. And God opens a big, big book and every-thing—EVERYTHING we have done is written there."

The little dog tried to look intelligent. He blinked his eyes and cocked his head. He raised one ear and then he raised his other ear. He shifted this way and he shifted that way. He tried patiently to follow what his master was saying.

"Do you see this finger?" Habibi said, wiggling his forefinger for the little dog to see.

Yow perked up and began wagging his stubby tail. He thought the lecture was over. He thought Habibi was ready to play.

"This is no play," Habibi said sternly. "Just look at this finger. Every night it goes to heaven and writes in a big, big book all the things I have done all day, good and bad. On Rosh Hashanah, when the big, big book is open, everything is written there. Not a single thing is hidden, not one thing is forgotten. Our own finger writes all our good deeds and all our bad deeds in that big book."

The little dog began at last to understand. He had visions of a huge book hanging overhead.

"Does my forepaw go to heaven each night?" he wondered, glancing down at his little black paw. "Is there a record of all things I have done? Did my forepaw write about the little squirrels I chased and their nuts that I scattered in the park?" His face became troubled and serious.

"Beginning today, we have ten days in which to make good the wrongs we have done," Habibi continued solemnly. "We have ten days before the great day of Yom Kippur when we fast and ask God to forgive all our sins. If we want God to forgive us, we must go to those whom we have wronged and get their forgiveness. And we must resolve never, never to repeat our sins."

Habibi was impressed with the sound of his own voice. He sounded so grown-up and important. In his ears still quivered the shrill sounds of the *shofar*, "T-T-T-Tooooo!" and the sweet singing of the choir.

"*Le-shanah tovah tikatevu!*" called Grandmother bursting into the room. "May you be inscribed for a good year!"

"Grandmother!" cried Habibi. "When did you come? I didn't hear you—"

"Of course you didn't," said Grandmother. "You were too busy with your little dog. We've come to have Rosh Hashanah dinner with you. We're all here."

To be sure they were all there, two grandmothers, two grandfathers, aunts, uncles, and cousins. They were greeting each other joyfully:

"*Le-shanah tovah tikatevu*, a good and happy year.

"*Le-shanah tovah tikatevu*, a year of health and cheer."

The house was full of flowers which they had sent for Rosh

Hashanah, and stacks of New Year cards lay unopened on the desk.

Uncle Peter was starved, as usual. He was the first to go into the dining room.

"Round, red apples," he said, admiring the bowl of shining apples in the center of the table. "And honey, too!"

"Apples and honey for a round, sweet year!" said Mother.

Everything on the table was round. The *hallahs* were round. They were not twisted like the Shabbat loaves. The egg barley in the soup were round. The *teiglach*, the honey balls, were round. Even the honey cake was round today.

"Round and sweet for a round, sweet year," Habibi kept repeating. "Round and sweet for a round, sweet year."

Although the dinner was delicious and Yow sat in his Shabbat chair that Uncle Peter had built for him, the little spaniel was impatient for the meal to end. He wanted to get away, to run and frisk and bark.

When the last of the grace, the prayer after the meal, was said, out rushed the little dog, wagging his stubby tail and barking and barking at the top of his voice.

"Happy New Year!" he barked at a little girl.

The girl was frightened and began to cry.

"Happy New Year! Happy New Year!" barked Yow to a man, jumping up at him in the friendliest way.

"Go 'way!" said the man. "You're dirtying my suit with your muddy paws."

"Happy New Year! Happy New Year!" barked Yow at everyone who passed by, but no one understood him and everyone brushed him off.

He ran into the street.

"Happy New Year! Happy New Year!" he barked at the automobiles that drove by. But the drivers of the automobiles did not understand either. They scowled and swerved to one side to avoid running the little dog over.

"Get off the road, you crazy little dog! Do you want to get killed?" they shouted.

One after another the drivers of the automobiles skidded and scolded as Yow ran into their paths, barking and chasing each car. Yow barked louder and louder for he wanted the drivers to understand he was greeting them on this Rosh Hashanah day.

A little speckled setter soon joined him in the middle of the street. He knew what Yow was saying, so he barked "Happy New Year!" too.

Now there were two dogs chasing and barking at each automobile. What a noise they made barking together! They barked so loud, that a third little dog, a bushy brown collie ran into the street and added his greeting to theirs.

"Happy New Year!" they all barked together. "Happy New Year!"

The whole street was in an uproar. Three dogs barking together, automobile horns blowing, gears shifting and scraping, angry drivers shouting—what a turmoil!

One by one the automobiles lined up after each other, unable to proceed. The drivers got out of their cars and tried to force the three little dogs off the street, but the dogs barked louder and jumped up at them trying to make them understand.

It was precisely at that moment that Habibi appeared. He saw the long line of cars and heard the threats of the angry drivers. He spied his little dog, Yow, at once.

"Yow!!!" he cried, panic-stricken. "Yow! come here this minute!"

Yow was an obedient dog. Much as he wanted to continue his fun, much as he wanted to continue barking "Happy New Year," he knew that when his master calls, he must respond immediately.

"What's the meaning of this?" asked Habibi, very, very angry at his little dog. "Do you want to get killed? Haven't I taught you never to play in the street? Those automobiles could have run you over."

The other two dogs, seeing their leader leave his post, followed him off the street.

The automobiles started moving. Order and quiet were restored.

Yow followed Habibi into the house. Habibi would not speak to him. The little dog knew that his master was angry with him but he could not see where he had done any wrong. He looked pleadingly into Habibi's eyes and tried to tell him that this being Rosh Hashanah, he wanted merely to be friendly and to greet everyone "Happy New Year!" If Habibi would only understand. If Habibi would only smile and tell him he was forgiven. How *can* a dog celebrate the New Year? He cannot go to the synagogue to pray. He is not allowed to hear the blowing of the *shofar*. He can only be very happy and *bark* his New Year's greetings.

And that's how Yow celebrated Rosh Hashanah.[5]

A SWEET NEW YEAR*

LEVIN KIPNIS

(age level eight to eleven)

Far, far away where sky and earth appear to embrace each other the two sisters met.

The older sister, Lady Lastyear, was old and weary. Her face was wrinkled, her clothing shabby. She moaned and groaned as she came trudging down the mountain to the valley below.

Her sister, Miss Newyear, was young and pretty. Dressed in a charming sky-blue dress with a beautiful wreath of flowers on her head, she stepped gracefully on her way to the top of the high mountain.

Four angels accompanied Miss Newyear: one on her right, one on her left, one behind her, and one in front.

"Shalom, my dear sister!" Miss Newyear greeted the old lady. "Why are you moaning and groaning?"

Lady Lastyear leaned heavily on her cane and replied with a deep sigh:

"I am broken-hearted, dear sister! Things look very dark and hopeless!"

* All rights reserved by the author.

"And what can you tell me about our people in this wide world?" the younger sister asked.

"Oh, sad and bitter is their lot! Sad and bitter!" moaned the old lady.

Meanwhile, the sun began to set, and Lady Lastyear resumed her trudging down the mountain while the youthful Miss Newyear went briskly on her way to the top.

Miss Newyear walked, but the parting words of her sister rang in her ears and gave her no rest.

"What can I do to gladden and sweeten the lot of our people?" she asked herself.

A vineyard on the slope of the mountain came out to meet the New Year. Rows of vines stretched out their tendrils to the newcomer. Clusters of grapes filled with sweet juice lay hidden among the leaves.

"A Happy and Sweet New Year!" greeted the vineyard. "What worries you, my dear, and what makes you so sad?"

"Lovely vineyard!" replied Miss Newyear, "how can I stop worrying and be happy when the lot of our people is sad and bitter?"

"Forget your worries, my dear!" said the vineyard. "Pluck my sweet juicy grapes and sweeten with them the lot of our people!"

Miss Newyear motioned to the two angels on her right and left. They plucked the heaviest clusters of grapes and carried them on a staff on their shoulders, stumbling and tottering under the load.

Miss Newyear walked ahead, but she was still worried and saddened.

"What else can I do to bring joy and sweetness to our people?" she kept asking herself.

A pomegranate grove appeared on the side of the mountain. Rows of trees stretched on the sides of the grove and among their sparkling and glittering leaves hung red-cheeked pomegranates.

"A Happy and Sweet New Year!" wished the grove. "What causes you to look so sad and down-hearted, my dear?"

"My dear pomegranate grove!" replied Miss Newyear. "My heart aches and pains over the sad and bitter lot of our people all over the world."

"My pomegranates are ripe," said the grove, "and their juice is sweet. Take them and sweeten the lot of our people!"

At the command of Miss Newyear the third angel plucked the choicest pomegranates and carried them in a basket on his head.

Miss Newyear continued on her way, but could not put out of her mind her sister's words.

"Will these grapes and pomegranates be enough to gladden and sweeten the lot of our people who are scattered all over the wide world?" she asked herself.

Her thoughts were interrupted by the appearance of a huge beehive. A swarm of golden bees with transparent wings, big round eyes, and slender curved feelers surrounded the bewildered Miss Newyear and buzzed:

"Zzzz . . . A Sss . . .weet New Year! Why are you so sss . . . ad?"

"My dear hard-working golden honey bees," replied Miss Newyear, "I am very unhappy over the plight of our people in the world!"

"Zzzz . . . ," buzzed the bees, "we flew from flower to flower gathering sweet honey. We stood in line from morning until sunset and worked without a stop chewing, macerating and making the honeycombs. Our golden honey is sweet and its fragrance is heavenly. Take it, bring it to our people, and make their New Year as sweet as our honey!"

The fourth angel accepted the honeycombs and carried them in a large jug.

The first three stars appeared in the sky when Miss Newyear and her angels accompanying her reached the top of the mountain. The big city was decorated in their honor. All houses were whitewashed. Doors and windows were repainted and covered with colorful curtains. White and blue flags waved from the balconies and burning candles in each house spread cheer and merriment. Men and women were dressed in holiday clothes, and children wore their new suits and dresses. They filled the streets with laughter and songs.

Miss Newyear spread her wings over the city and sent her angels to deliver the sweets to every home. When the people returned to their homes from the synagogue, they sat around their tables, tasted the sweet grapes, ate the juicy pomegranate, dipped pieces of bread in honey, and wished each other:

"A HAPPY AND SWEET NEW YEAR!"

Translated by Israel M. Goodelman[6]

SIMON OBSERVES ROSH HASHANAH

DOROTHY F. ZELIGS

(age level ten to thirteen)

The congregation stood in hushed silence as the stirring call of the *shofar* sounded through the house of worship. It was a solemn moment in the service of Rosh Hashanah, one of the most holy days of the Jewish year. As the notes died away, the voice of the worshipers rose in prayer.

To Simon Levy, who was sitting in one of the front rows, it was a new experience to be in a synagogue like this. He had arrived in the city just a few days ago, from a small town in the West where there were only a few Jewish families. It was amazing to him that this vast congregation was made up entirely of Jews. In all his eleven years he had never been in such a large and stately synagogue.

After the services, a hubbub of greetings arose. "Happy New Year! Happy New Year!" flew from lips to lips. A number gave the greeting in Hebrew, according to the custom. "*Le-shanah tovah tikatevu,*" they said, which means, "May you be inscribed for a good year."

Simon walked out with his uncle and aunt, Dr. and Mrs. Jonathon, and his two cousins, thirteen-year-old Maurice, and

THE ROSH HASHANAH ANTHOLOGY

blue-eyed Ruthie, who was ten. It seemed as if everyone stopped and greeted them. "I want you to meet Simon, my nephew," his Uncle Phil was saying. "He is going to spend a whole year with us. His parents went to South America and so they loaned him to us."

The September air was brisk, and it was pleasant to walk leisurely home among the well-dressed holiday crowd. "You like it here with us, don't you, Simon?" Ruthie looked up at him with a gay smile that made her eyes and tilted nose crinkle up in a funny, delightful fashion.

"He doesn't like to be bothered with girls all the time, remember that," Maury told her with a superior air.

"Why—why," Ruthie was about to prove he was right by bursting into angry tears, but Simon squeezed her hand and said shyly, "Ruthie's O.K., Maury." And the rest of the way he kept hold of her hand.

When they reached home, they gathered around the attractive table, set with the best dishes and decorated with flowers in honor of Rosh Hashanah. Dr. Jonathon recited the holiday *Kiddush* over the silver goblet of wine. After saying the prayer in Hebrew, he repeated part of it in English. "Blessed art Thou, O Lord our God, King of the Universe, who createst the fruit of the vine. Blessed art Thou, O Lord our God, King of the Universe, who hast kept us in life, and hast taken care of us, and enabled us to reach this season."

Over the two loaves of white bread twists that lay at the head of the table, Dr. Jonathon chanted, "Blessed art Thou, O Lord our God, King of the Universe, who bringest forth bread from the earth."

On the table stood a dish of honey surrounded by slices of apples. Each one took a piece of apple, dipped it in the honey, and ate it, reciting the Hebrew blessing "Blessed art Thou, O Lord our God, King of the Universe, who createst the fruit of the tree."

"It is an old custom," Uncle Phil explained, "to eat something sweet on Rosh Hashanah as a symbol for a sweet New Year."

"What's the matter, Simon?" asked Aunt Elsa. "You look a little bewildered."

"I guess I am," the boy admitted. "At home, we didn't celebrate the Jewish holidays very much. Even on Rosh Hashanah, we didn't have all these interesting ceremonies. Last night, when the holiday began and you lit candles on the table and everything, it seemed sort of strange. But I like it very much," he added.

There was little conversation for a while as all settled down to the pleasant task of enjoying the holiday meal. But Simon continued to look thoughtful as he ate. "Just what do those words Rosh Hashanah mean, Uncle Phil?"

His uncle smiled at him. "The words are Hebrew and mean *head of the year*. Rosh Hashanah and the holiday which comes ten days later, Yom Kippur, are known as the High Holy Days, because they are the most solemn occasions of the Jewish year. They are occasions for thinking about our conduct and for repenting of our wrongdoings. Most of the time we are too busy to think much about how we are behaving to our family and friends, to the Jewish people, to the whole world, in fact. But on the High Holy Days we put everything else aside and spend the time in thought and prayer. We ask forgiveness for past sins and resolve to lead better lives in the future."

"I like to hear the blowing of the *shofar* in the synagogue," Maury said. "It's sort of exciting—like calling the people to arms or something."

"It is an important part of the Rosh Hashanah service," his father replied. "The *shofar* is made of a ram's horn, and it's a very interesting musical instrument. The Bible mentions it many times. As Maury suggested, it was used as a call to arms, in times of war. But it had many other uses. The *shofar* summoned the people together for an assembly in times of crisis. It was used to announce events of national importance, such as the crowning of a new king. But the call of the *shofar* was familiar to the people even in their ordinary lives. On late Friday afternoons, the sound of the *shofar*, blown from the housetops of the city, proclaimed the arrival of the Sabbath. And, of course, the New Year was greeted with the blowing of the *shofar*."

"On Rosh Hashanah, the call of the *shofar* might be regarded as a call to conscience," Aunt Elsa added. "It says, 'What ho, there! Stop rushing around so much and think more about where you are going. Are you on the right road? Are you making the most of your life?' It is a warning signal to 'Stop, Look, and Listen' to the voice of conscience."

"Very well said," Dr. Jonathon nodded.

But his wife was looking at Ruth.

"Ruth, what are you doing?" Aunt Elsa cried. "You've eaten every bit of that big dish of honey. I hope it doesn't make you ill."

"It's good," Ruth replied calmly as she daintily wiped her sticky fingers on a napkin. "Now I'll be sure to have a sweet year."

After dinner, the family wandered into the living room. "The High Holy Days always bring me back to the period of my boyhood," Dr. Jonathon remarked as he relaxed in an armchair.

"Tell us about it," Ruthie demanded.

"They were events of the greatest importance in our little village in Lithuania," her father began. "For a whole month before the holidays arrived, there was an atmosphere of solemn expectancy. People said their prayers more earnestly and watched their behavior more carefully. In all the little wooden cottages with their thatched roofs, preparations went on for days ahead of time. Floors were freshly scrubbed, the huge tiled stoves were made ready for the winter, the brass samovars where the steaming tea was boiled shone with cleanliness, and the silver candlesticks were polished until they gleamed.

"But far more important than these things was the preparation of one's soul. For it was believed that on Rosh Hashanah God judges one and decides his fate for the coming year. On Yom Kippur the decree is made final and the judgment is sealed."

"Tell Simon about the *Three Books*," Maury suggested.

"There is an old belief among Jews," Dr. Jonathon replied,

"that on Rosh Hashanah three books are opened in heaven. In one, the names of those who were completely wicked are inscribed; their fate is death. In another, the names of the righteous are written and sealed for life, while in the third book are put the names of those who were neither very wicked nor very good. For them, judgment is suspended until Yom Kippur. If by that time they have repented, their names are entered in the *Book of Life*. The days from Rosh Hashanah through Yom Kippur are called the *Ten Days of Penitence*.

"Some rabbis have explained this story in the following way. When we do good deeds we feel happy. There is a sort of warm glow around our hearts. We feel a greater joy in being alive. We have really inscribed ourselves in the *Book of Life* by right living, for our bodies are healthier when we are happy. But when we do wrong, sadness and fear creep over us. We worry about what will happen as the result of our bad acts. Often, these feelings actually make us ill. But if we are sorry for our misdeeds and try to correct the wrongs we have done, peace comes into our hearts once more, and new strength and hope. That is the real meaning of the story of the three books."

"Tell us more, daddy," Ruthie begged. "About the time when you were a boy, and Rosh Hashanah, and everything."

"Well, let me see." He closed his eyes and leaned his head against the chair. "One of the things that stands out very clearly in my mind when I think of this season of the year is the *Selihot* services. *Selihot* are special prayers asking forgiveness. They are recited several days before Rosh Hashanah, and also between Rosh Hashanah and Yom Kippur. *Selihot* are said in the early hours of the morning, long before dawn. How well I remember, especially the first *Selihot* service. When the quiet village street was still wrapped in sleep, the heavy thump, thump, thump of footsteps upon the wooden sidewalks would be heard. It was the sexton from the synagogue. In one hand he carried a heavy cane and in the other, a large lantern in which burned the dim, flickering light of a candle. Rapping sharply on the window shutters, he called out in a deep voice, '*Selihot*! Time to arise for *Selihot*! Arouse yourself to worship the Creator.'

"I remember with what a feeling of pleasant excitement I dressed hastily in the dark. With a strange, eerie feeling, I walked beside my father towards the synagogue. The flickering lanterns cast weird lights on other hurrying, shadowy figures, and footsteps sounded strangely loud in the quiet of the night. In the synagogue itself, the swaying figures in the dim light of the candles, the chanting tearful voices reciting the prayers, gave me a thrill of mystery and strangeness."

"Do people go to Selihot services at the present time?" Simon asked, much interested.

"Oh, yes," Maury interrupted. "We went to the first Selihot, didn't we, dad? That was before you came, Simon. I liked it. It seemed so strange, going to the synagogue late at night, after twelve o'clock. There was a cantor and a choir and they sang some beautiful hymns."

"And now," Aunt Elsa suggested, "I think an hour of rest might be a good idea for all of us, if we are going to pay some New Year calls later on."

"An excellent idea, my dear," Uncle Phil agreed.

As Simon curled up on the sofa in the living room, he picked up a pile of New Year greeting cards which were lying on a small table. "May I look at these, Aunt Elsa?"

"Of course. We received a good many this year."

"We made some in our class at the synagogue school," Ruthie told him. "I sent them to my friends."

"Will I go to school, too, auntie?"

"Surely," she replied. "You want to learn about the other Jewish holidays, don't you?"

"Yes," decided Simon. "I think I do."[7]

THE MIRACLE OF THE SHOFAR

based on a report by ALEXANDER SHAFRAN

(age level ten to thirteen)

It was 1941 in the city of Bucharest. The Malbim Synagogue (Malbim was a commentator on the Bible and the synagogue was named in his honor) was packed with worshipers. Wrapped in their praying shawls, tears flowing down their cheeks, the men swayed gently back and forth, praying to the Lord of the Universe for help against the human beasts who were tormenting them.

The doors of the synagogue suddenly opened. A dead silence fell upon the congregation. Petrified with fear, they watched a band of Iron Guards enter their house of worship. The Romanian Fascists were dressed in their uniforms and were fully armed. Their faces were hard with hatred. They tramped down the aisle to the front of the synagogue and stood gazing at the frightened assemblage with their cold eyes. The grating voice of the captain of the band tore the silence. "Take those hats off your heads," he barked. "Raise your hands and line up with your faces to the wall."

The Jews knew what this meant. They were to be shot in the back. Their prayers had not been answered.

Silently they took their skullcaps from their heads. With beating hearts, they ranged themselves against the walls of the synagogue and waited for the pistol shots to ring out.

They waited, scarcely breathing. And then again they heard the voice of one of their tormentors.

"What is this thing here?" the voice asked curiously.

They turned their heads to see. One of the Iron Guards was holding a *shofar* in his hand.

"It is a *shofar*," one of the men told him.

The Fascist jerked the last speaker toward him. "Let's see how you blow this thing."

"I must put my skullcap on first," the man said. And he reached into his pocket for it.

A heavy hand knocked the skullcap to the ground.

"You'll blow this thing without that Jew's hat," said the Iron Guard fiercely. "Here!" he went on. And he thrust the *shofar* toward him.

His hand still throbbing with pain, the Jew of Bucharest said mildly, "I cannot blow the *shofar* until I have put on my skullcap."

Six Iron Guards rushed forward. They threw the man to

the ground. They kicked and pummeled him. The man bit his lips to keep from crying out with pain. Finally they jerked him to his feet. His face had been bruised. Blood flowed from the corner of his mouth.

"Will you blow the blasted *shofar* now, or shall we kill you?" the captain snapped.

As calmly as ever the man said, "You will probably kill me anyway. I shall not blow the *shofar* until I put on my skullcap."

The captain drew back his fist, then seemed to change his mind. He let his hand fall to his side. "Put it on, then," he muttered. "I want to hear what it sounds like before we shoot you."

The man bent down, picked up his skullcap, carefully dusted it, and put it on his head. He took the *shofar* and mounted the *bimah*.

Through the silent synagogue the blasts of the *shofar* rang out. The man threw back his head, his eyes closed. Again and again he blew. The mighty blasts sounded like a rumble from the hills, like the voice of a prophet, like the sentence of justice.

Fear seized the Iron Guards. Their mouths fell open. Their hands hung slack at their sides. They looked at each other, trembling, their faces pale. Then, without a word, they turned and fled from the synagogue.

The amazed worshipers could hardly believe their eyes. They put on their skullcaps and returned to their prayers.

That evening the news of the strange miracle had spread to every corner of Bucharest. Wherever Jews lived, the tale of how the *shofar* had driven the Fascists from the house of worship was repeated over and over again.

Every year, since that day, on the Sabbath of Repentance, the worshipers of the Malbim Synagogue of Bucharest assemble to hear Rabbi Alexander Shafran tell the amazing story of the miracle of the *shofar*.[8]

THE LEGEND OF THE JEWISH POPE

as told by MICHA BIN GORION

(age level eleven to thirteen)

Once upon a time in the city of Mayence, which is situated on the River Rhine, there lived a famous teacher, and his name was Rabbi Shimeon. In his house there were three mirrors, and everybody could see in them what had happened in the world before and what would happen in the future. When Rabbi Shimeon died, a well sprang up from his grave. This was considered a great miracle, since the water had healing powers.

Rabbi Shimeon had a son and his name was Elchanan. When he was yet little, his father and his mother went to the house of worship and the boy was left under the supervision of a young maid. As usual, a woman from the neighborhood would come to prepare the stove for the family, and when she came, she took the child from the cradle, put him into her arms, and left. The maid thought nothing ill of it, for she believed that the woman had gone out to play with the child and would soon return. Yet return she did not, but took the child to a place far away and gave him to the priest of the church.

When Rabbi Shimeon and his wife returned they found neither child nor maid, for she had run out of the house to look for the boy. When she did not find him, she returned weeping and reported what had happened. Then the parents raised their voices and wept and cried out in overwhelming pain. Rabbi Shimeon fasted and chastised his body day and night. He prayed to God that He should return his son to him, but the prayers went unheeded. And the Lord refused to reveal the name of the place where the boy was.

In the meantime Elchanan grew up among the priests and his wisdom and his scholarship grew with him, for he took after his father and had an open and quick mind for learning. He went from one university to the other until his wisdom was exceedingly great, and at long last he came to Rome. Here he

THE ROSH HASHANAH ANTHOLOGY

learned many more languages than he already knew and acquired a great reputation as a scholar. Soon thereafter he was elevated to the position of cardinal. His fame soon extended all over the world and everybody wanted to see him because he was so handsome and so learned. It was at this time that the Pontiff of the Roman Church died and nobody was considered worthier to become his successor than the cardinal. Thus the son of Rabbi Shimeon of Mayence became the Pope of Rome.

There is no doubt that the new Pope knew about his Jewish origin and he even knew that his father was the great Rabbi Shimeon who lived in the city of Mayence which was situated on the River Rhine. But his reputation and the high position which he held forced him to disregard his yearning for his people and his desire to return to his faith. However, now that he had become the Pope his yearning grew more and more insistent, and he was anxious to see his father face to face. Thus he decided to use a ruse to bring him to Rome. He sent a papal decree to the Bishop of Mayence and asked him to inform the Jews of the city that from now on they would not be permitted to celebrate the Sabbath, to circumcise their newborn sons, and that the women were no longer allowed to observe the law of purity which had been held in high esteem by the Jews. The new Pope thought in his heart: when this decree is read to the Jews of Mayence, they will soon send a delegation of worthy men to ask me to rescind the order, and there is no doubt that the group will be headed by my father. That is what happened. The Jews of Mayence were frightened when the Bishop read the papal decree to them. They implored him to avert the evil, but he told them that he had no power to do so and advised them to see the Pope. The Jews of Mayence did penitence and fasted and prayed to the Lord, and then they elected two scholars who would accompany Rabbi Shimeon on his mission to Rome.

When the three delegates came to Rome, they went to the Jewish quarter and told their brethren of the purpose which had caused them to come to Rome. At first the Jews of Rome did not believe it, for the Pope had been known to be a friend of the Jews. But then Rabbi Shimeon showed them the papal decree, and the Roman Jews said: "Woe unto us, for the Lord is wroth at you." And they called a day of fasting and prayed for the welfare of their brethren from Mayence.

After this, they went to a cardinal who saw the Pope daily and told him about the matter. The cardinal advised that the Jews from Mayence should put their complaint in writing. He would then submit it to the Pope.

When the letter was given to the Pope, he looked at the signatures and discovered that Rabbi Shimeon, his father, was among the delegates. He invited them to come to the papal palace. Soon Rabbi Shimeon stood face to face with the Pontiff of the Roman Church. He prostrated himself before him, but the Pope asked him to rise and to sit on a chair. Then he asked him to make his plea. Rabbi Shimeon could hardly speak because of the tears that choked his voice, but he spoke freely about the decree which threatened his community. The Pope did not immediately respond, but he began to engage Rabbi Shimeon in a learned dispute, and the rabbi marveled at the scholarship of the Pontiff. Knowing that the rabbi was a famous chess player, the Pope invited him to play with him, and to Shimeon's amazement he beat him handsomely after only a few moves. But by then the Pope could no longer hold back. He asked everybody present to leave and then told Rabbi Shimeon that he was his son. He explained that the decree had been but a ruse to make him come to Rome so that he could see him. He gave Rabbi Shimeon a papal letter which rescinded the decree, bade him farewell, and let him return to Mayence in peace.

After many years had passed the Pope disappeared from Rome and clandestinely returned to Mayence. Return he did, not merely to the place of his birth, but also to the God of his fathers. It is said that before leaving Rome he had written a book disputing the verities of the Christian Church which he left in the papal chambers so that his successors could read it.

There is a hymn which is recited on the second day of the Jewish New Year, written by Rabbi Shimeon, describing the story of the Jewish Pope. Nobody should doubt its veracity for it really happened.

Translated by Joachim Prinz[9]

XXII

CHILDREN'S POEMS
FOR ROSH HASHANAH

ROSH HASHANAH

BEN ARONIN

Mother took some honey
And an apple, too.
Then she said, "Come here, my child;
I have a gift for you.

"Let's begin the New Year
With this little treat,
May the year be happy!
May the year be sweet!"

* * *

There was a sound so sweet and clear
It said to me, "The New Year's here."

It said, "Remember to be brave."
It said, "Remember to be good."

And when I heard the *shofar's* call
I stood up straight and said I would.

* * *

I dreamed about a great big book
That has your name and mine;
The name of everyone on earth
A name on every line
And when you do a kindly deed
God writes, "That child is fine!"[1]

LE-SHANAH TOVAH

Sara G. Levy

The postman's coming down our street
With letters very wee
I think they're *Shanah Tovah* cards
"Oh look! There's one for me."[2]

FOR A GOOD AND A SWEET NEW YEAR

Sadie Rose Weilerstein

Bees, bees,
Give us your honey!
Give us your honey, please.
We have special round bread,
Apples too, round and red,
That came from the orchard trees.
We'll eat them with honey,
All golden and sunny,
When Rosh Hashanah is here;
Honey, apples, and bread
When the blessing is said
For a good and a sweet New Year.[3]

A HAPPY NEW YEAR

SADIE ROSE WEILERSTEIN

A happy New Year, Uncle Dave!
Le-Shanah Tovah Tikatev!
Just see my suit and my tie—it's blue;
And my cap and shoes! They're all brand new.
You've been to *shul?*
Well, I've been too.
I was in there when the *shofar* blew,
It's a ram's horn, everybody knows.
Te-ki-ah! That's the way it goes.
If any wicked thoughts are 'round
They're frightened off at such a sound.
That's what it's for, my Daddy said,
To bring the *good* thoughts out, instead.
I guess I haven't been good—quite;
But I'm going to start the New Year right.
A happy New Year, Uncle Dave!
Le-Shanah Tovah Tikatev![4]

THE JEWISH YEAR

JESSIE E. SAMPTER

Our year begins with burnished leaves,
    That flame in frost and rime,
With purple grapes and golden sheaves
    In harvest time.

Our year begins with biting cold.
    With winds and storms and rain;
The new year of the Jew grows old
    In strife and pain.

When others say the year has died,
    We say the year is new,

And we arise with power and pride
  To prove it true.

And we begin where others end,
  And fight where others yield;
And all the year we work and tend
  Our harvest field.

And after days of stormy rain
  And days of drought and heat,
When those that toiled have reaped their grain,
  And all's complete.

Oh then, when God has kept his word,
  In peace we end our year.
Our fruit is certain from the Lord.
  We shall not fear.[5]

THE *SHOFAR* CALL

ELMA EHRLICH LEVINGER

Within the synagogue the light is dim;
  The air is hushed around;
Even the silence seems to pray until
  We hear the *shofar* sound.

O *shofar*, tell us we need not fear,
  Though long and hard the way;
O *shofar*, bind us with thy holy strain,
Till each young heart will share in Israel's pain,
  And like a trumpet clear,
Sound to the world the vow we pledge anew:
To bear with honor the name of Jew,
  Throughout the coming year![6]

THE NEW YEAR

ABRAHAM BURSTEIN

No bells ring through the midnight air
    No sound of vulgar revelry
But everywhere the trumpet blare
    Sends greetings over land and sea.

And in the Jewish household reigns
    A quiet born of pious thought;
And every Jewish heart attains
    A joy from festive feeling wrought.

No ribald shout, no coarse play
    Proclaims our Rosh Hashanah here:
But we hope and smile and pray
    In this wise greet the glad New Year![7]

XXIII

NEW YEAR PROGRAMS

According to tradition, preparations for Rosh Hashanah begin a month in advance; therefore it is appropriate to plan special programs that will inspire a deep appreciation of the significance of this holy day among both children and adults. Such activities should induce the proper mood for observing the Days of Awe in the synagogue and in the home.

ROSH HASHANAH INSTITUTE

In order to induce a receptive mood for the traditional observance of these solemn days, an adult institute may be arranged. Since Rosh Hashanah usually occurs before most organizations embark on their program season, the committee for the institute should be organized before the summer months to allow sufficient time for advance planning. It should be representative of all the adult groups in the agency sponsoring the institute. Careful planning by knowledgeable committee members in consultation with a rabbi or Jewish educator is required to prepare an adequate program. Considerable source material for such an activity will be found in this volume.

Several two-hour sessions or even a single day or weekend agenda may be scheduled during the month preceding Rosh Hashanah. The Saturday night preceding *Selihot* services is a propitious opening time for the institute, which can then be continued on Sunday.

A typical institute may include all or some of the following elements, depending on the needs and interests of the participants and the available leadership:

Lecture on the background and significance of the High Holy Days

Discussion on the current relevance of the Days of Awe

Study of the pertinent laws and customs (see chapter on "Rosh Hashanah in Jewish Law")

Analysis and interpretation of selected prayers of the *mahzor* (see chapter on "Selected Prayers")

Congregational singing of traditional chants and melodies

Demonstration of preparing Rosh Hashanah dishes (see chapter on "The Culinary Art of Rosh Hashanah")

Playing of High Holy Days liturgical music recordings (see Bibliography)

Showing of kinescope or filmstrip (see Bibliography)

Exhibit of *mahzorim*, ceremonial objects, greeting cards

Quiz program at the conclusion of the institute

DISCUSSION THEMES

In order to insure a knowledgeable discussion, the leader and some of the participants should be encouraged to read pertinent literature in advance of the session. The leader may initiate the discussion by raising challenging questions based on some of the selections in the chapter "Rosh Hashanah in Modern Prose."

One or more of the following themes should be adequate for the discussion period:

Rosh Hashanah—The Birthday of the World: Its Universal
Message
The Jewish Concept of Divine Forgiveness
Repentance: Retrospection and Soul-searching
The Efficacy of Prayer: The Rosh Hashanah Liturgy
The Contrast between the Jewish New Year and the Secular
New Year
The Modern Relevance of Rosh Hashanah
The Meaning of the *Shofar*
The Threefold Elixir: Repentance, Prayer, and Charity
Looking Backward: The Old Year in Retrospect

STORY-TELLING HOUR

Young children particularly will enjoy Rosh Hashanah stories.
Some stories may stimulate interest in other activities. In
addition to the children's stories in this volume, some of those
for adults are easily adaptable for narration to youngsters.
Other suitable children's stories are listed in the Bibliography.

CREATIVE DRAMATICS

Rosh Hashanah with its numerous traditions and colorful
history presents many possibilities for creative and significant
dramatic projects. Many of the vivid accounts in the chapter
"Rosh Hashanah in Many Lands" as well as the two chapters
of stories in this volume may well serve as sources for plots.
Improvisations for the spontaneous creation of a dramatic
scene, charades, pantomimes, and shadowgraphs are dramatic
forms that may be employed to generate a better understanding
of Rosh Hashanah.

EXHIBITS

A number of different kinds of exhibits can be arranged to
deepen the meaning and enhance the beauty of Rosh Hashanah.
The local library may display adult and juvenile books that
include material on the High Holy Days. A gift shop may
feature Rosh Hashanah and Yom Kippur *mahzorim*, recordings
of liturgical music, New Year greeting cards, Rosh Hashanah
stamps from Israel, and Jewish calendars.

A model Rosh Hashanah table arrangement, using a white linen cloth set with white napkins and elegant silverware and china, may be conspicuously displayed. A wine decanter, wine cups, candlesticks with lit candles, round *hallot* with an attractive cover, a bread knife, a dish of honey, a plate of apples, and a plate of *teiglach* should be prominently exhibited. As a centerpiece, a vase of flowers surrounded by a few attractive Rosh Hashanah cards may be arranged.

ROSH HASHANAH POST OFFICE

To encourage and facilitate the exchange of Rosh Hashanah greetings, Jewish schools and community centers may establish a "post office," manned by volunteer postal clerks, to sell handmade and commercial cards and stamps. This may be a booth in a conspicuous part of the lobby. If the cards are to be delivered by "postmen," Jewish National Fund New Year stamps may be used. Letter boxes, appropriately decorated, may be set up in class and club rooms for the deposit of cards. The "postmen" will collect the cards and either deliver them by hand or send them through the mails.

VISIT TO A SYNAGOGUE

Prior to Rosh Hashanah a visit to a synagogue might be arranged to give children an opportunity to observe its architecture, the ark, the eternal light, the appurtenances of the Torah scroll, and the other physical objects. At the same time they may be introduced to some aspects of the special Rosh Hashanah rituals and liturgy.

ARTS AND CRAFTS

Shofar: A *shofar* may be made from a ram's horn at least six inches in length, which can be purchased at a slaughterhouse or ordered from a butcher store. The inner bones of the horn are removed by boiling it in a pot of water for about two hours until they soften. The bones can then be extracted with the help of pliers and a chisel or pick. If the end of the horn requires straightening, which may not always be necessary, it should be placed over a flame until it is softened and then bent, using force if necessary, until it is the proper shape. Hold the horn in a press until it is hardened. (To make sure that the pressure of the press will not crack the horn, fill it with plaster. The plaster can be cracked by a flow of cold water and then scooped out.) The narrow end of the horn should be cut off with a coping saw and a hole bored in it with an electric drill, using a ⅛-inch bit. Then place this end of the horn over a flame or in boiling water for softening. When supple, expand the narrow end (the mouthpiece) by pushing in a chisel or other implement and shaping into an oval. Both the interior and the exterior of the horn can be smoothened with sand-paper.

Model Shofar: A variety of craft techniques can be effectively utilized to make a model *shofar,* such as clay modeling, soap and wood carving, and papier-maché.

Greeting Cards: Many interesting possibilities present themselves for creating original artistic Rosh Hashanah greeting cards. Among the media adaptable for this purpose are linoleum and potato block prints, spatter and finger paints, stencils, crayons, sprays, watercolors, and cutouts of colored construction paper. Greetings may express original messages in prose or verse or one of the following customary salutations in Hebrew and English: "May You Be Inscribed for a Good Year," "A Happy New Year," "New Year Greetings." For further suggestions for legends and for designs, see the chapter on "Rosh Hashanah Greeting Cards."

Honey Dish: A special dish for honey can be made by decorating an ordinary saucer or small bowl with enamel paints. Another method is to crayon designs on tissue paper, place the tissue on a glass saucer, and cover it with a coat of clear shellac. Honey dishes may also be made by chiseling a block of wood into a small bowl or by shaping a piece of copper into a bowl, which may then have a design etched on. "A Good and Sweet Year" or "A Land of Milk and Honey" may be worked into the design.

Mahzor *Jackets*: A book jacket for the Rosh Hashanah *mahzor* is easily made with a sheet of wrapping paper or heavy colored paper. The title and design may be inscribed with crayons, finger paints, or watercolors. More durable *mahzor* jackets can be created by embroidery on silk or some other cloth or by leather tooling.

Hallah *Cover*: A special *hallah* cover for Rosh Hashanah can be made by drawing a design on a sheet of paper, tracing it onto a piece of unbleached muslin, linen, or cotton, and then embroidering the design. Watercolors or fabric paint that does not spread on cloth may be substituted. Covers can be embellished with a Hebrew version of "For a good and sweet year," "Sound the *shofar* at the new moon," or "Inscribe us in the book of life."

Jewish Calendar: A twelve-page (thirteen in a Jewish leap year) calendar may be quite simply or elaborately designed. The name of each Hebrew month should be put on the top of each page. There should be ruled spaces for each day of the month, in which are inserted the day of the week, the number of the day of the month, and any holiday that may occur. An examination of printed calendars will provide further suggestions. After the copy is filled in, the pages should be stapled, two holes should be punched at the top for a string, and the calendar is ready for use.

Wall Decorations: Large murals, paintings, and posters are some of the wall decorations that can be used to convey Rosh Hashanah messages. Well-designed posters can bear such legends as "The *shofar* calls: Awake, you sleepers from your slumber and consider your deeds," "Return, O Israel," "Rosh Hashanah—the Day of Judgment, the Day of Remembrance, the Day of Sounding the *Shofar*," "Repentance, Prayer, and Charity Avert the Evil Decree," "May you be inscribed and sealed in the book of life for a good year," and "May you enjoy a happy and sweet year." Posters may also be used to announce the schedule of the High Holy Days services.

NOTES

I ROSH HASHANAH IN THE BIBLE

1. Selections from the Pentateuch have been taken from *The Torah:
   The Five Books of Moses: A New Translation* . . . *According to the
   Masoretic Text* (1962) and those of the other biblical books are
   from *The Holy Scriptures According to the Masoretic Text* (1917),
   both published by The Jewish Publication Society of America,
   Philadelphia.

II ROSH HASHANAH IN POSTBIBLICAL WRITINGS

1. *The Apocrypha*, trans. by Edgar J. Goodspeed, University of Chicago
   Press (Chicago, 1938), pp. 371–372.
2. Ibid., p. 276.
3. Charles, R. H., ed., *The Apocrypha and Pseudepigrapha of the Old
   Testament*, Clarendon Press (Oxford, 1913), vol. 2, p. 31.
4. *Philo*, with an English translation by F. H. Colson (Loeb Classical
   Library), Harvard University Press (Cambridge, Massachusetts,
   1937), vol. 7, pp. 425–427.

III ROSH HASHANAH IN TALMUD AND MIDRASH

1. Selections from the *Midrash Rabbah* are from the translation under
   the editorship of H. Freedman and Maurice Simon, Soncino Press
   (London, 1939–1951).

2. Selections from *The Babylonian Talmud* are from the translation under the editorship of Isidore Epstein, Soncino Press (London, 1935–1950).
3. *Pesikta Rabbati: Discourses for Feasts, Fasts and Special Sabbaths*, trans. by William G. Braude, Yale University Press (New Haven, 1968), vol. 2, pp. 701–702.
4. Ibid., pp. 703–705.
5. *The Midrash on Psalms*, trans. by William G. Braude, Yale University Press (New Haven, 1959), vol. 1, p. 209.
6. *Pesikta Rabbati*, pp. 874–875.
7. *Midrash on Psalms*, vol. 2, p. 293.
8. *Pesikta Rabbati*, p. 779.
9. *Midrash on Psalms*, p. 94.

IV ROSH HASHANAH IN MEDIEVAL JEWISH LITERATURE

1. Al-Harizi, Judah, *The Tahkemoni*, trans. by Victor Emanuel Reichert, Raphael Haim Cohen's Press, Ltd., Publishers (Jerusalem, 1965), vol. 1, pp. 107–108.
2. *Zohar*, trans. by Harry Sperling and Maurice Simon, Soncino Press (London, 1931–1934), vol. 5, p. 127.
3. Ketko, Shlomo, ed., *A Handbook for Jewish Youth Leaders: The Month of Elul*, Youth and Hechalutz Department, Zionist Organization (Jerusalem, 1955), p. 22.
4. *Sefer Avudarham* (Amsterdam, 1726), p. 100.
5. Albo, Joseph, *Sefer ha-Ikkarim*, trans. and ed. by Isaac Husik, Jewish Publication Society of America (Philadelphia, 1929), vol. 1, pp. 64–67.
6. Ibid. (1930), vol. 4, pp. 235–239.
7. Bachya ben Joseph ibn Pakuda, *Duties of the Heart*, trans. by Moses Hyamson, Bloch Publishing Co. (New York, 1945), vol. 4, pp. 45–46, 50–51, 55–56.
8. Yonah ben Avraham of Gerona, *The Gates of Repentance*, trans. by Shraga Silverstein, Yaakov Feldheim (Boys Town, Jerusalem, 1967), p. 3.
9. Saadia Gaon, *The Book of Beliefs and Opinions*, trans. by Samuel Rosenblatt, Yale University Press (New Haven, 1948), pp. 220–223.
10. Ibid., pp. 227–228.
11. *Karaite Anthology: Excerpts from the Early Literature*, trans. by Leon Nemoy, Yale University Press (New Haven, 1952), pp. 192, 194.
12. Abraham Bar Hayya, *The Meditation of the Sad Soul*, trans. by Geoffrey Wigoder, Schocken Books (New York, 1969), pp. 87–88. (The author's name is usually spelled Hiyya.)
13. *The Authorised Selichot for the Whole Year*, trans. and annotated by Abraham Rosenfeld, I. Labworth & Co. (London, 1957), pp. 141–142.

V ROSH HASHANAH IN JEWISH LAW

1. *Maimonides' Mishneh Torah,* ed. and trans. by Philip Birnbaum, Hebrew Publishing Co. (New York, 1967), p. 38.
2. Ibid., pp. 39–41.
3. Ibid., pp. 43–44.

VI SELECTED PRAYERS

1. *The Union Prayer Book for Jewish Worship: Newly Revised Edition: Part II,* Central Conference of American Rabbis (New York, 1962), p. 8.
2. *Seder Avodah,* trans. by Max D. Klein (Philadelphia, 1960), pp. 11–13.
3. Solis-Cohen, Solomon, *When Love Passed By and Other Verses,* Rosenbach Co. (Philadelphia, 1929), pp. 102–103.
4. *The High Holyday Prayer Book: Rosh Hashanah and Yom Kippur,* trans. and arranged by Ben Zion Bokser, Hebrew Publishing Co. (New York, 1959), p. 124.
5. Abrahams, Israel, *Festival Studies,* Julius H. Greenstone (Philadelphia, 1906), pp. 19–21.
6. *High Holyday Prayer Book,* trans. and annotated by Philip Birnbaum, Hebrew Publishing Co. (New York, 1951), pp. 32–36.
7. Arzt, Max, *Justice and Mercy: Commentary on the Liturgy of the New Year and the Day of Atonement,* Holt, Rinehart and Winston (New York, 1963), pp. 100–102.
8. Birnbaum, p. 38.
9. Abrahams, pp. 23–24.
10. Bokser, p. 134.
11. Kieval, Herman, *The High Holy Days: A Commentary on the Prayerbook of Rosh Hashanah and Yom Kippur: Book One: Rosh Hashanah,* Burning Bush Press (New York, 1959), p. 77.
12. Bokser, pp. 139–141.
13. Greenstone, Julius H., *Jewish Feasts and Fasts* (Philadelphia, 1945), pp. 20–23.
14. Martin, Bernard, *Prayer in Judaism,* Basic Books (New York, 1968), p. 203.
15. Ibid., p. 204.
16. Birnbaum, pp. 18–20.
17. *The Orthodox Union,* vol. 8, no. 2 (November–December, 1940), p. 8.
18. Bokser, pp. 202–208.
19. Arzt, pp. 159–160, 109–111, 184–187.
20. Bokser, pp. 187–188.
21. Arzt, p. 165.
22. Bokser, pp. 188–190.
23. Arzt, pp. 166–168, 171.
24. Adler, Herbert M., and Arthur Davis, trans., *Service of the Synagogue: New Year,* George Routledge & Sons (London, 1904), pp. 151–152.
25. Martin, p. 213.

26. Leftwich, Joseph, trans. and ed., *The Golden Peacock: A Worldwide Treasury of Yiddish Poetry*, Thomas Yoseloff (New York, 1961), pp. 699–700.
27. Harlow, Jules, ed., *Yearnings: Prayer and Meditation for the Days of Awe*, Rabbinical Assembly (New York, 1968), p. 14.

VII THE SCRIPTURAL READINGS

1. Jacobs, Louis, *A Guide to Rosh Hashanah*, Jewish Chronicle Publications (London, 1959), pp. 34–42.
2. Greenstone, Julius H., *Jewish Feasts and Fasts* (Philadelphia, 1945), pp. 14–16.
3. Simon, Ernst, "The Birthday of the World," *Commentary*, vol. 20, no. 3 (September, 1955), pp. 200–202.

VIII THE *Shofar*

1. Lowenthal, Marvin, *A World Passed By: Scenes and Memories of Jewish Civilization in Europe and North Africa*, Behrman's Jewish Book House (New York, 1938), pp. 30–31.
2. Arzt, Max, *Justice and Mercy: Commentary on the Liturgy of the New Year and the Day of Atonement*, Holt, Rinehart and Winston (New York 1963), pp. 153–154.
3. Hirsch, Samson Raphael, *Judaism Eternal: Selected Essays*, trans. by I. Grunfeld, Soncino Press (London, 1956), vol. 1, pp. 8–9.
4. Hirsch, Samson Raphael, *Horeb: A Philosophy of Jewish Laws and Observances*, trans. by I. Grunfeld, Soncino Press (London, 1962), vol. 1, p. 140.
5. *Hadassah Magazine*, vol. 50, no. 1 (September, 1968), pp. 13, 34.

IX THE SYMBOLIC CEREMONY OF *Tashlikh*

1. Greenstone, Julius H., *Jewish Feasts and Fasts* (Philadelphia, 1945), pp. 17–19.

XI HASIDIC TALES AND TEACHINGS

1. Parts of this chapter are reprinted, in revised form, from *Rejoice in Thy Festival: A Treasury of Wisdom, Wit and Humor for the Sabbath and Jewish Holidays*, by Philip Goodman, Bloch Publishing Co. (New York, 1956).

XII ROSH HASHANAH IN MODERN PROSE

1. Hertz, Joseph H., ed., *A Book of Jewish Thoughts*, Bloch Publishing Co. (New York, 1926), p. 227.

2. Joseph, Morris, *Judaism as Creed and Life* (London, 1903), pp. 250-253.
3. Glatzer, Nahum N., ed., *Franz Rosenzweig: His Life and Thought*, Schocken Books and Farrar, Straus and Young (New York, 1953), pp. 328-330.
4. Liebman, Joshua Loth, *Peace of Mind*, Simon and Schuster (New York, 1946), p. 198.
5. Knox, Israel, "Solemn Days: An Ethical-Humanist View of Rosh Hashanah and Yom Kippur," *Point of View*, vol. 1, no. 2 (Autumn, 1961), pp. 3-4, 8; reprinted in *The Jewish Spectator*, vol. 27, no. 7 (September, 1963), pp. 7-9.
6. Hirsch, Samson Raphael, *Horeb: A Philosophy of Jewish Laws and Observances*, trans. by I. Grunfeld, Soncino Press (London, 1962), vol. 2, pp. 390-391.
7. Metzger, Alter B. Z., trans., *Rabbi Kook's Philosophy of Repentance*, Yeshiva University Press (New York, 1968), pp. 25, 39, 84, 107.
8. Berkovits, Eliezer, "When Man Fails God," *Great Jewish Ideas*, ed. by Abraham Ezra Millgram, B'nai B'rith Department of Adult Jewish Education (Washington, D.C., 1964), pp. 193-195.
9. Wiesel, Elie, *Night*, Hill and Wang (New York, 1960), pp. 72-74.
10. Feierberg, Mordecai Zeev, *Whither?*, trans. by Ira Eisenstein, Abelard-Schuman (New York, 1959), pp. 49-51.

XIII ROSH HASHANAH IN ART

1. Roth, Ernst, "Das Schofarblasen," *Allgemeine Zeitung der Juden in Deutschland*, vol. 17, no. 27 (1962), p. 17; Metzger, Mendel, "Le chofar et sa signification dans l'art juif," *Bulletin de nos Communautés*, vol. 15, no. 18 (1959), pp. 1-4; Roth, Ernst, "Machsor-Handschriften in der Bayrischen Staatsbibliothek," *Von Juden in Munchen*, ed. by H. Lamm (Munich, 1958), pp. 43-49; Roth, Ernst, "The Footstool in Shofar Blowing and in the Jewish Oath," *Yeda-'Am*, vol. 8, no. 26 (1962), pp. 3-8.
2. Metzger, Mendel, "L'Aquéda dans l'illustration de Mahzor médiéval," *Bulletin de nos Communautés*, vol. 20, no. 17 (1964), pp. 12 f.
3. Spiegel, Shalom, *The Last Trial* (Philadelphia, 1967), p. 152.
4. *Monumenta Judaica*, Catalog of exhibition held at Kölnisches Stadtmuseum, October-March 1964 (Cologne, 1964), D 599 and D 616-20; Gutmann, Joseph, *Jewish Ceremonial Art* (New York, 1964), pp. 23-24; Kayser, Stephen S., *Jewish Ceremonial Art* (Philadelphia, 1959), pp. 65-67, 114-116, 178; Finesinger, Sol B., "The Shofar," *Hebrew Union College Annual*, vols. 8-9 (1931-32), pp. 193-228.
5. Cf. Kirchner, Paul C., *Jüdisches Ceremoniel* (Nürnberg, 1726), pp. 109-115; Bodenschatz, Johann C. G., *Kirchliche Verfassung der heutigen Juden* (Erlang, 1748), vol. 2, pp. 171-198; Rubens, Alfred, *A Jewish Iconography* (London, 1954), pp. 5 ff.; Ben-Ezra, Akiva, *Minhage Hagim* (Jerusalem, 1962), pp. 9-26; Lauterbach, Jacob Z., "Tashlikh, A Study in Jewish Ceremonies," *Rabbinic Essays* (Cincinnati, 1951), pp. 299-433.

XIV THE MUSIC OF THE ROSH HASHANAH LITURGY

1. Literally: from Sinai. Since approximately the thirteenth century (see *Sefer Hasidim*, ed. by J. Wistinetzky [Berlin, 1891], #817), rabbis have attributed Sinaiitic origin to the synagogue tunes in order to emphasize their importance. Although at first this appellation was applied to cantillation only, it gradually was transferred to the melodies of the liturgy. These are also known as Scarbove tunes—from the Latin *sacra* or, more likely, from the Polish *skarb*, "treasure."

2. *Tune* and *melody* are here used interchangeably. *Motif* refers to a brief melodic phrase.

3. Generally accepted utilization of modes and melodies applied to the various sections and texts of the synagogue service.

4. This melody is also employed on Simhat Torah.

5. In this mode are also chanted the introductory paragraphs to the Torah reading (*Veya'atzor, Vetigaleh*) throughout the year.

6. For an analysis of the *Adonai Malakh*, as well as other synagogue modes, see *Jewish Music*, by A. Z. Idelsohn (New York, 1929), and *The Music of the Synagogue*, by Max Wohlberg, National Jewish Welfare Board (New York, 1947).

7. See *The Voice of Prayer and Praise*, by F. L. Cohen and D. D. Davis (London, 1933), and *Synagogue Melodies for the High Holy Days*, by Israel Goldfarb and Samuel E. Goldfarb (Brooklyn, 1926).

XV ROSH HASHANAH IN MANY LANDS

1. Schauss, Hayyim, *The Jewish Festivals: From Their Beginnings to Our Own Day*, trans. by Samuel Jaffe, Union of American Hebrew Congregations (Cincinnati, 1938), pp. 143–149.

2. Kobrin, Leon, *A Lithuanian Village*, trans. by Isaac Goldberg, Brentano's (New York, 1920), pp. 29–38.

3. Levin, Shmarya, *Forward from Exile: The Autobiography of Shmarya Levin*, trans. and ed. by Maurice Samuel, Jewish Publication Society of America (Philadelphia, 1967), pp. 65–67.

4. Chagall, Bella, *Burning Lights*, trans. by Norbert Guterman, Schocken Books (New York, 1946), pp. 73–81.

5. Schwab, Hermann, *Jewish Rural Communities in Germany*, Cooper Book Co. (London, 1956), pp. 26–27.

6. Cohen, Israel, *Travels in Jewry*, Dutton & Co. (New York, 1953), pp. 321–323.

7. *Hadassah Magazine*, vol. 50, no. 1 (September, 1968), pp. 37–38.

8. Kehimkar, Haeem Samuel, *The History of the Bene-Israel of India* (Tel Aviv, 1937), pp. 171–172.

9. Mandelbaum, David G., "The Jewish Way of Life in Cochin," *Jewish Social Studies*, vol. 1, no. 4 (October, 1939), pp. 454–456.

10. *Igeret Lagolah* (Jerusalem), no. 28 (August, 1946), pp. 10–16.

11. *South African Jewish Chronicle*, vol. 44 (September, 1946), pp. 43, 54.

12. Ben-Zvi, Rahel Yanait, *Coming Home*, trans. by David Harris and Julian Meltzer, Herzl Press (New York, 1964), pp. 90–92.

13. Kaplan, Chaim A., *Scroll of Agony: The Warsaw Diary of Chaim A.*

Kaplan, ed. and trans. by Abraham I. Katsh, Macmillan Co. (New York, 1965), pp. 202–203.

14. Shoskes, Henry, *No Traveler Returns*, ed. by Curt Riess, Doubleday, Doran and Co. (Garden City, New York, 1945), pp. 58–59.
15. Hersey, John, *The Wall*, Alfred A. Knopf (New York, 1950), pp. 392–393.
16. Flender, Harold, *Rescue in Denmark*, Simon and Schuster (New York, 1963), pp. 15, 53–54, 61–64.
17. Barish, Louis, ed., *Rabbis in Uniform: The Story of the American Jewish Military Chaplain*, Jonathan David (New York, 1962), pp. 99–101.

XVI ROSH HASHANAH IN POETRY

1. Misch, Marion L., ed., *Selections for Homes and Schools*, Jewish Publication Society of America (Philadelphia, 1911), pp. 231–232.
2. Lazarus, Emma, *The Poems of Emma Lazarus*, Houghton Mifflin Co. (Boston, 1888), vol. 2, pp. 1–3.
3. *Supplementary Prayers and Readings for the High Holidays, Part I*, Jewish Reconstructionist Foundation (New York, 1960), pp. 49–50.
4. *Anthology of Modern Hebrew Poetry*, selected by S. Y. Penueli and A. Ukhmani, Institute for the Translation of Hebrew Literature and Israel Universities Press (Jerusalem, 1966), vol. 2, p. 357.
5. Mintz, Ruth Finer, ed. and trans., *Modern Hebrew Poetry: A Bilingual Anthology*, University of California Press (Berkeley, 1966), p. 298.
6. Harlow, Jules, ed., *Yearnings: Prayer and Meditation for the Days of Awe*, Rabbinical Assembly (New York, 1968), p. 16.
7. Kruger, Fania, *The Tenth Jew*, Kaleidograph Press (Dallas, 1949), p. 95.
8. Brin, Ruth F., *A Rag of Love*, Emmett Publishing Co. (Minneapolis, 1969), p. 38.
9. Ibid., p. 37.
10. Ibid., p. 39

XVII ROSH HASHANAH IN THE SHORT STORY

1. Howe, Irving, and Eliezer Greenberg, eds., *A Treasury of Yiddish Stories*, Viking Press (New York, 1954), pp. 231–233.
2. Agnon, S. Y., *The Bridal Canopy*, trans. by I. M. Lask, Doubleday, Doran & Co. (New York, 1937), pp. 63–64.
3. *Ma'aseh Book: Book of Jewish Tales and Legends*, trans. by Moses Gaster, Jewish Publication Society of America (Philadelphia, 1934), vol. 2, pp. 514–518.
4. Samuel, Maurice, *Prince of the Ghetto*, Alfred A. Knopf (New York, 1948), pp. 181–188.
5. Peretz, I. L., *The Book of Fire: Stories*, trans. by Joseph Leftwich, Thomas Yoseloff (New York, 1960[?]), pp. 137–140.

6. Ausubel, Nathan, ed., *A Treasury of Jewish Humor*, Doubleday & Co. (Garden City, New York, 1951), pp. 82–86.
7. *The Jewish Chronicle* (London), New Year Section, no. 4,875 (September 28, 1962), pp. 31–32.

XVIII ROSH HASHANAH GREETING CARDS

1. *Rosh Hashanah* 16b.
2. *Sefer Maharil, Yamim Noraim;* Steinman, Sidney, *Custom and Survival: A Study of the Life and Work of Rabbi Jacob Molin . . .* , Bloch Publishing Co. (New York, 1963), p. 88.
3. Golnitzki, Heshil, *Be-Mahzor ha-Yamim: Moed ve-Hol be-Omanut uve-Folklor* (Haifa, 5723), pp. 44–45.
4. *Jewish Encyclopedia*, vol. 6, p. 89.
5. Persky, Daniel, "Tashri," *Hadoar*, vol. 29, no. 38 (September 23, 1949), pp. 988–990.
6. Nissenbaum, Isaac, *Ale Heldi* (Warsaw, 5689), pp. 110–111.
7. Tzidkoni, Jacob, "*Kartise Berakhah le-Rosh ha-Shanah*," *Mahanaim*, no. 60 (5722), pp. 170–177.
8. Aronsfeld, C. C., "It's on the Cards," *Jewish Affairs* (Johannesburg), vol. 20, no. 9 (September, 1965), pp. 87–89.
9. "Some New Year Cards: Humorous and Original," *The Jewish Chronicle* (London), no. 1,798 (September 18, 1903), p. 28.
10. Ibid., no. 4,767 (September 2, 1960), p. 25.
11. Tzidkoni, p. 177.
12. Parts of this article originally appeared—under the title "New Year Cards Have Long History," by Philip Goodman—in *The Jewish Exponent* (Philadelphia), vol. 140, no. 11 (September 9, 1966), p. 19.

XIX THE CULINARY ART OF ROSH HASHANAH

1. *Bereshit Rabbah* 68.4.
2. *Sefer Maharil, Rosh Hashanah;* Steinman, Sidney, *Custom and Survival: A Study of the Life and Work of Rabbi Jacob Molin . . .* , Bloch Publishing Co. (New York, 1963), p. 89.
3. *Orah Hayyim* 583.
4. *Keritot* 6a; *Horayot* 12a, Rashi.
5. Finesinger, Sol B., "The Shofar," *Hebrew Union College Annual*, vols. 8–9 (1931–1932), p. 198, note 12.
6. *Sanhedrin* 108b; Bergman, Yehudah, *Ha-Folklor ha-Yehudi* (Jerusalem, 5713), p. 108.

XX ROSH HASHANAH MISCELLANY

1. *Rosh Hashanah* 1.1.
2. Ibid., 16b.
3. *Soferim* 19.5.
4. *Betzah* 16a.

5. *The Special Laws* II. 188.
6. *Rosh Hashanah* 11a.
7. Ginzberg, Louis, *Legends of the Jews*, Jewish Publication Society of America (Philadelphia, 1925), vol. 5, p. 107.
8. Ibid., p. 136.
9. *Rosh Hashanah* 10b.
10. Ginzberg, p. 252.
11. *Book of Jubilees* 31–32; Ginzberg, p. 317.
12. *Rosh Hashanah* 11a.
13. Ibid., 11a–b.
14. Ibid., 11b.
15. Baron, Salo W., *A Social and Religious History of the Jews*, Jewish Publication Society of America (Philadelphia, 1957), vol. 5, pp. 30–31.
16. Ibid., vol. 8, p. 195.
17. *Jewish Encyclopedia*, vol. 1, p. 141.
18. Roth, Cecil, *A Jewish Book of Days*, Edward Goldston (London, 1931), pp. 215–216.
19. *Jewish Encyclopedia*, vol. 11, p. 221.
20. Baron, pp. 28–29; Wahrmann, Nahum, *Hage Yisrael u-Moadav*, Ahiasaf (Jerusalem, 1959), pp. 23–26; Zeitlin, Solomon, "The Second Day of Rosh Hashanah in Israel," *Jewish Quarterly Review*, vol. 44 (1954), pp. 326–329.
21. Feldman, W. M., *Rabbinical Mathematics and Astronomy*, Hermon Press (New York, 1965), p. 193.
22. *Avot* 5.23.
23. Sofer, Tzvi, "*Ve-Kakh Hayu Meorerim le-Selihot*," *Yeda-Am*, vol. 1, no. 1 (January, 1948), p. 14.
24. Feuchtwanger, H., "*Meorer ha-Shahar*," *Yeda-Am*, vol. 3, nos. 2–3 (October, 1955), pp. 104–105.
25. Brauer, Erich, *Yehude Kurdistan*, Palestine Institute of Folklore and Ethnology (Jerusalem, 1947), p. 254.
26. Rivlin, Joseph, "*Yamim Noraim Etzel Edat ha-Mizrah*," *Mahanaim*, no. 60 (5722), p. 165.
27. Eshel, Yonah, "*Al Minhag Tashlikh be-Bolehov (Galitziah)*," *Yeda-Am*, vol. 3, nos. 2–3 (October, 1955), p. 145.
28. Israel ben Joseph Benjamin, *Sefer Masae Yisrael* (Lyck, 1859), p. 30.
29. Davidson, Efraim, "*Folklor Shel ha-Yamim ha-Noraim*," *Mahanaim*, no. 49 (5721), pp. 89–90.
30. *Yamim Noraim: Yalkut le-Rosh Hashanah vele-Yom ha-Kippurim*, Israel Defense Forces (Jerusalem, 5710), p. 19.
31. *The Jewish Chronicle* (London), no. 3,675 (September 15, 1939), p. 21.
32. Benari, Nahum, *Shabbat u-Moed: Nisyonot, Haarakhot ve-Tzione Derekh le-Itzuv ha-Demut Shel Shabbat u-Moed*, Ha-Histadrut Shel ha-Ovdim ha-Ivrim (Tel Aviv, 5707), pp. 38–40.
33. Spiro, Melford E., *Kibbutz: Venture in Utopia*, Harvard University Press (Cambridge, Massachusetts, 1956), p. 142.
34. *Yedion* (Vaadat ha-Tarbut ha-Benkibbutzi), no. 9 (September, 1965), p. 8.
35. From the prayer for dew recited on Passover.

36. *Yedion*, vol. 2, no. 7 (September, 1967), p. 14; *Rosh Hashanah*, Vaadat ha-Benkibbutzit le-Hivui u-Moed, 5726, pp. 22–24.
37. *Petahim* (Jerusalem), no. 2 (Kislev, 5728), p. 40.

XXI CHILDREN'S STORIES FOR ROSH HASHANAH

1. Weilerstein, Sadie Rose, *What the Moon Brought*, Jewish Publication Society of America (Philadelphia, 1942), pp. 4–12.
2. Weilerstein, Sadie Rose, *The Adventures of K'tonton: A Little Jewish Tom Thumb*, National Women's League of the United Synagogue (New York, 1935), pp. 71–75.
3. Epstein, Morris, *Tell Me about God and Prayer*, Ktav Publishing House (New York, 1953), pp. 31–34.
4. Epstein, Morris, *My Holiday Story Book*, Ktav Publishing House (New York, 1952), pp. 9–13.
5. Silverman, Althea O., *Habibi and Yow: A Little Boy and His Dog*, Bloch Publishing Co. (New York, 1946), pp. 27–32.
6. Kipnis, Levin, *My Holidays: Holiday Stories for Children*, trans. by Israel M. Goodelman, N. Tversky Publishing House (Tel Aviv, 1961), pp. 7–13.
7. Zeligs, Dorothy F., *The Story of Jewish Holidays and Customs for Young People*, Bloch Publishing Co. (New York, 1942), pp. 15–28.
8. *World Over*, vol. 8, no. 9 (February 21, 1947), pp. 10–11.
9. Prinz, Joachim, *Popes from the Ghetto: A View of Medieval Christendom*, Horizon Press (New York, 1966), pp. 17–20.

XXII CHILDREN'S POEMS FOR ROSH HASHANAH

1. Aronin, Ben, *Jolly Jingles for the Jewish Child*, Behrman House (New York, 1947), unpaged.
2. Levy, Sara G., *Mother Goose Rhymes for Jewish Children*, Bloch Publishing Co. (New York, 1945), p. 19.
3. Weilerstein, Sadie Rose, *The Singing Way: Poems for Jewish Children*, National Women's League of the United Synagogue (New York, 1946), p. 6.
4. Ibid., p. 7.
5. Sampter, Jessie E., *Around the Year in Rhymes for the Jewish Child*, Bloch Publishing Co. (New York, 1920), p. 12.
6. *Poems for Young Judaeans*, Young Judaea (New York, 1925), pp. 115–116.
7. Burstein, Abraham, *A Jewish Child's Garden of Verses*, Bloch Publishing Co. (New York, 1940), p. 27.

GLOSSARY OF ROSH HASHANAH
TERMS

AKEDAH (binding). Generally refers to the binding of Isaac by Abraham when the latter was ready to offer his son as a sacrifice. Genesis 22.1–24, which describes this episode, is the Scripture reading for the second day of Rosh Hashanah.

AMIDAH (standing). The prayers recited silently while standing.

ASERET YEME TESHUVAH (ten days of repentance). The ten-day period from Rosh Hashanah through Yom Kippur.

BAAL TEKIAH (master of blowing). The person who sounds the *shofar*.

DAYS OF AWE. See YAMIM NORAIM.

ELUL. The sixth Hebrew month preceding Rosh Hashanah, a prelude to the High Holy Days.

HATARAT NEDARIM (annulment of vows). Confession and annulment of vows and resolutions, traditionally performed on the eve of Rosh Hashanah.

HIGH HOLY DAYS. See YAMIM NORAIM.

KEROVAH (prayer). Poetical interpolation in the *Amidah*.

LE-SHANAH TOVAH TIKATEV VE-TEHATEM (May you be inscribed and sealed for a good year). Traditional greeting on the first night of Rosh Hashanah.

MAHZOR (cycle). Book of prayers for the cycle of holy days and festivals throughout the year; also applied to the individual parts of the yearly liturgy in which *piyyutim* are included.

MALKHUYOT (Kingship verses). A portion of the Rosh Hashanah liturgy

[359

which includes ten verses from the Bible depicting God as King and expressing the hope that all peoples will accept His Kingship.

NEW YEAR. See ROSH HASHANAH.

PIYYUT, pl. PIYYUTIM (poetry). A liturgical poem of praise recited on Rosh Hashanah and Yom Kippur.

RAM'S HORN. See SHOFAR.

ROSH HASHANAH (head of the year). The Jewish New Year, which falls on the new moon near the autumnal equinox, i.e., the first and second days of Tishri.

SABBATH OF REPENTANCE. See SHABBAT SHUVAH.

SELIHOT (penitential prayers). Prayers of penitence recited during the season of the High Holy Days, between midnight and dawn.

SHABBAT SHUVAH (Sabbath of Repentance or Return). The Sabbath between Rosh Hashanah and Yom Kippur; the prophetic portion that is read opens with "Return, O Israel" (Hosea 14.2).

SHEVARIM (broken sounds). One of the prescribed sounds of the shofar, consisting of three short notes.

SHOFAR. The ram's horn, which is sounded during the month of Elul, on Rosh Hashanah, and at the conclusion of Yom Kippur.

SHOFAROT (shofar verses). A portion of the Rosh Hashanah liturgy which includes ten verses from the Bible referring to the shofar and expressing the hope for the ingathering of the exiles of Israel.

TASHLIKH (you shall cast away). A ceremony symbolizing the casting away of sins into the depths of the waters in accordance with the prophet Micah (7.19), who said, "And Thou wilt cast all their sins into the depths of the sea." It is observed on the afternoon of the first day of Rosh Hashanah unless that is the Sabbath, in which case it is held on the second day.

TEKIAH (blowing). One of the prescribed sounds of the shofar, consisting of one prolonged, deep note.

TEKIAH GEDOLAH (large tekiah). A very prolonged blast, concluding a series of shofar sounds.

TERUAH (sound). One of the prescribed sounds of the shofar, composed of nine staccato notes.

TESHUVAH (repentance or return). One of the major themes of the High Holy Days.

TISHRI. The seventh Hebrew month, during which Rosh Hashanah and Yom Kippur occur.

YAMIM NORAIM (Days of Awe). The ten-day period from Rosh Hashanah through Yom Kippur.

YOM HA-DIN (Day of Judgment). One of the names for Rosh Hashanah.

YOM HA-ZIKKARON (Day of Remembrance or Memorial). One of the names for Rosh Hashanah.

YOM TERUAH (Day of Sounding). A name for Rosh Hashanah found in the Bible (Numbers 29.1).

ZIKHRON TERUAH (Remembrance of Sounding). Another name for Rosh Hashanah given in the Bible (Leviticus 23.24).

ZIKHRONOT (remembrance verses). A portion of the Rosh Hashanah liturgy which includes ten verses from the Bible recalling how God remembers His covenant with Israel.

BIBLIOGRAPHY

GENERAL REFERENCES

Abrahams, Israel, *Festival Studies: Being Thoughts on the Jewish Year*, Julius H. Greenstone, Philadelphia, 1906, pp. 19–24, 91–95, 139–144.

Agnon, Shmuel Yosef, *Yamim Noraim: Sefer Minhagot ve-Midrashot ve-Aggadot le-Yeme ha-Rahamim veha-Selihot le-Rosh ha-Shanah vele-Yom ha-Kippurim vele-Yamim she-Bentaim*, Schocken, Berlin, 5698, pp. 15–252.

——, *Days of Awe: Being a Treasury of Traditions, Legends and Learned Commentaries Concerning Rosh Ha-Shanah, Yom Kippur and the Days Between, Culled from Three Hundred Volumes Old and New*, introduction by Judah Goldin, Schocken Books, New York, 1965, pp. 11–147.

Amorai, Y., and Ariel, Z., eds., *Moreshet Avot* (*Entziklopediah "Mayan"*), Joseph Sreberk, Tel Aviv, n.d., pp. 45–63.

Ariel, Z., ed., *Sefer ha-Hag veha-Moed*, Am Oved, Tel Aviv, 1962, pp. 1–34.

Asaf, A., *Sefer Yamim Noraim*, Joshua Chachik, Tel Aviv, 5715, pp. 1–97.

Ausubel, Nathan, *The Book of Jewish Knowledge*, Crown Publishers, New York, 1964.

Ayali, Meir, ed., *Hagim u-Zemanim: Mahzore Kriah le-Moade Yisrael*, Gazit, Tel Aviv, 5715, vol. 2, pp. 1–80.

Baruch, Y. L., ed., *Sefer ha-Moadim: Rosh Hashanah ve-Yom ha-Kippurim*, "Oneg Shabbat" Society and Dvir, Tel Aviv, 1946, pp. 31–188.

Ben-Ezra, Akiba, *Minhage Hagim*, M. Newman, Tel Aviv, 5723, pp. 9–26.

——, ed., *Yamim Noraim ve-Sukkot*, Mizrachi National Education Committee, New York, 1949, pp. 1–19.

Ben Yehoshua, Hagi, ed., *Yamim Noraim: Reshimah Bibliografit*, Muni-

cipality of Jerusalem Department of Education and Culture, Jerusa-
lem, 1966.
Bernards, Solomon S., *The Living Heritage of the High Holy Days*,
Anti-Defamation League of B'nai B'rith, New York, n.d., pp. 5–13.
Bial, Morrison David, *Liberal Judaism at Home: The Practice of Modern
Reform Judaism*, Temple Sinai, Summit, New Jersey, 1967, pp. 107–
111.
Birnbaum, Philip, *A Book of Jewish Concepts*, Hebrew Publishing Co.,
New York, 1964.
Chomsky, William, *Ha-Yamim ha-Noraim: Rosh ha-Shanah ve-Yom ha-
Kippurim*, Jewish Education Committee of New York, New York,
1960, pp. 1–32.
Cooper, Martin, ed., *The New Year Companion*, Association for Jewish
Youth, London, n.d., pp. 1–21.
Ehrmann, Elieser L., *Rosch ha-Schana und Jom Kippur: Ein Quel-
lenheft*, Schocken Verlag, Berlin, 1938, pp. 5–35.
Eisenstein, Ira, *What We Mean by Religion: A Modern Interpretation
of the Sabbath and Festivals*, Reconstructionist Press, New York,
1958, pp. 43–61.
Eliner, Eliezer, ed., *Keseh ve-Asor*, Religious Section of the Department
of Education and Culture in the Diaspora, World Zionist Organiza-
tion, Jerusalem, 1951, pp. 5–68, 91–205.
Freehof, Lillian S., and Bandman, Lottie C., *Flowers and Festivals of the
Jewish Year*, Hearthside Press, New York, 1964, pp. 48–55.
Frishman, Isaiah, ed., *Rosh Hashanah—Yom ha-Kippurim: Homer
Hadrakhah le-Morim be-Bate ha-Sefer ha-Memlakhtiim*, Ministry of
Education and Culture, Jerusalem, 5727, pp. 1–64.
Gaster, Theodor H., *Festivals of the Jewish Year: A Modern Interpreta-
tion and Guide*, William Sloane Associates, New York, 1953, pp.
107–134.
Goldin, Hyman E., *The Jewish Woman and Her Home*, Jewish Culture
Publishing Co., Brooklyn, 1941, pp. 193–202.
Goldman, Alex J., *A Handbook for the Jewish Family: Understanding and
Enjoying the Sabbath and Holidays*, Bloch Publishing Co., New York,
1958, pp. 1–34.
Golnitzki, Heshil, *Be-Mahzor ha-Yamim: Moed ve-Hol be-Omanut uve-
Folklor ha-Yehudi*, Haifa, 1963, pp. 44–47.
Goodman, Philip, ed., *New Year and Day of Atonement Program Material
for Youth and Adults*, National Jewish Welfare Board, New York,
1952, pp. 1–90.
Goren, Shlomoh, *Torat ha-Moadim: Mehkerim u-Maamarim al Moade
Yisrael le-Or ha-Halakhah*, Avraham Zioni, Tel Aviv, 5724, pp. 9–104.
Greenberg, Betty D., and Silverman, Althea O., *The Jewish Home Beauti-
ful*, National Women's League of the United Synagogue of America,
New York, 1941, pp. 42–43, 89–93.
Greenstone, Julius H., *The Jewish Religion*, Jewish Chautauqua Society,
Philadelphia, 1929, pp. 74–86.
———, *Jewish Feasts and Fasts*, Philadelphia, 1945, pp. 7–23, 297–301.
Hag u-Moed: Divre Iyun, Mekorot, Ha-Kibbutz ha-Artzi, ha-Mahlakah
le-Tarbut, Tel Aviv, 5727, pp. 50–65.

Hage Tishri: *Homer Hadrakhah le-Gane ha-Yeladim ha-Memlakhtiim*, Ministry of Education and Culture, Jerusalem, 5727, pp. 1-25.

Hakohen, Menahem, ed., *Mahanaim*: *Masekhet le-Haile Tzahal le-Yamim ha-Noraim*, Tzava Haganah le-Yisrael, no. 49 (5721), pp. 8-180.

Hakohen, Shmuel, Shragai, Eliahu, and Peli, Pinhas, eds., *Yamim Noraim*: *Yalkut le-Rosh Hashanah ve-Yom ha-Kippurim*, no. 6, Tzava Haganah le-Yisrael, no. 6 (5710), pp. 3-63.

Hamiel, Hayyim, ed., *Yamim Noraim*: *Alef*: *Maasaf le-Inyane Hinukh ve-Horaah*, Department of Torah Education and Culture in the Diaspora, World Zionist Organization, Jerusalem, 5728, pp. 1-330.

A Handbook for Jewish Youth Leaders: *The Month of Elul*: *Source Material for Discussion and Dramatization in the Youth Movement*, Zionist Organization, Jerusalem, 1955, pp. 18-47.

Hirsch, Samson Raphael, *Selected Essays on Rosh Hashanah*, ed. and trans. by Ismar Lipschutz, Atereth Tzvi Publication, New York, 1954, pp. 1-63.

———, *Horeb*: *A Philosophy of Jewish Laws and Observances*, trans. by I. Grunfeld, Soncino Press, London, 1962, vol. 1, pp. 136-141; vol. 2, pp. 385-391.

———, *Be-Magle Shanah*, trans. by Aviezer Wolf, Netzah, Bne Berak, 1965, pp. 45-109.

Jacobs, Louis, *A Guide to Rosh Ha-Shanah*, Jewish Chronicle Publications, London, 1959, pp. 1-74.

Jacobson, Bernhard S., ed., *Yamim Noraim*: *Arbeitsplan und Staffsammlung*, Tenuat Tora Wa'Avoda in Deutschland, Berlin, n.d., pp. 1-117.

The Jewish Encyclopedia, 12 vols., Ktav Publishing House, New York; articles on Life, Book of . . . ; New Year; Penitential Days; *Selihot*; *Shofar*; *Tashlikh*.

Joseph, Morris, *Judaism as Creed and Life*, George Routledge and Sons, London, 1903, pp. 247-254.

Kaplan, Mordecai M., *The Meaning of God in Modern Jewish Religion*, Jewish Reconstructionist Foundation, New York, 1947, pp. 104-148.

Kitov, Eliyahu, *Sefer ha-Todaah*: *La-Daat Huke ha-Elokim u-Mitzvotav Hage Yisrael u-Moadav*, Alef Makhon le-Hatzaat Sefarim, Jerusalem, 1964, pp. 7-28.

———, *The Book of Our Heritage*: *The Jewish Year and Its Days of Significance*: vol. 1: *Tishrey-Shevat*, trans. by Nathan Bulman, 'A' Publishers, Jerusalem, 1968, pp. 15-59.

Lauterbach, Jacob Z., "Tashlik: A Study in Jewish Ceremonies," *Hebrew Union College Annual*, vol. 11 (1936), pp. 207-340; reprinted in his *Rabbinic Essays*, Hebrew Union College Press, Cincinnati, 1951, pp. 299-433.

Lehrman, S. M., *The Jewish Festivals*, Shapiro, Vallentine & Co., London, 1938, pp. 89-108.

Leshem, Haim, *Shabbat u-Moade Yisrael be-Halakhah, be-Aggadah, be-Historiah, be-Hove, uve-Folklor*, Niv, Tel Aviv, 1965, pp. 77-153.

Levi, Shonie B., and Kaplan, Sylvia R., *Guide for the Jewish Homemaker*, Schocken Books, New York, 1964, pp. 83-93.

Maimon (Fishman), Yehudah Leb Hakohen, *Hagim u-Moadim*, Mosad Harav Kook, Jerusalem, 1944, pp. 19-39.

Markowitz, S. H., *Leading a Jewish Life in the Modern World*, rev. ed., Union of American Hebrew Congregations, New York, 1958, pp. 144-159.

Massekhet Rosh Hashanah, Talmud Bavli, Wilna, 1895.

Max, Mosheh, *The Way of God*, Feldheim Publishers, New York, 1968, pp. 179-198.

Melamed, Deborah M., *The Three Pillars: Thought, Worship and Practice for the Jewish Woman*, National Women's League of United Synagogue of America, New York, 1927, pp. 77-88.

Mervis, Leonard J., *We Celebrate the High Holy Days*, Union of American Hebrew Congregations, New York, 1953, pp. 2-16.

Midrash on Psalms (Midrash Tehillim), trans. by William G. Braude, Yale University Press, New Haven, 1959.

The Mishnah, trans. by Herbert Danby, Clarendon Press, Oxford, 1933, pp. 188-194.

Montefiore, C. G., "Rabbinic Conceptions of Repentance," *Jewish Quarterly Review*, o.s., vol. 16 (1904), pp. 209-257.

———, and Loewe, H., *A Rabbinic Anthology*, Macmillan and Co., London, 1938.

Morgenstern, Julian, "The Three Calendars of Ancient Israel," *Hebrew Union College Annual*, vol. 1 (1924), pp. 13-78.

Newman, Louis I., and Spitz, Samuel, *The Talmudic Anthology*, Behrman House, New York, 1945, pp. 391-394.

Pearlmutter, Jacob, ed., *Themes for Daily Study: Selections from the Bible, Talmud, Midrash and Shulhan-Aruch for Study: Part I: Rosh Hashanah and Yom Kippur*, Bloch Publishing Co., New York, 1941, pp. 1-21, 33-41.

Press, Chaim, *What Is the Reason: An Anthology of Questions and Answers on the Jewish Holidays*: Vol. 1: *Rosh Hashanah*, Bloch Publishing Co., New York, 1965, pp. 1-94.

Rosh Hashanah, trans. by Maurice Simon, *The Babylonian Talmud*, Soncino Press, London, 1938.

Roth, Cecil, ed., *The Standard Jewish Encyclopedia*, Doubleday & Co., Garden City, New York, 1959; articles on New Year, Rosh Hashanah, *Shofar, Tashlikh*.

Sachs, A. S., *Worlds That Passed*, Jewish Publication Society of America, Philadelphia, 1928, pp. 149-171.

Sack, Eugene J., *Rosh Hashanah*, National Jewish Welfare Board, New York, 1954, pp. 1-14.

Schauss, Hayyim, *The Jewish Festivals: From Their Beginnings to Our Own Day*, Union of American Hebrew Congregations, Cincinnati, 1938, pp. 112-118, 143-149.

Seidman, Hillel, *The Glory of the Jewish Holidays*, ed. by Moses Zalesky, Shengold Publishers, New York, 1969, pp. 68-92.

Shechter, S. Zvi, ed., *Moade Yisrael: Pirke Kriah ve-Nigun*, Ministry of Education and Culture Youth Department and Henrietta Szold Institute, Jerusalem, 1966, pp. 49-63.

Shragai, Eliyahu, and Alfasi, Yitzhak, eds., *Be-Yeme Din: Perakim le-Yamim Noraim*, Tzava Haganah le-Yisrael, no. 11 (5711), pp. 8-50.

Snaith, Norman H., *The Jewish New Year Festival: Its Origin and Development*, Society for Promoting Christian Knowledge, London, 1947, pp. 1–230.

Soltes, Mordecai, *The Jewish Holidays: A Guide to Their Origin, Significance and Observance*, National Jewish Welfare Board, New York, 1968, pp. 4–7, 25–26.

Sperling, Abraham Isaac, *Reasons for Jewish Customs and Traditions*, trans. by Abraham Matts, Bloch Publishing Co., New York, 1968, pp. 216–231.

Stolper, Pinchas, ed., *Yamim Noraim Manual*, Union of Orthodox Jewish Congregations, New York, 1961, pp. 9–31.

Thieberger, Friedrich, ed., *Jüdisches Fest: Jüdischer Brauch*, Jüdischer Verlag, Berlin, 1936, pp. 145–197.

Tishri: Textes pour Servir à la Préparation des Fêtes de Rosh Hashanah, Kippour et Soukkoth, Editions des E. I. F., Paris, 1945, pp. 9–64.

Tverski, Shimon, ed., *Moadim: Massekhet le-Yamim Noraim vele-Hag Sukkot*, Tzava Haganah le-Yisrael, no. 15 (5713), pp. 3–26.

The Universal Jewish Encyclopedia, 10 vols., ed. by Isaac Landman, Ktav Publishing House, New York, 1968; articles on Rosh Hashanah, Selihot, Shofar, Tashlikh.

Unterman, Isaac, *The Jewish Holidays*, 2nd ed., Bloch Publishing Co., New York, 1950, pp. 23–55.

Vainstein, Yaacov, *The Cycle of the Jewish Year: A Study of the Festivals and of Selections from the Liturgy*, World Zionist Organization, Jerusalem, 1964, pp. 96–104.

Wahrmann, Nahum, *Hage Yisrael u-Moadav: Minhagehem u-Semelehem*, Ahiasaf, Jerusalem, 1959, pp. 11–39.

———, ed., *Moadim: Pirke Halakhah, Aggadah ve-Tefilah le-Khol Moade ha-Shanah*, Kiryat Sefer, Jerusalem, 1957, pp. 24–38, 164–173, 232–233.

Werblowsky, R. J. Zwi, and Wigoder, Geoffrey, eds., *The Encyclopedia of the Jewish Religion*, Holt, Rinehart and Winston, New York, 1966; articles on *Akedah*, Festival Prayers, Rosh Ha-Shanah, *Shophar*.

Werfel, Yitzhak, ed., *Yerah ha-Etanim: Yalkut . . . Mugash le-Hayil ha-Ivri*, Mosad Harav Kook, Jerusalem, 5702, pp. 4–190.

Wouk, Herman, *This Is My God*, Doubleday & Co., Garden City, New York, 1959, pp. 65–75.

Yonah Ben Avraham of Gerona, *Shaare Teshuvah: Gates of Repentance*, trans. by Shraga Silverstein, Yaakov Feldheim, Boys Town, Jerusalem, 1967, pp. 1–390.

Zobel, Moritz, *Das Jahr des Juden in Brauch und Liturgie*, Schocken Verlag, Berlin, 1936, pp. 55–77.

ROSH HASHANAH IN JEWISH LAW

Berman, Yaakov, *Halakhah la-Am*, Avraham Zioni, Tel Aviv, 1962, pp. 118–186.

Caro, Joseph, *Shulhan Arukh, Orah Hayyim*, "Hilkhot Rosh Hashanah," 581–603.

Eisenstein, Judah D., *Otzar Dinim u-Minhagim*, New York, 1917.
Ganzfried, Solomon, *Code of Jewish Law*, trans. by Hyman E. Goldin, Hebrew Publishing Co., New York, 1927, vol. 3, pp. 70–81.
Hurwitz, S. L., *Sefer Dine Yisrael u-Minhagav le-Yamim Noraim*, New York, 1924.
Laws and Customs of Israel, trans. by Gerald Friedlander, Shapiro, Vallentine & Co., London, 1934, pp. 361–368.
Moses Ben Maimon, *Mishneh Torah*, Amsterdam, 1702. See *"Hilkhot Teshuvah," "Hilkhot Shofar."*
Shpriling, Abraham Isaac, *Sefer Taame ha-Minhagim u-Mekore ha-Dinim*, Eshkol, Jerusalem, 5721, pp. 300–325.
Zevin, Shlomoh Yosef, *Ha-Moadim be-Halakhah*, 2nd ed., Betan Hasefer, Tel Aviv, 5707, pp. 26–61.

THE LITURGY OF ROSH HASHANAH

Adler, Cyrus, "The Shofar: Its Use and Origin," *Journal of American Oriental Society*, 48 (1890); reprinted in Smithsonian Institution Report, 9 (1892), pp. 437–450.
Adler, Herbert M., and Davis, Arthur, trans., *Service of the Synagogue: New Year*, George Routledge & Sons, London, 1904.
Arzt, Max, *Justice and Mercy: Commentary on the Liturgy of the New Year and the Day of Atonement*, Holt, Rinehart and Winston, New York, 1963, pp. 1–188.
Barish, Louis, *High Holiday Liturgy*, Jonathan David, New York, 1959, pp. 1–95.
Birnbaum, Philip, trans., *High Holyday Prayer Book*, Hebrew Publishing Co., New York, 1951, pp. 1–462.
Bokser, Ben Zion, trans., *The High Holyday Prayer Book: Rosh Hashanah and Yom Kippur*, Hebrew Publishing Co., New York, 1959, pp. 1–237.
———, *Selihot Service*, United Synagogue of America, New York, 1955.
Dembitz, Louis N., *Jewish Services in Synagogue and Home*, Jewish Publication Society of America, Philadelphia, 1898, pp. 155–164.
Elbogen, Isaac M., *Toldot ha-Tefilah veha-Avodah be-Yisrael*, Dvir, Jerusalem/Berlin, 5684, part I, pp. 99–106.
Feinberg, Louis, trans., *Selihot for the First Day*, Behrman House, New York, 1950.
Finesinger, Sol B., "The Shofar," *Hebrew Union College Annual*, vols. 8–9. (1931–1932), pp. 193–228.
Freehof, Solomon B., *The Small Sanctuary: Judaism in the Prayerbook*, Union of American Hebrew Congregations, New York, 1942, pp. 162–171, 244–248, 254–255.
Glatzer, Nahum N., ed., *Language of Faith: A Selection from the Most Expressive Jewish Prayers*, Schocken Books, New York, 1967, pp. 270–279, 292.
Harlow, Jules, ed., *Yearnings: Prayer and Meditation for the Days of Awe*, Rabbinical Assembly, New York, 1968.
Hertz, Joseph Herman, *The Authorised Daily Prayer Book*, Bloch Publishing Co., New York, 1952, pp. 838–889.

Hoenig, Sidney B., "Origins of the Rosh Hashanah Liturgy," *The Seventy-fifth Anniversary Volume of the Jewish Quarterly Review*, Philadelphia, 1967, pp. 312–331.
Idelsohn, A. Z., *Jewish Liturgy and Its Development*, Henry Holt and Co., New York, 1932, pp. 34–46, 205–223, 272–274.
Kaplan, Mordecai M., Kohn, Eugene, and Eisenstein, Ira, eds., *High Holiday Prayer Book with Supplementary Prayers and Readings and with a New English Translation*, Jewish Reconstructionist Foundation, New York, 1948, vol. 1.
————, *Supplementary Prayers and Readings for the High Holidays*: Part I—*Rosh Hashanah*. Part II—*Yom Kippur*, Jewish Reconstructionist Foundation, New York, 1960, pp. 1–68.
Kieval, Herman, *The High Holy Days: A Commentary on the Prayerbook of Rosh Hashanah and Yom Kippur*: Book One: *Rosh Hashanah*, Burning Bush Press, New York, 1959.
Klein, Max D., trans., *Seder Avodah: Service Book for Rosh Hashanah and Yom Kippur*, Philadelphia, 1960, pp. 1–377.
Levy, Eliezer, *Yesodot ha-Tefilah*, Betan Hasefer, Tel Aviv, 5712, pp. 245–256.
Liebreich, Leon J., "Aspects of the New Year Liturgy," *Hebrew Union College Annual*, vol. 34 (1963), pp. 125–176.
Martin, Bernard, *Prayer in Judaism*, Basic Books, New York, 1968, pp. 181–218.
Munk, Elie, *The World of Prayer*: vol. 2: *Commentary and Translation of the Sabbath and Festival Prayers*, Philipp Feldheim, New York, 1963, pp. 169–216.
Pool, David de Sola, ed. and trans., *Prayers for the New Year According to the Custom of the Spanish and Portuguese Jews*, Union of Sephardic Congregations, New York, 1937.
Rosenfeld, Abraham, trans., *The Authorised Selichot for the Whole Year . . . Hebrew text and English translation*, London, 1957.
Rubinstein, A. L., *A Companion to the Rosh Hashanah & Yom Kippur Machzor*, Glascow, 1957, pp. 1–62.
Sendrey, Alfred, "Shofar," *Music in Ancient Israel*, Philosophical Library, New York, 1969, pp. 342–365.
Silverman, Morris, ed., *High Holiday Prayer Book*, Prayer Book Press, Hartford, 1951, pp. 1–190.
Steinbach, Alexander Alan, ed., *Supplementary Prayers and Meditations for the High Holy Days*, Temple Ahavath Sholom, Brooklyn, 1961, pp. 3–43.
The Union Prayer Book for Jewish Worship, newly rev. ed., part 2, Central Conference of American Rabbis, New York, 1962, pp. 6–122.

HASIDIC TALES

Buber, Martin, *Tales of the Hasidim: The Early Masters*, trans. by Olga Marx, Schocken Books, New York, 1947.
————, *Tales of the Hasidim: The Later Masters*, trans. by Olga Marx, Schocken Books, New York, 1948.

Goodman, Philip, *Rejoice in Thy Festival: A Treasury of Wisdom, Wit and Humor for the Sabbaths and Jewish Holidays*, Bloch Publishing Co., New York, 1956.
Kariv, Avraham, ed., *Shabbat u-Moed be-Derush uve-Hasidut*, Dvir and Oneg Shabbat Society, Tel Aviv, 1966.
Lipson, M., *Mi-Dor Dor*, vol. 3, Dorot, Tel Aviv and New York, 1938.
Newman, Louis I., and Spitz, Samuel, *The Hasidic Anthology: Tales and Teachings of the Hasidim*, Bloch Publishing Co., New York, 1944.
———, *Maggidim & Hasidim: Their Wisdom*, Bloch Publishing Co., New York, 1962.
Silverstone, Abraham, *Mi-Maane ha-Hasidut: Midot u-Moadim*, ed. by Robert Gordis and Morris D. Margolis, Rabbinical Assembly of America, New York, 1957.
Unger, Menashe, *Chasidus un Yom-Tov*, Farlag Chasidus, New York, 1958.
Zevin, Shlomoh Yosef, *Sipure Hasidim . . . le-Moade ha-Shanah*, Avraham Zioni, Tel Aviv, 1958.

SERMONS FOR THE HIGH HOLY DAYS

This bibliography is limited to sermons published in books and does not include the many High Holy Days sermons issued in pamphlet form by organizations and congregations. With some exceptions only books published since 1940 are included.

Amiel, Mosche Avigdor, *Unto My People (El Ami): A Book of Sermons for the High Festivals Period*, trans. from Hebrew by L. Rabinowitz, M. L. Cailingold, London, 1931. 170 pp.
Avigdor, Isaac C., *Ten for Two: Sermons for All Holidays of the Year*, Jonathan David, New York, 1960, pp. 19–119.
Berkovits, E., *Between Yesterday and Tomorrow: Sermons*, East and West Library, Oxford, 1945, pp. 84–88, 100–115, 140–145.
Bosniak, Jacob, *Interpreting Jewish Life: Sermons and Addresses*, Bloch Publishing Co., New York, 1944, pp. 16–24, 48–62, 69–77, 107–120.
Brodie, Israel, *A Word in Season, 1948–1958*, Vallentine, Mitchell, London, 1959, pp. 17–30, 36–44, 53–55, 66–67.
Calisch, Edward Nathan, *Three Score and Twenty: A Brief Biography: Selected Addresses and Sermons*, Richmond, Virginia, 1945, pp. 88–96, 100–114, 132–148.
Chiel, Samuel, *Spectators or Participants*, Jonathan David, New York, 1969, pp. 3–17, 27–37, 67–71, 129–135, 156–162.
Cohon, Beryl D., *From Generation to Generation*, Bruce Humphries, Boston, 1951, pp. 17–49.
———, *My King and My God: Intimate Talks on the Devotions of Life*, Bloch Publishing Co., New York, 1963, pp. 16–22, 40–66, 198–213.
Donin, Hayim, *Beyond Thyself: A Collection of Sermons*, Bloch Publishing Co., New York, 1965, pp. 1–57, 62–95, 120–127.
Dresner, Samuel H., *The Jew in American Life*, Crown Publishers, New York, 1963, pp. 50–61, 253–261.

Elfenbein, Israel, *The American Synagogue as a Leavening Force in Jewish Life and a Collection of Select Writings*, ed. by Abraham Burstein, Bloch Publishing Co., New York, 1966, pp. 29–35, 84–90.

Elton, Michael, *The Challenge of Destiny*, Exclusive Books, Johannesburg, 1961, pp. 184–198.

Epstein, Harry H., *Judaism and Progress: Sermons and Addresses*, Bloch Publishing Co., New York, 1935, pp. 1–92.

Epstein, Reuben, *The Blueprint of Creation*, Rachman, New York, 1943, pp. 11–22, 41–58, 76–85.

———, *The Torah Testifies: Essays and Sermons on Jewish Faith*, Philipp Feldheim, New York, 1958, pp. 175–178.

Gartenberg, Leo, *Torah Thoughts*, Jonathan David, New York, 1964, pp. 3–79.

Gerstein, Israel, *Reveille or Taps? Sermons, Essays and Addresses*, Bloch Publishing Co., New York, 1945, pp. 1–29.

Goldfarb, Solomon D., *To Stand Alone*, Jonathan David, New York, 1957, pp. 20–27, 81–87, 110–121, 141–164.

———, *Windows in Heaven*, Jonathan David, New York, 1960, pp. 1–4, 14–16, 21–23, 30–45, 61–63, 68–72, 85–87.

———, *Torah for Our Time: Sermons and Studies Based on Biblical Texts for Sabbath and Holidays*, Bloch Publishing Co., New York, 1965, pp. 154–164.

Goldstein, Israel, *Toward a Solution*, G. P. Putnams's Sons, New York, 1940, pp. 153–161.

———, *Tradition Years: New York-Jerusalem, 1960–1962*, Rubin Mass, Jerusalem, 1962, pp. 207–215.

Gordis, Robert, *Leave a Little to God: Essays in Judaism*, Bloch Publishing Co., New York, 1967, pp. 3–247.

Gordon, Solomon, *Voice of the Heart*, Bloch Publishing Co., New York, 1965, pp. 19–30.

Greenberg, Sidney, *Adding Life to Our Years*, Jonathan David, New York, 1959, pp. 1–43, 54–70, 84–156, 174–194.

———, *Finding Ourselves: Sermons on the Art of Living*, Jonathan David, New York, 1964, pp. 3–133, 145–258.

Hailperin, Herman, *A Rabbi Teaches: A Collection of Addresses and Sermons*, Bloch Publishing Co., New York, 1939, pp. 19–60.

Halpern, Abraham E., *A Son of Faith: From the Sermons of Abraham E. Halpern*, ed. by Bernard S. Raskas, Bloch Publishing Co., New York, 1962, pp. 10–51, 70–79, 90–100, 109–114, 119–137, 141–146, 156–159, 166–169, 228–233.

Hammer, Louis, *A Word in Season*, Judaica Publishing Co., Brooklyn, 1944, pp. 17–93.

Heller, Abraham Mayer, *Jewish Survival: Sermons and Addresses*, Behrman's Jewish Book House, New York, 1939, pp. 13–22, 75–114, 167–214.

Hershman, Abraham M., *Israel's Fate and Faith*, Bloch Publishing Co., New York, 1952, pp. 53–99.

Hertz, Joseph H., *Early and Late: Addresses, Messages, and Papers*, Soncino Press, London, 1943, pp. 25–36.

Hyamson, Moses, *The Oral Law and Other Sermons*, David Nutt, London, 1910, pp. 18–49.
———, *Sabbath and Festival Addresses*, Bloch Publishing Co., New York, 1936, pp. 157–173.
Jacob, Ernest I., *Paths of Faithfulness: A Collection of Sermons*, Pittsburgh, 1964, pp. 7–123.
Jakobovits, Immanuel, *Journal of a Rabbi*, Living Books, New York, 1966, pp. 291–381.
Jick, Leon A., *In Search of a Way*, Temple Books, Mount Vernon, New York, 1966, pp. 8–13, 25–28, 33–49, 55–60, 74–79, 110–128.
Jung, Leo, *Living Judaism*, Night & Day Press, New York, 1927, pp. 283–307, 331–341.
———, *Toward Sinai! Sermons and Addresses*, Pardes Publishing House, New York, 1929, pp. 3–95.
———, *Harvest: Sermons, Addresses, Studies*, Philipp Feldheim, New York, 1956, pp. 95–127.
Kahana, S. Z., *Heaven on Your Head: Interpretations, Legends and Parables, Comments on the Torah and the Holidays*, ed. by Morris Silverman, Hartmore House, Hartford, 1964, pp. 217–237.
Kellner, Abraham A., *A Rabbi's Faith: Sermons of Hope and Courage*, Albany, 1945, pp. 1–40.
———, *Strangers at the Gate: Sermons for Today and Tomorrow*, Bloch Publishing Co., New York, 1954, pp. 9–55.
———, *Tomorrow's Religion: Sermons and Studies*, Gertz Bros., New York, 1957, pp. 9–58.
———, *With Perfect Faith: Sermons for the Sixties*, H. F. Epstein Hebrew Academy, St. Louis, 1962, pp. 17–41, 51–58, 65–76.
Kertzer, Morris N., *The Art of Being a Jew*, World Publishing Co., Cleveland, 1962, pp. 70–78, 109–121.
Kirshenbaum, David, *Feast Days and Fast Days: Judaism Seen through Its Festivals*, Bloch Publishing Co., New York, 1968, pp. 23–88.
Klappholz, Kurt, *The Power within Us*, Torah Institute, Brooklyn, 1961, pp. 74–81.
Kohler, Kaufmann, *A Living Faith: Selected Sermons and Addresses . . .* , ed. by Samuel S. Cohon, Hebrew Union College Press, Cincinnati, 1948, pp. 42–69.
Kolatch, Alfred J., *Sermons and Sermon Snacks*, Jonathan David, New York, 1963, pp. 1–75, 87–109, 130–150.
———, *Sermons for the Sixties*, Jonathan David, New York, 1965, pp. 11–15, 26–36, 41–45, 93–120, 130–135, 153–157.
Levinthal, Israel Herbert, *Steering or Drifting—Which?: Sermons and Discourses*, Funk & Wagnalls, New York, 1928, pp. 3–61, 77–122, 139–149.
———, *A New World Is Born: Sermons and Addresses*, Funk & Wagnalls, New York, 1943, pp. 7–66, 122–128, 141–147, 155–161, 173–179, 194–200.
———, *Judaism Speaks to the Modern World*, Abelard-Schuman, New York, 1963, pp. 19–25, 32–43, 50–76.

Lookstein, Joseph H., *Faith and Destiny of Man: Traditional Judaism in a New Light*, Bloch Publishing Co., New York, 1967, pp. 1–174.
Margolies, Morris B., *Torah-Vision: Sermonic Essays for Our Time*, Philipp Feldheim, New York, 1961, pp. 221–231.
Maybaum, Ignaz, *The Faith of the Diaspora*, Vision, London, 1962, pp. 43–48, 61–71, 75–83, 115–117.
———, *The Face of God after Auschwitz*, Polak & Van Gennep, Amsterdam, 1965, pp. 61–64, 69–76, 93–96, 100–103.
Minda, Albert G., *Over the Years: Papers and Addresses*, Bloch Publishing Co., New York, 1957, pp. 28–51.
Narot, Joseph R., "The High Holy Day Sermon," *Israel Bettan Memorial Volume*, Central Conference of American Rabbis, New York, 1961, pp. 110–131.
———, *For Whom the Rabbi Speaks: A Collection of Sermons and Articles*, Rostrum Books, Miami, 1966, pp. 24–29.
Newman, J., *Speak unto the Children of Israel: Sermons for Every Sabbath and Festival of the Year for Jewish Children*, Bloch Publishing Co., New York, n.d., pp. 138–146.
Newman, Jacob, *The Eternal Quest*, Bloch Publishing Co., New York, 1965, pp. 1–49, 54–92.
Newman, Louis I., *Sermons and Addresses*, Bloch Publishing Co., New York, eight volumes, 1941–1954: vol. 2 (1941), pp. 8–67: vol. 3 (1941), pp. 94–101, 145–150; vol. 4 (1943), pp. 20–27, 64–66, 74–80, 118–125, 139–183; vol. 5 (1946—title: *Biting on Granite*), pp. 107–117, 284–327; vol. 6 (1950—title: *Becoming a New Person*), nos. 1–3, 9–14; vol. 7 (1952—title: *Living with Ourselves*), pp. 7–34, 133–148, 165–174, 185–226; vol. 8 (1954—title: *The Search for Serenity*), pp. 59–104, 119–128, 134–159.
Pilchik, Ely E., *Jeshurun Sermons*, Bloch Publishing Co., New York, 1957, pp. 237–261.
The Rabbinical Council Manual of Holiday and Sabbath Sermons (early volumes entitled *Manual of Holiday and Occasional Sermons* and variations), various editors, Rabbinical Council Press, New York, vols. 1–27 (1943–1969): 1943, pp. 7–79; 1944, pp. 9–73; 1945, pp. 7–47; 1946, pp. 9–66; 1947, pp. 9–45; 1948, pp. 9–76; 1949, pp. 9–80; 1950, pp. 9–102; 1951, pp. 9–130; 1952, pp. 13–101; 1953, pp. 15–183; 1954, pp. 17–146; 1955, pp. 28–141; 1956, pp. 19–106; 1957, pp. 15–108; 1958, pp. 17–124; 1959, pp. 29–146; 1960, pp. 19–150; 1961, pp. 19–155; 1962, pp. 21–95; 1963, pp. 17–139; 1964, pp. 17–165; 1965, pp. 17–108; 1966, pp. 17–115; 1967, pp. 15–126; 1968, pp. 17–91; 1969, pp. 15–64.
Rabinowitz, Louis I., *Out of the Depths: Sermons for All Sabbaths and Festivals*, Eagle Press, Johannesburg, 1951, pp. 307–347.
———, *Light and Salvation: Sermons for the High Holy Days*, Bloch Publishing Co., New York, 1965, pp. 14–349.
Roodman, Solomon, *The Vaccine of Faith*, Jonathan David, New York, 1957, pp. 1–14, 28–36, 43–48, 88–94, 102–107, 113–118, 137–142, 157–165.
———, *The Suburbs of the Almighty: Sermons and Discourses*, Jonathan

THE ROSH HASHANAH ANTHOLOGY

David, New York, 1962, pp. 7–14, 31–42, 121–127, 141–148, 154–165.
Rosenberg, Stuart E., *Man Is Free: Sermons and Addresses*, Bloch Publishing Co., New York, 1957, pp. 29–55, 99–105.
——, *A Time to Speak: Of Man, Faith and Society*, Bloch Publishing Co., New York, 1960, pp. 126–155, 172–177.
Rosenblatt, Samuel, *Our Heritage*, Bloch Publishing Co., New York, 1940, pp. 3–92.
——, *Hear, Oh Israel: Sermons and Addresses* . . . , Philipp Feldheim, New York, 1958, pp. 145–230.
Scheinberg, Abraham, *Man and Robot: Lectures and Sermons*, Bloch Publishing Co., New York, 1952, pp. 46–121.
Selig, Harris L., *The Eternal Fount*, Hebrew Publishing Co., New York, 1941, pp. 243–253.
——, *Links to Eternity: Jewish Holidays and Festivals*, Bloch Publishing Co., New York, 1957, pp. 1–85.
Sermonic Talks on Jewish Holidays and Festivals for Lay Leaders in the Armed Forces of the United States, Commission on Jewish Chaplaincy, National Jewish Welfare Board, New York, 1967, pp. 1–13.
A Set of Holiday Sermons, Union of American Hebrew Congregations and Central Conference of American Rabbis, New York (pamphlet published annually from 1905 to 1964).
Silver, Abba Hillel, *Therefore Choose Life: Selected Sermons, Addresses and Writings*: vol. 1, ed. by Herbert Weiner, World Publishing Co., Cleveland, 1967, pp. 22–29, 60–66, 77–84.
Silverstein, Baruch, *A Jew in Love*, Jonathan David, New York, 1966, pp. 11–18, 29–64, 74–92, 146–154.
Singer, Joseph I., *Margin for Triumph: Timeless Answers to Timely Questions*, Bloch Publishing Co., New York, 1958, pp. 17–95.
Spero, Shubert, *God in All Seasons*, Shengold Publishers, New York, 1967, pp. 9–38.
Steinbach, Alexander Alan, *Sabbath Queen: Fifty-four Bible Talks to the Young*, Behrman House, New York, 1936, pp. 155–157, 164–168.
——, *Through Storms We Grow and Other Sermons, Lectures and Essays*, Bloch Publishing Co., New York, 1964, pp. 17–52.
Steinberg, Milton, *A Believing Jew*, Harcourt, Brace and Co., New York, 1951, pp. 196–201, 213–228, 243–271, 282–305.
——, *From the Sermons of Rabbi Milton Steinberg: High Holydays and Major Festivals*, ed. by Bernard Mandelbaum, Bloch Publishing Co., New York, 1954, pp. 3–92.
Stern, Harry Joshua, *Martyrdom and Miracle: A Collection of Addresses*, Bloch Publishing Co., New York, 1950, pp. 22–49.
Stitskin, Leon, *Judaism as a Religion: A Series of Holiday Sermons*, Bloch Publishing Co., New York, 1939, pp. 3–48.
Swift, Harris, *Because I Believe: Sermons, Addresses and Essays*, Bloch Publishing Co., New York, 1954, pp. 27–33, 335–358.
Tabak, Israel, *Treasury of Holiday Thoughts: High Holy Days and Pilgrim Festivals*, Twayne Publishers, New York, 1958, pp. 27–112.
Teplitz, Saul I., ed., *Best Jewish Sermons*, Jonathan David, New York: 5713, 1953, pp. 1–108; 5714, 1954, pp. 52–56, 102–124, 139–148; 5715–5716, 1956, pp. 1–18, 24–57, 61–69, 79–94, 123–129, 136–183,

196–210; 5717–5718, 1958, pp. 12–21, 33–40, 57–63, 74–80, 92–107,
123–145, 156–189, 195–201, 208–245; 5719–5720, 1960, pp. 11–30,
39–45, 61–72, 97–110, 124–142; 5721–5722, 1962, pp. 19–39, 47–56,
75–84, 101–107, 122–145, 155–161, 172–181; 5723–5724, 1964, pp. 7–
34, 54–59, 69–92, 101–116, 139–145, 152–165, 172–181, 191–211;
5725–5726, 1966, pp. 1–16, 28–45, 71–127, 134–150, 158–164, 174–
202, 218–224, 245–276; 5727–5728, 1968, pp. 19–29, 37–43, 52–63,
111–126, 159–168, 183–196, 225–232.
Weinstein, Jacob J., *The Place of Understanding: Comments on the
Portions of the Week and the Holiday Cycle*, Bloch Publishing Co.,
New York, 1959, pp. 147–156.
Weisfeld, Israel H., ed., *The Message of Israel*, Bloch Publishing Co.,
New York, 1936, pp. 1–111.

COLLECTIONS WITH ROSH HASHANAH MUSIC

Baer, A. *Baal Tefillah*, J. Bulka, Nürnberg, 1930, pp. 215–293.
Binder, A. W., *The Jewish Year in Song*, G. Schirmer, New York, 1928,
pp. 6–7.
Cook, Ray M., *Sing for Fun: Book II*, Union of American Hebrew Con-
gregations, New York, 1957, pp. 18–21.
Coopersmith, Harry, ed., *Hebrew Songster for Kindergarten and Primary
Grades*, Jewish Education Committee of New York, 1948, pp. 30–31.
———, *The Songs We Sing*, United Synagogue Commission on Jewish
Education, New York, 1950, pp. 85–90.
Eisenstein, Judith Kaplan, *The Gateway to Jewish Song*, Behrman House,
New York, 1939, p. 70.
———, and Prensky, Frieda, eds., *Songs of Childhood*, United Syna-
gogue Commission on Jewish Education, New York, 1955, pp.
192–197.
Ephros, Gershon, ed., *Cantorial Anthology of Traditional and Modern
Synagogue Music*: vols. 1 and 6; *Rosh Hashanah*, Bloch Publishing
Co., New York, 1948, 1969.
Goldfarb, Israel, and Goldfarb, Samuel E., *Synagogue Melodies for the
High Holy Days: Arranged for Congregational Singing*, Brooklyn,
1926, pp. 6–49.
Idelsohn, Abraham Zevi, *The Jewish Song Book*, Publications for Judaism,
Cincinnati, 1938, pp. 186–247, 409–416, 526, 528–532.
Levy, Sara C., *So We Sing: Holiday and Bible Songs for Young Jewish
Children*, music by Beatrice L. Deutsch, illus. by Anita Rogoff, Bloch
Publishing Co., New York, 1950, pp. 13–17.
Saminsky, Lazare, *A Song Treasury of Old Israel*, Bloch Publishing Co.,
New York, 1951, pp. 3–4, 8–10, 23, 25.
Union Hymnal: Songs and Prayers for Jewish Worship, third ed.,
Central Conference of American Rabbis, 1940, pp. 167–173, 510–525.
*Union Hymnal: Songs and Prayers for Jewish Worship: Part II—Musical
Services*, Central Conference of American Rabbis, 1936, pp. 362–382.
Union Songster: Songs and Prayers for Jewish Youth, Central Conference
of American Rabbis, New York, 1960, pp. 131–141, 151–156.

Vinaver, Chemjo, ed., *Anthology of Jewish Music*, Edward B. Marks
Music Corp., New York, 1955, pp. 99–136.
Wohlberg, Max, *High Holyday Hymns Set to Music*, Hebrew Publishing
Co., New York, 1959, pp. 4–17.

RECORDINGS

The Art of the Cantor. Sung by Joseph Rosenblatt, Samuel Vigoda, and
Moshe Kusevitzky. Victor CM–6173.
The Best Cantorial Works. Sung by Mordecai Hershman. Greater Record-
ing Co. 52.
Complete High Holiday Service. Sung by Jacob Hass. Torah Umesorah.
Gershon Sirota Sings a Holiday Service. Greater Recording Co. 66.
High Holiday Prayers. Sung by Moshe Kusevitzky. Famous Records 1023.
High Holidays and Autumn Festivals Album. Sung by Maurice Goldman.
Bureau of Jewish Education of the Los Angeles Jewish Community
Council. For children.
High Holy Day Selections. Sung by David J. Putterman. Park Avenue
Synagogue 35.
The High Holy Days. Message of Israel Album. Union of American
Hebrew Congregations.
The High Holy Days. Sung by Gladys Gweirtz. Narrated by Eve Lippman.
House of Menorah H–5. For children.
Midnight Selihot Service. Sung by Leib Glantz. Famous Records 1015.
90 Minutes with Yossele Rosenblatt. Sung by Joseph Rosenblatt. Shirim
1001.
Original Compositions. Sung by Zavel Kwartin, International Records
LP–11.
Rosh Hashanah. Sung by Joseph Rosenblatt. Collectors Guild 652.
Selected Music for the High Holy Days. Sung by Frederick Lechner with
choir conducted by Lazar Weiner. Union of American Hebrew
Congregations 6583.
The Sound of the Shofar. Sung by Ray Smolover. Tikvah Records T 21.
Two Master Cantors. Sung by Moshe Ganchoff and Sholom Katz. Greater
Recording Co. 40.

ROSH HASHANAH IN THE SHORT STORY

Agnon, Shmuel Yosef, "The Orchestra," trans. by Jules Harlow, *Ariel*,
Jerusalem, no. 17 (Winter, 1966–67), pp. 109–115.
Levin, Meyer, "The Prophecy of the New Year," *Classic Hassidic Tales*,
Citadel Press, New York, 1966, pp. 138–145.
Peretz, Isaac Loeb, "Joyful Rejoicing," "The *Shofar*," *The Book of Fire:
Stories*, trans. by Joseph Leftwich, Thomas Yoseloff, New York,
1960(?), pp. 55–59, 137–140.
Reisen, Abraham, "The Poor Community," trans. by Charles Angoff,
A Treasury of Yiddish Stories, ed. by Irving Howe and Eliezer Green-
berg, Viking Press, New York, 1953, pp. 275–279.
Samuel, Maurice, "Ecstasy on the New Year," "And Even Beyond," *Prince*

of the Ghetto, Alfred A. Knopf, New York, 1948, pp. 181–188, 191–208.

Sholom Aleichem, "Mr. Green Has a Job," *Some Laughter, Some Tears: Tales from the Old World and the New,* trans. by Curt Leviant, G.P. Putnam's Sons, New York, 1968, pp. 233–236.

CHILDREN'S STORIES AND DESCRIPTIONS
OF ROSH HASHANAH

Alofsin, Dorothy, "The Clay Lamp," "A Holy Pilgrimage," *Happiness for Sale: Stories of Jewish Life,* Bloch Publishing Co., New York, 1946, pp. 127–133, 134–139.

Bregoff, Jacqueline, "Rosh Hashanah," *Holiday Time,* Bookman Associates, New York, 1957, unpaged.

Bronstein, Charlotte, *Tales of the Jewish Holidays as Told by the Light of the Moon,* illus. by Art Seiden, Behrman House, New York, 1959, unpaged.

Bugatch, Simon, "The Man of Mysteries," *High Holidays,* Board of Jewish Education, Baltimore, 1938, pp. 13–15.

Cedarbaum, Sophia N., *Rosh Ha-shono: Yom Kippur: The High Holy Days,* illus. by Clare and John Ross, Union of American Hebrew Congregations, New York, 1962, pp. 4–17.

Cone, Molly, *The Jewish New Year,* illus. by Jerome Snyder, Thomas Y. Crowell Co., New York, 1966.

———, "The Trumpet That Isn't a Trumpet," *Stories of Jewish Symbols,* Bloch Publishing Co., New York, 1963, pp. 51–53.

Edidin, Ben M., *Jewish Holidays and Festivals,* illus. by Kyra Markham, Hebrew Publishing Co., New York, 1940, pp. 45–55.

Eisenberg, Azriel, "Thirty-five Minutes That Rocked the Jewish World," *The Story of the Jewish Calendar,* Abelard-Schuman, New York, 1958, pp. 53–55.

———, and Robinson, Jessie B., *My Jewish Holidays,* United Synagogue Commission on Jewish Education, New York, 1958, pp. 11–26.

Engle, Fannie, *The Jewish Holidays and Their Favorite Foods: With Easy Recipes for Mother and Daughter,* illus. by Dorothy M. Weiss, Behrman House, New York, 1958, unpaged.

Epstein, Morris, *All about Jewish Holidays and Customs,* illus. by Arnold Lobel, Ktav Publishing House, New York, 1959, pp. 20–24.

———, *A Pictorial Treasury of Jewish Holidays and Customs,* Ktav Publishing House, New York, 1959, pp. 24–30.

Fine, Helen, "A Happy New Year," *G'dee,* Union of American Hebrew Congregations, New York, 1958, pp. 20–27.

———, *G'dee's Book of Holiday Fun,* Union of American Hebrew Congregations, New York, 1961, pp. 2–8. An activity book.

Fischman, Joyce, *Holiday Work and Play,* Union of American Hebrew Congregations, New York, 1961, pp. 1–8. An activity book.

Freehof, Lillian S., "The Lopsided Challah with the Crooked Crown," *Star Light Stories: Holiday and Sabbath Tales,* Bloch Publishing Co., New York, 1952, pp. 11–20.

Gamoran, Mamie G., *Days and Ways: The Story of Jewish Holidays and Customs*, Union of American Hebrew Congregations, Cincinnati, 1941, pp. 28–38.

———, "Four New Years," *Hillel's Calendar*, illus. by Ida Libby Dengrove, Union of American Hebrew Congregations, New York, 1960, pp. 30–36.

———, "A Happy New Year!," "In the Evening," "On the Sea," *Hillel's Happy Holidays*, illus. by Temima N. Gezari, Union of American Hebrew Congregations, Cincinnati, 1939, pp. 21–36.

Garvey, Robert, "The Third Good Deed," *Happy Holiday!*, illus. by Ezekiel Schloss, Ktav Publishing House, New York, 1953, pp. 11–15.

Ginsburg, Marvell, and Pins, Arnulf M., *My Rosh Hashanah Prayerbook: A Picture Prayerbook for the Very Young*, illus. by Robin King, Behrman House, New York, 1962.

Goldberg, David, *Holidays for American Judaism*, Bookman Associates, New York, 1954, pp. 134–143.

Goldin, Hyman E., *A Treasury of Jewish Holidays*, illus. by Resko, Twayne Publishers, New York, 1952, pp. 20–29.

Golub, Rose W., "Let's Make Up," *Down Holiday Lane*, illus. by Louis Kobrin, Union of American Hebrew Congregations, Cincinnati, 1947, pp. 3–10.

Halpern, Salomon Alter, "S . . . O . . . S . . . ," "The King's Men," *Tales of Faith*, Boys Town, Jerusalem, 1968, pp. 173–176, 205–208.

Isaacs, Abram S., "The Old Shofar," *Under the Sabbath Lamp: Stories of Our Time for Old and Young*, Jewish Publication Society of America, Philadelphia, 1919, pp. 23–38.

Ish-Kishor, Sulamith, "How Bennie Went to Look for the New Year," *The Heaven on the Sea and Other Stories*, Bloch Publishing Co., New York, 1924, pp. 31–37.

———, "Little Joey Honey-Pot," *The Stranger within Thy Gates and Other Stories*, Shoulson Press, New York, 1948, pp. 197–205.

———, "A Dream of the New Year," *The Palace of Eagles and Other Stories*, Shoulson Press, New York, 1948, pp. 165–173.

———, *Pathways through the Jewish Holidays*, ed. by Benjamin Efron, Ktav Publishing House, New York, 1967, pp. 9–24.

Katsh, Abraham I., ed., *Bar Mitzvah: Illustrated*, Shengold Publishers, New York, 1955, pp. 59–65.

Kipnis, Levin, "A Sweet New Year," "Oded's New Year's Card to His Father," *My Holidays: Holiday Stories for Children*, trans. by Israel M. Goodelman, illus. by Isa, N. Tversky, Tel Aviv, 1961, pp. 7–21.

Kranzler, Gershon, ed., *Jewish Youth Companion: Stories, Poems . . .* , Merkos L'Inyonei Chinuch, Brooklyn, 1957, pp. 71–73.

Learsi, Rufus, "Sins upon the Waters," *Kasriel the Watchman and Other Stories*, Jewish Publication Society of America, Philadelphia, 1936, pp. 174–182.

———, "Shimmele Turns to Good Deeds," *Shimmele and His Friends*, Behrman's Jewish Book House, New York, 1940, pp. 77–91.

Levinger, Elma Ehrlich, "The Dawn of Freedom," *Playmates in Egypt*, Jewish Publication Society of America, Philadelphia, 1940, pp. 33–40.

———, "A New Page," *Jewish Holyday Stories: Modern Tales of the*

American Jewish Youth, Bloch Publishing Co., New York, 1932, pp. 23-41.
———, "The Man Who Came Late," *In Many Lands*, Bloch Publishing Co., New York, 1923, pp. 13-21.
———, "A New Year for Berthold," "The Rabbi and the Bishop," *Tales Old and New*, Bloch Publishing Co., New York, 1926, pp. 13-31.
Margolis, Isidor, and Markowitz, Sidney L., *Jewish Holidays and Festivals*, illus. by John Teppich, Citadel Press, New York, 1962, pp. 27-36.
Markowitz, Samuel H., *Leading a Jewish Life in the Modern World*, Union of American Hebrew Congregations, New York, 1958, pp. 144-159.
Mindel, Nissan, *The Complete Story of Tishrei*, Merkos L'Inyonei Chinuch, Brooklyn, 1961, pp. 1-98.
Morrow, Betty, and Hartman, Louis, *Jewish Holidays*, illus. by Nathan Goldstein, Garrard Publishing Co., Champaign, Illinois, 1967, pp. 21-25.
Peretz, Isaac Loeb, "Even Higher," *Modern Jewish Life in Literature*, ed. by Azriel Eisenberg, United Synagogue Commission on Jewish Education, New York, 1948, pp. 26-29.
Pessin, Deborah, "*Peh* and His Friend the *Shofar*," *The Aleph Bet Story Book*, Jewish Publication Society of America, Philadephia, 1946, pp. 130-136.
———, and Gezari, Temima, *The Jewish Kindergarten: A Manual for Teachers*, Union of American Hebrew Congregations, Cincinnati, 1944, pp. 59-76.
Robinson, Jessie B., *Holidays Are Fun*, Bloch Publishing Co., New York, 1950, pp. 10-14. An activity book.
Schwab, Hermann, "The *Shofar* That Could Talk," *Dreams of Childhood: Stories for Jewish Children*, trans. by Joseph Leftwich, illus. by Sigismund Freyhan, Anscombe, London, 1949, pp. 7-8.
Shulman, Nisson, "The *Shofar* That Wouldn't Blow," *Stories for Jewish Juniors*, by Doris B. Gold, Jonathan David, New York, 1967, pp. 3-7.
Simon, Norma, *Rosh Hashanah*, illus. by Ayala Gordon, United Synagogue Commission on Jewish Education, New York, 1959.
Smith, Harold P., "The World Has a Birthday," *A Treasure Hunt in Judaism*, Hebrew Publishing Co., New York, 1950, pp. 49-57.
Spiro, Saul S., and Spiro, Rena M., *The Joy of Jewish Living*, Bureau of Jewish Education, Cleveland, 1965, pp. 55-63, 189-190.
Stadtler, Bea, "Dan and the *Shofar*," *Once upon a Jewish Holiday*, illus. by Bill Giacalone, Ktav Publishing House, New York, 1965, pp. 12-16.
Tchernovitz, Temima, "A New Year's Story," *Gan-Gani: Let Us Play in Israel*, ed. by Levin Kipnis and Temima Tchernovitz, trans. by Leslie Daiken, N. Tversky, Tel Aviv, 1952, pp. 26-29.
Weilerstein, Sadie Rose, "Danny and David Go Up and Down," *What Danny Did: Stories for the Wee Jewish Child*, illus. by Jessie Berkowitz Robinson, Bloch Publishing Co., New York, 1944, pp. 27-33.
———, "Happy Birthday, World!" "For a Good and a Sweet Year," *What the Moon Brought*, illus. by Mathilda Keller, Jewish Publication Society of America, Philadelphia, 1942, pp. 4-20.

PROGRAM AND AUDIO-VISUAL MATERIALS

PLAYS

min. = approximate performance time in minutes; m = number of male parts; f = number of female parts

Citron, Samuel J., "If Not Even Higher," *Dramatics the Year Round*, United Synagogue Commission on Jewish Education, New York, 1956. 5 m, 3 f, extras, ages 10 and up. 15 min. Adaptation of the story by I. L. Peretz.

Kabakoff, Dorothy, "Comrades All," *Dramatics the Year Round*, ed. by Samuel J. Citron, United Synagogue Commission on Jewish Education, New York, 1956. 12 m or f, ages 8–13. 10 min. Rosh Hashanah and the months of the Jewish year engage in a dialog.

Linsky, Fanny B., *Happy New Year*, Union of American Hebrew Congregations, New York, 1929. 16 m or f, extras, ages 9–12. 20 min. A fantasy in which the wonders of the universe express themselves.

Mindel, Joseph, *The High Places*. Eternal Light radio script, no. 598, September 14, 1958. Jewish Theological Seminary of America, New York. 25 min. Youth and adults. Commemorating Rosh Hashanah, this program tells of a crisis arising because of man's limitations when confronted with natural law.

————, *Let There Be Light*. Eternal Light radio script, no. 671, September 18, 1960. Jewish Theological Seminary of America, New York. 25 min. Youth and adults. Written for Rosh Hashanah, the conflict centers around the theme of man's sin against his fellowman.

————, *Take with You Words*. Eternal Light radio script, no. 559, September 22, 1957. Jewish Theological Seminary of America, New York. 25 min. Youth and adults. The moving story of a Jew who had renounced his religion to escape the terror of the Inquisition in Brazil and then fled to New Amsterdam. There he learned the meaning of repentance and forgiveness on Rosh Hashanah.

————, *Tears of Paradise*. Eternal Light radio script, no. 705, September 10, 1961. Jewish Theological Seminary of America, New York. 25 min. Youth and adults. Written in observance of Rosh Hashanah, this is the story of the beginning of man and his right of choice.

Segal, Samuel M., "The Voices of the *Shofarot*," *On Stage Everyone*, Jonathan David Co., New York, 1957. 3 m, 1 f, extras, ages 10–13. 20 min. A fantasy for Rosh Hashanah.

Wishengrad, Morton, *As a Wind That Blows*. Eternal Light radio script, no. 436, September 26, 1954. Jewish Theological Seminary of America, New York. 25 min. Youth and adults. Story of the bitterness of a mother whose son died in 1798 fighting an epidemic in New York.

Zweig, Esther Sommerstein, "Holiday Minstrels," *Dramatics the Year Round*, ed. by Samuel J. Citron, United Synagogue Commission on Jewish Education, New York, 1956. 12 to 16 m or f, ages 7–10. 7 min. Rosh Hashanah and Yom Kippur scenes.

FILMSTRIP

The Story of Rosh Hashana. By Samuel J. Citron. Jewish Education Committee of New York, 1952. 51 frames, black and white, narration. The celebration of the festival at home and in the synagogue and school and a depiction of Peretz's "If Not Higher."

KINESCOPES

Days of Awe, by Shimon Wincelberg. 16 mm, sound, black and white, 30 min. National Academy for Adult Jewish Studies of the United Synagogue of America, New York. Based on the book of the same title by S. Y. Agnon.

If Not Higher. 16 mm, sound, black and white, 30 min. New York Board of Rabbis. An adaptation of the story about the Rabbi of Nemirov, by I. L. Peretz.

MOTION PICTURE

With All Thy Heart. 16 mm, sound, black and white, 13½ min. Jewish Chautauqua Society, New York. The story of a grudge between a man and his cousin and the influence of the High Holy Days in resolving it, starring Shepperd Strudwick.

ARTS AND CRAFTS

Sharon, Ruth, *Arts and Crafts the Year Round*, United Synagogue Commission on Jewish Education, New York, 1965, vol. 1, pp. 58–77.

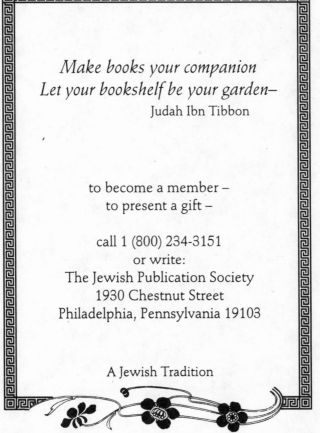

Make books your companion
Let your bookshelf be your garden–
Judah Ibn Tibbon

to become a member –
to present a gift –

call 1 (800) 234-3151
or write:
The Jewish Publication Society
1930 Chestnut Street
Philadelphia, Pennsylvania 19103

A Jewish Tradition